THE U

THE TRAGEDY OF HUMAN RIGHTS

VOLUME I

Kadiro Amae Elemo

THE EAST AFRICAN PRESS
WWW.THEEASTAFRICANPRESS.COM

The East African Press, LLC
Shakopee, Minnesota

© Kadiro Amae Elemo, 2013

All rights reserved. No portion of this publication may be reproduced, stored in a retrieval system or transmitted in any form or by any means electronic, mechanical or otherwise without the prior written permission of the publisher.

Printed in the United States of America.

ISBN-10: 1940181003 (paper)
ISBN-13: 978-1-940181-00-4 (paper)

Library of Congress Control Number: 2013939707

Cover design by Fuad Siraj (Barreedduu Pro)

THIS BOOK IS DEDICATED TO the memory of my younger brother Abdulkarim Amae Elemo. Abdulkarim was a little boy of ten years old. He was adored and loved for his boyish charm, love of stories, music and cattle. He took our cows to bush before he went to school every morning, and looked after them every weekend. One Saturday was a bad day for him. A secret assassin hired, by local officials, to kill a member of our family confronted him with a loaded gun. The gun belonged to one of "our" leaders, who disliked our family political views. He did not have to use the gun to kill the little boy. He slaughtered him with a knife. The promising boy, who barely had sympathy for politics at his age, except a natural love for his language and culture, killed because of something he never had known. The killer brought to justice after years. Unfortunately, none of the people who masterminded the crime held accountable for their action. I also want to dedicate this book to the memory of all nameless victims of the Ethiopian tyranny.

Contents

Acknowledgement vii

Prologue ix

Preface 1

Introduction 9

(1) The Rhetoric and Reality of U.S. Foreign Policy 21

(2) The Making of Minilik Empire 27

(3) The Prelude to the Formal Relations 38

(4) The Inauguration 45

(5) The U.S. Ignoring/Covering the Abyssinian Thriving Slave Trade 75

(6) Can Abyssinia Change? Reforms that Challenged Abyssinia and the West 81

(7) A Dilemma: Tafari or Mussolini? 91

(8) Favoring Mussolini? The Interruption of Ties 107

(9) The Resumption: Building a Post Mussolini 'Semi-Fascist' Empire 121

(10) Challenges and Responses 157

(11) The Failure of Triangular Axis and a Road to Communism 203

(12) The Culmination of Misguided Policy: The Death of the Lion 209

Summary 228

Bibliography 232

Glossary 251

Maps & Photos

(1) Horn of Africa Map xii

(2) Administrative Map of Ethiopia 20

(3) President William McKinley 24

(4) Theodore Roosevelt 26

(5) A Group of Borana Immigrants 35

(6) A Borana Immigrant Man 36

(7) Emperor Menelik 42

(8) A Group fo Abyssinian Warriors Escorting the Americans 49

(9) Minilik Receiving the Americans 50

(10) President Roosevelt on Elephant Hunt 58

(11) A Group of Oromo Slaves from Abyssinia 78

(12) Emperor Iyyasu 85

(13) Emperor Iyyasu and Ras Tafari 89

(14) General Taddasa Birru & Nelson Mandala 184

(15) General Waqo Gutu Usu 188

(16) Hayla Sillase removal from the palace 224

Acknowledgement

FIRST AND FOREMOST, this is a work of passion, a passion instilled in me being a member of the great family of the Gada (Oromo) Nation and from my conversations with peoples from the wilderness of Dassanach to the great land of Afar, from the land of Sheikh Khojele al-Hassan of Bella Shangul to the land of Abdille Hassan of Ogaden, from the tracing land of Konso to the coffee birthplace of Kafa. These peoples thought me the history that never was in the Empire of Ethiopia, and the history that inspired this work. My deepest gratitude goes for to all these uncertified scholars.

My brother, Dr. Ibrahim Elemo, deserves special thanks for relentlessly urging and encouraging me to put my perspective in the market place of ideas than to wait (or dream) for perfection. Putting his resources at my disposal, he simplified a lot of my burdens. Reading the whole manuscript, he also gave me valuable comments. I would like to take this opportunity to express my thanks to Bora Jarso, Gammachu and Qanani Amae, to my mom, the whole Elemo clan, my relatives, and my friends here and back home.

Passionate she is about Oromo issues better than most Oromos; Bonnie Holcomb is a wonderful asset. She deserves many thanks for her comments and editing part of this work. Dr. Mohammed Hassen, a selfless advocate of the Oromo cause, deserves a special mentioning for reading the manuscript and his helpful comments. Professor Mekuria Bulcha inspired and helped me to accomplish this work. I am highly indebted to Professor Wiessner and Dr. Roza Pati for their helps.

Many individuals contributed in different ways in the realization of this work. I am grateful to Amane Hussein, Abdalla Hussein, Hawwa Hussein, Taff Fayyisa, and Rayya Jimjimo for their encouragements, enduring friendships and uncompromised courtesies. Life in America is a demanding job, yet my friend, Abdurahman Ibrahim, is supportive, faithful, and regularly calls me, not giving upon me even when I frequently missed his calls. Faud Siraj designed a cover for this book, for which I am most grateful. Abarra Ture (Dr. Google), a self-made doctor from Google searches, merits special thanks, particularly for his whimsical yet entertaining jokes, diagnoses, and prescriptions. I should say had I consumed all dosages of vegetables and fruits he prescribed for me, I would have produced a different book. There is a family I want to thank, but if I enumerate their names I need a book for that; many thanks Jimjimo family.

I would like to express my indebtedness to Abdulatif Amae Elemo, Abdurahman Ahmad, Adunya Iddosa, Ayyub Jimjimo, Bati Dahessa, Darara Gubbo, Dassalany Boranto, Dr. Angelique Montgomery, Dr. Asafa Jalata, Dr. Roya Laghaie, Gannat Hurrisa, Haydee Gonzalez, Hussein Rone (Muzee), Ismael Ibrahim, Jama Rone, Robert Laghaie, Sena Jimjimo, Sofiya Bokku, Tamu Abdi, and Zaytuna Bati.

There are several brilliant scholars who invested a wealth of their intellectual capital to provide us unique perspectives on the Horn of African issues. Bonnie Holcomb and Sisai Ibssa are the people that I tapped into their acumens and intellectual treasures. Dr. Amanda McVety has a fascinating and unique insight and perspective always. Michela Wrong is immensely helpful for her highly engaging book, *I Didn't Do It for You.*

Last but not the least, there are many Ethiopianist scholars, whom I disagree with on some issues, but I respect their opinions. My work has been enriched by their researches and documentation, for which I am highly indebted. In this regard, Professor Theodore Vestal, Professor Harold G. Marcus, Dr. John H. Spencer, Professor Getachew Metaferia are among a few worth mention ones. That all said; I want to make clear that the views reflected herein are solely mine, and I am the only person responsible for it.

Kadiro Amae Elemo
Chicago, Illinois
June 2013

Prologue

THE TUMULTUOUS HORN OF AFRICA, as one might style, the Middle East of Africa, is a region that epitomizes winner-take-all politics, bloody regime change, civil wars, and lack of democracy and human rights protections. Its peoples had suffered and are suffering from the brutalities of their leaders: from Siad Barre to Mangistu, from Issayyas to Mallas, from Id-Amin to Al-Bashir. Perennial natural catastrophes, environmental challenges, famines, and droughts are the hallmark of this area. It is a corner of the world where superpowers, particularly the U.S., deeply put their fingers.

Today, this area is experiencing dramatic political developments. Born out of these developments are new hopes, at least, a hope to hope for the better future, but one marred with uncertainties, fears, and the same old challenges.

The expulsion of Al Shabab militants from their last stronghold of Kismayo, by Kenyan forces, gives a new hope for the area. This is a positive step for the peace of Somalia, which is emerging from the state of anarchy to a nascent stability. To have an influence in evolving Somali politics, Ethiopia has sent her military into Somalia for the second time in four years. Though Ethiopia and Kenya have commonalities of interests in defeating the militant group, they have competing interests and support different factions in Somalia. Washington has rendered *de jure* recognition for the government of Somalia for the first time in more than two decades.

Eritrea is in terrible shape. Unresolved conflicts with neighboring countries, lack of political space and repression, yawning economy, and U.N. sanctions are fermenting discontent. If the regime is not reforming itself, explosion is the only a matter of time. As an omen of things to come, an army mutiny laid siege to the Ministry of Information recently.

The ruling Omar Guelleh family, which ruled Djibouti in a royal fashion since the independence, hardly addressed the Afar issue. Inspired by the Arab Spring, they are increasingly challenging the legitimacy of the ruling elite of the country that hosts an American task force responsible for combating terrorism in the Horn of Africa and the Arabian Peninsula.

Lately, Kenya has carried out peaceful, successful, and credible elections. On one hand, this gives a new hope for the region. On the other hand, a victory of democracy posed a threat to human rights. Both President Uhuru Kenyatta and Vice President William Ruto are wanted by the International Criminal Court in relation to atrocities committed on the aftermath of the 2007 elections. This placed the U.S. in a dilemma, a dilemma of walking a tightrope between human rights and respecting the Kenyan sovereignty (and thereby maintaining security cooperation). Oddly, the U.S. was amongst the first countries to congratulate the winners.

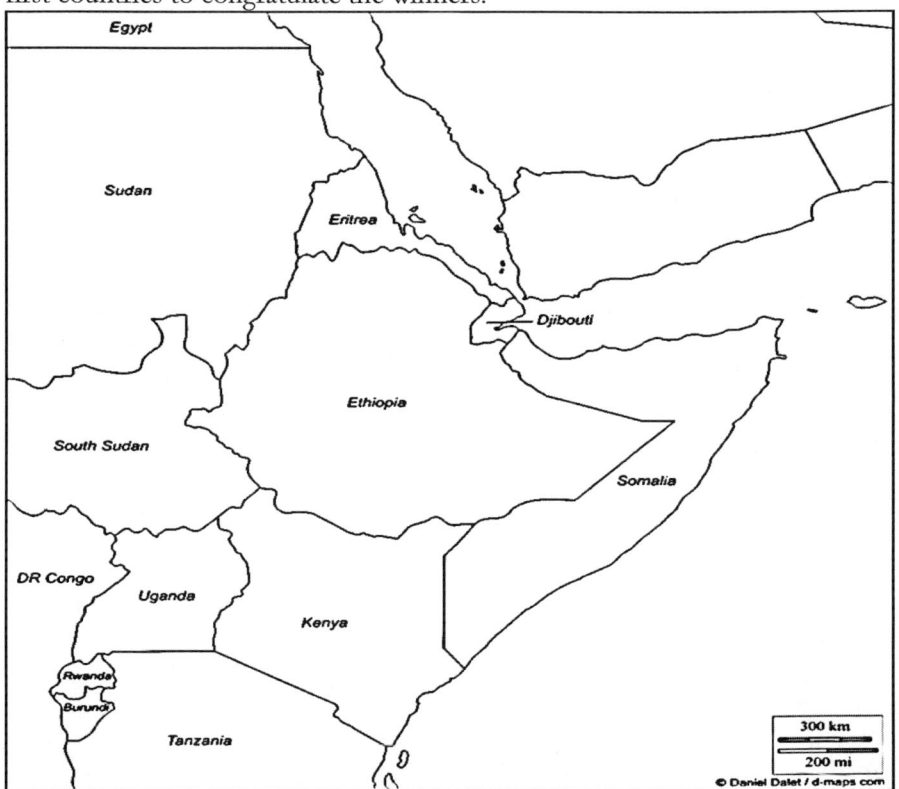

Fig 1. Horn of Africa Map. Courtesy of d.maps.com

The long civil war of Sudan has come to an end yet a newly born state of South Sudan is not on its feet. In addition to tribal (regional) tensions, it has some outstanding sharp issues to resolve with Sudan. With an ongoing Darfur Crisis and a loss of the oil revenue, Sudan has also potential for instability despite a government promise to open up political space for oppositions.

The future of a U.S. client state of Uganda is unknown after the departure of the strongman of the country, Yuweri Museveni. Moreover, the most wanted fugitive, Joseph Kony of the Lord Resistance Army (LRA), is on loose even evading capture by U.S. commandos.

Most importantly, when this book was at an embryonic stage, Ethiopia announced the death of Prime Minister Mallas Zenawi. He ruled the country with an iron fist for more than two decades. Regardless of his domestic human rights records, he secured a robust approval from the U.S. thanks to his centrality in the global coalition against terrorism. While the U.S. lost a strong ally in the region, Ethiopia is at a crossroad once again.

The announcement confirmed widely circulated rumors in the Ethiopian diaspora, who anticipated either an Arab spring style popular uprisings or breakdown of the EPRDF, and an opportunity for democracy to flourish overnight in the nation of some ninety million people. Some opposition groups even formed a government in exile and sought international recognition.

The hope for democratization and human rights under the Tigrayan minority rule has evaporated. Indeed, it has written a golden constitution, which incorporates most individual and collective rights one can ask for, to the extent of guaranteeing the right of self-determination including secession. Superficially, there is a separation of powers, periodic elections, a parliament, free press, and, in short, Ethiopia is a federation of "autonomous" ethnic-states. All of these rights hardly add up to a working and a meaningful reform of a despotic state. The chance of opposition parties mounting a successful challenge to the rule is minimal. The regime had effectively destroyed them to the extent of winning the 2010 elections with the margin of 99.8 percent. Moreover, built around a Tigrayan command structure, the TPLF is in a firm command of the army, the strongest institution in the country. Political groups of the largest nation of the country (Oromo) are in disarray, ineffective, shattered, and swing between opposing narratives back and forth. However, the face of Ethiopia has changed forever; the diaspora based Ethiopianist political doctors are prescribing to multiple failures of the country the same old prescriptions, which caused her ailments, in the first place. Despite rebranded and decorated with the human rights rhetoric, they are running on the political platform of the past, going back to the old Ethiopia minus the throne. Ethiopia can hardly be the old Ethiopia again, no matter their nostalgia for their "glorious" past.

Thanks to the late premiere's megalomaniac propensity of inhibiting the growth of viable personalities even within his own nucleus party, the power slipped from the TPLF to a nominal partner within the ruling coalition (the EPRDF), the South Ethiopian Peoples' Democratic Front (SEPDF). Hayla Maryam Dassalany ascended to power from the Walayta ethnicity. For the first time in the Ethiopian history, someone without the "Solomonic blood,"

Orthodox Christianity, a military or a *naftanya* background came to the helm of power. His breaking of a glass ceiling of power in Ethiopia calls for celebrations and festivities for the oppressed peoples of the nation; however, his ineffectiveness inhibits such festivities.

The oppositions often describe the new prime minister as a technocrat, docile, amateurish, underdog, and colorless person. In fact, we do not need a strong leader in Ethiopia, but we need strong institutions. Perhaps, the fact that he has a master's degree in organizational leadership might be helpful to achieve that goal. He has to prove his competence by setting the country on a democratic course or choose to remain, as some contend, under the tutelage of his TPLF bosses who cut their teeth on the guerilla style of rule. Will they let him act freely, or guide him remotely? How independent, confident, and ambitious he will be to break from the corruption of the past?

The fact that the premiere hails from the most heterogeneous member of the coalition with the softest power base makes him more dependent on the center [the TPLF]. Let alone in the EPRDF, his position in his power base is weak. His removal from the presidency of the Southern Nations, Nationalities, and People's Region (SNNPR) was because of a political defeat of his Walayta group at the hand of a Sidama group. In fact, this was a door opener for him to come to the office of the prime minister, and his rise to vice prime minister.

Likewise, the power base of Vice Premier Dammaqa Makonninfrom the Amhara National Democratic Movement (ANDM) is fragile in his own party. Being a Muslim, he is not an Amhara per se. An axis of Amhara identity is Orthodox Christianity, and, Amharas consider their identity and a Muslim identity as a mix of water and oil in a glass. He has to look to the center to get assurances to his power. Hayla Maryam and Dammaqa's chance of relying (defecting) to their power bases to counter influences of the center is minimal. Their vulnerabilities at their power base and their reliance on the center for their survivals make the centripetal force stronger than the centrifugal force.

Furthermore, Hayla Maryam is from minority yet the surging protestant church, which is, with its appeal to modernity, eroding a youth base of the Ethiopian Orthodox Church. In the world of the Ethiopian cyberspace, there was a rumor that the Orthodox Church was reluctant to recognize powers of the prime ministers that did not fit into pigeonholes of the traditional Ethiopian polity.

For now, the succession averted the feared succession chaos, proved naivety of the dawning of democracy and fostered the sham of a working democracy in Ethiopia. However, the death of the strongman uncovered acute differences within the ruling front (the EPRDF) and increased the assertiveness of sleeping members of the front such as the Oromo People's Democratic Organization (OPDO). Denied chief ministerial portfolios during the succession deal, the OPDO emerged as the worst performer on the aftermath of the succession deal lending itself to a serious disappointment. The OPDO amasses almost half of the front membership base; it putatively represents the largest ethnic group and Oromiya, the largest region and a backbone of the Ethiopian economy. Rubbing salt into its wounds, the TPLF dictated its internal matters and purged contumacious members from the organization. Paternalistic TPLF as usual downplays the resilience of the OPDO as a storm in a teacup, and silences them as the OLF sympathizers whenever they came up with legitimate demands.

Rumored widely was the discontent and ongoing tension within the TPLF, which felt the hard won power through bitter struggles wrung from its jaws. To address this discontent, the regime has engineered a polycephaly of the office of the vice prime minister. Ethiopia has three deputy prime ministers: Muktar Kadir of the OPDO, Dabratsiyon Gabramikael of the TPLF, and Dammaqa Makonnin of the ANDM. As it is true with Hayla Maryam and Dammaqa, the support base of Muktar in the OPDO is precarious as he hails from an ethnic minority (Yem or Janjaro) in Jimma Zone of Oromiya State. Making a meteoric rise to power, Dabratsiyon has eclipsed a symbolic head of the TPLF, Abbay Waldu.

The plurality of posts of the vice prime minister not only showed the succession drama, but also raised constitutional complexities and ambiguities since, according to the reading of Article 75 (1) of the constitution, the post is one and indivisible. Who will, out of the three, represent the prime minister during his absence or succeed him if anything happens to him. Perhaps, the arrangement is a fallback plan for the TPLF because if anything happens to the premier, the Tigrayan Dabratsiyon, who is *primus inter pares*, would take the helm of the country. Hence, a danger of power falling in hands of non-Tigre and Muslim would be averted.

Loyalist and submissive as only a handpicked successor can be, the administration of the new premiere does not show any break from that of his predecessor so far. His ascension to power did not orchestrate by pardons (amnesties). Nor does he follow a new approach in dealing with land grab issues. Nor does he pursue a peaceful approach to address ongoing Muslims' protests. His regime infamously called their legitimate and peaceful questions a terrorist agenda and tagged them with all nasty terrorist labels. With its erroneous and thoughtless approaches, the government is not only sowing the seed of hatred between Christians and Muslims, but also radicalizing Muslims and trying to make another al Shabab out of the non-violent Muslim resistance.

Let alone defending the rights of Muslims, according to some stories, the new prime minister is incapable to defend his religious liberty from his Tigrayan masters. There is a claim that they banned his Sunday mass at the National Palace after his pastor proclaimed, on the sermon, receiving a revelation about "the late Meles Zenawi walking in Paradise with Jesus."

Allegedly, the prime minister responded by bursting into shouting "halleluiah" to the embarrassment of his Albanian-Marxist masters (Getahun, 2013).

Instead of introducing reforms, the new premier consistently and vociferously vowed to follow his predecessor's path without an iota of deviation. It is these proclamations of strict adhesions and uncompromised loyalties to the ghost of the late prime minister that puzzled Lefort (2012) if, indeed, "Meles rules from beyond the grave."

> The new Prime Minister, Hailemariam Selassie [sic], endlessly repeats that he will pursue 'Meles's legacy without any change'. He has replaced not a single cabinet minister. It could be said that the regime is running on autopilot, with the Meles software driving the leadership computer. Plunged into disarray, the governing team is hanging on to this software like a lifebelt (Lefort, 2012).

In a short, the East Africa is undergoing intense political changes with fragile and hardly predictable future. For stability centered policy of the U.S., there is so much at stake in the region. The least thing it needs to see in the region, in general, and in Ethiopia, in particular, is stability. The stability of Ethiopia is essential for the stability of northeast Africa. Ethiopia is a fulcrum of the U.S. security policy on the Horn of Africa. It is a home of U.S. drones and U.S. Africa command (Africom). It has deployed peace keepers in a disputed border of Sudan and South Sudan. One might also surmise that the U.S. stronger presence in Ethiopia (Nile diplomacy) is necessary to arm-twist Egypt if its Sharia-minded leaders decided to go "rogue."

Africa is still a playground for superpowers. The U.S. and China are the main actors today. This battle is not defined by ideology or Cold War proxy wars, but it is the battle for natural resources and regional influences. The notion of a revolutionary democracy (development at the cost of democracy and human rights), which was championed by the late Prime Minister of Ethiopia, came from none other than from the Communist China. Being the capital of Africa, Ethiopia plays a crucial role to contain influences of the assertive China in Africa. Furthermore, with the victory of Kenyatta putting the U.S. policy makers in an awkward position, the U.S. might resuscitate Ethiopian surrogacy in Somalia.

These rapid changes necessitate investigating the U.S. foreign policy in Ethiopia. Will these changes require a dynamic approach from the U.S. or it will keep doing business as usual? I shall examine if the U.S. is going to achieve stability through democratization or through maintaining the *status quo*. What will be the future of democracy in Ethiopia and roles of the U.S.?

Preface

This book is about the what, the how, and the why of the United States foreign policy towards Ethiopia, from the vantage point of promotion and protection of human rights. It studies factors that shaped it, and, it draws how it impacted political dynamism of the nation with diverse cultural and religious landscape. It unravels its deficiency in promotion and protection of human rights in the ages of imperialism, Cold War antagonisms and fighting terrorism. It argues that the U.S had-and-has wrong diagnoses of human right problems in Ethiopia and hence applied wrong prescriptions. Based on the wrong prescriptions and myopia in the foreign policy, the U.S. offered *carte blanche* for the discriminations of the ruling class of Ethiopia instead of playing positive roles on promoting the rights of diverse linguistic and ethnic groups in Ethiopia. The wrong prescriptions perpetuate and exacerbate human rights violations and damage the reputation of the U.S. as the champion of freedom around the world.

The U.S. alliance with Ethiopia entertains irony of the U.S. strong pledge to put its weight in a global arena to promote human rights on one hand, and its silence to the atrocities committed by the Ethiopian government, on the other hand. Perhaps, it is not an exaggeration, if I may say that only a few countries match Ethiopia in demonstrating a discrepancy between the rhetoric and reality of human rights in the U.S. foreign policy. Ethiopia symbolizes a mecca of contradictions between human rights and national security within the foreign policy. It provided footing for U.S. adventurism into Africa during the inauguration of diplomatic relationship during the Menelik era; it became a robust partner in halting the spread of communism by providing a spy base of Kagnew during the Hayla Sillase period, and it turned into a headache for U.S. policy makers by defecting to the communist bloc during the Darg era. Today, Ethiopia is all about its status as a regional ally in a fight against terrorism and hub for predatory drones, a U.S. weapon of choice in the fight against terrorists. In this national security driven diplomacy, the human rights causes are forsaken, naturally lost in the gray and often offered as the sacrificial lamb.

The modern concept of human rights postulates that states have a responsibility to respect and protect natural and inalienable rights of individuals. Accordingly, states have to undertake preventive measures to discourage occurrence of violations of human rights and take remedial measures, on the event of breach, to redress the wrongs. From its formation, Ethiopia was-and-is a textbook example of "predatory state" with all connotations and denotations the phrase implies. Accordingly, Ethiopia is a police state and antithesis to the concept of human rights itself. Naked tyranny and a culture of impunity are everyday experiences. Its government is hardly accountable to its own people; power comes from bullet, not from ballot. If there is a ballot, a ballot is not a bullet proof for the ballot justifies the bullet. Often, the ballot process lends itself to the bullet process as the former lacks creditability and transparency.

The U.S is the most powerful nation on the face of the earth. She has an enormous influence in the international financial institutions such as the World Bank and International Monetary Fund. Her cultural [soft] power captivates the imagination of the world, for good or bad. She lures us not only with her flamboyant rhetoric, but also with her voracious consumptions, and she even exports her "craziness" as Ethan Watters *Crazy Like Us: The Globalization of the American Psyche* vividly showed. In Ethiopia, except some unfortunate times, we covet the U.S. for her power, economy, strong media, for everything, but especially for its democracy and human rights protections. It is imagined as a land of "dollar tree," a land where one kisses miseries goodbye. In short, it is a Heaven on earth. I will explain this with my personal experience.

Believing myself that I was well-informed, I did not expect for surprises in the U.S., such as collecting dollars from a "dollar tree" and remitting to my unhappy kinsmen. My sub-conscious (unconscious) fooled me; it abruptly awakened me from a deep sleep, one night. In my dream, I got the chance to go to the U.S.; I looked through the window; I saw a radiant light of the Chicago skylines; poor-me-one. Perhaps, the America my subconscious expected was greater than the one I saw. Alas! My teacher once told me, in high school, he would have rather preferred being a cow in the U.S. than being a man in Ethiopia. "How about India, you would be worshipped," I interjected. He told me that the noble America is all about animal welfare, and, a subsidy for a 'happy' cow is greater than our per capital income. He would have rather preferred being a tree in America because it is watered daily and protected from cutting, a 'tree right'. Being a pet in Americans would have been the finest thing because he would have lived the luxurious life of our prime minister, a dictator of comfort.

"The Ethiopian coffee gives a drinker gastritis; the American coffee gives the drinker happiness," he told me. "Come on, are not we the home of the world premium coffee," I impolitely interrupted him. I wondered; "Are you telling me about a hot pepper or coffee?" "Our coffee is good; America makes it better," he replied. "Thus, Americanized coffee is drinkable; one can drink a liter of coffee in the U.S., but only few small cups in Ethiopia," he explained. He even told me that citizens have the right to insult their president, the most influential person on the face of the earth. Perhaps, he wanted to say that citizens have the right to criticize the president because the culture of criticizing rulers in Ethiopia is unknown and intolerable.[1] In the middle of the hot conversation, he stumbled on a rock; he enchanted with America more because, in the innocent America, there are no such mean stones because technology had destroyed them, meaning roads are asphalted. Wow, the magic of America!! An America in the mind of my teacher, a land of happy cows and happy trees, is different from a real America.

Seriously, America is a powerful, influential and prosperous country. Why are her leverages compromised on the aid-hungry-nation like Ethiopia? Why is the U.S. end up buttressing the perpetrators of fragrant violators of human rights? Why did a noble America provide weapons for dictators, with which they kill, petrify, traumatize, terrorize, and rule their people? What is wrong with the U.S. human rights policy on Ethiopia? This book addresses that dilemma by investigating the foundations of American policy toward Ethiopia.

The turbulent Horn of Africa has grabbed fair attentions from researchers. A handful of these works has been dedicated for the bilateral relations of the U.S. and Ethiopia. Getachew Metaferia [*Ethiopia and the United States: History, Diplomacy, and Analysis*, 2009] and Negussay Ayele [*Ethiopia and the United States: The Season of Courtship*, 2003] have written by far the most comprehensive history and analysis of the U.S.-Ethiopia relations. Bonnie Holcomb and Sisai Ibssa [*The Invention of Ethiopia*, 1990] have shown how the U.S. maintained, if not invented, the Ethiopian autocracy for its hegemonic purposes. Jeffrey Lefebvre's *Arms for the Horn* gives a remarkable analysis on a flow of superpowers arms into Ethiopia and Somalia during Cold War rivalries. The late Professor Harold Marcus's *The Politics of Empire* sketches the United States-Ethiopian relations from the Second World War to the collapse of the regime of Hayla Sillase. Professor Theodore Vestal's *The Lion of Judah in the New World* extensively discusses the relations between the government of Hayla Sillase and successive administrations of the United States. The late

---

[1] The power of the king is above the earthly law since he is *Siyyuma Igzi'abiher, Elect of God*. Disobeying him was disobeying God. An Abyssinian proverb says, *Banigus sim qum sibbal inkwan saw, waraj wuham yiqomal* [When demanded to stop in the name of the King, flowing water stops flowing, let alone a man]. The Oromo democratic tradition asserts that *Qaalluu Waaqa se'ee, biraan baanan beeke* [I thought the King is God when I came near he is not]. This democratic culture is the culture Abyssinia rendered backward and liquidated.

John Spencer has commented on the relations between the U.S. and Ethiopia at length in his memoir, *Ethiopia at Bay*. Recently, Amanda McVety's *Enlightened Aid* has polemically elucidated on how the massive aid the U.S. poured into coffers of the Imperial Ethiopian government failed to deliver its purported goal of democratization and defection into the Communist bloc.

Some of these scholarly works are the mirror image of the historiography of Ethiopia or one can say the Ethiopianist perspective on the U.S. Ethiopian contact. Most Ethiopianist scholars begin with showing Ethiopia's "uniqueness" from the rest of black Africa and her "unique" orientation to the West and vice-versa. It is a norm for them to blend the image of Ethiopia as a beacon of "black independence" with biblical allegories and sell it as such. Revealing the suffering and suffocation caused in the region because of deeds of the empire builders is non-starter. They praise the "glories" of Ethiopian sovereigns, their "unique" diplomatic ties with the U.S., and enumerate the successful diplomatic, financial, military supports or sometimes mention, with the heartbrokenness, those declined.

Confronted with the question about the destination of all these weapons, they have no ready answer except coming with lists of imaginary external threats. For these scholars, Ethiopia is in the middle of her unnatural spot, nothing to do with the Negroes to the south and Muslims to the north. Not only geographic besiegement and religious isolation, but also she is in the state of constant threats from her antagonistic and belligerent neighbors. In a nutshell, the innocent Ethiopia is caught in a perpetual quagmire of a no-war-no-peace situation. However, Ethiopian rulers' ongoing wars to rule their citizens at the gun point merit exceedingly rare commentary.

Josh Rushing, a Gulf War veteran, who later became a correspondent for the Aljazeera television once asserted, 'CNN films the launch of the missile; Al Jazeera films what happens where it lands' (quoted in Khogali and Krajnc, 2009). Similarly, Ethiopianist scholars talk about the gift of weapons; I will talk about the victim of the weapons. They talk about the glories of those sovereigns; I shall remember the agonies of the peoples, who lost glories and history, because of the conducts of those sovereigns. I will comment on how the blank-checks and blankets of helps the U.S. rendered them exacerbated the torments of the voiceless victims. I remember them, as the novelist George Santayana aptly remarked, "Those who do not remember the past are condemned to re-live it" (quoted in Robinson, 2006, 4). I remember them, not for the sake of remembrance, but Ethiopia has to change a century of agonies and discriminations and move to a new chapter of equality. In this regard, the U.S. policy has to shift from a century of benign negligence of the plight of the second class Ethiopians. It has to encourage if possible, or to pressure if necessary, the Ethiopian government for genuine democratic reforms. The U.S. foreign policy towards Ethiopia should move from partisanship to facilitating a platform for various actors and stakeholders on the Ethiopian politics to have a dialogue on the future of the country. That said; let me sketch a panorama of Ethiopianist scholars' discourses on the U.S. and Ethiopia relations by taking a few samples.

Negussay Ayele (2003, 19) captures the image of Ethiopia as a symbol of black independence in this polemic way, "In the minds of the peoples of African descent at large Ethiopia symbolized their collective entitlement, supplication to God, their eternal redemption as well as their emblem of identity, liberty, and dignity wherever they are." Getachew Metaferia (2009) also follows the same trajectory. This is so true because the African diaspora imagined Ethiopia as an emblem of black liberation with the Battle of Adwa. It is so true at the time that the entire African continent was covered with colonialism and wanted inspiration, and, it is so true that the Ethiopians of Cush has such sensational appeal in the bible.

Whereas both writers are good at sketching the African-Americans enchantment with Adwa they never mentioned unrecognized Ethiopians, who were disenchanted with the result of their collective success against the racism of White man. They unequivocally condemned the sufferings of the African-Americans; they hardly cited the African-Americans in our backyard, the people Abyssinia colonized and enslaved, the "Shanqilla." If racism merited abomination, shouldn't we suppose to condemn or highlight the plight of those Ethiopians, who were ridiculed and dehumanized because of their complexion? Was not calling a certain race *bariya* (slave) worse than calling a race "Negro"? Was not a case of an industrial scale slave trade in Ethiopia and depopulation of the native peoples worse than segregations in the U.S.?

In fact, Getachew's shibboleth is racism, unraveling the endemic racism in the U.S., at the time. He deserves a credit for his well-articulated argument on that. According to his supposition, the "race relations [in the U.S] shocked most Ethiopians," for "Ethiopians [were] never colonized" and they "were unable to comprehend it" (Getachew, 2009, 27). He enumerates catalogues of what he calls the "concerns between Ethiopia and the US" relations since his Ethiopia is not only the symbol of black renaissance but also the drum major for their rights in diaspora. Thus, a certain Ethiopian aristocrat publicized racial discrimination in the U.S.; and a certain Ethiopian feudal lord horrified by segregation and discrimination (ibid, 26-7). Above all, racist it was, the U.S. denied Ethiopia the right to purchase types and amount of weapons she wanted (ibid, 31-2). I was frustrated by his sheer negligence of widespread discrimination in Ethiopia, but I kept reading because the book is well written and fun to read. I also deceived myself believing that he would drop in the epilogue, in the best traditions of the Ethiopian historiography. From alpha to omega, he was silent, and I was deadly proved wrong.

I came to the issue of slavery. Again, he follows the same pattern; perhaps, this one is worse. My impression is he argued that the whole issue of slavery was a farce and a conspiracy to deny Ethiopia the right to purchase weapons and her place in the club of "civilized" nations. Unfortunately, a third of Ethiopians traded as chattels and almost universal peasant servitude in the country did not merit a single line from this anti-racist scholar, let alone criticizing the U.S. and Ethiopia for failing to do their assignments. Getachew is from Illubabor (ibid, 57), and, he admires "enlightened" Manziyan Governor Tasamma Nadaw (ibid, 26). His enlightened governor was notorious for his earth-shattering manipulation of the peasants' coffee even to the extent of a grand looter, Minilik, inhibiting his behaviors when the coffee export dropped (Garretson, 2000, 121-2). I might guess that he might have a clue about peasants' embezzlement and land expropriation, but, he never stated it at all, except lambasting the *Darg* for a "radical" land nationalization policy (see, Getachew, 2009, 132).

Suddenly, his eyes are wide opened on the issues of slavery. He saw the "modern form of slavery" in the form of smuggling and airlifting of Beta Israelis, which "raised questions about the abuse of the human rights" (ibid, 56-7). Good observations! What about the bondage [bigotry] they passed through since the alleged destruction of the Aksum civilization by a certain Jewish queen (Gudit!)? He lamented how the Eritrean referendum was framed as a choice between independence and slavery, and "thus denying them other choices as had been accorded to them during the previous referendum" (ibid, 82). For the historical record, there is one and only one referendum. Otherwise, Eritrea was a gift of U.S. diplomacy to Hayla Sillase. As we shall see later, the "referendum" he talked about was a handful of hearings by the United Nations Commission in the urban centers. Above all, he hardly comments on the unspeakable abuses the Eritrean people suffered at the hands of either Mangistu or Hayla Sillase.

The late Paul Henze, a national security expert on the Horn during the Carter administration, a man who played a crucial role in propping the current government of Ethiopia, follows the same classic topos of "peculiarity" and "victimization" of Ethiopia. Asked about "America's strategic and economic interests in the Horn of Africa," he had to explain how the Portuguese saved Ethiopia from "Arabs" in the Sixteenth century. What was a link here? Does that mean the U.S. has to save Ethiopia from her invisible enemies surrounding her? In his word, '*Ethiopia might well have become an Arab country at that time had the Portuguese not come in*' (Henze, Episode 17). For that reason, 'the United States did commit itself to give Ethiopia a substantial military aid' since both countries have "a special relationship" (ibid). Therefore, as he unwittingly yet aptly implied, the pillars of the bilateral relations are Ethiopia's peculiarity from Africa, and lavishing a "besieged" nation with marvelous gifts of death machines.

Professor Vestal's approach is preoccupying himself with the praise of Hayla Sillase, who is not only a good guy at home and an inspiration for the world, but also the one who dismantled racial inequality in the U.S. His latest book, *The Lion of Judah in the New World*, is glorifying Hayla Sillase from a beginning to an end. He even tries to show how he changed Americans' perception of Africa and contributed for the election of the first black president. In his words, "The image that the Americans people developed during Hayla Sillase's prominence played a significant role in the election of Barack Obama as president in 2008" (Vestal, 2011, 196). When Americans think of "a son of Kenya" running for the highest office of the country, the images of the emperor's visits immediately clicked in their minds (ibid). In my view, as opposed to the votes of the generations of 1950s or 1960s, Obama carried the votes of minority, young generation, immigrants and women. Here, I am not disputing his claims, and this is not the crux of the matter of my subject. I might agree, to a certain extent, with him that a dazzling light of American media attention that the "Lion of Judah" secured might in some ways contribute for shifting the racial stereotypes. Nonetheless, my main disagreement with Professor Vestal is his reluctance to address the inequality in Hayla Sillase's Ethiopia because his idol was a "just" ruler. Thence, he rarely mentioned egregious violations of human rights committed by the regime. I should add that Professor Vestal is not only a passionate and committed Ethiopianist but also a "human rights" activist. He is amongst the foremost critique of the current government of Ethiopia, especially its "ethnic" policy since ethnicity is good for waging a guerrilla war, not for running a country (Vestal, 1999).

John Spencer, a 'white Ethiopian', who diligently served Hayla Sillase for good four decades, approach was an obsequious praise of the emperor. His Hayla Sillase was a "gentle," "thoughtful to the point of anticipating the needs or desires of others," "rendering many kindnesses with no thought for advantage or return," "grateful for small favors," "forgiving," and a "dynamic head of state." He even praises his megalomaniacs, 'holding the destiny of Ethiopia in his hands' (Spencer, 2006, 135-6). Although no white man on earth had witnessed expansionist tendencies and byzantine politics of the emperor, he ended his aforementioned memoir with the Herodotus' image of the righteous king of the ancient Ethiopia. This king neither "coveted a land which is not his own, nor brought slavery on a people which never did him any wrong" (ibid, 369).[1]

---

[1] The spillover effect of romanticism with the Ethiopian tyrants is also seen in American popular cultures. Karen Mercury, in her fiction, *The Four Quarters of the World*, reinforces the Amhara version of history, Oromo as invaders and illegitimate to rule the nation. The Tewodros' Empire was nation where, "hundreds of thousands of warriors defending their homes against pagan Galla intrusions," which Tewodros says, "Before I came to the throne ruled our country of the Amharas" (Mercury, 2006, 302). They worried more about the Oromo invaders than the British invaders, who came to defeat Tewodros. The

Thus, despite the fact that there are copious works produced to enlighten us on the U.S. and Ethiopian relations; there is a paucity of emphasis on the U.S. foreign policy impact on the dynamism of power play within Ethiopia's complex political landscape. Relevance of human rights discussion is reduced in importance to a sidekick. With the exception of a few writers, it is a trend to address the relations in abstract—as relations purely between two artificial personas [states]. This approach neglects the public of both countries as both the beneficiaries and victims of the policy. The relationship is not created in the vacuum; it involves human life at the both ends of spectrums. Irrespective of their flourishing or deterioration, the peoples of both nations have to pay the cost somehow; Americans through their taxes and Ethiopians through their lives and freedoms. Unfortunately, the American public is uninformed about the impact of their pocket on unhappy masses of Ethiopia. The American media never gets hold of the egregious violations of human rights committed there, nor do stories other than hunger or coup win the media coverage. This book will try to explore the untold aspects of the U.S. and Ethiopia relations.

---

fiction also narrates about the passion of killing, "*geddai.*" "A man could brag for forty geddai, the murder of forty men. [...] A lion is good for four men, and rubbing out a hated Galla was sufficient for a whole ballad" [ibid. 2]. In the book, Oromos are known by the pejorative name; however, it was published in 2006. Their trademarks are "heathenism;" "Mohammedanism;" exotic horses; wonderful eunuchs serving Tewodros loyally, and their cruel swordsmen whom the emperor uses to decapitate men. The book is full of "Tewodros' mercurial caprices" and his mercilessness, "I shall send their bodies to the grave and their soul to hell" (ibid. 244). Still, she 'loves' her hero character because "Tewodros was an incredibly magnetic and dynamic" Christian King of Kings; although, some people style him 'the crazed'. The press release of this fiction asserts that it "is a fresh, historically accurate, and exciting new take on the classic story of Emperor Tewodros of Abyssinia" (Press Release, 2006).

Introduction

DURING THE TURN OF the twentieth century, the United States was coming out of an age of isolationism, ready to join imperialist powers in overseas adventure, ready to espouse 'manifest destiny' as a rationale to civilize the world, ready to export the values of a master race through trade. In short, it was poised to begin the hunt for markets for its rapidly expanding industries. One prime target, the African continent, was at that time in the jaws of European colonialism. The U.S. responded by sending a diplomatic expedition to Ethiopia. Ethiopia had just defeated the Italian bid for colonization at the Battle of Adwa by defeating the European power. For some people, she turned out to be the "Japan of Africa" or "Switzerland of Africa," and for others she became synonymous with 'anticolonial' movement. Even though Abyssinia had "civilization" mission of its own underway at home, it was seeking recognition to reject a potential "civilization" mission from European powers. Commissioner Robert Skinner led the first U.S. mission to Abyssinia. Based on biblical allegories, he regarded Abyssinia as a "Caucasian" and a Christian civilization.

This contact made in 1903 gave rise to one of oldest diplomatic liaisons the U.S. established with the African continent.[1] The milestone diplomatic relations benefitted both parties. While the U.S. bestowed a diplomatic morale boost to the throne of Ethiopia, in return, Ethiopia provided foothold for U.S. adventurism in Africa.

---

[1] The U.S. diplomatic relations with Abyssinia was the third oldest diplomatic liaisons with the African continent. The first diplomatic contact was the Eaton Mission to the Bashaw of Tripoli, on the aftermath of the Barbary War in 1805. The second one was with Liberia. Some writers argue that the relationship with Ethiopia was the second one after Liberia. Maintaining that Liberia is the creation of the U.S., Ambassador Aurelia Brazeal, argues that the U.S.-Ethiopian contact was the first tie the U.S. formed with Africa (see, Skinner, 2003, 1).

The U.S. was among the first nations to be colonized by Europe, and it was the first nation to break the shackles of colonialism. It became a beacon of democracy and of human rights by virtue of being the first nation built upon a constitution and the Bill of Rights. Sooner, the U.S. grew into as an exuberant, affluent, modern nation based on technologically-driven capitalism.

Notwithstanding the fact that America is a product of European civilization, once it cut the umbilical cord from Great Britain in 1776, its political identity of isolationism and exceptionalism provided a counterpoint to European culture. America represented a 'New World' that had severed paternal ties with the corrupt Old World system rejecting their claim of divinity to rule, 'supremacy of the blood aristocracies', and 'power politics with its intrigues and wars' (Rossini, 1999, 14). "Others were held in bondage by the privileged classes, but America was the land of opportunity where demonstrated individual worth rather than birth was the test of a man" (Hill, 2007, 197). Furthermore, its image flourished as "God's elect;" noble America was regarded as "the vanguard of humanity;" poised to usher mankind into a new chapter of civilization. As Rossini (1999, 18) demonstrates, the U.S. portrayed itself as anything but a champion of liberty, a beacon of democracy, a messenger of peace. America at that era was championed to be the "city on a hill," i.e., "the model republican society that the rest of the world could emulate" (ibid).

Nonetheless, when the United States formed diplomatic relations with Abyssinia, there were well-formed myths on both sides of this partnership. America's republican ethos of democracy and equality served the Darwinian doctrine of the time, 'the survival of the fittest,' and promotion of self-interest.

These nations were connected by a thread of cultural imperialism. [1] Amharization/pacification of the surrounding peoples in Northeast Africa through conquest by Ethiopia and introducing Americanization through

---

[1] At the time, racism was a norm in the U.S. On President Roosevelt's 'unequivocal racism' towards Indians, refer to chapter four. He had similar view on Americanization of immigrants, "We must Amercanize them in every way, in speech, in political ideas and principles, and in their way of looking at the relations between Church and State. We welcome the German or the Irishman who becomes an American. We have no use for Germans or Irishman who remains such. We do not wish German-Americans and Irish Americans who figure as such in our social and political life; we want only Americans, and provide they are such, we do not care whether they are of native or of Irish or of German ancestry" (Roosevelt, 1897, 24). We should add that blacks were a fraction of human being in some part of the U.S. Also refer to chapter four on the Jim Crow laws.

global adventurism by the U.S. served as overriding cultural ideologies, a confluence of the imperialist ambitions. Native Americans at, the time, had to be 'Americanized,' which implied dispossession of their land and uprooting of their cultures. Non-Abyssinians in the Ethiopian Empire were also regarded as non-Ethiopians, and had to be civilized with "superior" values based on a culture, language, and religion of the Amhara people, the dominant cultural group of the emerging Ethiopian polity. While Native Americans soon became a tiny minority of the U.S population; non-Abyssinians were and remain the absolute majority in Ethiopia

The U.S. was/is prosperous and emerging as a global power. Citizens of all backgrounds had a fair shot at the American dream. Freedoms of speech, of the press, and of religion were taken for granted. Contrarily, Abyssinia was a predatory, feudalistic, bastion of slavery; a poor; war-torn, intrinsically undemocratic nation. The concept of human rights was foreign to the empire; the kings ruled by divine grace. Upward mobility by a non-Abyssinian was possible only through self-denial.

However, Ethiopia had a different appeal abroad; it was a romantic appeal, indeed. Let me explain this image with my personal experience. One day, I had a fantastic conversation with a certain white American scholar. He is a biology teacher, who baptized in the holy water of evolution. He is a young, well read, passionate and broadminded person. In a nutshell, he is an American, who is interested in talking about the staff of 'planet' out of America.

He said, "Where are you from originally?" I replied, "As your family was originally from Europe, I am originally from somewhere in Africa." He continued, "Where in Africa?" I replied, "A country called Africa as allegedly Sarah Palin said." "Come on, she is damn, Africa is a vast continent," he said. I responded, ok, somewhere in East Africa. He said, "Give me a hint?" You have to guess; you are smart; I said. "Nigeria," he said. No, that is West Africa, I replied. "South Africa," he continued. South Africa is south; I noted. Morocco, Ghana, Egypt, he was all over the map. "Kenya," he said. No, I am not the one who brought a birth certificate of Obama from a hospital in an African jungle, I replied. "That is not me, it is Donald Trump," he said. I could see his intellectual rambling to make sense of his flimsy geography knowledge. To make a long story short, I am from the Oromo country. It got worse. He had no clue. Ok, I am from Ethiopia.

Suddenly, his face shined. He was amazed how he forgot it. He gushed: I know that you guys are Jews, Christians, custodians of the Ark of Covenant; Hayla Sillase was a terrific guy; your Prime Minister [Mallas Zenawi] changed the country, and he was our ally. I patiently tried to listen to this gentleman because he is so cool, passionate, polite, and sincere. I asked him sources of all these information or misinformation, particularly about the Prime Minister.

He saw from newsflash about his funeral from a local television. I explained my position to him calmly.

This gentleman could not help but loving me more. He repeated so many times, "I love you." I was confused. I found a little bit of an American psyche in myself. I failed to understand a relationship outside the context of sex. I am not a gay, I whispered in my mind. Tell me why, I asked him softly, but not romantically. He is a citizen of Ethiopia like me because Ethiopia is a "cradle of humanity." "We all are the children of Lucy, Viva Lucy," he chanted. His only difference from me, he lectured me, I am carrying a passport of Ethiopia.

My sense of humor came. The only problem, I said, we issue the passport for a person who naturally born on the Ethiopian soil (Jus Solis) since our land is limited to accommodate the whole world population. "You see, your large country is even not large enough, or your politicians do not like to accommodate Latinos," I remarked. "Fair enough," he nodded. "We are citizens of one earth, we are all leaves of one tree, and we are the fruits of one branch as Abdul-Baha championed," I remarked. Humanity everywhere has one goal, I insisted, to live a happy life, but greed impedes a human family from understanding their unity and harmony.

Most of the views of my American friend are typical views of Americans politicians at the early twentieth century. Ethiopia was all about her status as a unique nation, Semitic outpost (Orient in Africa), Caucasian, next door to Black, noble, Christian, homogenous nation, and all of its peoples speak a language called Ethiopian (Ethiopic). Of course, there are images of famine and war that flourished later, but there was no attempt to correlate them with inhumane policies of the empire than simply presenting as facts of nature. Her diversity is at best discovered through lenses of anthropologists and linguists, who either interested for the sake of appreciating diversity or justifying the "civilization" mission of the ruling elites.

Therefore, the U.S. politicians' perception of Abyssinia fitted squarely with the myths Europeans had propagated about that empire grounded in a version of history that the Abyssinian ruling elites had fabricated. This image of Ethiopia was fundamentally in error and consequently led to misguided policy, which shaped all subsequent relations between the U.S. and peoples in the region, peoples who were actively oppressed by Ethiopia. American racial biases and outright prejudices were written undiplomatically and blatantly at the time. We learned these from the writings of the U.S. plenipotentiary diplomat, Robert Skinner, and of President Roosevelt himself. Nothing drives this point home more than Skinner's assertion that the Caucasian Abyssinia came of age by triumphing over the "savage" tribes who arrested her development and severed her connection with the "civilized" world (Skinner, 1906, 187). Tragically, the "savages" were the people Abyssinia conquered, enslaved, brutalized, killed, exploited, dehumanized, evicted from their lands, made into the second class citizens, turning a numeric majority into a political, economic, and cultural minority.

For the protagonists of this paradigm, Ethiopia was a certain throne, and the U.S. foreign policy towards this country was measured by its commitment to that throne. For this paradigm, the country became synonymous with Hayla Sillase, and thus, his visits were spiced up with a dazzling light of American media or the diplomatic razzle-dazzle while the agonies of his subjects were kept in darkness. Therefore, he got weapons without conditions.

Likewise, pan-Africanists had similar fascination for this country. Ethiopia is "a granite monument, a living exponent of the black race, the shrine enclosing the last sacred spark of African freedom, the impregnable rock of black resistance against white invasion, a living symbol, an incarnation of African independence" (quoted in Magubane, 1987, 165). The same is true about Arab historiographers who appreciated the Abyssinians as "the people of the scriptures," and their land as the land of "just" monarchs. To sum up, as John Hotten well-said, *'About no part of the habitable world has there been such prolonged misconception and ignorance as about the country of the Habese [Habasha], or, as we style, Abyssinia'* (Hotten, 1968, 13).

Ethiopia is different from what people in the West know, feel and imagine. This country, which is situated between latitudes 3°N and 15°N and longitudes 33°E and 48°E, was formed by force a century ago and maintained as such still today. It is a home of ethnic mosaic, and they are of predominately of non-Semitic stock. The occupied peoples extend from the Sudanese border in the west to the Somali border in the east. They extend from the Kenyan border in the south and occupy the center of the country including Addis Ababa. The Abyssinians proper occupy only three provinces in the northern Ethiopia. Equally, she is a home of diverse religions, and even after a century enforced conversion, almost half of its population follows faiths other than Christianity. Inasmuch as she is early recipient of Christianity in the world, she was the oldest happy home of Muslims.

Ethiopia, the "cradle of humanity," is not a cradle for all of her children. In other words, she has never been all embracing mother because she is based on the principle that 'some of her children are more equal than others.' She lionized some of her children as "chosen" to rule the country and denied the same right to the majority of them. This made the conquered people a social and political out-cast in their very own country. Her monarchs were compassionate and generous to their loyalists and power base [an alliance of the Church and the Amharic nobility] to the extent of robbing the conquered nations and giving them. Contrarily, they ruled the conquered people by cruelty. They ruled with gun [*naft*], and hence, they replaced their indigenous institutions with an administrative system based on "the rule by gun," the *naftanya* system.

Therefore, the quintessential feature of Ethiopian diplomacy is all about gun, "the gun diplomacy" or the *naftanya* diplomacy. Good staffs such as trade, tourism and investment take a backseat of her diplomacy.

So, Ethiopia garnered 80 percent of the U.S. military aid allocated to Africa since 1950s till 1970s (Skinner, 2003, 43; Lefebvre, 1991, 13-4). *To put into perspective, she received four times U.S. military aids to the rest of African countries (some fifty plus countries) put together.* On the other hand, she received only ten percent of development assistances the U.S. donated to the continent (Skinner, 2003, 46). For instance, Ethiopia, along the coalition of the UN, saved South Korea from the communist takeover in 1950. The Koreans learned democracy and development from the U.S. and miraculously leapfrogged from poverty in twenty years. Nonetheless, it lives on the same Peninsula with a nuclear armed hawkish North Korea.

This gun diplomacy (heavy machinery) neither benefitted the Ethiopian people did it nor save the throne that worshiped it. Nor did it prevent Eritreans from severing ties with a "motherland." The western gift of heavy machine is a gift of white elephant. It overburdens, wounds, bleeds, agonizes, destroys the country. The result of gun diplomacy is only deaths and defeats, nothing else.

During the formation of relations, the intention of the U.S. was to transform Abyssinia through belief in the ability of commerce to lead to a positive chain reaction, i.e., the assumed premise that commerce promotes wealth; wealth promotes modernity; modernity promotes democracy and human rights. Transformation of Ethiopia was also a double-edged sword since Washington wanted it to transform into a leading consumer nation for America's mushrooming industrial production. Besides countering the influence of "unfriendly" European colonial powers by allying with the U.S., Ethiopia had also a keen interest to avail herself of U.S. science and technology for her modernization and nation building.

Ultimately, the U.S. was neither successful in inspiring Abyssinia through technological innovations (democratization), nor did it discover a veritable treasure trove of the raw materials (or market) it wanted. It did confer unequivocal sanctification for the Abyssinia's pacification crusade on her "heathen" neighbors, however, always presuming that the "Caucasian" Abyssinian race was "superior" to her "Negro" neighbors. In this book, it is my argument that where America, as the self-proclaimed messiah of freedom and democracy underpinned a racist ideology in its dealings with the emperor, it permanently undermined its ability to champion human rights in the region. The emperor had already legitimized his power through overt racism. In the end, the United States foreign policy towards Ethiopia was based on the same colonialist assumptions as Europeans rather than being informed by the liberalism and idealism it claimed to promote. The diplomatic genesis between the United States and Ethiopia was devoid of human rights concerns, and the relationship has remained locked in that erroneous position without correction [or reversal] to the current day.

The prevalent wrong perceptions about Ethiopia are demolished if one properly understands the formation of Ethiopia, and examine the relationship between its components thoroughly. The slogan of the Gestalt psychologist says, "The whole is greater than the sum of the parts," but the whole has never been a holistic enough in case of Ethiopia as Ethiopia means Amhara. Professor Donald Levine (1974) characterized the *Greater Ethiopia* as a synthesis of dialectics between a unification thesis, spearheaded by the Amharas, and a colonization antithesis, championed by the Oromos. In my view, the idea of the Ethiopian synthesis is more of wishful thinking. If there is a synthesis, it is an incomplete, inadequate, imperfect, and failed synthesis. What is the synthesis between Amhara and Ogaden except the synthesis of violence? What is their relationship after a century of the occupation, a mix of water and oil in a glass? What is a synthesis between Amhara and Anyuak except mainly the synthesis of exploitation? What is the synthesis out there when the country is maintained together at the gun point? Thus, it is through analyzing the relations (experiences) between the conquered and conquerors that one understands the egregious violations of human rights committed in the name of Ethiopia and the fierce urgency of addressing them now. In this case, the U.S and Ethiopia relationship is not only evaluated through the throne it sustained for a long time, but also through the plights of the voiceless victims of the throne it sustained. I call the latter as the dark side of the U.S-Ethiopian relations. My mission is to illuminate that dark side, which kept in the darkness for so long in literary, media, and policy world. This dark side will never be brighter if I do not bring into the spotlight the dark side of the Abyssinia history, i.e., political developments within the empire, and, what that meant for its diverse peoples.

The Second World War heralded a new era of the U.S. position in the global politics. The U.S. emerged as a global leader with a powerful army, largest and vibrant economy, and net creditor to the rest of the world. Above all, in order to safeguard its position in the post war world order, it developed interests in all corners of the world (Hubbard, 2011, 1). In spite of the fact that the U.S. foreign policy profoundly suffered from inconsistencies and double standard, the U.S. played a crucial role in the birth of the first convention on earth that enshrined the principles of universal human rights, the United Nations Charter in 1945. The U.S had a lion's share in the passage of the Universal Declaration of Human Rights in 1948 despite its reluctance to embrace economic rights.

During this period, the Soviet Union that the U.S. assisted to resist Nazi aggressions became forceful in spreading its ideology. Beyond the ideological antagonisms, it sooner rivaled the U.S. in terms of military capabilities, to the extent of leapfrogging over it in the areas of space technology. Then, the entire U.S. foreign policy was hijacked by Cold War hostilities.

Subsequently, the U.S. and Ethiopia relations entered a new chapter. This was a marriage between the U.S. desire to secure influence in the region, and Hayla Sillase's strategy to survive by strengthening his ironclad grip on power. The nature of this diplomatic milieu left no room for developing policies based upon rationality and the mutual benefits of the peoples of both countries.

In the context of Cold War tensions, nothing was as necessary to the U.S. as containing Communism and Arab nationalism; for which the "Christian" Abyssinia appeared to be the best candidate to be used as a regional surrogate in return for American weapons, money, and diplomatic support. Thus, Ethiopia catapulted to among the top client states and beneficiaries of the U.S. assistance programs. Although security cooperation was at the center of the aid packages, there were also crucial programs like technical assistance programs and Peace Corps. Through these, U.S. administrations undertook interventions in the areas of education, health, public administration, airlines, and so on. Clientelism developed at two levels: firstly, at international level, Hayla Sillase as a client and the U.S. as a patron; secondly, at national level, Hayla Sillase as the patron and his supporters as clients. At the first level, rather than lifting the poor out of poverty, it vitalized the ruling class power, increased their parasitic propensities by allowing them to control the Ethiopian economy. Their symbiotic relationship with the Anglo-American corporations led to accumulation of wealth in the hands of a few.

In this liaison, whereas the U.S. secured a robust agent in geopolitically significant region of the Red Sea by running Kagnew spy station, it underwrote the emperor's government–both militarily and economically. Despite the fact that U.S. aids were instrumental in militarization; U.S. contributions in fostering a culture necessary for a humane political order in Ethiopia were negligible. In addition, U.S responses to the Empire gross breaches of principles of human rights and self-determination enshrined in the aforesaid international instruments were lukewarm. Thus, unconditional external assurances to his throne made Hayla Sillase aloof and unresponsive to demands of his subjects. Of course, domestic legitimacy was unnecessary because external legitimacy and divine grace were sufficient for the "Conquering Lion of Judah" to conquer his subjects indefinitely with impunity. He did this both metaphorically and literally.

At the second level, those ostensibly nice educational and development projects funded by the U.S. favored only Hayla Sillase supporters, excluding the vast majority of Ethiopians from the benefits. Though they were beneficial in principle, their distribution and administration perpetuated a fundamental inequality among the ethnic and religious groups of the country.

In short, during this period, Hayla Sillase was a force to be reckoned with, and his empire became a nerve center for U.S. imperialist agendas in the region. The U.S. viewed him as a good friend; visionary; reformer; modernizer; and a deal broker. Although his international image was impeccable, his house was not in order. He chose to preside over internal fault lines, which did not bother him as much as his imagined external threats. Taking the sustainability of his throne for granted, the U.S. National Security commentaries had mainly obsessed with the succession chaos upon his "natural" death. Beyond providing unwavering support to his regime to check the advance of communism, Washington rarely pressed him for domestic reforms. Unbeknownst to him, a demise of his power was none other than the result of his own makings.

However, the U.S. was providing unwavering support to the regime of the Emperor to check the advance of communism; Communist leaning military officers overthrew his rule. When Ethiopia switched sides at the heyday of the Cold War, Washington found itself in a diplomatic nightmare. Surprisingly, U.S. priorities in the region turned into containing Ethiopia and her Red Emperor, Mangistu Hayla Maryam. Why did the U.S. policy on Ethiopia fail in such terrible way? Why did the Ethiopian political elites and the intellectuals, whom the U.S. baptized with the anti-communist curricula, choose the course of radicalism and antagonism to their former master? What did precipitate the Ethiopia's 180 degree diplomatic turn? This book addresses that dilemma by investigating the foundations of American policy toward Ethiopia.

In overview, this work has two volumes. The first volume addresses the relations from the inauguration of diplomatic relations to the downfall of the Hayla Sillase's rule in 1974. It consists of 12 chapters.

A daunting challenge of studying U.S. foreign policy in general and towards Ethiopia in particular is the absence of uniform policy, there are variegated and amorphous policies; different yardsticks for a friend and a foe in a similar situation. This is double standards. Sometimes, what works for the world never works for the U.S., American exceptionalism. Though mythicized as the el-dorado of human rights and democracy, the U.S. is sometimes a role model for human wrongs and dictators through setting poor examples such as Guantanamo, Abu Ghraib, waterboarding, and wiretapping. What is wrong with the U.S. foreign policy? Therefore, chapter one introduces some historical and paradoxical legacies within the U.S. foreign policy. By finding out the subtle and fundamental factors that outline the U.S. foreign policy, we shall try to establish the basis for the understanding of U.S. foreign policy towards Ethiopia.

Whereas the doctrine of isolationism was a dominant theme of U.S. foreign policy, we shall examine a metamorphosis the U.S. made from a 'model republican state' to a 'republican empire', at the turn of the twentieth century. In a parallel development, in chapter two, we shall see the formation of the modern Ethiopia, a transition from "Christian kingdoms" to an "Amhara Empire." Then, we draw attention to the subsequent power relations among its components, that is, between the conquerors and conquered peoples. Then, we shall comment on how the formation of Ethiopia set the stage for diplomatic relations with the U.S. But, before a formalization of diplomatic contacts, there were informal contacts between the peoples and governments of both nations. Thus, chapter three will bring that into the spotlight.

One understands Ethiopia's foreign policy and diplomatic alignment if one has a decent grasp of her myths, which played extremely powerful roles in defining Ethiopia for foreigners. These are the myths which created in the minds of the Westerners the images of Ethiopia as a Semitic outpost and a Christian Island in the nucleus of heathens and infidels. In relation to the inauguration of diplomatic ties, chapter four tries to highlight the footprints of Ethiopia myths on the relations. It tries to provide how those pseudo historic facts dominated and impacted the relations.

Chapter five presents U.S. silence about addressing the smoldering human rights issue of the time, the slave trade, which was an endemic—a flourishing epidemic—in Abyssinia during the onset of this key diplomatic contact. Contrarily, the U.S. connection provided a cover for Ethiopian slavery in the early days. Hence, the human rights of millions in Ethiopia living in bondage never bothered the U.S. One cannot help but entertain the irony of the U.S. pledge to champion human rights when its plenipotentiary diplomat denied the existence of slavery while, at the same time, he offered a biblical edict to justify the Abyssinian enslavement of the subdued peoples. The sixth chapter deals with the U.S.-Ethiopian complex relations during the era of Iyyasu V (1913-1916). I draw attention to his reforms, and how the confluences of interests of the Church, nobilities, and the West led to his downfall and the rise of Ras Tafari, the future Hayla Sillase.

Chapter seven focuses on the relations from the rise of Ras Tafari to the Italian aggression of Ethiopia. In this episode, we shall grasp a U.S. dilemma of choosing between two emerging dictators, Ras Tafari and Mussolini. We shall offer an observation on Ras Tafari's strong inclinations to form stronger relations with the U.S. to counterbalance European influences, and, on the other hand, we shall see, how Mussolini ascended to power in Italy with the strong support of the U.S. I will also comment on how Hayla Sillase's total control of the country's resources contributed to expansion of his court, which he used to his advantage by purchasing weapons and consolidating powers unprecedented in the history of Ethiopia. We shall also see how lukewarm he was to the international calls for eradicating slavery from his empire.

Chapter eight discusses the interruption of diplomatic relations by the Fascist aggression. We shall discuss the U.S. government and public reactions to the invasion. We shall focus on the universal anger Mussolini encountered from African-Americans, and how the double identity of Abyssinia, black or white, bewildered them.

Chapter nine focuses on the resumption of bilateral relations. I shall discuss contributions of the U.S. in dismantling fascism and creating a 'totalitarian empire' and a totalitarian dictatorship of Hayla Sillase. In this light, I shall offer observations on the U.S. role in building military, higher education institutions, airlines, national currency... etc. It discusses how a guilt mentality of President Roosevelt (reluctance to help Hayla Sillase before the war) and the victim image of Hayla Sillase (helpless prey of the Fascist bully) contributed to the victimization of the Ethiopian peoples by resulting in unconditional support from the U.S. for a tyrant. Chapter ten explains the growth of the bilateral relations amidst the growing mutual dissatisfactions. We shall explain the challenges posed by the emergence of Somalia, Arab nationalism, and communism. We shall also see how the unchecked power of Hayla Sillase gave rise to the escalation of provincial oppositions. In chapter eleven, we shall see student activism and road to socialism. The last chapter fill focus on a logical conclusion of misguided policy, that is, the overthrowing of the Lion of Judah.

That all said, some general remarks and caveats should be entered about this work. The question whether the U.S. stands for human rights or human rights stands for U.S. national interests has been debated seriously. We are not going to indulge into this complex debate. It is tough yet to evade that entrapment since the U.S. foreign policy poses such a formidable challenge because of murkiness of a demarcation between human rights and national interests.

The book neither argues that U.S. is a prime mover and shaker of events in Ethiopia, nor does it argue that the U.S. policy on Ethiopia is a force for bad. It argues that the U.S. policy, on balance, is more helpful to the ruling elite as opposed to the large masses. It has to support the aspirations of Ethiopians for democratization and human rights. If the U.S. foreign policy is based on right premises and purposes it espoused to stand for, it will be meaningful and can positively impact the lives of the masses. I should also note that it is my central belief that the destiny of Ethiopia is in the hands of the Ethiopians, and the ruling elites are primarily responsible for making or breaking the country.

Let me throw a few lines on the scope of this work. This book is about exploring the U.S. foreign policy towards Ethiopia. There was the absolute majority of Ethiopians that the Ethiopian ruling class considered and rendered foreigners in their own country. Thus, I decided to deal with both ways: the U.S. foreign policy towards Ethiopia and the Ethiopian foreign policy towards the majority of its own people. Accordingly, some of the issues and events, in this book, are highlighted not to illuminate the U.S and Ethiopian relations, but to throw light on the nature of the Ethiopian Empire, the empire America underpinned and undergird blindly. Finally, I tried to organize the events in this book according to a chronological order to the extent it was possible. Fragmentations of discussions and ideas are natural in this approach. I will try to make connections as much as I can. Making a loose distinction between Abyssinia, a cluster of Christian kingdoms, and Ethiopia, an Amharic Empire, I use both terms interchangeably.

Orthography of Ethiopian words is highly inconsistent and difficult. For example, Menelik, Menelek, Menilek, Minilik, Menyelek, Menyelik are variants of transliterations used for the emperor of Ethiopia. Some is true for geographic places: Walo, Welo, Wello, Wallo, Wollo, and Wolo….is the transliteration an Oromo name for a place. Of course, none of them is scientific and gives accurate pronunciation for a foreigner. Nor the transcriptions I embraced are scientific/accurate. Otherwise, all I can say is I tried to be as consistent as I can.

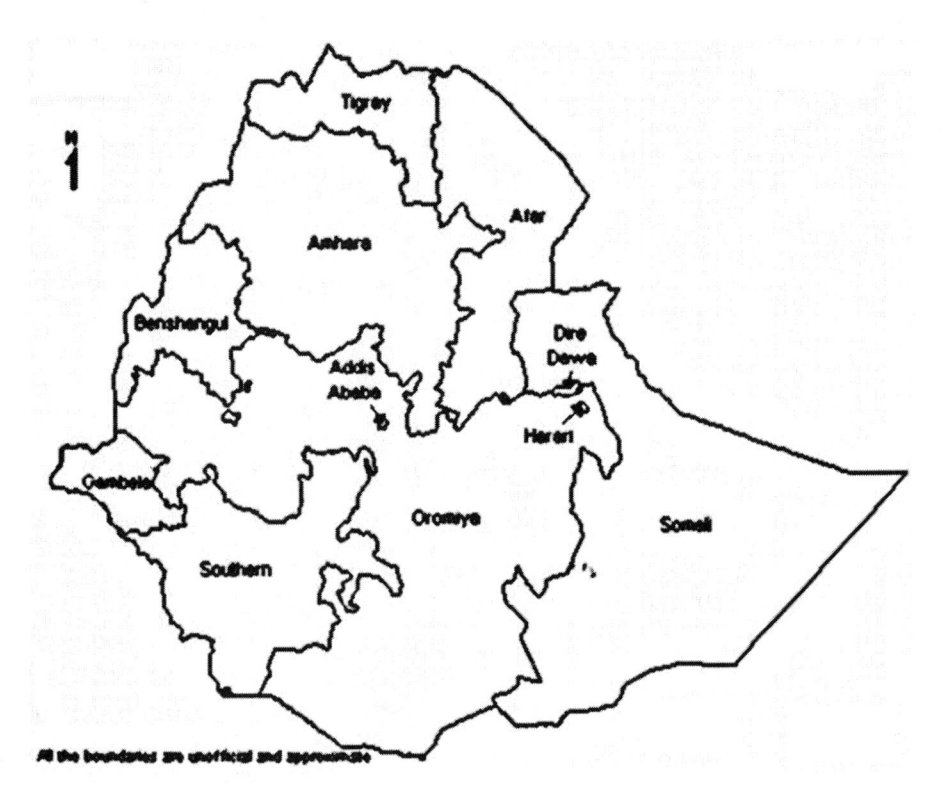

Fig 2. Administrative Map of Ethiopia. Courtesy of Fao.org

1   The Rhetoric and Reality of U.S. Foreign Policy

Puritans with their emphasis on the moral virtuousness and American exceptionalism shaped how the public looked at their government during the early days of the birth of the republic. They played a crucial role in defining what America stands for. America epitomizes utopia of human rights and democratic essences as the nation bed-rocked on a constitution and the bill of rights unmatched elsewhere, which some claimed divinely guided.[1] By virtue of its cultural and moral superiority, America has a divine mission (manifest destiny) to spread the flame of liberty and freedom to the world (Chambers, 1999, 273). This utopian view was informed by "the enlightenment's faith in reason, progress, the essential goodness of human nature, popular sovereignty, and the benefit of equal access to opportunity" (ibid). Adlai Stevenson, ardent proponent of American exceptionalism, underlined this idealism in these words: "America is much more than a geographical fact. It is a political and moral fact" (ibid).

Thus, the human right rhetoric was at the heart of U.S. foreign policy since independence from the colonial shackles of Great Britain as witnessed by the writings of various American prominent political figures. 'A bill of rights,' Jefferson explained, 'is what people are entitled to against every

---

[1] The Puritans had a strong belief that God played a significant role in the making of the Constitution. Alexander Hamilton, one of the founding fathers says, "For my own part, I sincerely esteem it a system which without the finger of God, never could have been suggested and agreed upon by such a diversity of interests." See, George Frater, Our Humanist Heritage (Nashville: Thomas Nelson Publishers, 1978), 139.

government on earth, general or particular, and what no just government should refuse, or rest on inferences' (Bernstein, 2003, 72). The Declaration of Independence splendidly confirms "life, liberty and the pursuit of happiness" as "self-evident" truth and "inalienable rights" given by the creator. Tom Farer noted, "concern for human rights has been a prominent theme in the rhetoric of American foreign policy" since "the revolutionary war of independence to this day" (quoted in Kommers and Loescher, 1779, 263). These and other statements made at different times have been the manifestation of the U.S. government's commitment, at least rhetorically, for upholding the cause of individual freedom, self-determination and civil liberties globally as part of its foreign policy.

The America idealism promoted the doctrine of isolationism. A quintessential feature of this doctrine was an absolute abnegation of entanglement in global affairs, except in the cases of commerce. Thus, participation in any regional or global organization or formation of an alliance with any country contravenes with the principle of non-entanglement. A famous diplomatic historian Perkins argues that the Declaration of independence was 'an act of isolation, a cutting of ties with the Old World... which existed on the other side of the Atlantic' (Perkins, 1952, 10). George Washington, however, set clear tone for it. In his farewell address of 1796, he admonished a fresh and exuberant country from entanglement. He said, 'It is our true policy to steer clear of intimate permanent alliances, with any portion of sovereign world' (Washington, 1892, 318). His rejection of entanglement was strong that he compared it to slavery. "The nation which indulges towards another a habitual hatred or a habitual fondness is in some degree a slave. It is a slave to its animosity or its affection, either of which is sufficient to lead it astray from its duty and its interest" (ibid, 312). Credit goes for the Monroe Doctrine which drew a line in the sand between the New World and the Old. Monroe's "quest for American identity" and requesting European nations to recognize her laws and voice was a "diplomatic declaration of independence" (Perkins, 1993, 169).

Inferring from this, a grand champion of individual freedoms should keep her distance from the rest of the world since on balance the detriment of the interaction outweighs the benefit (Rossini, 1999, 13). America, the possessor of superior culture hardly gains anything in return from an intercourse with inferior cultures that have a potential to vitiate the purity of American ideas. In a way, isolationism was accentuation of the racist Anglo Saxons weltanschauung which Americans borrowed from their European ancestors and injection of social Darwinism into international relations (ibid). Whereas the utopian idealism that mutated into the "manifest destiny" underpinned America's westward expansion that resulted in the seizure of Native American lands; it forbade America into carrying that experimentation into the global scale.

America had never been all about the idealism. Political realism was a subset of foreign policy, for that matter, the prominent one. It originates from a dualistic approach of the founding fathers who appealed to justice whilst they pursued energetic defense of national interest (Hill, 2007, 197). Although the founding fathers were Lockean in their understanding of domestic affairs, they were Hobbesian in their understanding of the state of world affairs and international law. Exaltation of liberty and a moral consideration of state's decision in the international arena come auxiliary to promoting and defending national prosperity, privilege and power (Chambers, 1999, 273). The political realism allows entanglement in international affairs, but only for protection of self-interest.

Hence, the foreign policy debate essentially revolves along the orbits of moral idealism and political realism that underpins two entirely contradictory worldviews. Contrary to buttressing each other, these pillars are in the constant state of tension, which underlies the intrinsic paradoxes between "principles and interests" and between "moral purpose and military primacy" (ibid, 272). The foreign policy often swings along the pendulum of human rights and national security depending on the side that happened to possess more gravitational force at the time. As Neilsen (1969, 245) said: "American policy early and steadily reflected a duality of approach, intertwining of idealistic declamations with hardheaded pursuit of national interests."

The doctrine of isolationism yielded for the political realism during the presidency of William McKinley, who capitalized on flexing military muscle abroad. This brief hiatus was at the best characterized by the reification of the expansionist penchants of Henry Cabot Lodge known as "Large Policy." Senator Lodge dreamt of "making the United States the indisputably dominant power in the Western hemisphere, possessed of a great navy… and contesting on at least even terms with the greatest powers, the naval and commercial supremacy of the Pacific Ocean and the Far East" (quoted in Hendrickson, 2009, 285). In 1895, Lodge bragged of the imperialist achievement of the country often portrayed itself as an emblem of republican ethos as follows, "We have a record of conquest, colonization, and expansion unequalled by any people in the Nineteenth Century. We are not to be curbed now… For the sake of our commercial supremacy in the Pacific we should control the Hawaiian Islands and maintain our influence in Samoa" (quoted in Williams, 1962, 34).

In 1898, when the Cubans started the war of independence against their Spanish colonizers, it opened the door for the U.S. to carry out a "humanitarian imperialism." The U.S. intervened to end the plight of Cubans but smartly ripped off the war booty by occupying Philippines, Puerto Rico, and Guam. The Spanish-American War widely opened the door for exporting the "manifest destiny" overseas. The U.S. catapulted to a "colonial empire" or an "industrial empire" or an "imperial democracy" or a "second empire."

A "first empire" or a "republican empire" being the continental expansion completed in 1850 (May, 1961, 220; Restad, 2010, 29).

Fig 3. President W. McKinley, 1986. Image: Courtesy of Courtney Art Studio.

The heyday of American imperialism raised multitudes of burning questions such as the constitutionality of the territorial expansion and how far the constitution follows the flag. 'Expansionism and imperialism are at war with the best traditions, principles, and interests of the American people' and undermines "the schemes of a republic which our fathers formed," declared the prominent constitutional scholar, Professor William Graham (quoted in Raustiala, 2009, 79). For some, the U.S. adventure abroad was part of America discharging its manifest destiny to civilize the world by exporting the values of the master race. Senator Beveridge of Indiana noted:

> God has not been preparing the English-speaking and Teutonic peoples for a thousand years for nothing but vain and idle self-contemplation and self-admiration. No! He has made us the master organizers of the world to

establish [a] system where chaos reigns. He has given us the spirit of progress to overwhelm the forces of reaction throughout the earth. He has made us adepts in government that we may administer government among savage and senile peoples. Were it not for such a force as this world would relapse into barbarism and night. And of all our race He has marked the American people as His chosen nation to finally lead in the regeneration of the world. This is the divine mission of America, and it holds for us all the profit, all the glory, all the happiness possible to man. We are trustees of the world's progress, guardians of its righteous peace (quoted in Schirmer & Shalom, 1987, 26).

The U.S. eruption in the global scene in no way satiated the imperialist lust of U.S. politicians at the time. Complaints of Washington being left out from the global market and commercial prosperity were commonplace experience. "We must have the market [of China] or we shall have revolution," or "we are driven from the markets of the world," or "[w]e are on the eve of a very dark night" were some of the memorable quotes said by politicians at the time (Williams, 1964, 34). Coming under enormous pressure at home, McKinley's Secretary of State circulated a series of notes dubbed "open door policy" to major powers that had an interest in China from 1899-1990 underscoring the need for "sharing" Chinese trading rights while respecting its administrative and territorial integrity.

Emboldened by "unexampled prosperity" America witnessed as a benediction of his policy, McKinley delivered one of the finest speeches at the Pan American Exposition at Buffalo. He declared America's departure from the policy of isolationism. His 'dinner-pail industrialism' failed to pay a dinner for all. On the next day after his speech, he was assassinated by the anarchist that uses 'violence and political assassination as a means to force a change in social relations between the haves and have-nots' (Skrabec, 2008, 184).

McKinley's successor, Teddy Roosevelt, the youngest president in history of the U.S., embraced his signature foreign policy achievements, i.e., use of force if necessary on the foreign soil to "exercise international police power." Roosevelt underlined the importance of force to advance America's interest in global arena using an African maxim, "Speak softly and carry a big stick; you will go far" (quoted in Davison, 2003, 9). James Morgan contends that while Roosevelt was portrayed as a disciple of the 'big stick', a hallmark of the adage 'speak soft' was totally lost in the black hole. In his argument, presenting Roosevelt—who never used the big stick at home or abroad—like "a bully, looking for a trouble, and spoiling for a fight" was a big distortion of his key diplomacy, 'speak softly' (Morgan, 1919, 217).

Whatever was the merit of the argumentations, Roosevelt embraced imperialists' insatiable demands for market expansions overseas. He joined a subtle version of the 19th century British Imperialism, the "imperialism of free trade'" or "informal imperialism" (Louis, 2006, 912). Gallagher (1982, 15) argues that the rebranding imperial agendas as "trade not rule" was nothing but the same strategy destined to extend control, 'informal empire if possible, formal empire if necessary'.

On December 2, 1902, in his Second Annual Message to the Congress, Roosevelt laid a blueprint for his new foreign policy based on adventurism abroad as follows, "We may either fall greatly or succeed greatly, but we cannot avoid the endeavor from which either great failure or great success must come." He underlined a new desire for larger global influence, "As a people we have played a large part in the world, and we are bent upon making our future even larger than the past" (Roosevelt, 1902). Learning from deeds and misdeeds of his predecessor, Roosevelt, who inherited America with overseas wars and military virility, pursued a new approach to make "America great among nations." Instead of policing uncivilized powers, he chose to civilize them through commerce since the "United States will hold the key" for "unlocking the gates to the commerce of the world, and closing them to war" (Williams, 1962, 34). Creation of a secretary of commerce and entering into reciprocity treaties were wisdoms of the day.

Theodore Roosevelt, 1898. Image from the United States Library of Congress's Prints and Photographs division under the digital ID cph.3b14493.

2 The Making of Minilik Empire

ETHIOPIA IS A NAME that conjures up, and arouses passion in faraway places for different reasons since time immemorial. She is often depicted as the birthplace of mankind, a Christian nation, a Semitic outpost, the land of Prester (Presbyter) John…. Wedding Ethiopia to antiquity is a norm both at home and abroad. Indeed, the sensational portrayal of Ethiopia became more radiant after the Battle of Adwa since Ethiopia turned out to be a quintessential beacon of blacks' freedom. This had got more colors when Ethiopia became the only internationally recognized country in Africa by joining the League of Nations, and when she became a symbol of the failure of collective security of the League. This is the image celebrated at home and projected abroad. Do all these depictions convey an actual reality about that country? Is she as old as she claimed to be? Is she as captivating, as she is imagined from distant place, for her children at home? We do not go into the image issue in this work as we shall treatise about that in a separate publication, but it is advisable to keep that perspective in minds since it will illuminate our discussion of the formation of the Empire of Ethiopia. To understand the anomalous birth of this amorphous nation, let's start by having some dose of a history lesson about northeast Africa.

The northeast Africa has a rich and a deep history. According to corpuses of archeological findings, the area is believed to be the cradle of human kind and civilization. The indigenous peoples of the region (Cushitic, Nilotic, Omotic stocks) are among pioneers of farming and domestication of animal. Being at the cross road of Asian and African continents, the area is a melting pot of peoples from both continents. As per the widespread historical assumptions, the Semitic stock (Abyssinian race) migrated, from the southern Arabia, to this area around 10th century BC. They introduced their Judeo-Arabic influences and Geez language (and script) to coastal areas of the Red Sea. Perhaps due to external pressure or search for fertile land, they later moved southward. Superimposed on the indigenous sub-strata of the Nilotic and Cushitic people of the area, a cluster of Semitic languages (Amharic, Tigre, Tigrinya...) emerged from the Geez language.

A foundational myth of Abyssinia was encapsulated in the Abyssinian "holy book" of *Kibra Nagast* [Glory of the Kings]. The myth claims that Abyssinia has a continuous history of three thousand years of nationhood since Minilik I, a son of King Solomon and the Queen of Sheba, formed a Kingdom of Aksum in the tenth century B.C. Abyssinia also asserts that Minilik I smuggled, from Jerusalem, to Aksum the most powerful totem on the face of the earth, the Ark of Covenant. Hence, Abyssinians are "unique" in the region since they are a Caucasian people (racially superior) and since they are bearers of well-placed civilization. These entitle them to rule the entire humanity. Therefore, they have a "divine" mandate to expand through peaceful means if possible and through coercion if necessary.

Contrary to what the myth alleges, the Kingdom of Aksum only emerged after the first century AD and embraced Christianity in the fourth century. For surety, this dynasty was eclipsed by the Zagwe dynasty that buried the fable of superiority of the Abyssinian race through their remarkable architectural achievements. In 13th century, the Amhara kingdom of Yikonno Amlak reinvented itself through the use of force as a legitimate claimer of "Solomonic" throne (see, Reid, 2012).

All myths about the "uniqueness" of Ethiopia were not the result of Ethiopian ingenuity, indeed. As Acemoglu and Robinson (2012, 235) remarked, maintaining that Abyssinia was a Christian kingdom in the heartland of heathenism, it became a "natural target" for European myths. For centuries, they romanticized about it as an exotic land of adventure, i.e., a domain of Prester John, a medieval fabulous monarch, who presided over, among others, on 'horned men' and 'men with eyes in front and back'.

The North Eastern Africa had been characterized with protracted history of conflicts, population movements, and migrations. Whereas Abyssinia was an expansionist entity since its formation; equally, there were expansions and migrations in the region almost from all directions. Prior to the introduction of European death machines into the region, the balance of power in the region and victories were changing hands from time to time depending on resources, seasons and organizations of belligerent groups. Suggestive of the fact that the Abyssinians had no better military formations, they were repetitively warded off by the indigenous peoples. The Bejas, Agaws, and the Jews of Lasta repelled the Kingdom of Aksum at various times; the Muslims defeated the "Solomonic" Kingdom in the 16th century until the Portuguese came to their rescue. The Oromos, under its *gada* military formation and without being supported by any power on earth, defeated them incessantly for more than two centuries. In its encroachment for millenniums, Abyssinia hardly advanced south of the Shawan plateau.

During the age of Scramble for Africa, the destinies of freedom loving peoples of the region began to change forever like elsewhere in Africa. Unlike the rest of Africa, the major contenders for the continent, Britain and France, reached a deadlock in the race for engulfing the area. They backed off from a direct confrontation. They agreed that the "barbarian" races of this region had to be civilized somehow. Considering that Abyssinians were closer to civilization than the Negroes of the "Dark Continent," Europeans had turned the Christian Abyssinia into a storehouse of modern weapons. Britain supported a Tigray warlord, and the delicate Italy gambled on Minilik of Shawa, and France took the short cut when relations between Minilik and Italy began to deteriorate (see, Holcomb & Ibssa, 1990).

None other than Minilik made the biggest capital out of the arms flow into the region. From 1880-1900, he imported 1 million rifles and 47 million cartridges from Europe (Yohannes, 1991, 200). He managed to mobilize 700,000 armies, and their dependents (wives, children, slaves, concubines, priests, and *tabots*), to conquer the neighboring lands (see, Shillington, 2005, 874). In 1989, when the Tigray warlord, Emperor Yohannes killed while trying to execute the British agenda in Sudan, he emerged as a sole runner for the throne of Solomonic Ethiopia. He proved his military virility by defeating European power using the European technology.

He vigorously crusaded the Abyssinian "civilization" mission into the lush green of the south to bring to an end "savagery" of the native peoples. Therefore, law and order, 'Pax Abyssinica', would prevail in the conquered areas (see, Naty, 1994). The military formations of traditionally equipped peoples, who have no other weapons but their bravery, a lance, a knife and a shield, hardly matched the Abyssinian well-equipped army with European death machines (Marcus, 1975, 64). His brutal army swallowed up the host of self-governing states: in most cases through violent confrontations or rarely through cooption of the ruling elites. Thanks to immeasurable treasure troves of gold, ivory, coffee, musk, hides and skins, and slaves he procured from these areas, he formed a symbiotic relationship with the European merchants of death. This helped him to maintain his control over the conquered areas with the same harshness without having the need for accommodation of the demands of the conquered peoples in the empire.

The rich resources of the Oromo lands had brought a relief to the Abyssinian nomadic warriors who were constantly on the move in search of loot (see, Teshale, 1995, 34). As a result, Abyssinia abandoned a tradition of moving capital. Minilik created a modern city, Addis Ababa (the new flower), by removing the indigenous Oromo people, who call the area Finfinne, the land of spring water.

Thanks to the resources of the south, the Europeans introduced a western modernization to the empire in return for raw materials from the occupied territories. They wanted to convert Abyssinia into a modern consumer nation. At a certain time, Empress Taytu asked the Europeans, 'Where will our poor country find the resources to satisfy the needs you create? Do you think our people will be happier than they are now?' (Prouty, 1986, 219). Thanks to the agencies of Europeans and the abundant resources of the south, Emperor Minilik had introduced elements of modernization to Abyssinia. He formed a facade of a western style ministerial cabinet. He built hospitals, roads, railroads, school, banks, telegraphs, and schools. Most of investments were for *Ketemas*, garrison towns for his soldier settlers. The roles of the occupied peoples were sustaining the pace of modernization, and the Abyssinian rule over them felt by slave and stock looting expeditions, tribute extractions, land annexation, cultural dislocation, and forceful imposition of alien culture.

Unlike the Abyssinian myth states, a contemporary Ethiopia is, therefore, a product of the late nineteenth century conquests. Whereas Ethiopianist scholars dub the conquests merely as "unification" projects, other scholars depict the same events as "colonization" projects. Whatever label one uses, the brutalities of the conquests, the orgies of plundering, the manners of exploitations, relations between the conqueror and conquered attest that Minilik's projects not only had affinity to colonial projects elsewhere in Africa but also exceeded them with violence.

For instance, the Minilik army killed about 100,000 people during its relentless onslaughts, for six years, to conquer the Arsi country (Gada, 1980, 43). To break their resistance, the conquering army engaged in amputations, beheadings, summary executions, and poisoning of water wells. If it is not called Holocaust or genocide, the Arsi peasants have coined a term for the sheer slaughtering of the Amhara conquerors, "warradomsa" (see, Østebø, 2011, 78). *Warradomsa* is a portmanteau, from *warra*, which means family, hearth, or people, and *domsa*, which means making [a knife] dull. *Warradomsa* means people who kill until a knife turns dull. According to a local tradition, the Minilik army killed over one hundred thousand people in the course of the Walayta conquest (Vaughan, 2003, 253). Vanderheym, a Frenchman who joined the Minilik army, reported what he saw as follows: "One had the feeling of witnessing some kind of infernal hunting where human beings rather than animals served as game" (quoted in Bahru, 2001, 65). The Minilik army triumphantly returned to Shawa with 18,000 Walayta slaves, who carried grains and drove cattle looted from the area (Strecker, 1994; Teshale, 1995).

Correspondingly, devastating impacts of the conquest on the Arbore was put in this ways: "All four Arbore villages were burned to the ground, the men massacred and women and children taken as slaves. Arbore tradition recalls this calamity: 'Menelik's army swarmed over Arbore land. Hyenas ate the dead as well as the living" (Markakis, 2011, 104). Evelyn Waugh, in his book, Waugh in Abyssinia, indicated that "The pagan peoples of the south and west were treated with wanton brutality unequaled even in the Belgian Congo" (Waugh, 2007, 24). In his work, *Sport and travel: Abyssinia and British East Africa*, Lord Baron Hindlip put what he saw in Abyssinia as follows,

> Menelik, instead of being checked, has been encouraged to extend his territory southwards in an uninterrupted march—redolent of lust, oppression, and crime. His chiefs ruling, or rather oppressing, the wretched Gallas living south of Adis Abeba, are little better than leaders of robber bands, living on what they take from the inhabitants, collecting revenue in the shape of cattle, sheep, and grain, and where elephants are to be found, indiscriminately killing males, females, and calves, and sending the ivory to the capital. Slaves are sent up, usually boys, who are brought for about sixty shillings at head at the capital. (Hindlip, 1906, 73-4).

According to Lord Hindlip, "The Abyssinians above all things excel in cruelty, both to mankind and animals…Their treatment of natives….is of too repulsive a nature to be dealt with in a book of this kind" (ibid, 70-71).

A Russian lieutenant—who campaigned with Minilik army in the Oromo land—dubbed the conquests as the "dreadful annihilation of more than half the population" of the Oromos (Bulatovich, 2000, 68). According to de Salviac (1900)—the French Capuchin missionary and traveler—the conquests claimed half of the Oromo population, which he estimated a reduction from 10 million to 5 million people.

The Minilikan army looted about 66,000 heads of cattle from the Arsi plateau (Mekuria, 1988, 102); about 18,000 from Walayta (Teshale, 1995, 57); about 50,000 from Jijiga (Markakis, 2011, 102); and about 40,000 from the South Omo (ibid). Minilik extracted unreasonable taxations and tributes from those areas that submitted with less resistance such as Jimma, Limmu, Gera, and Guma. Each paid $200,000 per annum in a tribute (Cahiers d'études africaines, 1962, 49). The prominent authority on the Scramble for Africa Thomas Pakenham designated the Abyssinian conquests as follows: "It was imperial expansion and Realpolitik, African style, and it brought greater rewards than any European war in Africa" (Pakenham, 1991, 486)

The Minilik march increased the Abyssinia's landmass more than threefold; the conquered peoples considerably outnumbered the Christian Abyssinians (Markakis, 1974; Levine, 1974; Mekuria, 1988; Salviac, 1900). The ethno-linguistic ecology and composition of the country has changed once for all, and the country became a home of more than 80 languages and a tapestry of cultures, which Carlo Conti-Rossini described "a museum of peoples." His description won him praise as "one of the greatest of all

Ethiopianists" from Levine (1974, 19) and 'the greatest authority on Ethiopian culture and history' from Woolbert (1935, 340).

Ethiopia was never complacent with being the museum of peoples because the conquered peoples were not "true Ethiopians," meaning: they were neither Christians nor the Amhara-type. Abyssinia considered them as the wild people without culture, religion, history, a prominent ancestor (such as King Solomon). Cultural chauvinism was embedded into every fabric and the very psyche of the Abyssinian society. Some of these offensive claims were written into the law and school books until recently. However, Abyssinia lacked sophistication to produce a "scientific racism;" the Abyssinian's hate machines equally fabricated and sustained countless myths about the conquered people to justify their discriminations. Gebru Tareke (1991, 71) eloquently noted this factor in this fashion:

> Paternalistic and arrogant Abyssinian looked upon and treated the indigenous people as backward, heathen, filthy, deceitful, lazy, and even stupid—stereotypes that European colonialists commonly ascribe to the African subjects. Both literally and symbolically, southerners became the symbol of scorn and ridicule.

Offensively, some tribes were described (even believed) as cannibals (saw ballawoch) or as stench as human feces (Donham and James, 1986, 107-8).

As part of the so-called the Abyssinian civilization mission, the empire supplanted traditional rules and institutions the occupied peoples with Abyssinian politico-administrative institutions of *naftanya* [neftegna] system. Thus, in addition to looting, they lost their land and became tenants on their very land. Haile Selassie and Volker (2000, 12) succinctly put this phenomenon in this way:

> In order to sustain rule and domination in the newly conquered regions, an institutional order called 'Neftegna' was put in place, which would become instrumental in perpetuating control and preponderance through systematic violations of human rights for nearly a century. Neftegna literally translated means 'gunman', denoting that the communication between the neftegnas and local inhabitants was regulated and expressed by guns. Most of the neftegna army that took part in during the campaigns to subjugate the inhabitants of the conquered areas settled in the newly established garrison towns known as 'ketemas' under the leadership of neftegnas. Eventually, a classic feudal socio-economic order was imposed, whose effective functioning involved the continuity of military, social, religious, political and other coercive methods of subjugations. With the establishment of this feudal edifice and the concomitant institutions of dominations in the newly conquered territories, abuse of rights became commonplace.

The Abyssinians considered conquered lands *terra nullius* since they treated the native peoples as idle, lazy and worthless vagabond (*Zallan*), who deserved no right to own land. Teshale Tibebu explains this point as follows:

> Two concepts epitomize the Menelikan Christian-Amharic conquest: *Agar maqnat*, and *dar agar*. *Agar maqnat* refers to colonization, cultivation, (and Christianization) of land defined as "empty," waiting to be made use of. Dar agar (frontiers) pertains to the end of horizons of the expansion, the boundary of colonization. Accordingly, the term "Galla agar" [Oromo Country] came to be identifies with a fictitious empty land. With that came the idea of the "idle, lazy Gallas," not working on the land they possess, a land wasted for lack of hard-working people, a land occupied by "infidels" (Teshale, 1995, 40).

The occupied peoples were stripped of their traditional usage of land; denied access to their shrines and resources thereof. Their accumulated wisdom for millennia on treating land and natural resources disappeared altogether. For instance, the Oromo peoples' practice of venerating and preserving trees, mountains, and rivers were banned. Therefore, the environmentally friendly Oromo tradition, a "pagan" civilization, failed to pass the test of Christianity. The Christian culture of cutting and burning millions of trees every year known as *damara* was promoted and universalized. Today, the Oromos of Shawa burn trees with their fellow Orthodox Christians once in a year and after a week march to their rivers and forests for their traditional rituals and perhaps to repent for the burned trees.

By prohibiting the traditional usage of lands, Abyssinia instituted a *chisanya- gabbar* system (serfdom) in the occupied territories. This involved confiscation of lands from the indigenous peoples and distribution among the Minilik's victorious settler-soldiers (*naftanya*) as war booty. An Amharic term for the "tenancy" is *chisanya*, "smoke." This signifies the ease with which peasants evicted from their land (Donham and James, 1986, 5). This system works in this manner: "Between 75 and 80 percent of the lands were seized by Minilik while the remaining 20 to 25 percent were distributed to cooperating chiefs" (TransAfrica Forum, Volume 9, Issue 1, 1992, 59). The annexed land "was quickly disposed in a wholesale manner to various groups of claimants from the north" (Markakis and Nega, 1978, 23).

In addition to this, these claimants had to procure corvée labor from the indigenous peoples; men have to work on land; build houses, fences, churches; children have to serve in households and look after animals; and women have to ground grains and fetch water, not to mention their raping by soldiers (TransAfrica Forum, Volume 9, Issue 1, 1992, 59). The relationship of the conquered people and the settlers was of that of slave and lord. For that matter, the corvée labor of peasants to settler soldiers was dubbed as *hudad*, the same word for Lenten Fast, which means a relationship of lordship and slavery was equated to one of God and His worshippers (see, Donham and James, 1986, 6). The corvée labor extractions cost the peasant 30 percent of their total farm production. Besides, the tenants have to pay harsh taxation of as high as 25 percent of their produce. Paradoxically, the southern peoples, who castigated as heathen, have to tithe from their meager produce to the church, which owned a third of the empire's land. The corvée, high rate of levy, and the tithe claimed more than two thirds of the produce of the tenants. If a peasant failed to pay taxes for three years, the land was considered abandoned, even though, he had effective possession of it. "Usually a person paying taxes for three years on such abandoned land may file a claim of ownership, which he is likely to acquire" (Lipsky, 1964, 471).

The abundant wealth found in the newly acquired places enticed more northerners to migrate and boosted the *naftanya* system. Joining Minilik army's monumental plundering and acquiring slice of booty was a classical Abyssinian dream. It was plundering in a broad day light. As the Thomas Hobbes's state of nature theory explains, it is the "unrestrained savagery of the plundering soldiers," when the plundering converts into a right (Schmitt, et. al., 2008, 24). Tibebu Teshale captured the Abyssinian loot as such:

> The saying *yaabateh bet sizaraf abrah zeraf* (when your father's property is looted, join the looting) is a recognition of how plundering was a means of livelihood not only of the warriors, but also of some peasants who, unable to stop the looting, would join the looters. 'Indeed part-time soldiering was almost the only way a farmer could escape for a time from being prey to others by participating in the plunder.' The common practice of peasants hiding their grain in deep pits outside their homes so as to save it from looting by the warriors was typical form of class struggle in the conditions of predatory appropriation (Tibebu, 1995, 35).

Owing to the lucrative looting tradition, and pervasive accounts of military fame, it was a dream and passion of every Abyssinian to attain the status of the landlord through the feasts of great bravery in war (Donham and James, 1986, 7). As Skinner aptly articulated, "The opulent Abyssinian is not born with a silver spoon in his mouth, but with a gun in his hand" (1906, 175).

Whereas the Minilik court flourished, wanton destructions and slavery wrought untold miseries to the invaded people. When the conquered territories were converted into the slave-mart of the invading army, and when the local people became a homeless in their home country, and when their traditional administrative system banned and replaced by the Abyssinian tyranny, they began to flee from the brutalities of the empire. The Horn of Africa demonstrated what ensued in this way: "The first exodus of refugees fled Oromo land in the late 1880's following the incorporation of Oromia into the Abyssinian Empire. Able bodied men left their wives and children, opting to live under British colonialism in surrounding countries rather than fall victims to nihilistic policies of land-hungry Emperor" (quoted in Mekuria, 1988, 41).

This is an image of Borana immigrants from Southern Ethiopia, Ellis Island, New York City, 1902. We do not know exactly the reason why they came to the U.S. but they came in 1902, which was five years after the Minilik army occupied the Borana country. Many native peoples were evicted from their land by the conquerors. Also countless people fled to the British colonies to escape from the Abyssinian slave raids.

Source: Augustus F. Sherman (2005). *Ellis Island Portraits, 1905-1920/ Historical Essay by Peter Mesenhöller*, New York: Aperture. Image Courtesy of the Ellis Island Immigration Museum and the Aperture Foundation.

A Borana man from Southern Ethiopia, Ellis Island, New York City, 1902. Source: Augustus F. Sherman (2005). *Ellis Island Portraits, 1905-1920/ Historical Essay by Peter Mesenhöller*, New York: Aperture. Image Courtesy of the Ellis Island Immigration Museum and the Aperture Foundation.

The Abyssinian "civilization" mission neither introduced a better civilization, such as a modern form of cultivation nor animal husbandry to the occupied areas. Nor the native peoples learned a work culture from them since the Abyssinians were "lazy" and dependent on them for food. The only profession of the Abyssinians was holding gun (*naftanya*) to loot and maintain the central rule. Augustus Wylde, who traveled through Abyssinia, at length, commented as follows,

> No harder worker than the Galla [Oromo] peasant of Abyssinia exits... No more truculent, worthless, conceited, lazy, useless creature than the Abyssinian soldier, who both formerly and now preys on the defenseless cultivator and breeder whenever a chance crops up (quoted in Hindlip, 1906, 72).

Lord Baron Handlip had also related observation about the Abyssinians:

> Next to the Abyssinian's cruelty comes his snobbishness, love of display, and admiration of shallow and cheap show in others... His laziness is only equaled by his contempt of the hardworking Gallas [Oromos], who grow his grain and raise his cattle, or rather their grain and cattle which he annexes (ibid, 71)

The lasting impact of the Abyssinian civilization mission was "the universalization of slavery" (Yohannes, 1991, 200),[1] their scorched-earth pillaging and destructions of ecosystems. For instance, in some areas, the peasants switched from farming by oxen to hoe since they lost their cattle to the Abyssinian warriors. This happened in the Arsi plateau (Markakis, 2011, 98). Similarly, parts of Hararghe lost their oxen. Harar sanga is delicious for an Abyssinian "bloody banquet," otherwise known as *qurti!* Even so, they had to give 75 percent of the produce to the warriors. Nor, even the Abyssinians had a desire to proselytize the conquered peoples properly except forceful imposition of their religion and dehumanizing and exploiting them on the basis of their adhesion to an inferior religion, "heathenism."

Another aspect of the Abyssinian civilization mission was replacing the indigenous justice systems, such as the *gada* system, with the Abyssinian justice systems. One of such system was *Leba shay*, a practice of intoxicating and walking a young boy, in the neighborhood, to detect a thief. In the Abyssinian sense of justice, an owner of a house (property) where the unfortunate boy collapsed, unfortunately, became guilty of theft (Naty, 1994; Bahru, 2001). The devastating impact of this institution on the indigenous peoples has been aptly demonstrated in Alexander Naty's article, *The Thief-*

---

[1] We shall deal with slavery in chapter five, in extended fashion and in relation to Abyssinian application to the League of Nations, as well.

Searching (Leba Shay) Institution in Aariland. He indicated how "it resulted in disruption of local societies," and how Aari children were taken as slaves for this otherwise "modern" Abyssinian justice system (ibid, 261). Similarly, a *quranya* system, a custom of chaining a defendant and plaintiff together until a case settled, mushroomed all over the conquered areas. Abyssinia also introduced a system of collective punishment for a crime committed by individuals known as *Afarsata*. According to an description of an American diplomat a crime for hiding a suspected criminal were 'confiscation of herds and destruction of the villages of the native peoples' (Skinner, 1996, 136). It was an ordinary experience for them to hand over one of their luckless comrades to redeem the entire villagers, women and children, from collective doom.

It was this Ethiopia that became a global sensation after the Battle Adwa. Whereas Adwa dominated international news, countless battles of Menelik against the defenseless indigenous peoples of the south "remained unknown to the wider world" (Strecker, 1994). Adwa was a psychological coup and diplomatic triumph over Italy and the invisible hand of Britain. Therefore, the talk about Abyssinia in European diplomatic circles changed from colonizing to coopting, from downgrading to promoting, and from unrecognized power to co-equal in the Scramble for Africa. In the eyes of the Westerns, Minilik instantly morphed from the symbol of barbarity into, at least, the symbol of semi barbarity if not fully civility. Lord Edward Gleichen portrayal of Minilik was emblematic of his perception in the western world. He depicted him as a man of prophetic mien, of "almost superhuman activity," "extra-ordinarily well acquainted with what is going on in the world, not only from a political, but from a general and even scientific point of view." His manners were "pleasant," "dignified," "courteous," "kindly," an "Oriental potentate," a pious Christian who "rises every morning at 3 a.m., goes to early morning chapel" (Gleichen, 1898, 151-153).

In short, diplomacy with Abyssinia became a popular vocabulary. Italy, Russia, France, the U.K., among others, had signed treaties, and, some had acquired concessions. An American diplomat based in Marseilles, who knew Ethiopia from biblical allegories, insisted the U.S. to pay homage to the Court of Minilik. So did a black tycoon William Henry Ellis.

3   Prelude to the Formation of the Formal Relations

FOLLOWING AN ANGLO-SHAWAN treaty of 1841, an informal contact between the U.S. and Abyssinia emerged. A head of the American Foreign Policy Agency advised the House of Representatives of the importance of opening, extending and protecting American interest in the east. In that connection, sending a similar mission to Abyssinia to seek commercial status of the same footing to that of Britain was essential. The U.S. dispatched Emanuel Weiss, a former employee of the East Indian Company and a man who lived for the eighteen years in the east, to the Red Sea region to evaluate business opportunities with Abyssinia. A Swiss traveler produced a detailed analysis of the trade of the Red Sea, but he dismissed doing business with Abyssinia as a non-starter since "neither Abyssinian nationality nor Abyssinian domination extends to the sea coast." But he indicated that the Hawash River basin would be in the future 'the highway for commerce and civilization of the Oromo nation' (Brownson, et al., 1850, 132-8; see also, Skinner, 2003).

In 1968, Henry Stanley, a naturalized American citizen from Wells, a restless wanderer, and the best war correspondent of his time, approached the New York Herald to commission him to report the Maqdala campaign. He described the motif for his adventurism as follows: "I had seen Americans fight: I had seen Indians fight; I was glad the opportunity to have of seeing how Englishmen fought" (Stanley, 1874, iii). He hardly saw them fighting as Tewodros conceded defeat, but he saw his brutalities and a British victory. His memoir provided detailed accounts of cruelties of the violent king, particularly against Wallo. For instance, he demonstrated how "30,000 men, women, and children were destroyed by crucifixion, the relentless courbach [a whip made out of hippopotamus hide], or by shootings, stabbings, or decapitation, within three months" by Tewodros (ibid, 358). He described him as a dictator who declared "I will have no capital; my head shall be the empire, and my tent my capital" (ibid, 372).

In November 1872, Emperor Yohannes IV wrote a letter to a U.S. president as part of soliciting "aid and sympathy from the Christian world." General Kirkham, a British commander-in-chief of Yohannes and his special envoy to the U.S. and Europe, submitted the letter to the U.S. consulate in London in 1872. The letter commences with the typical Abyssinian diplomacy of playing the victim. It reads:

> In all of Abyssinia we have nearly 8,000,000 Christians. They are the prey of Mussulmans, and as sought as slaves. For many centuries the Turks and Egyptian have succeeded in seducing and coercing them into bondage, and the function of Christian Abyssinia is considered to be the slave-mart for the Turkish Empire [...] America has lately given [the] freedom to 4,000,000 of slaves; can she not also give her moral support to 8,000,000 of Christians honestly struggling out of African bondage and barbarianism?

The writer was too smart by half. As the letter shows Abyssinia was not as such a prey but a predatory, as well. At the time, the Emperor was trying to subjugate the Wallo Oromo. The letter says, "Egypt in order to further her schemes against Abyssinia, undertook a hostile expedition against Emperor Yourness [sic] when *His Majesty was absent in the Azebo-Galla country endeavoring to suppress a rebellion*" [italics added]. Enumerating the miseries of the pioneers of Christianity in Africa, the letter explains why Abyssinia needed to be helped: "While the United States are nobly looking for the development of heathens Japan in the West [sic], it does seem to me that they cast a sympathetic glance at Christians Abyssinia to the East [sic]." Yohannes wanted U.S. supports against the Egyptian invaders, against Wallo in the name of abolishing slavery, access to the sea and a commercial treaty. Ethiopia needed the help of the U.S. because other Christian nations had helped and still helping it. "When Abyssinian rulers applied to the Portuguese kings," the letter says, "those monarchs had listened to the entreaties of Abyssinia" (Congressional Serial Set, 1873, 311). Recovering from the wounds of the civil war, the isolationist U.S. lacked appetite to form a diplomatic contact with Abyssinia.

In the same decade, American mercenaries recruited by Khedive Ismael Pasha, along Egyptian troops, fought Emperor Yohannes forces at different battles. Surgeon Major Johnson was captured by Yohannes army becoming the first U.S prisoner of war on the Abyssinian soil. In 1877, Yohannes soldiers captured an American civilian geologist affiliated with the Egyptian forces named L.H. Mitchell. According to Ambassador David Shinn, Mitchell might be the U.S. first citizen to have an audience with an Ethiopian ruler, although, not as a diplomat, but as a prisoner (Skinner, 2003, 6).

On the death of Yohannes, the Amhara-centered Empire of Minilik came into prominence. In March 1896, he defeated the Italian colonizers at Adwa setting a stage for black diaspora fascination with Ethiopia. A Pan-Africanist, Edward Wilmot Blyden, described the ancient Ethiopia as "the most creditable of ancient peoples," who had attained "the highest rank of knowledge and civilization" (quoted in Weisbord, 1998, 152). W.E.B. DuBois put Ethiopia as the "sunrise of human culture" and the "cradle of Egyptian civilization" (ibid). In short, Ethiopia became synonymous with black liberation, self-determination, renaissance, and inspiration.

The black activists flocked to Ethiopia to seek blessings (guidance) for their missions and to establish the emperor as the towering figure of pan Africanism, unbeknownst to them his self-denial. One of such figure was a Haitian apostle of Pan-Africanism, Benito Sylvain, who abandoned his Paris based newspaper, "La Fraternité," to become "a knight leaving for a Crusade" when the Adwa war broke out between Italy and Ethiopia (Jonas, 2011, 282). He envisioned Minilik as "African's first personality with a truly global stature" and "a redemptive figure" (ibid). Connecting Haiti, a home of the first successful slave rebellion, with Ethiopia, the first nation that successfully thwarted European colonialism on African soil, was his intention (ibid). In his wildest dream, Emperor Minilik was "the greatest black man in the world" for advancing the cause of "the general amelioration of the negro race" (Skinner, 1906, 131). Whatever was the framework and platform, buttressing Minilik was crucial for French colonial agendas, and thus, France facilitated Sylvain trip to Africa. In January 1897, he reached Addis Ababa, but Minilik was lukewarm to his initiatives. He never gave up. He came back with the same plan in December 1903. This time, Minilik's response was affront to him. Robert Skinner reported as follows: "Yours is a most excellent idea, my young friend. The Negro should be uplifted. I applaud your theory, and I wish you the greatest possible success. But in coming to take the leadership, you are knocking at the wrong door, so to speak. *You know, I am not a Negro at all: I am a Caucasian*" [italics added] (ibid).

However, although Skinner failed to mention, "Menelik was more 'negroid' in appearance than most Ethiopians" (Skinner, 1979, 280). Emperor Minilik, who was brainwashed by the Abyssinian court to deny his color, was, as the matter of fact, an illegitimate child born of a slave woman. As John Gunther aptly commented, no matter what their complexion told them, the Amhara ruling elites considered themselves to be white (1954, 255). Therefore, the Abyssinian whiteness was not because of their complexion but because of their self-definition, and a mere racial propaganda fabricated to conquer and dominate their adjoining nations whom the Abyssinians considered black (bariya or slave).

Emperor Menelik. Image courtesy of James William Young of Aden.

Despite Emperor Minilik's discourteous response, nothing diminished the enthusiasm of the black diaspora, for the God has spoken: "Princes shall come out of Egypt; Ethiopia shall soon stretch out her hands unto God" [Psalm 68:31]. Joseph Vitalien, a pan-Africanist and West Indian doctor from Guadeloupe, came to Addis Ababa to serve as a personal physician and advisor to Minilik. He helped Ethiopia to establish hospitals in Harar and Addis Ababa and mentored Ras Tafari.

A missionary from Missouri named Daniel Alexander was the first African American to settle in Shawa. He became quite prosperous from a farming business with many servants and cattle near Addis Ababa. Not only winning the trust of Minilik, he became his personal favorite (The Crisis, Vol. 40, No. 11, Nov 1933, 262).

Another prominent personality in cementing U.S. informal bonds with the Empire of Minilik was African-American magnet William Henry Ellis. Born in 1864 into an African-American family in predominantly Mexican-American part of Texas, Ellis worked as a cowboy in Texas and Mexico before joining college in Tennessee. In 1886, he entered a hide and wool trade in San Antonio, Texas. Fluent he was in Spanish, he decided to take his business to south of the border. He rechristened himself Guillaume Enriques Ellesio by translating his name into Spanish. He embarked on a cotton plantation business and his plan of colonizing African-Americans in Mexico. (See, US Department of State Dispatch, 1992; Hales & Haeussler, Ellis). His plan eventually proved fiasco because of bad organization, cultural clashes and diseases (Harlan, 1979, 462).

Then, he turned his attention to other business sectors, becoming a Wall Street stockbroker and a world traveler. In 1897, he moved to New York becoming the first African-American entrepreneur, who defied an established economic order by joining the club of a Wall Street stockbroker. Successful he was, he rented offices in the Drexel building along J.P. Morgan and Co. He came to be known as "the only Negro who ever invaded Wall Street" (McVety, 2011, 206). The New York times put Ellis as a "cowboy, boom town explorer, capitalist, receiver of water supply corporations in New York, a moving spirit in Central American and West Indian trading companies, a high liver, a mirror of extreme and gaudy fashion, and a side figure in the famous Fayne Moore badger case" (quoted in Menelik's Journal, Vol. 27, No. 1, 2011, 7)

In 1902, Henry Ellis caught up with the Pan-Africanist Sylvain in London, during the coronation of King Edward VII. Thereby, he found a chance to have an audience with Ras Makonnin who invited him to visit Ethiopia. Cutting his career *rite de passage* on a hide and wool trade in Texas, he knew a whole world of business opportunities Abyssinia would offer. Hoping that he was the best candidate to be named emissary to Abyssinia, he attempted to familiarize himself with the history and culture of the country. In December 1902, he spent three thousand dollars at a New York book seller to publish a book about the Ethiopian history. He was a believer that Ethiopia, like Egypt, was a pioneer of civilization that predates and surpasses European civilization. A self-made black millionaire he was, Ellis disproved the assertion that race was a barrier for the advancement of an individual or a country. As a consequence, he championed the idea of establishing commercial relations with Ethiopia. He underlined:

> Abyssinia is the richest country on the earth in gold, silver and copper, iron, rubies and I understand diamonds. There are great quantities of coal within two days of the capital, but nothing has yet been developed. The field of American trade in Abyssinia is

practically unlimited. There is a great deal of American manufactured stuff used there, in fact, the Abyssinian has discarded his leather clothes, and now stands robed in American cotton goods, but all of it passes through three or four hands, and finally reaches the Abyssinian at about four times the real value (The New York Times, Jan. 1, 1904).

He wrote to Secretary of State John Hay that all Abyssinia "need is good advice and teaching from a friendly nation which I am satisfied that they will get at the hands of this great nation" (McVety, 2011, 205). Ellis was convinced that he was the best candidate to represent the U.S. and seek a treaty with Emperor Minilik. Thanks to the wrong perception that Abyssinians were dark-skinned Caucasian, the U.S. opted for sending a white emissary to Addis Ababa. Ellis protested the decision by writing letters to the New York Times, the Baltimore Sun, and Washington Post, and all major black newspapers (Sotiropoulos, 2009, 145).

Knowing the futility of lobbying Washington to reverse the decision, he organized his own trip to Ethiopia ahead of a U.S. diplomatic mission. In 1903, Ellis, along with his friend Benito Sylvain, departed for Addis Ababa to explore repatriation of African-Americans to Ethiopia along with business and development initiatives (US Department of State Dispatch, 1992, 140). Being a political activist affiliated with the Republican Party, which was a pro-black party at the time, he approached Minilik with an intention to establish "a colored lobby" (Harlan, 1979; Adejumobi, 2007); unbeknownst to him his claim of whiteness. Ellis hoped that Minilik would be a defender of rights of Africans all over the world. When he invited him to make a statement, he proclaimed:

> As our American motto is, America for Americans, Monroe Doctrine, so I hope your motto will soon be Africa for Africans, Menelik Doctrine, and Europe for Europeans" (The New York Times, January 1, 1904).

Regardless of Minilik's perception of his own color, a black capitalist had won his confidence regarding the need to enter a treaty with America. Ellis reported his enthusiasm to receive a U.S. mission in this fashion, "I will welcome them in God's love: That is what I long for—connection with a nation that is not looking to get some of my territory" (ibid). The forthcoming chapter will throw light on the formalization of the U.S. and Ethiopia relations.

4   The Inauguration

WE HIGHLIGHTED THE TRANSFORMATION of American into an "industrial empire" around the turn of the twentieth century in chapter one. The boom in industrial development demanded market scavenger hunting in the foreign lands. Africa had spotted for its immense potential to enlarge U.S. market abroad. Indeed, the West Africa market alone was assumed to be "only second in importance to that of China" (Monthly Consular and Trade Reports, 1901, 437). Nonetheless, penetrating into the African market had never been an easy assignment as the compartmentalization of African continent into the sphere of influences and formation of custom authorities reached its zenith in this period. The last self-governing African countries that Washington had nascent commercial intercourses with had gone. France had claimed the Island of Madagascar by exiling the last king of Merina monarchy. The American cotton market once seemed to be indomitable had almost been taken by Europeans. Thanks to the agency of American Henry Stanley, King Leopold II of Belgium had turned the Congo Free State into his private colony. This was an enormous loss of market for America's gray shirting, otherwise known as *Americani*. Apparently, the Congo trade was a U.S. trophy for its participation, albeit in an observer role, in the Scramble for Africa at the Berlin Conference of 1884-85 (Feldmeth, et al., 2011, 178).

Liberia and Ethiopia were the only two "survivors" in the Scramble for Africa. Liberia was a colony founded by the Americo-Liberian settlers and a traditional sphere of influence of the United States in Africa (Duignan and Gann, 1987, 187). Annihilating the Italians at Adwa, Menelik made a name for himself as a single and serious stakeholder, from African soil, in the European project of Scramble for Africa. Desperately desirous for the market share of the continent widely known for its diverse flora and fauna, virgin and unexploited mineral resources, Ethiopia was the last spot left for U.S. trade in Africa. Being the last unclaimed territory, the trade with Abyssinia had become a shibboleth in Europe. The magic of her potential for the business had caught the attention of Americans alike. Some consular reports used hyperboles to express the world of business opportunities Abyssinia would provide. 'A very thriving trade with the Abyssinian Empire is perhaps the most promising to our people of all portions of Africa, and the least known,' insisted a U.S. consular intelligence report (United States Congressional Serial Set, 1902, 206). A consular intelligence report published in 1901 noted that the Eastern Africa was the last bastion of American's gray shirting, and, export from this area was totally in the hands of Americans. It mentions that skins, ivory, ghee (clarified butter), high-quality meat, hide and skins, mother-of -pearls, pearls, and salt were the exports of this area. It also noted the exports of coffee beans capable of indefinite expansion and favorable for the production of Mocha. The report, therefore, concluded that:

> The trade is worth now $661,844, and if the Harar trade is kept it will increase as the resources of the protectorate, and especially of Abyssinia, are developed. There is a whole of the protectorate and tracts to the east of it, the Ogaden and the country to the south, the southern portion of Abyssinia, and the Galla country, to be supplied with this commodity, now an ordinary requirement of life (Monthly Consular and Trade Reports, 1901, 137-8).

Similarly, an Italian Consular report, which put emphasis on the size of Ethiopia's population 10 million, "whose capacity of consumption merits the consideration of exporting nation," had fired the interest of doing business with Abyssinia in the U.S. (Monthly Consular and Trade Reports, 1902, 592). By 1902, a trade volume between Ethiopia and the U.S had vindicated these consular intelligence reports. It had reached $2.3 million of which the U.S had 59 percent share (Skinner, 2003, 8). Whereas the U.S. monopolized the import of the Ethiopian coffee, *Americani* had an absolute control of the Ethiopian market. In short, the U.S. had more than half of the small trade of the empire. This market was in jeopardy since Europeans were rushing to Abyssinia to seek export/import concessions. No wonder then why the U.S. had to defend its last remaining market in the continent divided by colonialists on paper. Consul Robert Skinner, an American adventurous career diplomat in France, developed a serious interest in preserving trade with Abyssinia. Who was Skinner and what motivated him? The next discussion will shade some light on his background.

Robert Skinner: An Engine of Relations and a Believer of Myths

Skinner was born in Massillon, Stark County, Ohio, on February 24, 1866. During his salad days, he became an editor and owner of a local newspaper called *The Independent*. Foreseeing a victory of a rising star, he joined an election campaign of William McKinley, a native of Niles, Ohio, for presidency. In 1897, Skinner married to his wife Helen Wales, a woman who hailed from a notable Massillon family with a deep connection to a political establishment. In the same year, he got the best honey moon gift from President McKinley when he appointed him U.S. Consul in Marseille, France. A newly married couple, Mr. and Mrs. Skinner, left Massillon to enjoy life in the land of romance. In 1901, Skinner was promoted to the position of Consul General (PoliticalGraveyard.com, 2013; massillonmuseum.org/66).

Came at the time when France was gripped with joy of their paw (Abyssinia) triumphing over Italy and the Britain invisible hand, Skinner quickly caught up in the mood of his time, fascination with Abyssinia. When he learned about Abyssinian's war-making qualities, he saw the spark of a "Caucasian" civilization from a far land in the heart of "darkness." According to the school of thought he belonged to, deaths and destruction [a power to control means of violence] and skin colors were the hallmark of the so called civilization.

Skinner was cognizant of a rapid transformation in the U.S. foreign policy under the administration of his friend William McKinley. Above all, based in Marseilles, a French colonial nerve center, he was cognizant of intensification of Scramble for Africa. At the time, France had an ambition to build a great transatlantic empire in Africa, running from Dakar on the Atlantic Ocean to the Gulf of Tadjoura on the Red Sea. Minilik was a key to a French plan since through Abyssinia it would secure source of the Nile River and deal a death blow to the British control of Egypt.

To achieve that, he had given a major concession for a French company to build a railway from Djibouti to Sudan. This project would take away Muslims traditional advantage over the caravan trade and eases the empire access to weapons. Skinner was familiar with a huge impetus of partial completion of the railway in enhancing commercial intercourse with the landlocked nation. The appeals of securing the market for *Americani* and importing the world class coffee and exploiting untapped mineral resources and abundances were particularly strong.[1] "Ethiopia," Skinner noted, "is

---

[1] Gibbon said, 'Ethiopia contains more gold than the mines of America' (1843, 282). Skinner repeated similar tone, "Gold is hidden away in the mountains in quantities which can be estimated by no exiting data" (1906, 187). He put Ethiopia as the "land of milk and honey."

wealthy in resources beyond the power of any man to calculate. Gold, silver, asphalt, petroleum, iron, and coal exist in combination with a salubrious climate, agricultural productiveness, and a population of singular docility" (1904, 166).

Beginning from 1900, Skinner was insisting the McKinley administration to commission him to negotiate a treaty of commerce with Minilik, "a Bismarck of Africa." "The United States has maintained friendly official relations with a number of small powers with which we have no commerce, but none with Ethiopia, where for years we had profited by a flourishing trade," asserted Skinner (1905, 413). Engrossed in the overseas wars and possibly interested more in open annexations, the administration found a little incentive for sponsoring an expensive expedition for a little return. Thus, it shelved his proposal.

President Roosevelt's new vigor for entering reciprocal trade arrangements with foreign nations threw a strong momentum behind the Skinner's resolve. In 1903, when he put forward his plan, the response was overwhelming and prompt.

On 25 October 1903, a year after Roosevelt promised to play "a large part in the world," a Skinner's expedition left Marseilles for Abyssinia for a threefold mission: opening a diplomatic relationship, inviting Minilik to participate on the St. Louis Exposition, and conducting a scientific research on behalf of the Department of Agriculture (The New York Times, October 18, 1903). His longtime friend, surgeon Dr. Abraham Pease and his brother-in-law, Secretary Horatio Wales, joined him at Naples, Italy. A contingent of marine guards selected from the USS San Francisco and the USS Brooklyn, the U.S. Navy Mediterranean squadron, went on board of the gunboat Machias, at Beirut, Lebanon. There were 19 mariners commanded by Captain George Thorpe and six Navy Bluejackets directed by Lieutenant Hussey.

On November 21, they reached Djibouti. Rested for two days, they boarded a steam locomotive destined for Dirre Dawa. Keeping two sick marines in there, they arranged their forty two caravans of camels and mules, and, they left for Finfinne, an autochthonous Oromo name for Addis Ababa, on November 29, 1903. After twenty-two days of the arduous journey through the desert, they arrived on 18 December 1903. Cognizant of the emperor arranging a 5,000 men guard of honor for them, the mariners dressed their blue uniforms as they came approached the city. Warriors embellished with leopard and lion skin mantles heralded the arrival of the Americans into the city with music, dances, noises of trumpets and horns.

According to Skinner only "the bright rifle barrel" differentiated the Minilik's army from their ancestors who accompanied the Queen of Sheba to Judea. The colors and melodies of bizarre music spellbound them 'the fall of Jericho' and "the Yankees at the Court of King Arthur" (1906, 76). Mounted on their horses, the Abyssinian warriors ushered the Americans to the emperor's palace. The Europeans trained Abyssinian artillery men welcomed the guests with a 21 gun salute. Minilik, as Skinner described, "sat in Oriental fashion, ...wore diamond eardrops, and several rings upon his hands, his face was full of intelligence, and his manners those of a gentleman as well as a king" (ibid, 78). Minilik, a Bismarck of Africa, "confounded American expectations" since he happened to be "anything but an isolated, provincial leader." Nonetheless, "Skinner was immediately struck by the emperor's kindness, intelligence, and wit—and skill at diplomacy [and…] impressed by the emperor's interest in them and their country" (US Department of State Dispatch, 1992, 140). The emperor organized a fabulous feast of honor for his American guests. The European style marching band and marching infantrymen escorted the delegation to a camp designated for their stay, Ras Walda Giyorgis compound, provisionally rechristened "Camp Roosevelt."

Abyssinian Warriors escorting the American mission to the palace. Source: Skinner's Memoir, 1906. Image: Courtesy of R.P. Skinner

From the viewpoint of Ethiopian emperors, who were suspicious of white men (colonizers), to the extent of proverbial saying of a certain monarch[1] ordering the washing of their shoes to prevent taking of Ethiopian soil, the reception of the Court of Minilik to the American mission was unprecedented and miraculous. In Negussay Ayele's words, "The most

---

[1] Tewodros was the one who ordered the event according to Getachew (2009, 10-11). Did he control Massawa even by proxy? It was Yohannes who humorously said it when he released Egyptian prisoners of war.

important and spectacular aspect of this first official American mission was the way it was received by the people and government of Ethiopia. No other foreign mission before or after was accorded such warmth, enthusiasm, lavish, hospitality and colorful pomp and pageantry every day of its stay, as was the American mission led by Consul Skinner in December 1903" (2003, 19).

Minilik Receiving the Americans. Source: Skinner's Memoir, 1906.
Image: Courtesy of R.P. Skinner

According Daugherty (2009, 60-1), the marine mission to the Court of Abyssinia was "one of the most unusual diplomatic missions in its entire history" and "one of the most interesting and perhaps the most exotic diplomatic missions Marines participated in up to that time." The journey was eventless and extraordinarily enjoyable, albeit, exhausting. They enjoyed a hunting party, scenery and cultural diversities and beauties. Although Skinner claims that the savage's "supreme joy is to kill his fellow-man" (1906, 134) and although he claimed that "a white man has ten times the value of a black one as a victim" (ibid, 36), a friendly reception began once they landed at Djibouti, a typical "savage" land. He hardly helped but admiring the "savages" for their peacefulness and politeness when he passed through their land. In fact, he used oxymoronic expressions such as "polite savage" or "amiable savage" or "uncivilized friend" to characterize their trips through the lands of "savages. It should be indicated that almost all of his assistants during the trips were the sons of "savages."

However, their trepidation was intense. For instance, one night during the trip, they heard the strange sounds, which put them in a life-or-death condition. They prepared their 175 rounds of ammunitions per person, and even considered the possibility of retreat to Dirre Dawa. Skinner speaks: *"Melodrama was now succeeded by comedy, for the mysterious enemy on the hilltops was found to be, not bloodthirsty savages, but an army of huge monkeys disturbed by the sentinel's gun-shot...It was their chattering that we had mistaken for human voices"* [italics added] (1906, 42).

Henry Ellis, who visited Finfinne in the same year, said, "The country is just as safe for a foreigner as Broadway is." What was the rationale for sending a guard of marines with Skinner? Ellis says, "It is policy to carry a gun and let natives see it, but one never has any occasion to use it" (The New York Times, January 1, 1904). Thus, the fear of savagery of the natives was simply a fabrication of the ruling class, which used the same pretext to conquer them.

Signing of a Treaty of Amity and Commerce

When the pomp and the ceremony of a diplomatic inauguration was out of the way, they immediately began negotiation for signing a trade compact. They expected protracted negotiations with the emperor who was in a "difficult position" in balancing influence against influence (US Department of State Dispatch, 1992, 140). Contrarily, he impressed them with amiability and keenness towards their country. Learning from intelligence sources that the emperor was monolingual, Professor Enno Littmann, a German Orientalist, "probably the only one in the United States familiar with Amharic", as Skinner (1906, 83) asserted, drafted a treaty in Amharic. **The professor carried out protracted archeological excavations in Aksum, and he had never been to the Amharic speaking part of Abyssinia.** Whereas Skinner passed the Amharic version to Minilik for his comments; he started to work on a French version along with Chefneux, a former arm dealer turn a counselor of the state for his client (Minilik). "In an empire permeated with the spirit of intrigue it was a satisfaction to be in the presence of a man of affairs, accustomed to dealings with a business propositions in a businesslike way," commented Skinner about Chefneux (ibid, 74). At the time, Alfred Ilg, a Swiss engineer, a mover of Abyssinian foreign policy, was in Europe.

This engagement culminated in birth of the treaty of commerce and amity between Emperor Minilik and Robert Skinner, on the ninth day of their stay in Finfinne, 27 December 1903, which came into existence earlier than the date the delegation anticipated. Minilik threw a huge celebratory banquet of 3,000 people to welcome a birth of the treaty. Why did the American mission garner such a fantastic attention, messianic welcoming, and the birth of the treaty did come before the time they did expect?

Indeed, as we addressed previously, W.H. Ellis, an informal U.S. emissary to Ethiopia, had done a terrific groundwork for the treaty to be a reality. He reported the enthusiasm of Minilik to receive the delegation of 'the nation that is not looking to get some of his territory'. To that effect; he even carried a Minilik's personal letter addressed to President Roosevelt, which says, "All Americans come to visit me and my country, we shall accept you in love: our aim is one-Christianity and independence" (The New York Times, January 1, 1904).

Another factor for the popularity of the relations was the fact that it was purely for commercial purposes devoid of considerations such as politics or human rights. According to Skinner the warm greeting emanated from the fact that "for the first time in the modern history of Ethiopia has a foreign mission visited the country upon an errand peace and amity, bringing no vexed question of territorial integrity or national honor to decide, and neither asking nor granting anything to which both sides could not gladly accede" (Skinner, 1904, 165).

Minilik applauded a purely business oriented and a unique diplomacy that singled out itself from the interest of European powers, which approached Ethiopia, according to his contention, as a son yearning for a testimony of a father to inherit his estate (Getachew, 2009, 18). The American approach was, indeed, a total break from European trickeries of signing treaties with Africans to colonize them.[1] Similarly, approaching the emperor with the disposition of negotiation—as opposed to colonial mentality of passivity of "savage" nations and hence imposition of one sided treaty—was a factor that contributed for the popularity of the treaty. The fact that the treaty was drafted in Amharic was gratifying for the monolingual Emperor who relied on the European interpreters.

The treaty had seven articles, precise, and transparent. Even, there was no provision envisaged to shield the American citizens from the Ethiopian courts. Article 1 reads, "The citizens of the two Powers [...shall submit] to the

---

[1] For instance, in 1885, the treaty of friendship signed between Sultan Sakwa Kavirondo (in German East Africa) and Karl Peter of Germany, the Sultan "begs" to relinquish his sovereignty. In the Central Africa, Russ signed a treaty with the King of Lobengula of Matabeleland in which the King agreed to cede to the British South African Company the right of exploitation of the mineral resources. Later, when the king understood the paper on which he put his thumbprint, he was shocked and fought them until he was killed in the fighting. See, J. Makong'o et al, History and Government Form 2 (Dar es Slaaam: East African Publishers, 2004), 2. Similarly, Italy maneuvered the Wuchale treaty to realize its ambition of claiming the last terra nullius of the colonial world except it was defeated at Adwa.

tribunals of the countries in which they may be located." Agreeing that Americans would be susceptible to the Ethiopian courts is different from the European style which, if not always, most of the time seeks extraterritorial jurisdictions, to save their citizens from the courts of "savage" nations. Enshrinement of a modification or a termination provision in the treaty was inbuilt means of securing the confidence of the vulnerable party in the diplomatic bargain. "[T]he two governments shall be able to modify all or any part of this treaty," stipulated in Article VI.

Minilik used this treaty as a model treaty in dealings with Europeans. For instance, in an Ethiopia-Austrian treaty of 1905, an Austrian delegation drafted and proposed a treaty in French on which Minilik declined to affix his seal unless an Amharic version accompanied it, which he deemed a controlling version on the event of contradiction between the two versions. He also requested the inclusion of the duration of a treaty, period of notification, and a provision for revision (Bairu, 1994, 98). These all were the elements envisaged in the U.S-Ethiopian treaty of 1903.

The most germane part of the treaty was the granting of the status of the most favored nation (MFN) for each other. The pertinent MFN provisions are Article I, Article III, and Article IV. According to Article I, "The citizens of the two Powers, like the citizens of other countries, shall be able freely to travel and to transact business throughout the extent of the territories of the two contracting Powers..." If they afforded to do so, the dark-skinned Caucasian Abyssinians had a privilege to mingle freely with white Americans at the time when segregation laws were in full force.

As I hinted above, the same article stipulates that the citizens of both nations would be submitting themselves to the tribunals of the countries in which they might be located. Theoretically, Americans would be susceptible to the Abyssinian justice systems, which included among other things, leba shay, quranya, afarsata or awchachiny…etc.

In article III, the U.S. sought nothing more than guarantees for non-discrimination, asking Ethiopia not to give any preferential treatment for any other nation at the cost of U.S. businesses. "Ethiopia," remarked Skinner, "being without a seaport and hemmed in by three European powers, each one striving to supplant our merchandize, we came none too soon to protect out trade by the negotiation of a treaty which should guarantee equal treatment to our merchandise, not only in respect to import duties, but, more important still, in respect to equal rates of transport" (1904, 166). Article IV says, "The citizens of the United States of America shall have the use of the telegraphs, posts and other means of transportation upon the same terms as the citizens of other powers." Some interpret the phrase other means of transportation was to protect American products against the impositions of discriminatory measures in respect to the charges of railway (Harper's weekly,

Jan. 21, 1905). Contrarily, Skinner expressed his fear about Europeans excluding the American interests once the train construction was over.

Notwithstanding that the treaty did not garner any concession in banking, financial, manufacturing, mining, or agricultural sectors, the Harper Weekly hailed it as a groundbreaking initiative. It pronounced that out of 64 diplomatic arrangements Roosevelt administration entered till 1905, the treaty with Abyssinia was "the most important of the commercial treaties" signed along the treaty with China [Open Door Policy](ibid).

As I have already pointed out, the treaty was negotiated, concluded, and signed by Consul Robert Skinner, on behalf of the United States of America, and Minilik. By virtue of the absoluteness of power of Minilik, the King of Kings, "supreme lawgiver," and the "fountain of justice," the treaty immediately became law in Ethiopia. In the case of the United States, it should pass through constitutional mechanisms, such as ratification, notification, and proclamation. Accordingly, upon the advice of the Senate on March 12, 1904, the President signed the treaty into law on March 17, 1904. To the dismay of W. H. Ellis, Kent J. Loomis, a brother of Assistant Secretary of State Francis B. Loomis, was assigned to carry the ratified treaty to Minilik. Because of his familiarity with the country and its culture, he chose Ellis to accompany him. Loomis mysteriously vanished from a German ship, Kaiser Wilhelm II, while crossing the English Channel, and after a week, his body washed ashore in France. However, his heavy drunkenness was known; the suspicion landed on Ellis because, as we discussed earlier, his desires were well-known. Ellis proceeded with the mission, and he delivered the ratified treaty to Minilik on August 2, 1904. He reported that Minilik appointed him a Duke of Harar and gave him two million acres of land for a mineral concession and a cotton plantation. Nevertheless, none of his grand projects ever came to fruition. When Ellis came to Washington carrying a copy of the ratified treaty, an internal probe by the State Department had cleared him of any foul play in an accidental death of his companion. Loomis, who lured by the exotic wonders of Abyssinia and who took the unfortunate trip at his own expense, fell from the ship because of a heavy drinking on the journey (Getachew, 2009; Harlan, 1979; Skinner, 2003).

As I have touched already, the treaty was bilingual; the U.S. proposed it in Amharic. The other language was French. Beyond being the language of the world of diplomacy at a time, French was the language of Minilik advisors and the second language of Consul Skinner. The treaty was ratified in Amharic and French. There was a third version, an English one, which was a verbatim copy of the French one. The fact that the treaty was drafted and signed in languages other than English is a bit odd from the viewpoint of the principle of the alternat. It is hard to conclude the relation of the English version *vis-à-vis* the French or Amharic versions. I have to leave this for American constitutional students.

Departure and Gifts

A "democratic" Skinner underlined that America as the "republic" was neither addicted to giving nor receiving gifts, and, therefore, he brought no elephant to Minilik like a British envoy did. Except types of materials, the republic followed the footprints of the empire in bribing Minilik. He carried various souvenirs to him as per the Abyssinia tradition, which he traced back to the biblical narrative of the wise men carrying gifts on the birth of Christ Child. He brought the signed portrait of President Roosevelt; the President's book on 'North American Big Game'; a magazine rifle of the latest model; type writing machine, and selected American garden seeds sent by the Department of Agriculture. Minilik was happy about the gifts. He "received the book with great respect;" although Skinner "feared that His Majesty will never be able to read it." He was fascinated with the gun, cartridges, and drills. As Skinner indicated, "the imperial eyes brightened with evident pleasure," Minilik immediately fired through the opened doorway to the great alarm of the audience that caused "a wild stampede." "The Emperor's eye showed that he appreciated the humor of the situation," wrote Skinner. He liked the type writing machine, and, he inquired, "Why cannot we have an Amharic type writer?" Chefneux responded, "Whereas we had only 26 letters in our alphabet, it would require 251 characters to represent Amharic language, and the construction of a machine containing so many figures presented practical difficulties" (Skinner, 1906, 119-122).

The diplomatic mission received gifts including a pair of elephant tusks, two lion cubs, and a baby hyena. Minilik decorated all the mission members including those left behind in Dirre Dawa with the medallions and ribbon of the Star of Ethiopia. As per the U.S. law, commissioned officers deposited their decorations the State Department on their return (ibid 204).

On their departure, on 27 December 1903, some two thousand spectators watched the 21-gun salute, and a local band played Hail, Columbia—the U.S. patriotic song—and the Marseille—the national anthem of France. Washington took some measures to cement the relations. Minilik was invited to take part on the St. Louis World Fair of 1904 meant to celebrate the centennial of the Louisiana Purchase and to showcase America's innovations and power to the world in the era of imperialism. Minilik was unable to show up for unknown reason; although, he promised to take part in the exposition, and, America assured him a necessary protection.

Imagining the Ethiopia of Roosevelt

In the previous discussion, we have seen how Consul Skinner was lobbying to go to Abyssinia since 1900, and how the McKinley government tabled his initiative. When the Consul asked the Roosevelt administration, it delivered a light-speed response. The President called him to Washington to lecture him on a list of tasks to be done during his mission to the 'Christian Empire'. Although he had a paucity of knowledge about Ethiopia, he was loaded for "intellectual ramblings" to spice up the Consul's exotic diplomatic trip to "the Eldorado of wonders." Both of them were ready to feed each other's imagination rapacity. Who did not have a piece of information about Abyssinia as the land of romantic wonders? Who did not have a piece of information about Abyssinia as a Christian civilization in the wilderness of Africa? Thus, the president did not miss two things: 'exotic wildlife', the portrayal popularized through the fable of Prester John, and the proverbial allusion of Abyssinia as a 'Semitic outpost' in Africa encapsulated in the narrative of *Kibra Nagast*.

A competent horseman, hunter, and conservationist he was, Roosevelt was personally interested in the trip to Abyssinia. He was unhappy that he could not see for himself a living Christian civilization and an exotic land of wonders. The 'electrified' Skinner narrated his vivid memory about the mood of conversation at the White House to the amusement of his wife, Helen Skinner. The president was roaming a room—in the style of mobile lecturing—and passionately talked at length about everything he knew and fantasized about that country (McVety, 2011, 192). He remarked: "He wished very much he could go himself, for there were lions and elephants; no, the Ethiopians were not negroes at all but of Semitic stock and proud of their ancestry; life there must be something similar to life in the time of Christ; how interesting to be able to study an early Christian culture" (ibid).

For Roosevelt, Ethiopia was anything but "a mysterious land" populated by "a primitive society which was much like society in the time of Christ" (US Department of State Dispatch, 1992, 138). No transformation for 1900 years! Ethiopia is nothing but a homogeneous nation as Minilik would love to make it. The real Ethiopia is a museum of peoples, with various languages, cultures, histories; of different stocks: Semitic, Cushitic, Nilotic and Omotic ones, and the land of different religions. To make the matter short, Ethiopia is haphazard collections of wild varieties of entities put together through violence and maintained as such. The American diplomats were incapable to see beyond biblical parables, their imaginations, and false dichotomies, and, that the world is either Negro and Caucasian, or Christian or savage. Even for those who saw Abyssinia, like Skinner, though they were proved wrong; contrarily, they felt what they saw vindicated them. Even when Skinner came back from Abyssinia, the content of discussions between the President and Skinner did not change. When Skinner told him some of the people he met, President Roosevelt inferred that 'he must be a Caucasian, a Scotchman'. Skinner agreed with him (see, Skinner, 2006, 21). They believed those myths like religious dogma to the extent of praying that they would stay unchanged forever. For instance, Skinner hoped, 'No historian will come along to demolish the myth of Queen Sheba and King Solomon with proofs of incontestable authenticity' (ibid, 184). President Roosevelt had similar fascination and obsession with Abyssinia since she was a "Christian civilization" and free from Negroes. Wildly excited about Abyssinia, he asserted, "Ethiopia is an Empire and must remain so" (Foreign Relations of the United States: Diplomatic Papers, 1964, 93).

The president's bizarre presentation about Ethiopia was a manifestation of westerns shallow-minded thinking and false consciousness about Ethiopia. His scanty understanding of Ethiopia and stereotypes are a mindset of an average American. Curt Keim, in his work, *Mistaking Africa: Curiosities and Inventions of the American Mind* (1999), argued that for most Americans, the reference of Africa immediately conjures up images of safaris, ferocious animals, impenetrable jungles, and tribesmen with fancy costumes. Even today, in the era of Cable Revolution, while pundits engage in endless cycles of repetitions and gossips, serious attempts to understand how people live presently in Africa are absent as televisions' obsessions never pass beyond exotic aspects of Africa, coup, famine, or wars (Keim, 1999). This simplistic stereotypical attitude hardly implies the need for seriously engaging Africans on issues of mutual benefit. We shall come to racial attitudes of Roosevelt towards Ethiopia later.

The adventurous Roosevelt told Skinner a shop-list of items to be carried from Abyssinia. Obviously, a treaty was a top priority, but he was desirous to acquire other staffs such as seeds of endemic plants and exotic African wild animals since it was possible to plant those seeds and to breed those animals in the uncultivated western United States (McVety, 2011).

Minilik sent two lion cubs, a symbol of his imperial authority, and a hyena to President Roosevelt as a diplomatic gift. Unfortunately, 'the over kindness, in the form of too much food,' killed one of the cubs, before it crossed Mount Asabot (Skinner, 2006, 199). "The grief of the lion-men was most pitiful, and indeed we were all depressed by the circumstances as the two animals were playful and gentle as kittens," wrote Skinner. 'They buried the cub with ceremony' since "lion in Ethiopia is almost a sacred creature." Substitution for a loss of the cub immediately came from Ras Makonnin, who gave them a lion and an oryx. Except an emotional breakdown with death of the cub, the journey back home was peaceful and "was incomparably more satisfactory than the one to Addis Ababa" (ibid, 207).

The real lions of Ethiopia, Panthera leo landed on the American soil before any "Conquering Lions of Judah" set their feet on the American soil. Theodore Roosevelt, who became a house hold name by conferring his nickname to popular animal bear, "Teddy bear," found an Ethiopian lion named after him, Felis leo rooseveltii.

According to the zoologists, the lion had a strong resemblance to the McMillan lions from Nairobi and Felis leo massaica, which convinced them that the lion was "brought to the emperor as a kitten by some of his subjects living in some far distant corner of Abyssinia" (Hollister, 1919, 165). It shared fewer similarities with Felis leo somaliensis (ibid, 164), and most likely captured from the wilderness of Borana country along the Ethiopia-Kenyan border. The lion was entrusted to the protection and public display at the National Zoo in Washington. Although it was denied the natural rights to enjoy the wilderness of its ecosystem, it served its captive country in an ambassadorial role, before it sent its ambassador to the U.S. It died on 14 November 1906, and the Smithsonian National Museum of Natural History kept its body. An Ethiopian hyena named Bill, Crocuta crocuta, lived in the White House briefly. Roosevelt taught it tricks, enjoyed its high pitched crackle and let it beg for table scraps (Brinkley, 2009, 561).

Teddy Roosevelt posing with an elephant he killed during safari in the British Kenya, 1909. Image courtesy of Edward Van Altena

These gifts were more than animal diplomacy. At the time, the Secretary of Smithsonian required all naval officers to carry exotic animals for the National Zoological Park in Washington DC after their visits abroad. This zoo was modeled after the Zoological Gardens in Regent's Park, in London, which filled with exotic animals from all over the world as gifts from princes, lords, consuls, and foreign rulers (Mullan, 1999, 109-111). The tradition of sending zoological specimen from Ethiopia to Washington was unabated even after the return of Skinner to Marseilles.

It was classical image that Ethiopia is the origin of the coffee plant and the word coffee itself. Unfortunately, westerns hardly knew the barbarity with which Abyssinia liquidated the people of Kafa to capture their coffee land.

Skinner wanted to procure this indigenous coffee beans known for its long berry and aroma suitable to introduce to U.S soil, particularly for Porto Rico. 'By getting the wild coffee plant, the habitat which is the province of Kafa, a new variety may be created, the value of which will be incalculable,' asserted Skinner (1904, 166). He hardly obtained it during his stay in Ethiopia. He ordered them to collect and ship to him.

Skinner had written about the King of Kafa who lost the battle to the Minilik's army and brought to Addis Ababa as a prisoner of war. He wrote about his arrogance, and how "in sign of object submissions [...] he fell flat and placed a stone upon the back of his neck" when he came before Minilik (Skinner, 1906, 141-2). Skinner barely set the pieces of the facts he saw together than echoing Minilik's version of the story and his racial belief all in the name of diplomacy. If he understood, the only crime of this king was the fact that he defended his coffee against the Abyssinian marching army.

Skinner was also craved for "a few of the fine large Grévy zebras to be found only in Abyssinia" (ibid, 28). Unlike he claimed, Grévy zebras spread in the Horn of Africa, but, Abyssinia became synonymous with it after King Minilik of Shawa donated to the President of France, François Paul Jules Grévy, in 1882. An attempt to obtain some for him was futile as their population was dwindling and hard to capture them alive. He left directions to his friends to seize and ship him these "beautiful animals." These precious animals were captured in this barbarous manner:

> In Ethiopia, driving animals was for years a favorite method of capturing them. An army of as many as 2,000 men would encircle a large tract of [a] country where, for example, zebra were known to be found. The locality picked would be one in the center of which was a dried-up riverbed, common to that country. The circle of men would then slowly contact, driving the zebras into the center. When the animals were corralled within the riverbed, a barbarous spectacle would take place. A thousand men would ride in and trash the zebra with long whips until the animals were thoroughly exhausted and their spirits broken. They were fastened by ropes attached to each of their legs and tied to posts—in a few days, they became quiet and tamed. Many men were often killed in the process (some might say poetic justice) (Livingston, 2000, 173).

In 1904, Minilik sent a zebra for Roosevelt; it was named Dan. Dan was an incredible and timely gift for the animal passionate Roosevelt to show off during his reelection (see, McVety, 2011, 204). It stayed for a while at the

White House. Later, it was kept at the National Zoo until his death in 1919. In 1905, Ras Makonnin sent Skinner a male and a female zebra on the French Consul.

During his last year in the White House [1908], Roosevelt invited Sir Harry Johnston, a British explorer, to provide him with advice on hunting trip to Africa. The Englishman convinced him to sail for the British Colony of Kenya, not to the "biblical civilization" of Abyssinia, a land free of Negroes. In 1909, he made safari to Kenya, and, he killed a host of wild animals.

Ethiopia learned the news immediately; including his lack of success to kill as many elephant as he would like. Crown Prince Iyyasu sent out an invitation for Roosevelt for "a splendid shooting program" in the land of "unrivalled elephant hunt." According to this hunting plan, "The Crown Prince will send out 5,000 horsemen to encircle an immense range of prairie and drive in the elephants. Hundreds, and possibly thousands of elephants could thus be assembled." Notwithstanding the Crown Prince was portrayed as an adventurous and skilled hunter, who spoke three European languages (English, French and German), and willing to welcome Roosevelt at the borders of his country, the invitation failed to materialize since they learned that he was too young, and Roosevelt declined numerous invitations from Europe (Everett, 2004, 422).

Receiving Consular Exchanges

Article V stipulates about receiving consular exchanges for perpetuating and strengthening bilateral ties. It says, "In order to perpetuate and strengthen the friendly relations which exist between Ethiopia and the United States of America, the two governments agree to receive reciprocally representatives acceptable to the two governments." The treaty gives wide latitude for the contracting parties to reject an appointed representative in which case it would be replaced. Nonetheless, the treaty is silent on a number of the center (s) for establishing the consulate.

Consul Skinner suggested himself to operate as an agent for Abyssinia from Marseilles for the purpose of facilitating communication between the two governments until such time that the railway constructions would be completed upon which an appointment of a permanent diplomatic and a consular officer should be considered. Frank Mower recommended the opening of a Consulate General 'to meet the expectations of the Abyssinian government and to promote American trade properly.' His idea prevailed, and, the U.S. opened the post on 19 December 1906. Mower became the first Consul General (Records of the Department of State, 1962). However, the decision dismayed Minilik since the post was inferior to a minister in terms of its diplomatic prestige and weight (Getachew, 2009, 19). On February 8, 1910,

Mower departed and the U.S. interest was passed to the British legation in Finfinne. In September 1907, Edward Valle came as the Vice Consul General, and he assumed the charge of his office in November 30, 1907 till his departure in the spring of 1908 because of his illness. Again, the interest of the U.S. was entrusted to the representatives in charge of British legation in Addis Ababa till 1909. Mower expressed his regret at relegation of the post and recommended upgrading to the level of legation. (Records of the Department of State, 1962).

On July 6, 1909, President William Taft appointed Hoffman Philip as the U.S. Minister Resident and Consul General in Addis Ababa. During his short stay in Ethiopia, Consul General Philip significantly contributed for the ethnological collection in Abyssinia; The Hoffman Philip Abyssinian Ethnological Collection was published by the Washington Printing Office on May 18, 1911. Walter Hough, a Curator of Ethnology at the U.S. National Museum remarked this about the collection: "Material from Abyssinia is exceedingly rare, and the collection of Mr. Philip, probably the first that has been brought to this country, is interesting on account of the survival which it exhibits from the ancient, culture of northern Africa, the neighboring Asiatic continent, and Eastern Europe" (Hough & Philip, 1911, 265).

Sooner, the relations with Addis Ababa lost relevance under the Taft's foreign policy orientation, which was geared "to improve financial opportunities," and thence dubbed "dollar diplomacy" (Winkler-Morey, 2003, 265). He pursued a new approach of using economic power to influence international relations unlike military adventures of his predecessors. Of course, Abyssinia had little lucrative deals to offer compared with Chinese market, or an American banking conglomerations penetration of Europe or control of Mexican oil or 20 percent control of Mexico's land, which was a recipe for the Mexican Revolution of 1910 (ibid). Thanks to "dollar diplomacy" Hoffman Philip posting lasted till February 8, 1910, and, the U.S. relegated the relationship to a Vice Consul General. In February 1910, Vice Consul General Guy Love came to Addis Ababa, and he served for three years until his death. Then, the Britannic Majesty's representatives in Addis Ababa entrusted with U.S. affairs.

Myths of Abyssinia and a Skinner's Memoir

Skinner elegantly wrote a memoir about his expedition to Ethiopia in 1906. To be fair, his memoir was neither an account of a historian nor a sociologist nor an anthropologist. Nor his presence in Ethiopia for less than two months permitted him to produce comprehensive information about the country and its peoples. Nor, bothered he was to know about some components of Abyssinia in the first place. Being the memoir, melodrama, exaggerations, and blemishing facts with quixotic aspects of Abyssinia and selling to voracious western readers were a norm for travelers.

Nevertheless, his memoir provided an excellent reflection of how Westerns, in general, perceived Abyssinia. It provides straight from the horse's mouth manner about Skinner's perceptions of Ethiopia, good and bad, reality and fiction, and prejudices and biases. It was among early works produced, on Abyssinia, by Americans, perhaps, like a Henry Stanley's book, *Coomassie and Magdala: the Story of Two British Campaigns in Africa*. The Skinner's book was republished under a title, *The 1903 Skinner Mission to Ethiopia: And a Century of Ethiopian-American Relations*, for a centennial celebration of the United States and Ethiopia diplomatic relations.

The memoir profusely deals with culture, history, legend, race, geography, flora and fauna, weather, agriculture, minerals, economy, justice, religion, relations with other countries, narratives of their journey to Ethiopia. It can be broadly categorized into three sections: the first part primarily provides vivid accounts of their sojourn; the second portion deals with receptions and courtesies. The third part was selective compilations about the greatness and glories of Abyssinia, and savagery of the native peoples. The aroma of his profound enthusiasm for Abyssinia strikes a reader from the first page of the book. His love for the Abyssinia rulers was idealistic, and he idolized it.

Before I embark on discussing contents of the memoir, it is appropriate to spell out some of my observations. Perhaps suggestive of their rivalry or ideological oppositions, Skinner never at all mentions W.H. Ellis in the memoir, nor recognizes his role in the success of the treaty. All the same, he mentions Benito Sylvain for his repudiation by Emperor Minilik when he told him that he was a Caucasian King. The memoir was mainly devoid of discourse of democracy and human rights. Nor, Skinner talked about the republican ethos and the revolutionary spirit of the French Republic, let alone making comparison and contrast with Ethiopia, an empire totally foreign to the notions of human rights and democracy. He did pretend to be a democrat at times.

At this junction, clarification of my standpoint is relevant. My disagreement with Skinner is not a personal. I believe that his opinions were also political. Firstly, he was a plenipotentiary diplomat of the U.S. who negotiated and signed the treaty on behalf of the president, the government, and the people of the United States of America. Secondly, more than being an embodiment of the sovereign power, he was a pathfinder to Abyssinia, and, he put Abyssinia on the map of U.S. diplomacy. In other parlance, he was the first U.S. diplomat who defined Abyssinia for Washington politicians. Being a trailblazer diplomat, his footprints on the U.S-Ethiopian relations are incomparable. With all due respect, he deserves a credit for pioneering the contact with Abyssinia, and, he has been glorified a lot for that. This work will offer some aspects of his dark legacy, how he wittingly or unwittingly underpinned racism in his diplomatic adventure.

Regardless of his journalistic background, perhaps my readers have already noticed the influence of biblical narratives on the Skinner's perception of Ethiopia. He tried to use every metaphor about the Cush Ethiopia said in the bible. A humble and an innocent member of the Episcopal Church that he was, he was extremely candid and prideful about that. He underlined, "The only really satisfactory report on Ethiopia known by US citizens was contained in the 10th Chapter of the First Book of Kings" (US Department of State Dispatch , 1992, 138). This is narrative that became a foundation stone for the corrupted myth of King Solomon and the Queen of Sheba. He put his Abyssinia in this way.

> We devote millions to the uncovering of ancient cities dead, and we neglect an ancient civilization living, a civilization which found its inspiration in Solomon's Court, and which, preserving its Christian faith through 1,600 years, and during many centuries cut off from all contacts with the outside world, hand itself down to us in all essential respects identical with that which prevailed in Bethlehem 2,000 years ago. We boast of our own Christian civilization, and we are undertaking with our railroads and other Western inventions to break down a civilization virtually like that in which Christ himself lived and moved; we boast of our law, and we send our agents to teach a land in which judges administer justice based upon precepts of the open Bible in their hand" (Skinner, 1906, viii).

In the same way, Skinner praised Minilik as a unifier, an intelligent, an amicable, a Bismarck, a McKinley and a reconciliatory (ibid, 141). He also presented the myth of Queen Sheba and King Solomon as a self-evident truth. Her famous diplomatic 'journey resulted in the negotiation of a treaty of commerce with Shawa (not Aksum),' similar to the one he negotiated with Minilik (ibid, 182). He also confirmed that 'there is enough in favor of the Ethiopian claim of the present Minilik's [1889-1913] direct descent' from the Queen of Sheba and King Solomon (ibid, 184). Thus, he established that 'Minilik is cousin of Christ and born of the race of David' (ibid, 182). The contents of memoir make us wonder if Skinner was an American diplomat or if he was an American Magi searching for the Abyssinian "King of Judah."

Skinner Adopting Name Ethiopia for Abyssinia

Skinner defined "Abyssinia" as "merely a fragment of the ancient empire of Ethiopia." Then he passed on to describe an etymology of "derogatory" term Abyssinia and how it passed like epidemic from "Moslem lips" instead of "her nobler designation of Ethiopia."[1] In his assertion, Abyssinians "have every historical and racial right" to the word "Ethiopia" (ibid, vii-viii). Had the word Abyssinia had a negative connotation, why he would have chosen a topic of his book "Abyssinia Today"?

In his Paris dispatch No. 766 of September 23, 1925 (123 SK3 /246), Skinner suggested abandoning the "derogatory" name Abyssinia in favor of "noble" Ethiopia.

> I respectfully suggest that it would be more strictly correct to abandon the use of the word Abyssinia in favor of Ethiopia. The government of the country considers Ethiopia to be its proper name. And it is under this name that our treaty appears in the official volume of Treaties, Conventions and International Acts. And in the body of the treaty Ethiopia alone is mentioned from time to time. I believe that it would be gratifying to the existing government of Ethiopia if the use of the word Abyssinia could be dropped." (Steffanson, et al., 1976, 32).

Allen W. Dulles, a Director of the Division of Near Eastern Affairs of the Department of State, adopted the name 'Ethiopia' for official use by the Federal Government. 'Abyssinia' was officially changed to 'Ethiopia' by the U.S. Board on Geographic Names that maintain uniform geographic name usage throughout the Federal Government on February 3, 1926 (ibid, 32-33).

Unlike Skinner claimed, the emperors, historians, and map makers called the Christian plateau Abyssinia until the twentieth century. The usage of 'Ethiopia' by the Amhara emperors only emerged and popularized with the expansion of Abyssinia southwards. At the time, they intended to create inclusive national identity; even if, the envisioned inclusive nation happened to be an "Amhara Ethiopia." (Markakis, 2011; Gebru, 1991). Robert Collins and James Burns expounded:

> Although the term "Ethiopian" was used by the ancients and lingered into the Christian era, it had nothing to do with the Ethiopians of the

---

[1] In British literature the reality stood opposite to what he said. According to Auf Der Maur, "Ethiopia first and foremost stands for sub-Saharan Africa as a whole," which conjures such imagery of "savage" Africa; contrarily Abyssinia was the helm of Prester John and enjoyed "nobler" designation, the "Orient" within Africa. See, Auf Der Maur, Lorenz, "Ethiopia and Abyssinia in English Writing Up To 1790," in Siegbert Uhlig, (ed.), *Proceedings of the 15th International Conference of Ethiopian Studies in Hamburg* (Wiesbaden: Harrassowitz Verlag, 2005), 552-54. In the words of an English diplomat, "The Abyssinians of to-day do not described themselves as such but as "Ethiopians," a description which we have learned to associate more readily with the negro or negroid races of the South Eastern Sudan, especially that part of it known as the Island of Meroe" (Rey, 1923, 82).

highlands; it was a generic term, often with pejorative connotations, for all black Africans. Throughout history the people of Ethiopia have been known as Abyssinians (Arabic, Habasha), and Abyssinia was the name of highlands until the twentieth century when Emperor Haile Selassie in his efforts to modernize insisted that 'Ethiopia' and 'Ethiopians' replace 'Abyssinia' and 'Abyssinians.' By the mid-twentieth century Abyssinia had ceased to be used by Ethiopians as a derisory term. (Collins & Burns, 2007, 64).

To set the historic record straight, Emperor Ezana of Aksum designated himself the 'King of Ethiopia' in 4th century. Ezana was the King of Kings of Aksum, Beja, Nubia (Ethiopia), Himyar, Raydan, Saba, and Salhen. In short, he was the king of everything he conquered from Africa to the Southern Arabia. One might wonder, the historic root of a name Ethiopia, then.

The name "Ethiopia" is a product of biblical translation of the Hebrew word Cush. Chapter 10 of the Genesis provides detailed information about a family tree of Cush, the first son of Ham, and Ham is the son of Noah. The children of Cush spread in Arabia, Egypt, Babylon, Median, and Palestine. To show the significance of color as their identity maker, the legendary expression goes, 'Can the Cush change his color?' (Jeremiah, 13:23]. Cush was the first black race known to the Hellenic Greek. Still, Cush means black (race) in Hebrew. When the bible was translated into the Greek language, the word Cush was replaced with word aithops, which means red face and/or from aitho plus ops burnt face. An English translation of the Bible (the King James Version) followed this trajectory when the word "Ethiopia" substituted the word "Cush." Similarly, the Geez bible adopted Ethiopia "widely and proudly" (Bromiley, 1915, 193).

The term Ethiopia, therefore, referred to all the land of the people of dark complexion. It has broader geographic representation when Homer says, "The distant Ethiopians, the farthest outposts of mankind, half of whom live where the sun goes down, and half where the sun rises" (Homer, 1950, 1). Implicit in his sensational 'faraway' Ethiopia is its divisions into the Eastern and Western Ethiopia. In this sense, the entire African landmass [south of Egypt] technically falls within the designation of the Western Ethiopia. When the Greeks became close to Egypt, Ethiopia enduringly wedded to the African landmass and the Ethiopians of East slowly disappeared. In a generic term, Ethiopia refers to all black people of Africa; or in a narrower sense, it refers to the Nubian Kingdom of Meroe. For instance, Oceanographer Sebastian Münster named the Southern Atlantic Ocean located on the western side of Africa Mare Aethiopicum (Ethiopian Sea), which later Gerald Mercator, in his famous world map, named Oceanus Aethiopicum [Ethiopian Ocean] (Murray, 1895, 49).

Once Nubia swallowed by Islam and its famous Christian kingdom eventually declined, it became imperative that the biblical "Ethiopian" had to become a Christian Abyssinia, not a Muslim Nubia. If we follow the genealogy of the bible and make Cush the hallmark of the definition of Ethiopians, it is the "conquered" peoples of Ethiopia, who deserve the designation because they are the ones who belong to the "Cushitic Stock" than the conqueror race, who is of the "Semitic Stock." Possibly, Skinner's exclusion of the "conquered" peoples from the definition of Ethiopia shows his lack of understanding of the etymological root of the word. Perhaps, he might deliberately play a role in usurpation of the "noble" name Ethiopia by Abyssinians so that the "savages" would not be entitled to that designation. That said on the usurpation of the ancient name "Ethiopia," let us see the Skinner's universe of Ethiopians. Who were his Ethiopians?

Accounts and Analysis of Skinner: Caucasian Vs. Savages Races

As we already highlighted, serious flaws of Skinner's accounts and analysis were conspicuous from the way he depicted the nature of Abyssinia and her relation to her conquered peoples. Skinner distinguished the existence of two races in Ethiopia, the Ethiopic (Abyssinian) race and the "savage" (non-Abyssinian) race. Ethiopians are the descendants of "the natives and the Jews who, according to tradition, followed the Queen of Sheba back after her visit to Solomon" (Skinner, 1905, 416; Skinner, 1906, 132). This race became the "conqueror" or the "Ethiopic race" or the "Abyssinian proper." They dwell in the kingdoms of Shawa, Tigre, and Gojjam. Their language is Amharic; hence, Amharic is "modern Ethiopic."

There is another race he saw on his way from Djibouti all the way to Addis Ababa. He labeled them the "savage" or the "conquered" race or the "natives." They include the Afars, Danakils, Somalis, and the Oromos. In his assertion, in the present day Ethiopia, "The primitive stock is of Ethiopic origin." Therefore, the "savages" are not Ethiopians per se. Instead, they "are ruled by Ethiopians" (see, Skinner, 1906, 132-3). For instance, he says, 'The Gallas [Oromo] share the hill country around Harar with the Ethiopians' (Skinner, 1906, 16). This race does not have a historic claim to the "nobler designation of Ethiopia." How did Ethiopians become only Abyssinians all of a sudden? Was not Abyssinia a portion of Ethiopia, according to what he told us?

Not only affirming the superiority of the Abyssinian race vis-à-vis the conquered race, he set the hierarchy of races in Ethiopia. Abyssinian proper is civilized race; "the Gallas are much more advanced towards civilization than either the Danakils or the Somalis" (ibid, 140). "The Somalis are finer in form and feature than Danakils" (ibid, 136). "The Danakils are exceedingly black" (ibid, 135). Mathematically speaking, the Abyssinian race>Galla

(Oromos)>Somalis> Danakils (Afars). Skinner only saw these four nations; he had never seen the rest of more than eighty Ethiopian ethnic groups.

According to Skinner, Abyssinia is "lands of romance and adventure—a land of grave faces, elaborate courtesy, classic togas, and Biblical civilizations." He lamented studying ancient civilizations while neglecting Abyssinia that was suspended in time "virtually like that in which Christ himself lived." He expressed his disappointment at travelers who "usually come back with grotesque tales" about "this interesting people of Caucasian ancestry" (Skinner, 2006, viii). "The Ethiopians are a fine, strong race, more usually of a copper hue than not, and are altogether different from the Negroes, with whom, however, they have frequently been confounded, but only because they were called a black people," wrote Skinner (ibid, 132)." He tried to justify distinctness of Abyssinia from the Negro race by scientific racism of Professor Littmann, who made an extended scientific research in Aksum. "Abyssinian type contains no negro blood whatever, and none of the Negro qualities, either physical or mental" (ibid, 164). John Gunther had capitalized on Ethiopia's isolation from its "Negro" neighbors when he said Ethiopia has "practically no contact, cultural or economic, with Black Africa." He claimed, "Kenya, although it borders on Ethiopia, seems farther away than Saskatchewan." In his view, the Abyssinians belong to another world, the world of the Middle East (Gunther, 1954, 255).

Skinner found the Caucasian origin of Abyssinia in their pictorial art, in which "the goods are always depicted as white men and the bad as black men" (ibid). He also noted, "Abyssinian complexion, and personal vanity is most highly flattered by possession of the lighter tints of the skin" (ibid, 130).

The Abyssinian race is 'vastly superior to any race in Ethiopia,' and "in the best estate" (Skinner, 1905, 413; Skinner, 1906, 133). They are 'orderly, peaceful personage, a professional warrior', 'extremely ceremonious people,' and 'possessed of innate courtesy' (Skinner, 1906, 16 & 58). Contrarily, the non-Abyssinian race is 'barbarous', 'constantly warring with each other, and knew no higher law than that of force' (ibid, 3). The savages were "held in constraint by a wholesome fear of the wise man [Minilik] at Addis Ababa" (ibid, 16). To exemplify the Abyssinian tough task of governing the "savages," he mentioned a miserable life of Ras Makonnin, a 'shrewd, very able person, and whom the savages count as father' (ibid, 3). He almost ran out of the breath, vainly, policing them (ibid, 3). Skinner said this on the "barbarity" and "backwardness" of Somalis and Afar:

> The savage of the desert says of his country: 'It is clean.' To him our cities are prisons, and our cheer an invention of the devil to stiffen his limbs and fatten his body. He prefers as a roof either the blue sky, or his hut made of four sticks and some brush; or, if he be a camel-driver, the shelter made by throwing the vegetable fiber mats upon which the 'charge' is laid over the boxes constituting the load itself. His supreme joy is to kill his fellow-man,

and having done so, he parades the fact to the world by wearing an ostrich feather in his hair. Pushed by necessity, he sometimes visits the miserable native villages; but if once installed therein, he returns with difficulty to his desert. Ordinarily he is unsociable (ibid, 134).

The Abyssinians are technology friendly. Emperor Minilik "has heard of Japan" and he "is trying to emulate that striking example" (ibid, 86). He mentioned a novelty in Addis-Ababa including the Court jeweler who decorated the trim of an emperor's 'shiny silky hat', which came from Paris, with a series of emeralds (ibid, 75). Contrarily, the sons of Islam consider technology a beast.

When the rails were first laid across the desert, the sons of Islam looked upon the locomotive as a beast, the like of which they had never seen before, and, being brave, they occasionally stood up before the monster and persisted in their attitude, just to see what would happen. And though engineers were careful and kind, a number of missing arms and legs in French Somaliland testify today to the futility of these duels between man and steam. When these experiences had once been noised abroad, the Issas bowed to what they believed to be a law of fate, and the locomotives circulated thereafter with perfect security (ibid, 4).

He appreciated the carefulness and kindness with which the engineers amputated the limbs of those victims than injustices done to them. He even made a distinction between the caravans of camels that transported their material and traveled with them. There were "fine Arab camels" driven by Arab drivers all the way to the Court of Abyssinia, and "Danakil camels driven by savages from the desert" to the start of the Ethiopian plateau, "the point where the real Ethiopia begins and the savage ceases to feel at home" (ibid, 125-6). The mission mistreated the Danakils, which Skinner called them, "servants of servants." They fired some of them since "there had to be a considerable number of similar boys to perform miscellaneous duties" (ibid, 12). The memoir did not mention whether the disbanded servants were paid. Nor, it did say a reason for disbanding them.

Firstly, as the diplomat from the "civilized" nation, Skinner should treat his servants with respect and dignity. Secondly, he was supposed to ask why the "savages" cease to feel at home in Ethiopia than justifying the Abyssinians discriminations. Should it not Ethiopian citizens feel free to travel within their country? Did not he negotiate for a free movement of Americans in Ethiopia?

Then again, the so-called Danakil savages were very friendly with them. He wrote, "The Danakil camel-drivers, who by this time were professing respect and affection for our persons, had devoted the day of rest to the rehearsal of a fantasia, or dance, which took place during the evening in front of my tent" (ibid, 49). Although he had written to convey the sense of justice of Minilik, Skinner had unintentionally explained the injustice of the Ethiopian justice system on the "Danakils" at the time. He wrote about a certain incident of a native from this tribe who allegedly killed a white man. The emperor sent his regiment to arrest a suspect. Skinner expresses: *"As the penalty for concealing the culprit involved confiscation of herds and destruction of their villages, the headmen finally acceded. The savage was hanged from a tree in the market-place at Addis Ababa, where his body remained until the vulture had carried it way"* [italics added] (ibid, 136).

Consul Skinner said everything about the Oromo nation from their savagery to their foreignness to Ethiopia, i.e., coming from the land of Somalis (ibid, 136). He reinforced the image of barbarity of the Oromo even when they were civilized by the Abyssinians in this style:

> The usual custom of the Abyssinian army is to advance in a half moon formation. ... When the battle becomes hot, and the final rush is made, sword and lance come into play, and the war cries of the ancient kingdoms are raised. 'Together, together!' cry the Choans [Shawans]. 'God pardon us, Christ!' cry the Godjamites. *The Gallas, lowest in the social scale, repeat twice, 'Slay, Slay!* [Italics added] (ibid, 176).

Surprisingly most of the European zealots, who came to support Minilik in subjugating of the native peoples, had moderate opinion about them compared to Skinner. A Russian Lieutenant Alexander Bulatovich—who marched with the Minilik army in the Oromo land—said:

> Southern clans had a republican form of government... Such was the form of government of Galla states up until their conquest by the Abyssinians. But from that time the peaceful, free way of life, which could have become the ideal for philosophers and writers of the eighteenth century, if they had known of it, was completely changed. Their peaceful way of life is broken; freedom is lost; and the independent, freedom-loving Gallas find themselves under the severe authority of the Abyssinian conquerors (Bulatovich, 2000, 68).

He further noted:
> The dreadful annihilation of more than half the population during the conquest took away from the Galla all possibility of thinking about any sort of uprising. And the freedom-loving Galla who didn't recognize any authority other than the speed of his horse, the strength of his hand, and the accuracy of his spear, now goes through the hard school of obedience (ibid, 68).

He then asked: 'What are the relations of the conquered to the conquerors?' He replied; "if "the Abyssinians skillfully and tactfully manage them, not violating their customers and religious beliefs and treating them lawfully and justly, they will with time blend with the Abyssinians" (ibid, 68-69).

If one juxtaposes the writings of the Russian mercenary to the assertions of the U.S. diplomat, it reveals how undiplomatic the diplomat was. At a different time, the same diplomat, who told as the war-likeness of Oromos, told us a different story about the Oromo when he thought that he was in "an African Switzerland," meaning in the land of the Abyssinian proper. He thought that he was in the land of Ras Makonnin, whose photo (as a typical Caucasian) emblazoned the cover of his memoir. He praised him as the man who 'possessed many of Scotch qualities and a Scotch name' (ibid, 21). [Did he confuse Makonnin for McKinnon or Mackinnon?]. Skinner penned, "We emerged upon the plateau, in the center of which stands Harrar, and from an African Switzerland we now entered upon boundless plains of rich and well-cultivated lands. Sorgho, barely, teff, all the vast variety of Ethiopian crops, grew about us, all the vast variety of Ethiopian crops." To his surprising, he learned that the farmers were Oromos, not the Abyssinians. This unexpected incident forced him to eat his words about their barbarity: *"The Gallas are a conquered race of excellent intelligence, and they are industrious farmers and safe citizens"* [italics added] (ibid, 16-7).

This never deterred him from regurgitating unsubstantiated allegations about the native people. Accordingly, they were liable for backwardness and disconnection of Abyssinia from the Christian civilizations. Indeed, the *raison d'être* for rushing to form a commercial link originated from Abyssinia's victories over them. Skinner says:

> They were cut off from communication with the over-sea Christians by the belt of lowland, inhabited by savage tribes, with whom they are constantly at war. *These tribes have now been brought under subjugation; regular trade routes have been opened, and the isolation of the past is over* [italics added] (ibid, 187).

Blindly blaming of these peoples for the backwardness of Abyssinia was taken none other than from the holy book of Edward Gibbon, who tried hard to appear more Catholic than the Pope. An assertion of this armchair historian certainly contributed for fostering the image of a "Christian Island of Ethiopia" besieged by infidels, who cut her from science, technology, art of the civilized world. He wrote, "Encompassed on all sides by the enemies of their religion the Ethiopians slept near a thousand years, forgetful of the world, by whom they were forgotten" (Gibbon, 1841, 281). It is not rocket science to understand his lamentation of the decline of the Roman Empire because of the defeat by the Ottoman Turkey. He said, "If a Christian power had been maintained in Arabia, Mahomet must have been crushed in his cradle, and Abyssinia would have prevented a revolution which has changed the civil and religious state of the world" (ibid, 123).

Gibbon was quite wrong and uninformed about the reality of Ethiopia. Firstly, the reading of "enmity" between Ethiopia and Muslim world, during Aksum and Agaw eras, was not proper historical characterization, to say the least. Secondly, the claim of Ethiopia sleeping was baseless in light of the flourishing of the Agaw civilization. Thirdly, the Ethiopia's pariah status in a wider Christian world happened long before the advent of Islam as she refused to recognize ecumenical validity of conciliatory meetings in the Byzantine world after the crisis of the Council of Chalcedon in 451 AD (McGuckin, 2010, 9). Fourthly, the rise of Islam was parallel development with a decline of prosperity and power of Aksum than something that caused it (Hussein, 2001, 33). In the world of Skinner, Gibbon's assertions and Abyssinian myths are self-evident truth and should be accepted as it is.

Skinner (1906, 142) lauded the brutalities and unspeakable crimes committed by Tewodros, Yohannes and Minilik as the "unmistakable tendency of Abyssinia to come out of the darkness of the ages." In short, except lionizing, and glorifying Abyssinia and its rulers, he never mentioned at all the plundering, killing, enslaving, exiling, and the forced conversion of the native peoples. The justice he did for them was ridiculing, dehumanizing, and regurgitating all justifications Minilik said about his conquests.

Racism in America at the Age of Diplomacy with Abyssinia

Race and religion hierarchies were not peculiar to Skinner, but it was part and parcel of the law of the USA. In 1892, an African-American individual was arrested in Louisiana for riding in the section of a train reserved for the white men in contravention of the Jim Crow laws. In May 1896, the Supreme Court in a landmark decision of Plessy v. Ferguson approved the doctrine of "separate but equal" treatment. Besides, President Roosevelt's 'unequivocal racism' towards Indians was emblematic of an epidemic of racism in the U.S. at the time. According to the collections of Roosevelt Memorial Associations, "He detested them for their cruelty, and even for their emphasis on cruelty as a virtue to be carefully developed as a white man might develop [a] sense of chivalry." "The most vicious cowboy has more moral principle than the average Indian" because of the image that they are "reckless, revengeful, fiendishly cruel, they rob and murder, not the cow boys, who can take care of themselves" (Hagedorn, 1921, 355). Roosevelt deplorably said, "The only good Indians are the dead Indians" (Mojica, 2009, 98). He adopted from the maxim of General Philip Sheridan who said: "The more we can kill this year the less will have to be killed the next year. They all have to be killed or be maintained as species of paupers" (Utter, 1993, 181).

Roosevelt believed that 'different races produce different responses for the same stimuli because of their intellect.' He wrote, "*A perfectly stupid race can never rise to a very high plane; the Negro, for instance, has been kept down as much by lack of intellectual development as by anything else*" [italics added]. He substantiated his assertion by citing Abyssinia and Haiti as examples. They are conservative Christian nations yet technological underachievers unlike their Western Christian counterparts since Christianity doomed to failure in civilizing them because of their race (see, Roosevelt, 1897, 343-5). For Roosevelt, Abyssinia turned out to be white after the battle of Adwa.

For Roosevelt, the decadence of Roman Empire was because of the Asiatic and African slaves." He wrote, "The immense damage done to the Italian husbandman by the importation of Asiatic and African slaves; which was in all probability the chief of the causes that conspired to ruin him" (ibid, 358). An archetypal Ethiopianist Abir uses similar language to show how the arrivals of Oromo in the Gondar Court marked the beginning of the worst chapter in the Abyssinian civilization, the Era of the Princes. He says, "Once the court of the Solomonic rulers in Gondar became dominated by Galla elements whose daughters the emperors married, it is no longer represented the Christian Semitized Ethiopia and was no longer able to provide the link which held the country together." (Abir, 1968, xxii).

Caucasian Image: Abyssinian Creation or Western Invention?

The discourse of "Caucasian Abyssinia" has got attention in two articles of Harold Marcus, *The Black Men Who Turned White* and *Racist Discourse about Ethiopia and Ethiopians before and after the Battle of Adwa*. Amanda McVety's article, *The 1903 Skinner Mission: Images of Ethiopia in the Progressive Era*, draws attention to a similar point. They developed strong argument that "white" or "Semitic" Ethiopia was an invention of Whiteman's racism. Correlating Adwa turning the classic paradigm of race relations upside-down and the affirmation of the Jim Crow laws by the Supreme Court's decision in May 1896, McVety maintains that U.S. politicians wanted to control the damage done by Adwa. According to Marcus, the African success at Adwa forced Europeans to "rationalize Menelik's victory, and they turned inevitably to the discourse without abandoning notions of racism, since such an admission would conflict the teleology of modern European imperialism," and thus, Ethiopia became white (Marcus, 1971, 235). "Ethiopians were white people and considered themselves superior to Negroes" was the conspiracy created "to dissuade Africans and persons of African descent from supporting Ethiopia," according to Asante (1977, 55). Even William Scott, whom an Ethiopian aristocrat derided as a slave (Scott, 1993, xv), maintains the same line of argument: "Maintaining that indigenous Africans lacked the capacity to create the complex state structured found among the Abyssinians, white commentators on African ethnography typically attributed a Caucasian rather than a Negro ethnicity to the Ethiopians" (ibid, 192).

According to McVety (2011), what came out of Adwa were two opposed interpretations in the world of race relations. For African-Americans, it epitomized the spirit of black resilience, renaissance, and disqualified the notion of superiority of whites over blacks; while white Americans portrayed it as a victory of "white" Ethiopia over the white Europeans, and thus, it had nothing to do with Negro race. Cyrus Veeser (2011) agrees with McVety by referring to 'instantaneous racial revisionism' when in few months after Adwa the New York Times called Ethiopia *the Switzerland of Africa* and Ethiopians "are not black, but are of Caucasian descent as pure as the Anglo-Saxon."

These scholars have accurately highlighted how whites, in general, and U.S. politicians, in particular, were bleaching Ethiopia to deny the psychological boost the African-Americans would have gotten out of Adwa. The whitening was so ubiquitous as they even tried to bleach trees in Ethiopia, a land of "honest trees." "What struck us most," wrote John Gunther, "we saw trees—not palms, not tropical shrubbery—but stout, honest trees" (Gunther ,1954, 247).

Of course, at the heart of the White Americans discourse on Adwa, as these scholars showed, there is an assertion that blacks are inferior, unintelligent, uncivilized, and ill-fated at resisting the colonial rule, and whites had a 'manifest destiny' to rule them. In the same fashion, Abyssinia presented itself as the Caucasian, as demonstrated by her myths, to rule over her allegedly darker neighbors. This is the other part of the equation missing from the analysis of the abovementioned scholars who characterized the "whiteness" of Abyssinia as an invention of westerns.

Contrarily, Ethiopia's rulers' claim of whiteness was clear from their title of the "Lion of Judah," and the myth of the Queen of Sheba and King Solomon. There are a plethora of recorded incidents to elucidate that point. What Emperor Minilik told Pan Africanist Benito Sylvain, who came to seek his guidance, is good to mention here; "I am a Caucasian." Indeed, the pronouncement of the Emperor and a Sylvain's lack of 'disconcert' were among the Skinner's proof for his claim of the "Caucasian" Abyssinia (Skinner, 1906, 131). Alberto Sbacchi contends that "Benito Sylvain has the distinction of being recorded in history as possibly the first Black from the West to be rebuffed by Emperor Menelik" and "recorded example of the Ethiopians denying racial kinship with African-Americans." Minilik considered African-Americans, according to Sbacchi, Shanqilla, the race Abyssinia enslaved (1997, 23). Sylvain never gave up; he went to Finfinne to celebrate the centennial of Haiti independence in the only independent black nation in Africa 1904. Minilik was not remorseful; he secretly left for countryside while Sylvain was organizing an honor guard of Ethiopian volunteers (Jonas, 2011, 283).

Minilik also boycotted all the pan-African conferences in the early twentieth century and refused to be a part of any association of the Negro race (Putnam, 2006, 156). Benito Sylvain attended the 1900 Pan-African Conference in London describing himself as an aide-de-camp to Emperor Minilik. It was unlikely that the latter sought the representation of someone whom he rebuffed his pan-Africanist ideology on the pan-African conference.

Rejectionist he was about Ethiopia's racial kinship with blacks, Emperor Hayla Sillase returned a letter of invitation on the International Convention of Negro Peoples in 1920 unopened (Weisbord, 1998, 162). When a prominent Nigerian nationalist Chief Hizekia Oladipo Davies approached him to draw an inspiration to search a vision for black peoples' renaissance, he told him "that Ethiopians were not, and did not regard themselves as Negroes" (Sbacchi, 1997, 25). Criticism for this came from none other than Marcus Garvey, who created such a sensational image about him in the heart and minds of Rastafarians to the extent of being worshipping him as a living God. The emperor recognized his blackness, not even after the fascist invasion of 1930s that galvanized universal back supports. When he addressed the Congress in 1954, he emphasized his empire's location in the "Middle East" and the root of its culture and social structures from the Arabian Peninsula. He realized his "blackness" after the resurgence of Arab nationalism in 1960s and Ethiopia ouster from the 'Middle East Club' (Spencer, 2006, 306). As Ambassador Edward Korry precisely noted, in 1960s, 'Ethiopia became the first nation in modern times, which succeeded changing its geography from an isolated Middle Eastern country to an African nation' (quoted in Vestal, 2011, 144). Haggai Erlick has similar observation about Ethiopia's self-awareness, image and identity as an African country. 'The peoples of historic northern Ethiopia never really identify themselves as blacks,' says Erlick, "The diplomatic road from marginal partnership in a dangerous Middle East to distinguished seniority in a continent of rising expectations was swift and clear" (2002, 156). Interestingly, Ethiopia also recognized Egypt, her alleged racial sister to the north, as an African nation in 1964 (ibid, 157). At the heyday of Hayla Sillase recognition of blackness of Ethiopians, he invited the Rastafarian immigrant from the U.S. and Jamaica to settle in Ethiopia. They established a colony in the vicinity of Shashamane, Malka Oda. This contributed for further eviction of the remnants of the Oromo people from their lands who were already evicted by the Amhara settlers (see, Robinette, 2012, 307).

In short, Abyssinian claim of "whiteness" was deep rooted. This resulted in association of blackness with evilness and whiteness with virtuousness in the pictorial art of Abyssinia. Even Abyssinian religious fathers had echoed the infamous and whimsical assertion that Jesus will come to turn black men into white and pagans into black (see, Levine, 1974, 104). Therefore, the notion of the Caucasian Abyssinia was not only because of the fabrication of Europeans/Americans, but also Abyssinians were "the quintessential Africans who reject African identity" (Sorenson as quoted in Asafa, 2002, 96).

5 The U.S. Ignoring/Covering the Abyssinian Thriving Slave Trade

ERADICATION OF SLAVERY was preponderant human right issue of the time during the flourishing of the landmark diplomatic contact between the United States and Ethiopia. From 1815 to 1957, the international community formulated over three hundred international conventions to combat the slave trade (Weissbrodt and De La Vega, 42). The Anti-Slavery Society that championed "the Universal extinction of slavery and the slave trade" was the oldest human rights NGO established on the planet, in the first half of 19th century (Oberleitner, 2007, 24). Abused though it was for the "civilization" mission, suppressing slave trafficking was a mantra and a matter of national honor for European powers.

Emancipating its millions of black slaves during the bloody civil wars, the U.S. played pivotal roles in those international initiatives to end the slave trades. After wars with the Barbary Pirates, in1803, in the shores of Tripoli, the U.S. entered fighting slave trade in Africa. In 1807, the U.S. joined Britain to prevent the slave trade by enacting statutes restricting the transatlantic slave trade (Worger, et al, 2010, 95). President Thomas Jefferson—who was uncompromised champion of liberty and who was ironically the principal owners of slaves among the founding fathers—signed this bill into law. Notwithstanding the underlying rationales for sending liberated slave to Africa and notwithstanding Americo-Liberians unfortunate history of enslaving the indigenous Liberians, the second relationship the U.S. formed with Africa was founding a homeland for liberated slaves, Liberia. One might plausibly contend that fighting the slave trade and piracy were the U.S. human rights foreign policy towards Africa at the time.

However, the U.S. had a claim to history in abolishing slavery from Africa; it was unconcerned about abolishing the slave trade on an extraordinary magnitude in Abyssinia, which was called "the commerce of the area" (Nicholl, 1999, 274). The U.S. plenipotentiary diplomat either denied the existence of slavery, or he tried to justify the Abyssinian race enslavement of the "savage" race. On the defiant King of Kafa, whose people were killed and enslaved, Skinner reinforced the conquerors' narrative about his arrogance and his slave ownership. He denied an elephant in the room in the case of the conquerors when he said, "slavery does not exist" (Skinner, 2006, 148). Contrarily, Donaldson Smith, a British traveler, who visited Abyssinia, reported:

> Never have the evils of slavery shown themselves in a more terrible light than that in which they are now manifesting themselves in Abyssinia; nor could o cruel a government be found in the world as that which is in store for the tribes among whom I journeyed (qtd. in Hindlip, 1906, 73).

Slavery was profoundly entrenched within the socio-economic fabric of the Abyssinians. It was as old as the Aksum civilization itself, and the wealth of Abyssinia was based on the slave trades and exploitations of indigenous peoples. The kings and nobilities were among the chief beneficiaries of this inhuman trade. Let us explain how slavery and the slave trade were intertwined with every aspect of the social fabric of Abyssinia. For instance, slave ownership was the symbol of the social status, method of paying tax and tributes, source of free labor, and source of income. Eunuchs, castrated slaves, for their docility, loyalty, and sharp feminine voices were popular for church services. Castrated men they were, eunuchs were good for serving women of aristocracies. Slave women served as concubines to nobilities. Slavery was part of the justice system. The Abyssinian novelty of detecting thief by intoxicating children with heavy drugs (leba shay) needed slaves. Slavery served as disciplinary or punitive measures. When a peasant failed to pay an annual tribute to a landlord because of a crop failure, the latter had the right to sell the former (his children) to compensate the loss of his revenue. During famines, which were rampant in Abyssinia, the peasants had to barter some of their children for survival bread. Acquiring slaves through slave raiding expeditions, conquests, and turning war captives into slaves were widespread experiences in Ethiopia (Levine, 1974, 56). On top of this, there was deep rooted and endemic problem of casts, which Herbert Lewis compared to the case of the caste system in India except a single lacking indicia of Hinduism (cited in Levine, ibid).

It is a classical Ethiopian historiography to treat Minilik as a progressive and an abolitionist historic figure; however, the slave trade showed "spectacular growth during his reign" (Markakis, 2011, 97). According to a distinguished historian, Emperor Minilik had a notorious reputation as "Ethiopia's greatest slave entrepreneur" (Marcus, 1995, 73). In addition to enriching his empire from the slave trade and its tax revenues, the emperor, along with his wife, owned as many as 70,000 domestic slaves (Markakis, 2011, 97).

Because of lucrativeness of the trade, Abyssinia organized repetitive slave raids into neighboring territories. From 1870 to 1895, Minilik annually exported 4,000 slaves via Somali and Eritrean coasts, and he captured about 8,000 slaves annually from Kafa (Yohannes, 1991, 201). Between 1898 and 1929, Abyssinia exported 360,000 slaves from the occupied lands (ibid). The fierce slave raids depopulated the newly conquered areas (Waugh, 2007, 24). The populations of Kafa, Kaficho, Maji, and Gimira were reduced almost to the point of extinction (Pankhurst 1968, 111). For instance, the population of Gimira reduced from 100,000 to some 20,000 (Yohannes, 1991, 201).

When depopulations resulted in decline of agricultural productivity, Minilik issued a handful of anti-slavery edicts so that the occupied people would farm and feed the Abyssinian warriors. Therefore, his edicts were not out of humanitarian concerns but to turn the conquered peoples from one mode of slavery to another, that is, "the value of the southern population was greater as cultivators than as commodities for export and immediate profit." (Clarence-Smith, 1989, 124). These proclamations accomplished, yet, very little if anything. In his work, *Modern Abyssinia*, Augustus B. Wylde reported this after having an extended trip through the Abyssinian realm:

> His [Menelik's] profession to the English Anti-Slavery Society were not sincere, and the only good he has done in this business is to forbid slavery in an open manner, that is, driving slaves caravans through the country; but his proclamations seems to have done little good, as Galla [Oromo] slaves in large numbers are still to be purchased in the Yemen and the Hidjaz, and the French do not bother themselves to put down the trade, which passes through their dominions, although they well know who the slave dealers are and that they carry the slaves across the Red Sea in boats flying the French flag (Wylde, 1901, 59).

Wylde also reported that that 'pretty Oromo girls' were a favorite for harems in the Southern Arabia (ibid, 66). A certain missionary who campaigned for the eradication of slavery lamented Minilik's reluctance in this way:

> I am very sorry to hear from the people that King Menelek again allows the traders to carry on their horrible business of the slave trade. This sad news was confirmed by the fact, that several slaves dealers brought six hundred young Galla [Oromo] girls, with many boys, and joined our caravan towards Tajurra (ibid, 472).

In 1910, when Ras Walda Giyorgis, the governor of Kafa and Maji, transferred to the Province of Begameder, he removed all the natives from their country as slaves (Markakis, 2011, 97). In May 1912, Crown Prince

Iyyasu organized 10,000 strong soldiers slave-raiding expedition to the south western corner of Ethiopia. They ransack the area and capture 40,000 slaves, including women and children. Half of the captives died on their way because of inhumane treatments, smallpox, dysentery, hunger and fatigue (Pankhurst, 1968; Zewde, 2001). According to Dr. Merab, a personal physician of Minilik, a third of the population of the country and a third of the population of Addis Ababa were in slavery in 1914 (cited in Pankhurst, ibid).

When an influenza epidemic (1919-1920) decimated the slave population of Abyssinia proper, Abyssinia organized repetitive slave raids in occupied territories. For instance, an Amhara governor of Maji pledged the entire population of his colony for slaves (Yohannes, 1991, 201). His successor plundered the whole area and captured countless slaves, 18,000 head of cattle, and 50,000 sheep (ibid). In a separate raid, his wife also captured 92 slaves (ibid). As we shall see later, the empire profiteering from slavery continued unabated throughout the first half of the twentieth century.

A group of Oromo slaves from Abyssinia liberated by a British warship in 1888 of the coast of Yemen. They were resettled in South Africa. One of the women, Bisho Jarsa had a daughter, Dimbiti, who married to David Alexander. They had a son, Neville Alexander, an anti-apartheid activist. He was arrested, along Mandela, at the Robben Island. He became a prominent educationalist. Source: Sandra Rowoldt Shell, *How an Ethiopian Slave became a South African Teacher*, 24 August 2011. <http://www.bbc.co.uk/news/world-africa-14357121>.

Though Skinner dismissed the existence of slavery in Ethiopia; he was familiar with the fact that peasants were in absolute servitude as one can discern from his writings. "Peasants are virtually in a state of serfdom, with this distinction they are not attached to the soil," noted Skinner (1906, 148). This will turn us to some other aspects of subtle form of slavery/peasant exploitations in the Empire.

Skinner wrote agreat deal about a prodigious courtesy, what he called "hospitality by law" of the people of "the land of milk and honey." Focal to this was a '*durgo*' culture, "the right in law to demand supplies and provisions of the inhabitant" by virtue of the guests of the emperor (ibid, 58). He informed us that the peasants who give a *durgo* in lieu of that secure concession from tax-gatherers when they establish that they complied with the law imposing "forced" hospitality. Skinner could have understood the near impossibility of the peasant to provide proof to get the tax-credit for the *durgo* in the nation where illiteracy was rampant, and the culture of recording (documentation) was unknown. He gave us a good testimony for that when he told us that he brought the parchment sheets for writing the U.S.-Ethiopian treaty of 1903 from the U.S. Contrary to Skinner's assertions, Bulatovich (2000, 9) frankly indicated a direct correlation between the *durgo* and slavery. He showed that the governors, who were coercing peasants to give the *durgo*, were themselves "nursed" by slaves. In this sense, they were extending the same right they enjoy to guests of the emperor in the form of *durgo*.

I believe that Skinner was familiar with individual rights and freedoms under the U.S. Constitution and the Bill of Rights. The Third Amendment of the Bill of Rights protects citizens from government quartering of troops in their houses. This was a culture of Abyssinian army who had the right to quarter in any house during the time of war and peace. According to Skinner (2006, 16), "Abyssinian proper is "professionally a warrior," and "he is not fond of work, but is *capable of obtaining work from others.*" How did they obtain work? Whom did they obtain work from? The dots he failed to connect were the Abyssinians "obtained work from others" through practices such as corvée and other types of forced labors. Furthermore, as the guest of the emperor, just like Skinner, the soldiers had the rights to the *durgo*. This means, all Abyssinians, "professional soldiers," were not salaried soldiers, but they had "been given the land to eat" (Markakis, 2011, 97). The adage goes, 'Soldiers ate the land; Oromo tilled the land.' The impacts of those soldiers on the natives were likened to the biblical locust of Egypt that Skinner knew it. "It is not an army," he said, "it is an invasion, the transplanting of the whole people." (Skinner, 1906, 176).

Notwithstanding his complete rejection of slavery in Abyssinia, the prevalence of slave-master relationship between the "conqueror" race and the "savage" race was clear to him, but the rights of the latter were worthless to him. The Abyssinian enslavement of the subdued people had a biblical ground when Skinner cited Abyssinian law: 'Let them become your servants, whom you take from the people around you, and the strangers who live with you.' "War and raids may cause some to serve others because it is a law of war that the conquered become the slaves of the conqueror" (ibid, 158).

The U.S. had clear information about the endemic of slavery in Abyssinia as various Consular reports showed at the time. A U.S. Consul from Cairo, John G. Long, stated this on June 27, 1901.

> A traveler, who has recently crossed Abyssinia, which he entered by the Zeila route and left by the Blue Nile, writes that he had an especially good opportunity of noting the present condition of [the] slave trade in that region. In that portion of the country which is completely under the control of Minilik, he informs me that slavery exits. [...] In the country of Godjam [...] the institution of slavery openly exists, and public sales take place in the ordinary weekly markets. The supply of victims for this traffic is principally obtained by organized raids upon the strip of country inhabited by mixed Shangalla [Shanqilla] tribes, which separates Abyssinia proper from the Anglo-Egyptian Sudan. (Monthly Consular and Trade Reports, 1901, 187).

Furthermore, the report specified that eunuchs—the worst form of slavery—were the brand Ethiopia was known for in the Arabian Peninsula (ibid).

In fact, the U.S. deserves credit for pressuring Italy to throttle the traffic of the slave trade along the Red Sea. On 31 October 1901, a U.S. Consul in Harput, Thomas H. Norton, thanked the Italian government for its "earnest, vigilant, and persistent" efforts to suppress trafficking of slaves along the Red Sea (ibid).

In a nutshell, while the U.S. was aware of the slave trade on an industrial scale in Ethiopia, it lacked gumption to criticize it let alone advocate for its abolishment. While the U.S. played a decisive role in establishing a homeland for liberated slaves in Liberia, aradoxically the relations with Abyssinia culminated in reinforcing the last bastion of slavery in Africa. For the nation touted as second to none in spreading liberty around the world, a consideration of human rights in dealing with Abyssinia was naught. As it is true today, Washington was in favor of promoting national interests than serving the cause of human dignity.

6   Can Abyssinia Change? Reforms that Challenged Abyssinia and the West

THE UNITED STATES WAS in an election drama that featured three candidates in 1912. Woodrow Wilson of the Democratic Party and the ex-President Theodore Roosevelt of the Bull Moose Party, for a third term, were running against the corpulent William Taft, the seating president from the Republican Party. What was unusual was not the third party running against the democratic and republican establishments, but it was the former president running as the third party candidate on particularly strong platforms and supports. With the split of the Republican Party, a political scientist and a son of an ardent supporter of the Confederacy, Wilson, easily triumphed.

By the same token, Abyssinia was equally in a political drama, in the same year. The drama emanated from the Abyssinian culture of secrecy and the lack of transparency of government internal workings. It was the drama of election in America; it was the drama of succession in Abyssinia. American media talked about their political drama, and the public determine the winner. In Abyssinia, only the inner circles of the Imperial Court, in a closed-door session, addressed the Abyssinian drama to determine the "Elect of God" for the country. In 1913, in spite of the deafening silence of the Court, the death of Minilik from syphilis attacks became an open secret.

Emperor Minilik groomed his grandson for the throne since he had no surviving male descendant of his own. His given name was Lij Iyyasu, which literally means Baby Jesus, and his baptismal name was Kifla Yaqob [share/part of Jacob]. Born in 1897, he was a son of Prince Shawaragga Minilik and Ras Mikael [née Mohammad Ali], a former Muslim cleric and leader from the Wallo Oromo. Would Ethiopia accept the Christian leader from a mixed background, like a son of the Confederate Army chaplain embraced by the U.S.? Would the Empire willing to heal wounds of violent conquests like the U.S. healed wounds of the civil war? Would the West, in general, and the U.S., in particular, support reforms in Ethiopia? Before considering a short reign of Iyyasu, let me point out relations between Ethiopia and the West prior to the succession, concisely.

When Emperor Minilik suffered a massive cerebral hemorrhage in 1906, there were widespread rumors about his death in the diplomatic world. In the same year, strong aspirants to the throne (i.e., Ras Makonnin of Harar and Ras Mangasha of Tigray) died suddenly. With an ironman in a life-death-condition, the discordant elements of Abyssinia revived; European advisors lost their influences at the Court. Europeans expected a succession wrangling. France, Italy, and Britain hammered out a Tripartite Treaty to recognize each other's sphere of influence to avoid potential clashes of interest in the event of disintegration of the Ethiopian state. Consequently, Britain safeguarded interests over the Blue Nile basin. France secured its economic dominance over areas around a main artery of Ethiopian business lifeline with the outer world, the Addis Ababa-Djibouti railway. Italy garnered green light to connect its colonies of Eritrea and the Italian Somaliland through Ethiopia. Expressing gratefulness for respecting the sovereignty of Ethiopia, Minilik expressed his indignation over European intrigues that ephemerally rescinded following Adwa (Luther, 1958, 19).

One of the reasons for the U.S. to seek diplomatic relations was to help Abyssinia to survive and thrive unmolested amidst encirclement by European powers. To that effect, Skinner wrote, "Years before, France, Italy and Great Britain had set up parched and dreary coastal colonies which effectively hemmed in Ethiopia from the sea, and were watching each other as they were now watching President Roosevelt" (quoted in McVety, 2011, 199). Therefore, besides internal developments, one of the external reasons that precipitated the Tripartite Treaty might be U.S. trade and diplomatic contacts with Ethiopia. Support for this assertion came from a statement of Commissioner Skinner on December 15, 1904 when he addressed the Department of the State concerning an additional construction of the Addis Ababa-Djibouti railroad. He addressed a danger of a Tripartite Treaty among France, Britain, and Italy "to be signed" that might exclude America's interests. He underlines, 'Our present [1904] trade interests in Ethiopia are greater than those of any of the three powers now legislating for that country.' By the "three powers," he was referring to France, Italy, and Britain; by "now legislating," he was indicating the Tripartite Treaty in the pipeline; and by "for that country," obviously Ethiopia. There was an asterisk placed on the statement of Skinner. It reads, "An agreement was signed by Great Britain, France, and Italy at London, December 13, 1906, containing articles relating to the Djibouti railroad, etc" (Records of the Department of State, 1962).

The U.S. presence in Ethiopia had somehow mitigated a threat of annexation of Ethiopia. The best example to explain that is the three powers unequivocal commitment to maintain the territorial integrity of Ethiopia in the treaty. Article 102 reads, "We the Great powers of Europe, France, Great Britain, and Italy, shall cooperate in maintaining the political and territorial *status quo* in Ethiopia as determined by the state of affairs at present existing and the previous [boundary] agreements" (quoted in Holcomb and Ibssa, 1990, 8). This was, however, a British traveler presented, "[T]here are moral considerations which should compel all the civilized people of the world to lend their support to crushing out of the Abyssinian power, and substitution of a humane government in the place of Menelik's rule" (quoted in Hindlip, 1906, 73).

According to Skinner, a trigger point for the Tripartite Treaty was the better deals the U.S. secured from Ethiopia. Contrarily, France had gained superior concessions including railway and agricultural exploitation of the Awash Valley, and, Britain had secured the banking sector. We should also indicate that Germany came to Finfinne signing a treaty with Minilik in 1905, and so did Austria. These two nations were core members of Triple Alliance. The Triple Entente born in 1907. Perhaps, we could safely argue that the treaty was a mechanism to get around the U.S. presence in Ethiopia. More fittingly, it was a mechanism to close the door on the late comers to the area. That said; let us turn to the ascension of Iyyasu to the throne of a clandestine nation beset with ethnic and religious inequalities.

Though he was sixteen-years-old at the time of his enthronement, Iyyasu was extraordinarily mature and ahead of his time by following the path of reforms incomparable in accommodating differences of cultures/religions in history of the nation. At his salad days, he embraced the progressive principle of non-sectarianism, if not secularism, by envisioning his "country a happy family" for his "people regardless of the question of religion" (Getachew, 2009, 21). According to Chris Prouty, he "held informal talks with the people of all faiths whether showing companion and interests in all his people whether Christian, Muslim, pagan, northerners or southerners" (quoted in Holcomb & Sissai, 1990, 158). He underlined that "he sought to release the energies of his empire's Muslim population which 'up to now has been abandoned and prosecuted'"(ibid, 161).

Trying to heal the historic wounds of harsh occupations of the peripheral populations was, indeed, a noble adventure of the maverick king. He tried to recognize their autonomy by reversing the trajectory of appointing exploitative Shawan nobilities to govern them. He restored land to the native peasants and allowed them the right to carry gun to defend themselves against the *naftanyas* (ibid, 159).

According to a preeminent Ethiopianist Richard Pankhurst, "Iyyasu was apparently the first Ethiopian ruler to draw a distinction between state property and the monarch's personal property" (Pankhurst, 2009, 139). This was a total break from the culture of considering the country itself property of the crown. This exploitative culture was discernible from a statement of Emperor Sayfa Ar'ad, 'God gave all the land to me' (quoted in Tamrat, 1972, 98). When Empress Tayitu approached Iyyasu (her grandson) to get a share of the estate of her deceased husband (Minilik), he replied: 'I assure you that the gold and silver in the Palace is for the government of the people, it is not the Emperor's or your private property' (Pankhurst, 2009, 140). To curb an endemic corruption in the empire, he introduced a system of auditing of government accounts.

He attempted to overhaul the draconian taxation systems by nullifying "the cumbersome system of tithes instituted by Menelik." His emancipatory tax-edict proclaims, "Let the peasant gather his harvest, and declare its amount under oath; tax collectors are not required." Excited with a new system, taxes collected from the peasants increased. He changed a tradition of the government taking properties of a person who dies childless even without providing him/her with a funeral service or expense. His new decree says, "Even if childless, let a person bequeath his or her property to a trusted relative, and let the latter provide a funeral service for the dead. The Government should no longer inherit such property" (ibid, 2009, 147).

Iyyasu also introduced earth-shattering reforms in the justice system. He abolished *leba shay* and *quranya* systems. In his short reign, Abyssinia got the first municipal police force (Bahru Zewde, 2001, 121-2).

The peripheral peoples welcomed the reforms of the feudal system with euphoria. "[W]hen the prince became emperor in his own right," insisted his supporter, "he would astonish everyone by his intelligence and by his system of government, which would be carried out according to some European criteria with justice, especially for the Galla [Oromo] population" (quoted in Marcus, 1975, 258). Nonetheless, the advocates of the *status quo* perceived his reforms nothing short of apocalypse. In the worldview of the Church and nobilities, the emancipation of peasants from their jaws was anything but Ethiopian lapsing back into savagery. They created a climate of hysteria, and, the reformer king faced a vitriolic criticism. They scandalized and vilified him. Accordingly, he was the worst womanizer [of almost a playboy character], a traitor who betrayed a cherished culture of the ruling class by converting to Islam, and a person who entombed the "sacred" myth of *Kibra Nagast*. As per Hayla Sillase's claim, he had created a family tree, which rivals the Solomonic root and cousinship with Jesus Christ. He styled himself a direct descendant of Prophet Muhammad (Haile Selassie, 1976).

As we noticed in chapter four, the death of Guy Love culminated in closing of the U.S. mission indefinitely. The British Legation in Addis Ababa was overseeing the U.S. interests in Ethiopia. The relegation of diplomatic contact to the lowest level came before the expiration of the treaty of

Commerce and Amity signed in 1903. Upon the expiration of this treaty, Consul General John Q. Wood came to Addis Ababa to negotiate a new commercial treaty in 1914. Owning to the uncertainties around succession and resurgence of European interests towards Ethiopia, the negotiation for a treaty was protracted. When Iyyasu requested for postponement of consideration of the treaty, Consul General Wood deferred it "for a month until His Royal Highness should be in a stronger position as there existed considerable political unrest in his country" (Papers Relating to the Foreign Relations of the United States, 1935, 232).

Emperor Iyyasu (1913-1916). Author: Unknown.

For the young emperor, who cut his diplomatic teeth by sending an invitation out for ex-President Roosevelt for elephant hunting, building a cordial relation with the U.S.'s highest diplomat originated logically for him. Hence, he addressed President Wilson as "my great friend" in response to his letter, in which Wilson also addressed him, "Great and Good Friend." "I am happy to avail myself of this opportunity to assure Your Royal Highness of my best wishes of your personal welfare and for the prosperity of Ethiopia," says the letter of Wilson. He ended the letter with prayer for the young monarch, "May God have Your Royal Highness in His wise keeping." Iyyasu replied, "I prayed from my heart to Almighty God for prosperity of the United States of America and for your personal welfare" (ibid, 242).

These correspondences and understanding between Consul General Wood and Iyyasu showed the warm relations between Ethiopia and the U.S. at the time. Accordingly, on 27 June 1914, the Consul General John Q. Wood and His Royal Highness Prince Iyyasu signed a treaty of commerce. This treaty was almost a mirror copy of the 1903 treaty except a few modifications. The first difference is a semantic one, the usage of the phrase "the most favored power" in Articles III and IV *explicitly* unlike the previous treaty. Article VI of the treaty stipulates that the duration of this treaty was for four years after the date of ratifications by the government of the United States. It also stipulated that if neither of the parties seeks termination, one year before expiration, it should remain in force for a further period of ten years.

The rationale for shortening of the treaty's duration was because of a controversial Franco-Ethiopian treaty of friendship and commerce and a Klobukowski treaty, which would expire in four years from the date of signing of this treaty. Interestingly, the French treaties extend the extrajudicial jurisdictions to the all-European consuls. Article IV of Klobukowski treaty reads, "The Ethiopian government is committed to granting French nationals and protégés all those rights, privileges that Ethiopia was able to grant, or that it will grant to nationals and protégés of the third power in the future, notably as concerns customs, internal taxation and jurisdiction" (Uhlig, 200, 782). Technically, whatever agreement/concession Ethiopia enters with the U.S. should be extended to France. Why did Ethiopia agree to these French treaties having rejected the Tripartite Treaty of 1906? Because France allowed them to import weapons through the port of Djibouti, which they needed for their rule (see, Adejumobi, 2007, 50).

The Senate advised ratification of the treaty on 15 September 1914, and, the President ratified it on September 19, 1914. Delivery of the treaty was entrusted to Colonel Charles H.M. Doughty-Wylie, Chargé d'Affaires of the Britannic Majesty at Addis Ababa. He delivered it on 20 December 1914. As per Article VI, the expiration of the treaty, a period of four years, ran from "the date of its ratification by the Government of the United States." Therefore, technically, it would expire on September 19, 1918. The treaty was proclaimed on 9 August 1920, which was more than six years after it came into existence, because it "was inadvertently placed in the Department's files and buried without being brought to the knowledge of the proper office" (Papers Relating to the Foreign Relations of the United States, 1935, 243). Could the treaty enter into force without a proclamation? Did the treaty expire before it was proclaimed? I wound contend that the treaty had entered into force with ratification and notification to Ethiopia. Firstly, Article VII says, "The present treaty shall take effect if ratified by the Government of the United States, and if this ratification shall be notified to His Royal Highness Prince Lidj Yassou." Both elements of ratification and notification had been satisfied. Secondly, since neither of the signatories sought the cancellation of the treaty one year before its expiration on September 19, 1918, according to Article VI, it automatically continued to be a law.

The Consul General Wood reasoned that most European powers operated at the level of legation either as a matter of prestige [or to impress Ethiopian government] or because of their status as adjacent colonial powers. These legations put the U.S. Consular General at a disadvantaged position because of the prestige of those powers operating at the level of legation enjoys. Showing also the cost of up keeping, he suggested that it was not worth having American legation because of "small trade with no immediate prospect of increasing." For Wood, "the post does not warrant any such expense in view of the commercial insignificance of the country and our own trade which cannot be increased to any appreciable extent by the presence of a consular representative" (Records of the Department of State, 1962). Consequently, the relations degenerated into desuetude.

In the meantime, Iyyasu found himself in a more delicate balance since the break out of the First World War would test his diplomatic shrewdness. Abandoned a Triple Alliance it formed along with Germany and the Austro-Hungarian Empire in 1892, Italy chose neutrality because of territorial disputes with the Austria. Through promising "lavish territorial gains," a London treaty of 1915 cajoled Italy into the war on the side of the Entente Powers. The nationalist defined taking part in the war as the commencement of a renaissance chapter to be a world power. Once again, Italy approached Ethiopia with the sphere of influence mentality despite the fact that Emperor Iyyasu sought normalization of relations with Italy by opening Ethiopia's first Consulate in Asmara in 1915 (Pankhurst, 2009, 142).

The German Reich wanted to fight Britain in Sudan and drive Italy out of Somaliland and Eritrea. It approached Ethiopia via a liaison of the Ottoman Empire to take part in the war on their side. Iyyasu already resented his country's encirclement by Britain, France, and Italian colonies, which denied it access to the sea; the same powers wanted to partition Ethiopia in the Tripartite Convention of 1906, the same powers promised a territorial expansion for Italy, at the expense of his country, in the London Agreement of 1915 (Pankhurst, e. al., 2004, 122). On the other side, he persuaded that the Germans, Austrians and Turks had no colonial ambitions in the region. Their success would drive expansionist Italy out of the Horn thereby Ethiopia getting the opportunity to expand its territorial possessions. Their success would also lead to an end of the British occupation in the region that would usher in amicable relations among neighboring nations. Besides, their "envoys were offering more economic assistance to Ethiopia than were the Allied Powers" (ibid; Robinson, 2004, 120).

Iyyasu's ship of state battered by conflicting reports of the outcome of the war and which side was good for Ethiopia's interest. Britain told him that a German victory means the end of Ethiopia's sovereignty. Iyyasu had tense relations with Britain because of his brutal slave raid when he was the Crown Prince and his retaliatory measures against the Afars when they attacked the Karrayyu tribe. A British Minister, Wilfried G. Thesiger, described him as "an arrogant, cruel youth, [who] took pleasure in watching executions and floggings. "[To] satisfy his lust," stressed Thesiger, "he massacred Shanqalla Negroes on the Abyssinian Sudan border, and slaughtered three hundred Danakils, including women and children." He lost relevance with the minister totally, and he became anything, but a blood addicted vampire who 'liked the sight of blood' (see, Thesiger, 1987, 47). Moreover, he drew the ire of Britain because of his alliance with Muhammad Abdullah Hassan [Mad Mullah], the father of Somali nationalism, who was fighting against Britain, Italy, and Minilik.

At this junction, proponents of *Kibra Nagast* and Prester John began to reinforce each other, to coalesce around the central belief of their myths—Ethiopia was the Christian nation and has to remain as such, however, unjust she was. The fact that a fair-minded Christian ruler wanted to make the country home for all its peoples was unacceptable for the *status quo* and their Western allies. Thus, the British Minister convinced that the reform of the young king was tantamount with "putting himself at the head of the Mohammadan Abyssinians, and of producing a Moslem kingdom that will stretch far beyond the frontiers of his present Empire" (ibid, 48). He reprimanded the Crown Council to either restrain him or face a punitive expedition similar to a Napier expedition against the defiant Tewodros (Pankhurst, et. al., 2004, 124). The protests from the westerns emboldened the rally from within to uproot the maverick king.

A man named Ras Tafari—a son of Ras Makonnin—rose to restore a "soul" of Ethiopia, 'the Christian identity of the court' (Robinson, 2004, 120). He was born in 1892 as the first generation *naftanya* settler in the vicinity of Islamic Holy City of Harar, in the Oromo country. In this land, his fellow Copts were only settlers like him. He was convinced that Ethiopia is only for the Christian Amharas. He 'outmaneuvered' Iyyasu easily. This was not because of his exceptional smartness but because of convergences of interests of the Church, nobilities, and Westerners.

Embattled at home and bewildered with unknown outcomes of the war, Iyyasu sought diplomatic cooperation with the U.S. that downgraded relationship with his country. At this junction, the otherwise apathetic United States in the Europeans infightings drawn into the war following the German submarines sinking of its merchant ships. To avoid potential abjuration from isolationists, Wilson defined the intervention as a parallel war against a mutual enemy—not in coordination with the Entente Powers (Rossini, 1999, 13). This showed ambivalence of the U.S. to entangle in international affairs even when its national security interests were at stake. The response for the Iyyasu's government open arms for the U.S. was absolute condescension since the "young boy" was simply passing a facsimile of a letter written by Turkish and German representatives in Fnfinne (Getachew, 2009, 22). Hence, the deduction that he lacked understanding of his duties. Consul General Wood described his administration in this way:

> [The] present Government is the worst travesty ever inflicted upon a people. The Government exits only in name and the worst type of plunderers that any government ever had. The Prince, a boy of 18 years, is a debauchee, sensual, syphilitic, ignorant, without any idea of his duties, a mere tool, at the present time, of the Minister of Foreign Affairs, a moat unscrupulous, lying blackguard... Other officials are of the same character only not quite so clever. (Records of the Department of State, 1962).

Emperor Iyyasu and Ras Tafari, 1915. Author: Unknown

Besides, Consul Wood described the Minister of Foreign Affairs as "unreliable, dishonest and grafting Minister." In short, he lambasted the people who surrounded Iyyasu as "immoral, unprincipled and [an] ignorant group" (ibid). The lackluster response to diplomatic overtures of the young king was appreciated against the background that the U.S. handed its diplomatic affairs to the British legation, which detested him for his "pro-Islam" dealings. Moreover, at this time, the U.S. relied on the perspectives and needs of European colonial powers to map out foreign policy towards Africa (see, Walton, 2010, 25). In general, Westerners gave a green light for the Crown Council to go ahead with excommunication of Iyyasu from the office. Probably, the Ottoman Turkey conflicts with Armenians had turned against him an influential Armenian diaspora in Ethiopia. It was none other than a certain Armenian photographer who forged a picture of Iyyasu in a Muslim garb (Oguibe, 2005; Waugh, 2005).

Iyyasu's apostasy, collusion with the Triple Alliance powers, and polygamy were pretexts for a palace coup on the commemoration of the discovery of the True Cross, September 27, 1916. An ex-communication edict read: "The Christian faith, which our fathers and hitherto carefully retained by fighting for their faith with the Muslims and by shedding their blood, Ledj Iyyasu exchanged for the Muslims religion and aroused commotion in our midst; in order to exterminate us by mutual fighting he has converted to Islam and, therefore, we shall not submit to him; we shall not place a Muslim on the throne of a Christian king" (Haile Selassie, 1976, 48).

Iyyasu's loyalists were unwilling to concede a defeat. His father (Negus Mikael) marched, from his stronghold of Wallo, to reverse the tide of power grab. He lost at the battle of Sagale in 1917. While Ras Michael was captured, Iyyasu remained at large, and a large-scale manhunt was launched. His fugitive life was short. He was captured, arrested, and vanished in a mysterious way a little before the Italian conquest.

The jubilant minister of the Britannic Majesty watched the triumphant parades of Tafari's troops, in Addis Ababa, with his family. "I have the honor to report," he wrote, "the defeat of and capture of Negus Michael, together the occupation of Dessie by Ras Waldo Giorgis and the definite adherence of Tigre to the Shoan cause." Therefore, "I think we have every reason to be satisfied with the course of [the] event" (Pankhurst, et. al., 2004, 127). Then, Thesiger (1987, 56) wrote this to his mother: "I had been reading Tales from the Iliad. Now, in boyish fancy, I watched the likes of Achilles, Ajax, and Ulysses pass in triumph with aged Priam, proud even in defeat. I believed that day implanted in me a lifelong craving for barbaric splendor, for savagery and colors and the throb of drums."

He found his-life-long-passion, a magnificent triumphal procession and barbaric splendor, after 32,000 people fell like dry leaves. The coup changed the rapprochement of the Solomonic Ethiopia with adherents of Islam and the relations between the center and periphery. Simply, experimentation with pluralism was lurched back in favor of an archaic unitary system. Perhaps, it had averted offering Ethiopia as war booty to Italy, or dividing according to the 1906 Tripartite Treaty or disintegrating like the Austro-Hungarian and Turkish empires. Would the Allied powers romance with Tafari last? We shall grasp with this question in the next chapter.

7 A Dilemma: Tafari or Mussolini?

THE DEMISE OF IYYASU led to a triumvirate rule of Empress Zawditu Minilik, Ras Tafari Makonnin, Heir Apparent, and Habte Giyorgis Dinagde, the influential War Minister. Tafari, a man who credited "destiny" for his success than his "abilities" showed an early syndrome of power obsession. A U.S. diplomat noted, "Ras Tafari wished to be made Prince Regent ... but the Council of Ministers have [sic] never actually made him more than Heir Apparent, because as Prince Regent he would possibly be able to dispute their own power" (quoted in Rubinkowska, 2004, 227). The empress officially recognized him "regent plenipotentiary" saying 'he had no parent, and she had no son that made their relations a relation of a son and a mother'. An insider who detected his alpha-dog character had foreseen a looming danger on her throne. He overtly told her, "He is your master" (ibid). She also dismissed the Council of Ministers in the same year.

Tafari had two qualities to overshadow her: firstly, his self-publicity was unparalleled to anyone in the court; secondly, he presented himself as a messiah who came for redemption of Ethiopia. Tafari was 'neither distinguished by the blood of Minilik nor any abstentious feet of arms', nor was he more than primus inter pares with other noblemen (Waugh, 2005, 4). For Tafari, who was facing an uphill battle against the legitimate successors, therefore, the modernization mantra was a deliberate weapon of choice to win the hearts and minds of nobilities, and above and beyond, it was a propaganda coup against the empress in the eyes of westerns. Whereas Europeans considered Tafari as a man longing for the Western style progress; she became a symbol of the status quo (Rubinkowska, 2004, 331). "Inevitable though it may be," Sir Charles Rey bemoaned, "the modernizing of this wonderfully beautiful old land must cause a pang of regret to any lover of the picturesque and the antique." He had a reason to panic because Tafari would end "the barbaric splendor of 2000 years ago that still exists in Abyssinia today" (Rey, 1924, 12). As Robinette correctly stressed, 'The myth of Tafari as a progressive enlightened monarch peacefully opening up to the modern world an Ethiopia that had been frozen for centuries had its origin in the Westerns' unshakeable bad conscience about Abyssinia' (2012, 320). Ironically, his reforms were nothing but restorations of nobilities' interests and intolerance towards the Muslim population.

The modernization, either for cosmetic or genuine purposes, implied the necessity for building closer ties with western nations, especially with the U.S. The closer relations the U.S. were necessary to protect Tafari's throne from Europeans influences. He commenced his role as the Crown Prince by writing a letter to President Wilson underlining the need for resumption of direct relations, creating robust friendship, and Ethiopia's aspirations to develop a U.S. model of modernization (see, Getachew, 2009, 22).

Mending Ethiopia's image dented as the Muslim ally by jockeying to the Entente powers was among his highest urgencies. He gravely insisted to join the World War First on their side to get armaments and for considerations of the postwar territorial settlements (Shuster, 2006; Marcus, 1994). His ambition failed to materialize due to an Italian opposition that counted Abyssinia as a reward for its contribution in war efforts. He dispatched congratulatory messages to the victorious Entente powers. Getachaw Abate went to Rome to congratulate the King of Italy. Governor Tasamma Nadaw of Illubabor led a four-man delegation to Britain.

Nonetheless, the Allied powers were not shy of redrawing the map of the world as part of the post war settlement plan during the Versailles Peace Conference of 1919. Their approach towards Ethiopia was offering for Italy as per the promise of the London treaty. Thanks to the self-determination rhetoric born out of the anti-imperialist tendencies of Woodrow Wilson, Italy failed to secure sphere of influence over Ethiopia. Wilsonian anti-imperialist outlooks were shaped by his Fourteen Point Proclamations of War Aims in 1918 that underpinned for redrawing the post-war maps in accordance with "recognizable lines of nationality" and 'the right of self-determination for every peace-loving nation' (Sikkenga, 2003, 608). This was a recipe for the birth of various nation-states in the Balkans from disintegrations of Austro-Hungarian and Ottoman empires.

The aforesaid delegation of Tasamma came to the U.S. to congratulate President Wilson. Empress Zawditu expressed her country's appreciation for U.S. initiatives to build world peace and order through launching of the League of Nations. To strengthen the bilateral ties, she requested Wilson to promote American businesses to conduct commerce with Ethiopia (see, Getachew, 2009, 22).

The visit came at the heyday of racism, when lynching and the Jim Crows laws were the ugly face of the U.S. domestic policy. To shield the

Abyssinian visitors from discriminations, the U.S. designated them "Caucasians" officials, in most cases, accompanied them. A U.S. diplomat noted, '*The honorable Abyssinians, with their traditional cloth and fine features, were different from American Negroes. Despite their skin color and hair texture, they belong to the Semitic race and had to be treated like white men*' (ibid, 25).

Still, their Caucasian tag never saved them from racial abuses, and, the National Democratic Club in the New York refused to serve them (Putnam, 2006, 157). In 1922, Hayla Sillase personal representative Heruy Walda Selassie tested the same vicious racism when he came to shop for military hardware. The "noble" Abyssinians, who never colonized except colonizing, who never faced racism except racially abusing others, who never enslaved except enslaving others tasted the evil deed of racism. However, the incidents opened their eyes about the broad day light nasty racism in the U.S.; it never opened their eyes about their pernicious racism and discriminations at home. These widespread racial discriminations stood against strong desires of Tafari to visit the U.S. in 1920s.

The U.S.-Ethiopian Relations under Harding and Coolidge

Wilson interventionism left bad test in the mouth of voters because of stuttering economy. His decision to invade Haiti, a symbol of black freedom in the Western Hemisphere, in 1915, alienated the black minority. Riding on a strong current of anti-interventionism and black support in the north, isolationists won a landslide victory in the Congress. Warren Harding who "knew nothing about international affairs" won the presidential election of 1920 with a landslide victory in an election widely considered as a referendum on internationalism (Somerville, 2004, 29).

As America slipped back to the mindset of isolationism, Harding changed a nascent experimentation with interventionism. America was in the economic hardship, struggling with a large influx of immigrant from the war-torn Europe, the crisis of alcohol prohibition, and lynching. He was a rubber stump president who signed every bill placed by the Congress on his table. Emboldened by the ceremonial role of the president on the foreign policy and delegation of his role to the Secretary of the State, the Senate considered foreign policy as its domain. Senator Boies Penrose emphatically asserted, 'The Congress would blaze the way in international affairs and would not be dictated to or led by the Secretary of State' (Buck, 2002, 50). The Senate pursued the policy of "return to normalcy" to seek "relief from the burdens that international engagement brings." The independent nationalism that emerged out of disenchantment with the WWI eroded American belief in internationalism and altruism "that America's mission should be one of magnanimous service to the rest of the world" (Wittkopf & Jones, 2008, 37).

Because of resurgence of a new wave of isolationism, the U.S. even disinterested in sending a representative to Ethiopia and closed its mission. "I am very sincerely sorry," Ras Tafari wrote to Harding, "that there was not appointed in Ethiopia a representative of your Government" (Records of the Department of State, 1962).

In August 1923, John Calvin Coolidge succeeded to the presidency upon the death of Harding. On November 16, 1923, Tafari wrote to President Coolidge, "I attach a very special importance in the establishment of relations of friendship and commerce between the United States and Ethiopia." He promised to strengthen the existing ties of friendship, as well as to develop upon a solid foundation for promotion of the mutual interests of both nations. He thanked the President for showing interest in Ethiopian students studying in the U.S. Of course, the Ethiopian students were none other than three of his sons at Muskingum College in New Concord, Ohio. "They will be able to render to their country signal services" because of "the sound education they may receive and the moral support that they have found in the United States." "America will be assuredly the ideal cradle of instructions of the Ethiopian youth" (ibid).

The diplomatic ties were improved during the presidency of Coolidge as he accepted Tafari's request for appointing a resident diplomat to Ethiopia. On December 8, 1923, the Department of States Divisions of Near Eastern Affairs made a positive recommendation for the office to be reopened in Ethiopia: to promote trade extensions and facilitations, for protection of the public health, to preserve the existing or potential American interests, to counteract the influence of Britain, France and Italy. Their presence in Ethiopia was good since the Department of Agriculture requires for issuing a certificate for import of hides and skins from the "country of origin" (instead of from Aden). In particular, it regretted entrusting U.S. interests to its principal commercial competitor, the U.K (ibid). This was fruitless due to opposition from the State Department over the cost of the mission and lack of appetite for internationalism. "I never could see anything for a minister in Abyssinia to do," Secretary Root insisted. He wanted to spend money "in the places where it counts" (Getachew, 2009, 23). We shall come back to this issue, but let us see some significant international developments, relevant to the bilateral relations, first.

The U.S., the League of Nations, and Fascism

In line with his modernization pretenses, Tafari's had obsession to secure external legitimacy for his throne. As elaborated above, Wilson foreign policy neither persuaded the American public to embrace internationalism nor did it swayed the Senate to join the League, the supranational organization he engineered to create a global rule of law. Tafari had to look to Europe to find a support for his ambitious scheme of bestowing honor and prestige on Abyssinia by joining the League of Nations. He filed a membership application in 1919 through the sponsorship of France. Due to the rampancy of slavery, Abyssinia denied admission. The denial for a place in the club of "civilized" world came as a slap on his face.

Meanwhile, the World War I threw Italy into economic shambles. Although Italy secured most of territories it wanted in Europe, nationalists regretted the lack of commitment to the London treaty and the rejection of a map redrawing plan. On the other hand, inspired by the Russian Revolution, socialists brought Italy into deadlock through their unrelenting waves of strikes and factory occupations. The Government of Giovanni Giolitti hardly stopped the wave of attacks against the factories and made a concession after a concession that disappointed employers.

A man named Mussolini came to prominence by making the biggest political capital out of the ineffectiveness of government systems. He formed fascist paramilitary groups called Squadristi (Black-shirts). He organized the Black-shirts under ras, from an Amharic term for chieftains. The Black-shirts and the ras were redolent of the ferocious black warriors at Adwa. Some speculated that it might be a manifestation of his intention to use their ferocity at home first and use against Abyssinia later (see, Finaldi, 2009, 17). The Black-shirts were ruthless in wiping out the socialist party, trade unions, and peasants' leagues. Mussolini pacified Italy through brutalities. The Black-shirts mushroomed all over Italy. The business owners, who breathed a sigh of relief, showered the fascists with funds that transformed fascism into a mass movement.

Fascism changed to a political party in 1921. While Mussolini was becoming a political heavy weight, the crisis was worsened. Now, Mussolini's confidence went through the roof. He declared to his supporters, "either we are allowed to govern or we will seize power by marching on Rome" to "take by the throat the miserable political class that governs us" (in Smith, 1983, 51). On 29 October 1922, Benito Mussolini, a staunch believer in the renaissance and restoration of the golden age of the Roman Empire, ascended to power in such enigmatic fashion.

Despite American newspapers carried horrific stories of fascist crimes, America "gave Benito Mussolini and his fascist dictatorship greater support than did the people of any other Western Nation" (LaGumina, 2000, 215). Mussolini was all about his status as a pacifier, bulwark against Bolshevism, and the savior of capitalism. In his book, *The Myth of American Diplomacy*, Walter Hixson underlined that "Italian fascism was perceived as meeting all the qualifications for U.S. support: promise of political stability, anti-Bolshevism, and increased trade with the United States." He stresses that though some advised against a danger of a rising brutal repression; the U.S.

praised Mussolini for his nationalist agendas, intelligence, commonsense and charm (Hixson, 2008, 143).

In his work, *The Culture of Make Believe*, Derrick Jensen meticulously presented the U.S. cordiality with and roles in supporting fascism. He argues that even when Mussolini abolished democracy altogether, a U.S. ambassador in Italy liked it. The ambassador wrote, "We are having a fine young revolution here. No danger. Plenty of enthusiasm. We all enjoy it." He even created the impression that the whole people were happy it since they were craving for a "strong leadership" and 'there has not been a single strike in the whole of Italy since the end of democracy'. "Fascism was praised by the ambassador as a growing, vibrant party willing to take action against the country's enemies, which included not only socialists, communists, and anarchists but also republicans" (Jensen, 2004, 544). Secretary of State Henry Stimson praised Mussolini as "a sound and useful leader" (ibid).

Jensen also demonstrated how American companies played pivotal roles in buttressing Mussolini, and how the mouthpieces of corporate America became a "missionary" for the cause of fascism. Jack Morgan of J.P. Morgan Company stated, "We had the great satisfaction of seeing Mr. Mussolini's Revolution." Judge Elbert Gary of United States Steel hoped, "we, too, need a man like Mussolini" (ibid). By 1930, U.S. firms had bankrolled the regime more than $460 million while direct investments alone surpassed $121 million (Hixson, 2008, 143). It was this unqualified support that Marcus Duffield of Harper's magazine lamented as "Mussolini's American Empire" (LaGumina, 2000, 217).

In related development, Tafari launched a second campaign for the League membership. Initially, Mussolini's Italy, which was the permanent member of the League Council, was inimical to the admission of Ethiopia. Swayed by whim, Mussolini approached Abyssinia with the gesture of friendship and good neighborliness. His friendliness towards Abyssinia was different from a hawkish approach of his predecessors as he pursued a new paradigm, "to kill Abyssinian independence by kindness" (Quinn and Sevareid, 159). At the infancy of his rule, he pursued the foreign policy of peaceful diplomacy with dynamic themes and aggressive intentions (see, Fry, et al., 2004, 214). A romance between Tafari and Mussolini was a classic example of prisoner's dilemma for both. Whereas Tafari was seeking the League admission to shepherd Ethiopia from Mussolini, the latter was ironically helping him to eat his empire softly.

Thanks to painstaking diplomacy of Mussolini, Britain that considered abolishing of slavery as a *sine qua none* of its foreign policy and that posed a formidable challenge to the Abyssinia's entry caved in as a gesture of goodwill to a traditional ally. The country that was called "uncivilized" for the admission suddenly changed to a "civilized" country with full honors that 'civility' implied (see, Quinn & Sevareid, 159)

The British support came despite Tafari unequivocally indicated to a British minister in Finfinne that he would oppose the League aids to wipeout slavery from his empire (Perham, 1948, 225). Therefore, his strategy was simply securing the admission while maintaining the *status quo* (ibid). To his delight, the unanimous admission with a considerable fanfare came in September 1923.

Nonetheless, the admission came with the proviso that Ethiopia would undertake measures "to observe the St. Germain Arms Convention of 1919, provide the Council with information on slavery and consider the League recommendations on obligations under the Covenant" (Quirk, 2011, 77). Ethiopia had to open its door to the recommendation of the League on abolishing slavery, and, it had to carry out a symbolic act of manumission, launching anti-slave agencies, furnishing the lists of freed slaves, and of prosecuted slave traders (Quirk, 2011; Greenidge, 1958).

These conditions put Tafari on notice that the sovereignty of his throne was in jeopardy unless he carried out a genuine reform to put an end to slavery. This placed him at a cross road. On one hand, a wealth of his nation, his Amhara elites, the church was based on slave system, and on the hand, he had to comply with the demand of the international community. "The Church in which priests and monks were considerable slave-owners appears to have been almost solidly against change in this direction" (Perham, 1948, 228). As Pankhurst (1968, 108) emphatically articulated, "Slavery was then as deeply ingrained as ever and its abolition involved nothing short of a social revolution." Tibebu (1995, 63) correctly said that the socio-economic ramification of eradicating slavery on slave owning aristocrats was anything but declaring a full-fledged war on them.

Tafari embarked on finding equilibrium between sustaining the system and deceiving the international community. Instead of introducing a comprehensive reform at once, he decided to pursue spasmodic and superficial reforms, which turned the problem underground. On 15 September 1923, he passed a decree banning the export of slaves to foreign countries. The preamble of the decree provides a fascinating glimpse of the empire's indulgence in this barbaric trade:

> [T]he reasons why some men were declared slaves (in the past) was [sic] that certain nations were at war with us, and this had caused money to be spent which these nations had to repay by their labour, and moreover, that they should learn virtue by communications with Christians. (quoted in Markakis, 2011, 98).

He issued a second decree, which outlaws selling and buying of slaves and emancipates slaves seven years after the death of their masters. The status of already existing slaves, forced labor, various forms of peasant exploitation mechanisms remained unabated.

In short, introducing an earth shattering reform was unthinkable for Tafari since, beneath his superficial declamations, there was a hard reality that he was a mover of the wheel of the system. In fact, on the aftermath of the so-called reforms, the population of a fertile province of Maji, which his nephew ruled, dropped from some thirty thousand to a few hundred (Perham, 1948, 220). By the mid-1920s, according to an Abyssinian official, the populations of rich provinces of Kafa declined from 250,000 to 10,000 (Yohannes, 1991, 201). "The fierce slave raiding in the area had spilled across frontiers, antagonizing" the adjacent British colonial officials (Marcus, 1994, 134). According to the 1932 report of the Anti-Slavery and Aborigines Protection Society, *a quarter of the population of Ethiopia was under the bondage. There were a minimum of two million slaves out of the estimated 7 to 8 million population of the country.*

Lackadaisical he was about eradicating slavery; Tafari wanted some twenty years to carry out full eradication (Perham, 1948, 227). He wrote his argumentum ad antiquitatem in this manner:

> No government in the history of the world was able to solve all problems at once and to straighten everything out miraculously. In fact, it takes a long time and consistent effort to carry out such a task. Yet, it was surprising that everything was exaggerated when it came to us. The most exaggerated accusation against Ethiopia was the issue of slavery… The institution of slavery was deeply rooted in tradition … Since far back in history, slavery had been practiced in the whole world; it was not an institution unique to Ethiopia. (Haile Selassie, 1994, 175).

While he criticized the West for their harshness on him, his mediocre reforms were good enough to obliterate autonomous regions and to consolidate his power. He scrapped the autonomy of the gold rich province of Asosa, and the coffee rich provinces of Sidamo and Jimma.

What was the role of Uncle Sam in throttling the slave traffic this time? Here again, dear Uncle Sam had lost the honor of global champion of freedom. For instance, a U.S. delegation that visited Addis Ababa under the Phelps-Stokes Fund to explore the possibility of cooperation in the educational sector was surprised by the reality of the slave trade in Ethiopia. The director of the fund reported that slavery was a severe problem in Ethiopia despite Tafari's assertion of opposing it (Skinner, 2003, 17).

Tafari Gravitating towards Europe

Tafari found himself in the limbo: firstly, the U.S. that would mitigate the fear of invasion was reluctant to have visibility in Ethiopia; secondly, the League requirement to abolish slavery placed him in a precarious position at home. He resorted to strengthening friendship with Europe, including to be friended with sooner-would-be unfriendly Italy. Thus, instead of totally eliminating the slave system, he chose an expensive globetrotting European tour to sell his piecemeal reforms and the image of "civility" of Ethiopia in 1924.[1] To avoid coup at home, his arch rivals, Ras Kasa Haylu of Gojjam and Ras Siyyum Mangasha of Tigray, escorted him for the trip of more than four months. He grabbed six lions and four zebras, as a diplomatic gift and to show to the world that he was the twentieth century *Prester John*.

European press praised him for his "devotion to modernization," Caucasian features, and Solomonic wisdoms. He was described as 'the thoughtful prince, intelligent, with extraordinary handsome face, next door to black, a fine hawkish nose, a person of striking refined appearance, the appearance of a deity receiving homage, serenely unmoved by the pomp of his welcome' (Asafa, 2002, 101; Vestal, 2011, 22). At times, he was described with the languages best reserved for describing the demeanor of angels. 'He has melancholy eyes, and beautiful, aristocratic hands, so tiny, so exquisitely shaped. …The moment one looks into his eyes, one realizes that he has a will of iron, an acute and alert mind, and the strength of purpose that can move mountains' (quoted in Robinette, 2012, 317). The famous Cambridge University honored him with an honorary doctor with infamous praises. Thus, "He follows in the footsteps of his ancestors and possesses knowledge exceeding that of Orientals and Egyptians. He explored all ancient and modern knowledge… the ancient Christian traditions…a modern science" (Ullendorf, 1976, 111).[2]

Along praises for his Caucasian features and wisdoms playing with the golden rules of selfishness was the business etiquette of imperialists. Thus, Tafari neither succeeded in selling the "civilization" of Ethiopia nor did he secure an access to sea. France—his main ally—was loath about his free port tour since it would make its primary business interest with Ethiopia—the railway—irrelevant (Marcus, 1994, 123).

Mussolini was looking for economic favor from him for supporting his country to become the League member. Britain and Italy joined forces, once again, to pressure him to accept the Tripartite Treaty of 1906. As a result, Britain consented to Italy's construction of railway from Somalia to Eritrea

---

[1] For the rejuvenated Italy, the rampancy of slavery was a good pretext to "civilize backward" Abyssinia should the a peaceful penetration stumbles.

[2] In reality, his Majesty was not even a majestic; and, most of the time, he was smart by half. He was 'exceptionally short', 'looked something like a mushroom', 'had rest his tiny feet on a cushion otherwise they would not have touched the floor', 'far below the average height', 'could not weigh more than 110 pounds, and 'had the fragility of a figurine' (Gunther, 1954, 250-1; Robinette, 2012, 319).

via Ethiopia, and its economic control over the rich western part of Ethiopia. In return, Italy agreed to British interests of building a dam on Lake Tana to provide electricity for its colonies and to facilitate better flow of water for irrigation projects. Tafari protested them before the League of Nations; they abandoned their efforts. He scored the first diplomatic victory over Mussolini who helped him to join the League (Pankhurst, 2004, 206-7).

Ethiopia, the U.S., and Nile Diplomacy

In 1927, President Coolidge assigned Addison Southard as minister resident in Finfinne. Tafari position at home was firm. As I noted before, establishing stronger relations with the U.S. was a panacea to overcome the economic and diplomatic stranglehold by European powers.

On the other hand, on 28 April 1928, Mussolini—who hailed in the words of Pope Pius XI as "the man whom Providence has made us meet" (Palla, 2000, 62), and whose domestic position became firm—delivered a bombastic speech. This time, his diatribe was not for a domestic consumption, but a harbinger for his stronger intentions to erupt on the global scene. He proclaimed, "Words are a very fine thing; but rifles, machine guns, warships, aero-planes and cannon are still finer things (…) because right unaccompanied by might is an empty word." "Fascist Italy," he declared to the world, "powerful armed, will offer her two simple alternatives: a precious friendship or an adamant hostility" (quoted in Hyde, 1988, 203). The speech indicated Mussolini's shift from a peaceful method of exerting influence over Ethiopia towards bellicosity.

On August 2, 1928, Tafari signed a treaty of perpetual friendship and arbitration for twenty five years with Italy. Mussolini wanted to use it as a Trojan horse for the soft penetration of Ethiopia if it worked. As Marcus noted, a Tafari's plan "was too clever by half … since Ethiopia's refusal to abide by the stipulations of the 1928 agreement led to frustrations and then to bitterness in Rome" (1994, 126).

Wishing to forge closer ties with the U.S. and other non-European powers, Tafari denied a market to Europeans, even to the friendly France. Historian Marcus (1994, 124) reasons that this was a radical turn for France and Britain to concede on Mussolini's free hand in Ethiopia. Thanks to India and Japan becoming the main exporting partner of Ethiopia the market for the U.S. cotton products, *Amercani*, had almost gone. Still, the U.S. was a significant buyer of Ethiopia's hides and coffee. What was in it for the "Yankee traders" to defend Ethiopia, hides and coffee? Therefore, it was a time for Tafari to play a card of Nile diplomacy.

Tafari sent Dr. Charles Martin (aka, Hakim Warqinah Eshete) to the State Department to seek the help of the U.S. to facilitate J.G. White Engineering Company to build the Lake Tana dam. The company secured a concession; however, an Italian company offered the lowest bid thanks to a subsidy of its government that dreamed for the economic soft-landing in Ethiopia. Britain supported Italy to take the work as part of the appeasement plan and to create economic interdependence between them. A Mussolini attempt to get a share of the American company was an utter failure (see, Tvedt, 2004, 161-3).

A company vice president met Ethiopian officials in Finfinne, in 1930. The sole outcome of the meeting was the company should undertake deep research on the engineering problems of the dam. Although it consented to the dam construction superficially, Britain unleashed its lower riparian colonies to face the project with a full force. It also indirectly put conditions for the plan. Firstly, it had to build a road from Sudan to the Lake Tana, which Ethiopia considered a highway for a colonial agenda than a technical one. Secondly, they wanted to have a control of the company. The company was ready register as a British agent, albeit, a futile one. Eventually, the plan collapsed and the survey team left Finfinne without visiting a project site. All the parties were virtual losers somehow, but Tafari was the worst of all. His action led to the curse of priests for selling their shrines, and, it even agitated regional rebellions (ibid).

The U.S., Tafari and the Gun Diplomacy

Domestically, Tafari tightened his control over resource rich areas of the south; his throne flourished with the export of coffee, and hide and skins. Ninety five percent of the national revenue generated from export came from the levies collected from the occupied peoples of the south (Lefort, 1983, 9). He had a strong resolve to spend this revenue to purchase advanced weapons, technologies, scientific and technical expertise.

However, Ethiopia agreed to prevent arm's buildup in Africa along abolishing of slavery as conditions for the League admission; France shielded it from the restrictions so that it could shop for modern weapons (see, Marcus, 1994, 123). Tafari acquired tanks and treasure troves of ammunitions and machine-guns from Belgium, Switzerland, Czechoslovakia, among other countries. He acquired six aircrafts (4 French Potez 25, an Italian Breda sports plane, and a German Farman monoplane) to kill and frighten his adversaries on the ground and from the air (see, Joseph, 2010, 20). He trained his elites Imperial Guard, *Kibur Zabanya*, in Europe. To create a favorable atmosphere for their missionaries to proselytize the conquered areas, the Swedish government supported the gun-hungry emperor with modern weapons and opened a cadet school at Holata. Later, the Belgium government also established a training center at Harar for the formation of two modern infantry battalions, squadrons of horse soldiers, camel mounted infantry, and armored cars (ibid). Besides, there were several European mercenaries willing to train the Ethiopia army on efficacious usage of those weapons (ibid, 19-20). In short, as Keller correctly stated, *"Ras Tafari expanded his army and provided it with the most modern weaponry his money could buy"* [italics added] (1989, 43).

That was too little for Ras Tafari, whose main legitimacy emanates from the use of force. He was convinced that America produced airplanes and tanks of superior quality to Europeans ones (Getachew, 2009, 31). Thanks to the coffee revenue of the south, he was ready "to pay cash in advance for American weapons" (ibid). To make the effective use of weapons, and to enhance the bilateral ties, he was prepared to pay for American experts (ibid). The U.S. was reluctant to feed his avarice for the superior and sophisticated weaponry because of the League restriction and British opposition. It should be noted that the overflow of gun in Abyssinia and smuggling into the adjacent British colonies had alarmed Britain. The U.S., however, maintained his cool by providing him with light weapons and ammunitions. Getachew (2009, 31-3) argues that Tafari's misfortune to get weapons bonanza from the U.S. left Ethiopia without a means to defend itself against the Italian aggression. The fact of the matter was the emperor mainly wanted those weapons to use against his own defenseless people because the *naftanya* system hardly survived without a gun (*naft*). I want to point out the emperor's pattern of power monopolization for which he needed those weapons.

In 1926, the death of the war minister led to a diarchy of the fragile Zawditu and the rising Tafari. Tafari doled out the general's estates among his loyalists and absorbed his army into his own army.

In 1928, he sacked Ras Balcha Safo. The accusation was he failed to comply with a new ordinance of taxation he issued to tighten his control on revenue of the south. He seized his estate and appointed his son-in-law (Dasta Damtaw) to control the coffee-rich province of Sidamo. However, Tafari fractured the old-guard for not conforming to principles of good book-keeping; it was impossible to determine the boundary between the government estate and his personal one (Robinette, 2012, 325). During this time, he "accumulated a considerable personal fortune and deposited the money in foreign banks," and he "recruited members of his own family to serve as his closest confidants" (Keller, 1989, 43).

On September 22, 1928, Ras Tafari "undermined the Empress's position by coup d'état" (Perham, 1948, 63). His modern army, who were "well-armed with newly imported rifles, machine guns, small cannons, and ....menacing tank" (Marcus, 1994, 128), encircled the palace and arrested the commander of her guard with a demand for the title of king (Perham, 1948, 63). The enfeebled empress could not help, but to sanctioned him a king with full powers on October 6, 1928. He became a *de facto* ruler of Ethiopia, in the eye of Western diplomats.

Ras Gugsa Walle was defiant to accept the authority of the man, who grabbed the power of his ex-wife. Too bad for poorly informed Gugsa, the modernizer Tafari ordered the preemptive airstrike on his forces at his hometown, *Dabra Tabor* (otherwise ironically known as the Battle of Anchim). A French mercenary pilot Andre Maillet was ready to drop death dealing weapon of the Potez-25 aircraft, nicknamed a *Bird of the Prince*. That was the first air warfare in the history of the empire. Gugsa's men hardly told whether it was wrath of God or an airplane attack; he died in the battle. The news came as a big shock to the Empress who mysteriously died the next day. The battle of *Dabra Tabor*, along with the battle of *Sagale*, ended a military balance in the empire and opposition of Wallo to the Shawan rule. *The Bird of the Prince* thereby subdued the rebellion of Raya Azebo against the *naftanya* settlers.

The above discussion answers whether Tafari's endless quest for weapons was for the national defense purposes or perpetuation of his domestic rule. By the time of Mussolini's invasion, Tafari left with a single aircraft (Joseph, 2010, 20). During this time, because of surpluses, Ethiopia had become a net exporter of guns to the people from neighboring European colonies. Whereas Ethiopia possessed at the time 560,000 stockpiles of rifles; Hayla Sillase sent only 60,000 against the Italians while he distributed the rest to his settler soldiers in the occupied territories to maintain order (Holcomb & Sissai, 1990, 112). When the country was invaded, he was not in the business of defending it. He ran away, indeed.

The Coronation of Hayla Sillase and African-Americans

On April 2, 1930, Regent Tafari ascended to the Imperial Throne of Ethiopia. President Hoover sent him a congratulatory message: "I have received Your Majesty's telegram informing me of your accession to the imperial throne of Ethiopia and assure you of the satisfaction with which I receive this announcement." (Public Papers of the Presidents of the U.S., 1999, 144). On November 2, 1930, Tafari, the 225th descendant of the Queen of Sheba and King Solomon, crowned Emperor Hayla Sillase, King of Kings, Lord of Lords, Conquering Lion of the Tribe of Judah, Elect of God and Power of Trinity, Light of the World. Traditionally, it was a 21-gun salute; but for this occasion a 101-gun salute wrung because it was a coronation of an 'unexceptional' man "blessed to be the King of Israel" (see, Vestal, 2011, 25). From the ceremony, he got what he wanted since the Time Magazine, in the same year, named him a "Man of the Year."

According to Evelyn Waugh, a reporter for *The Times* and the *Daily Express*, the lavish display and pageantry had two messages. Firstly, he desired to enhance the impression that Ethiopia was a civilized, powerful, and organized nation; not a mere collection of "barbarous" to be exploited by

Europeans. Secondly, "he wanted to impress his countrymen that he was not paramount chief of a dozen independent communities, but an absolute monarch recognized on equal terms by the monarchies and governments of the great worlds" (Waugh, 2005, 5). Waugh did not like the show off and the mismatch between the pomp and the reality of Ethiopia at the time. He wrote that "the whole country is policed with spies" (ibid, 3). Later, he authored a classic novel of his time, *Black Mischief*, in which he transformed 'Hayla Sillase into the buffoon emperor Seth, whose whimsical ideas produce one political disaster after another' (Schweizer, 2001, 48). Waugh also indicated that the crowning process, in the cathedral, was highly militarized because of his power grab. The Western press called it 'meditation behind machine guns' (2005, 24).

Hayla Sillase wanted the presence of large American mission on the occasion. Ambassador Herman Murray Jacoby and Brigadier General Hurts represented the U.S. They carried various gifts, inter alia, an electric refrigerator, a typewriting machine emblazoned with the royal coat of arms, a radio-phonograph console, 100 records of American music, 500 rosebushes, a three motion pictures, and a National Geographic report of Chicago Field Museum's expedition to Abyssinia (Adejumobi, 2007, 54).

The coronation augmented this atmosphere of African-American enchantment and self-identification with Ethiopia. We should state that the movement of Abyssinianism, which mixes religion and Black Nationalism, got a ground in the U.S. in 1920s. A notable event, at the time, was a certain Abyssinian leader "burned an American flag to symbolize the surrender of allegiance to the United States and the assumption of allegiance to Ethiopia." The slogan of this movement was "The Ethiopians [African-Americans] do not belong here and should be taken back to their own country" (Weisbord, 1998, 154). Hence, although they were uninvited; the coronation attracted an attention of blacks of Harlem. A Jewish activist named Rabbi Arnold Josiah Ford went to Addis Ababa to congratulate the emperor and seek settlement in Ethiopia. A black reporter Joel Augustus Rogers visited Ethiopia to cover the event for a black newspaper. Marcus Garvey convinced that occasion was the fulfillment of biblical prophecy of "Princes shall come out of Egypt; Ethiopia shall soon stretch forth her hands unto God." He already indoctrinated his followers to replace the photos of a white Christ and a white Madonna with a black Christ and a black Madonna, and, he already declared that white represented 'evil' for black people (Robinette, 2012, 312). For Rastafarians, thus, the coronation and titles of Hayla Sillase supported his "divinity," fulfillment of Garvey's prophecy, and for the larger Africa-America community it epitomized the "Last of Free Africa" (Weisbord, 1998, 155).

This was opportunity for Tafari to encourage the emigration of professional and skilled African-Americans to Ethiopia. He had already tried to achieve this via the agency of Malaku Bayyan, an Ethiopian student at Howard University and the British educated Dr. Charles Martin, an Ethiopian minister in London. This time, he sent Gabru Dasta, a mayor of Gondar, to lure professional and highly skilled African-Americans through promising good salary, free land, and settlement plan.

Consul Addison Southard strongly disapproved recruitments. He had observed Ethiopian racism. He emphasized that a "racist abuse lay the root of Ethiopia's tolerance" of African-Americans. 'The proper Ethiopian is a man of dark color but in temperament, character, and most other ways, is quite alien to the negro whom he regards as an inferior being to be exploited if and when possible.' Therefore, in his view, "Ethiopia could support neither white nor black pioneers" (quoted in Plummer, 1996, 39).

Nevertheless, a few hundred of Africa-Americans consisting of social workers, physicians, engineers, and skilled workers moved to Ethiopia. Believing that Abyssinia was a good window to escape from the economic depression in the U.S., some of them moved with inadequate fund and necessary skills and became a burden on the U.S.

A Road to One Man Rule

Whereas the emperor's power takeover was an established fact on the ground, he desired to make it a legal fact. In the empire, the absences of institutions lend themselves to the unchecked powers of emperors; however, creations of institutions under the watch of Hayla Sillase were to lay a foundation for the centralized state and bolster his autocratic style of governance than to relieve the empire from the fundamental and chronic problems (Uhlig, 2003, 62). Also, he was eager to have a constitution to showcase to the world that Ethiopia was on the equal footing with the "civilized" nations. This would sell the image that Ethiopia is a "constitutional nation" and dispel doubts lingering in some circles of "civilized" world about the civility of the country.

The modernizing document was blind to see the elephant in the room, addressing the issue of slavery that often put the country under a negative international publicity. Nor did it address the rights of the "subjects" in any meaningful way except embodying some democratic facades and trying to give a legal framework for the absolute power of the emperor.[1] Credited,

---

[1] Fasil Nahum (1997, 20) described the constitution as an "indirect coup d'état on traditional power institutions." Deliberative chambers presence in Addis Ababa alienated nobility from their power base and made them out of the equation of power play. The emperor filled the political vacuum by appointing his own confidantes. By incorporating the church created legitimacy myth in the supreme law of the land, Hayla Sillase curbed the role of the church in the theater of power play. Indirectly, the church became subordinate to the monarchy (see, Fasil, 1997; Keller, 1989). On the aftermath of the constitution,

however, for heralding a transformation of the country from the era of unwritten constitution to the era of written constitution (Fasil, 1997), the birth of the written constitution was not different from the old tradition of legendary lawgiver bestowing "rights" and "duties" on his subjects. Simply, he wanted to change his status from a traditional absolutism to a constitutional absolutism. His minister of finance espoused that it was "a gift from heaven" (Messing, 1972, 111), like the Heavenly Tablet of Moses, to bless his kingdom as "Heaven on Earth." Given of his own free will, without being requested by his subjects, the constitution was neither a contract between the public and the king. It neither envisaged a check and balance, nor did it limit an absolute power of the emperor. Nor did it envisage an exercise of popular sovereignty since sovereignty emanated from the personality of the emperor whose office is sacred, dignity is inviolable, and power is indisputable (article 5). Article 3 encapsulated a coke and bull legend of Abyssinia. It declared that 'the imperial dignity shall remain perpetually attached to the line of Hayla Sillase I whose line descends without interruption from King Solomon and the Queen of Sheba'. In consequence, he is the only line of "Solomon" to claim the honor of the "Lion of Judah" to the discomfort of all traditional rulers.

The emperor controlled a council of ministers collectively and individually, and gave titles and personal estates. He had the power to enter into treaties, pardon and commute penalties, declare peace or war. The façade structures of the senate and chamber of deputies were neither vested in them the power to arrest the absolute power of the monarch by enacting laws, nor did it envisage popular representation. As per article 31, the emperor appointed Senate members from the nobility. According to article 32, the only election envisioned in the constitution was for the Chamber of Deputies, which was nothing more than the election of nobilities for the house of nobility by nobility on behalf of the people until "people are capable of electing them."

Did the "civilized" nations accept Ethiopia's claim to a road to civilization? In other words, did it help to preserve the independence of Ethiopia? I shall deal with this question in the next chapter.

Hayla Sillase also obliterated the last autonomous regions of Jimma and Gojjam. Ethiopia effectively made a unitary state.

8   Favoring Mussolini? The Interruption of Ties

SINCE THE WALWAL incident of 1930, tension was flaring between Ethiopia and Italy. Both countries were locked in accusations and counter accusations over violating each other's territorial possessions on the League of Nations. At this time, the America's ship of state was deep in the Great Depression of 1929-1933. Twelve million people were unemployed and 18 million more were seeking assistance in 1932. It was unlucky to be the president of a powerful nation when its fortune was at a low ebb, and hence, Hoover was anything but changed into a national laughing stock.[1] Franklin Delano Roosevelt (FDR) of the Democratic Party won an election of 1932.

Wolfgang Schivelbusch has vividly demonstrated a cordiality of relations between *Mussolini's Italy* and *Roosevelt's America*. He claims that when he assumed office, one of the first acts of FDR was appointing his longtime political ally, Breckinridge Long, as U.S. Ambassador to Italy. Thanks to his personal closeness to FDR, the Ambassador was passing the standard procedures of the State Department and feeding information to him personally. "There seems to be no question," commented FDR, "that Mussolini is really interested in what we are doing, and I am much interested and deeply impressed by what he was accomplished and by his evidenced

---

[1] "Hoover-ville," meant a collection of tents, cardboard boxes for housing homeless; "Hoover blanket," meant an accumulated newspapers under which jobless (homeless) slept; "Hoover hogs," meant a situation of the shortage of food forcing people to eat small game, "Hoover shoes," meant shoes with visible holes in the soles; and "Hoover flags," meant 'empty pockets destitute people turn inside out to indicate that they are empty' (Young & Young, 2007, 240).

honest purpose of restoring Italy." At another occasion, he remarked, "I don't mind telling you in confidence that I am keeping in fairly close touch with that admirable Italian gentleman." Rexford G. Tugwell, a distinguished scholar and an architect of the New Deal policies, had a deep fascination with policies of fascism. He appreciated fascism as the "cleanest, neatnest [sic], most efficiently operating piece of social machinery I've ever seen. It makes me envious." He even liked Mussolini abolishing of the free press: "Mussolini certainly has the same people opposed to him as F.D.R. has. But he has the press controlled so they cannot scream lies at him daily." Lorena Hickok, an intimate friend of Eleanor Roosevelt, even expressed her willingness "to be the Joan of Arc of the Fascist Movement in the United States" (Schivelbusch, 2006, 31-2).

In his work, *Roosevelt: The Lion and the Fox*, James Burns claims that Ambassador Long strongly stated his passion for the fascist's project of "rejuvenation" of Italy. He did not only play a significant role in cementing the relationships between the U.S. and Italy, but also he was redrawing a map of the Horn of Africa to give a large chunk of Ethiopia to Italy as part of general European settlement (Burns, 1956, 256). Nonetheless, his appeasement plan was unsuccessful as Mussolini's drum of war rapidly drifted Italy into violent means to engulf Ethiopia. Roosevelt was lukewarm to Mussolini's bellicose approach and hardly moved beyond encouraging him to find a peaceful solution to the problem through negotiation.

On July 3, 1935, Hayla Sillase, as per the U.S.-Ethiopian arbitration and conciliation treaties, pleaded to the U.S. to use its good offices to secure Italy's observance of the Kellogg-Briand Pact. On January 26, 1929, when King Tafari and Consul Southard signed treaties of arbitration and conciliation, both nations agreed to advance 'the cause of arbitration and the pacific settlements of international disputes' (see, Papers Relating to the Foreign Relations of the United States, 1943, 981). In a preamble of the treaty of arbitration, both nations expressed "their condemnation of war as an instrument of national policy in their mutual relations [...and agreed] to hasten the time when the perfection of international arrangements for the pacific settlement of international disputes shall have eliminated forever the possibility of war among any of the Powers of the world." Similarly, Secretary Frank Kellogg and French Prime Minister Aristide Briand, in Paris, on August 27, 1928 singed the *Kellogg-Briand Pact* to prevent the use of war as a means of settling international disputes, to promote peaceful settlement of disputes, and to envisage use of a collective force in the event of aggression. It was hoped that the pact was a new chapter in the international law; "war to be a crime and it has been recognized as such by a large number of States" (Glueck, 2008, 78). The U.S. Senate ratified the treaty with a single dissenting vote and with the proviso that there would be no limitation on the right of U.S. to self-defense and that the U.S. was not forced to join force against countries that broke the treaty (Olusanya, 2004, 38). More than 60 nations including Germany, Italy, Japan, Ethiopia and the Soviet Union signed the Pact.

United States response to Hayla Sillase pleading for enforcement of the Brian-Kellogg Pact was downplaying the looming threat of war. On the other hand, it urged Americans living in Ethiopia, mostly missionaries, to pack. Mussolini interpreted this as the victory of his diplomacy and "as evidence of the United States' friendliness towards Italy and an American realization that his country is justified in its stand" (Harris, 1964, 34). As the last desperate act of convincing Britain and the U.S. to protect Ethiopia, Hayla Sillase granted a 75-year mineral concession encompassing half of Ethiopia to Anglo-American oil companies (ibid, 35-38). Perhaps, this only increased Mussolini's resolve to push with invasion. Hayla Sillase also hired a U.S. international legal scholar, John Spencer, a native Iowa, to help him on how to cater his message to the Western audience.

Meanwhile, Mussolini was ratcheting up a hyperbole of an imminent aggression on Italian colonies from Ethiopia while he was denouncing a plan to invade Ethiopia. He was looking for *casus belli*; Ethiopia was seeking the international community to issue a clear and a strong message for Italy to respect its territorial integrity and sovereignty. In the end, Hayla Sillase failed to convince the world, and Mussolini fooled the world. As their Italian political scientist Niccolo Machiavelli espoused, Il Duce had beast natures necessary for a politician: 'cunningness of a fox' and 'ferociousness of a lion'. At the end of the day, they contrarily worked against him.

Mussolini War came and Peasants Rose

As Hayla Sillase abolished the autonomy of Jimma under the pretext of abolishing slavery, now it was a turn for Mussolini to invoke the same pretext to abolish his throne to "civilize" "backward" Abyssinia under the "tutelage" of the European power (see, Quirk, 2011, 77). In the absence of a declaration of war, Mussolini invaded Ethiopia on October 3, 1935. Mounted on a white horse, General Emilio De Bono jubilantly entered the ecclesiastical capital of Ethiopia (Aksum) on October 15, 1935. In December 1935, he issued a proclamation from Maqale eradicating slavery from occupied territories. Foreign Secretary Samuel Hoare of Britain and Foreign Minister Pierre Laval of France architected a *Hoare-Laval Pact* to partition Ethiopia to appease Mussolini. Had the pact come to fruition, Mussolini would have maintained what he occupied by early December 1935, which was pretty much, the northern part of Ethiopia, and Ogaden as a bonus. The southern part of Ethiopia would remain free but under indirect Italian economic hegemony. In return, Ethiopia assured an access to the sea, "a corridor for camels."

France assented to Mussolini's takeover of Ethiopia and awarded him with a share of the main Ethiopian trade artery, the railway.

When Mussolini was considering the plan, the information leaked to the press under controversial circumstances. Ensued was a spontaneous public outcry, which forced both countries to abandon the plan and both ministers to resign to save faces of their governments. The Italo-Ethiopian crisis kept unfolding. Rewarded than scolded through this plan, Mussolini pushed with his goal of complete occupation of Ethiopia. A critical historian of Europe Alan Taylor publicly declared, "The League died with it ... [I]t was only effective in negation" (Wrigley & Taylor, 2006, 100).

Mussolini replaced the War General De Bono with Badoglio, and instructed him to employ all means of fighting including the use of a banned mustard gas to kneel down a disobedient Abyssinia. Mussolini claimed "civilization" mission, but Ethiopia littered with dead bodies, summary executions, tortures, aerial bombardment and a carpet use of toxic gases banned by international conventions. In general, Ethiopia became a testing ground for the modern Italian arsenal.

Hayla Sillase's "black army" was only good against his "black" people; they were helpless in the face of the Black-shirts of Mussolini, who were equipped to the teeth with sophisticated and death dealing weapons. The last attempt of his army to check the Italian advance at the Battle of Maychaw, on 31 March 1936, collapsed. For the rebellious Raya Azebo, it was time for a sweet revenge when they destroyed the retreating army in disarray. They killed Minister of War, Ras Mulugeta. According to Ambassador Richards, Hayla Sillase "suffered a breakdown; he withdrew from reality and entered the mystical world of religion and faith" (quoted in Marcus, 1995, 160). Worse, the custodians of the throne, Hayla Sillase Gugsa and Ras Siyyum Mangasha of Tigray jumped from the emperor's battered ship of state by colluding with the invaders (see, Markakis, 2011, 113). Hayla Sillase's once dreadful and indomitable empire, his "Jerusalem," turned out to be a cursed Tower of Babylon. It crumbled like a house of cards right in front of his eyes. The "Conquering Lion" tucked its tail between the legs, like frightened hyena, and fled into exile. On 2 May 1936, he left Finfinne boarding an overloaded train to Djibouti for an exile to Europe. Blatta Takla Hawaryat and other noblemen, who cherished the tradition of warrior emperors, condemned fleeing before an invading enemy as an act of "disgraceful cowardice" (Wrong, 2005, 154). The international legal scholar Antonio Damato sarcastically asked, "Was the real 'Ethiopia' walking around Great Britain in the person of a heavily bearded gentleman named Hayla Sillase?" (Damato, 1994, 5).

Now, one could tell a winner and loser. The U.S. had to play its classic diplomacy. Wait and see, and throw support behind a winner. When the "Conquering Lion" fled the country, the Secretary of State Cordell Hull urged

Mussolini "to have his forces enter Addis Ababa swiftly" (quoted in Negussay, 2003, 98). On May 5, 1935, Badoglio entered Finfinne. Mussolini proclaimed the restoration of "the Fate of hills of Rome," and the King of Italy Victor Emanuel III and his wife Queen Elena proclaimed the Emperor and Empress of Ethiopia by dismissing "Haile Selassie as a discard on the rubbish heap of history"(Spencer, 2006, 80). At least, the triumph of the Black-shirts "erased" a shameful memory of the Adwa defeat. Italy raptured with jubilations; Italian wives followed the footsteps of the Queen Elena by donating their wedding rings to the father's lands, and the parish priests launched a massive propaganda network to maintain a support on the home front (Palla 2000, 105).

Although Hayla Sillase issued an injunction against looting during the war period, George Steer's account of the war compared his army to a "trail of brown ants…eating up everything" (quoted in Teshale, 1995, 36). The conquered people rose to defend themselves against the looters, the settler soldiers. The rule of the empire immediately collapsed throughout the country. Hayla Sillase appointed his cousin Immiru Hayla Sillase as prince regent. He found no-where to rule. He advised him to establish government in Gore, Illubabor, but he learned that he was a *persona non grata* in Oromo land since the peasant rose to claim their freedom from the shackles of *naftanya* rule. When he approached Gore, the peasants had forced the Amhara governor of Illubabor to flee with his soldiers to Sudan. The uprising of Oromos "formed the decisive coup de grace to Ethiopian sovereignty"(Lentakis, 2005, 68). In fact, thirty-three Oromo leaders were clamoring for recognition and protection from Britain after forming a 'Western Oromo Confederation'. A British Consul in Gore, Captain Hubert Erskine, dispatched this message:

> The Galla provinces have disarmed the Amhara officials and soldiers in their areas and the Galla hereditary chiefs have assumed control of the government in their areas. All Galla chiefs have sent seals and signatures and delegations asking the League of Nations to place the provinces of Western Abyssinia under British mandate (quoted in Markakis, 2011, 113).

The Oromos also sought representation in London: "All the Galla chiefs refuse to be represented by their enemies and oppressors—that is, the Amhara delegation now present in London" (quoted in Lentakis, 2005, 67). Since the Britain wanted to have stronger and healthier relations with Italy and since Britain wanted to secure the flow of Nile River without obstacles, it rejected the request of the Oromo chiefs. In the meantime time, when Ras Immiru moved to Jimma area; the peasants chased him and he ran to Sudan. Sheikh Mustafa el Tur, a chief Bella Shangul, liberated Asosa from the Amhara rule (ibid).

The peasants in the south similarly rejected the rule of the Empire. "When a government comes, I welcome it, when it leaves I say farewell, like a guest," proclaimed a Selte chieftain who shares no emotional attachments to the Hayla Sillase's Ethiopia (Markakis, 2011, 113). The Guji tribe exulted when the Empire perished: 'We were jailed and released by Atala [Italy]'. They rose with their spear and shield asserting, "We were jailed and bitten by Habasha; now it is our time, we have the opportunity to retaliate against them" (ibid).

Mussolini made a good reading of the atmosphere in the country. He presented himself as a friend of the victims of the Empire. He passed a second proclamation that abolished slavery from the whole country on April 12, 1936. He also destroyed *leba shay, quranya,* and *Afarsata* systems. Italy brought to an end the *Naftanya* and *Gabbar* systems, distributed the royal land to the landless, and acquitted Hayla Sillase's prisoners. It metaphorically and literally liberated peasants from an open air prison, the rule of the empire. As Markakis appropriately said, the Italian occupation "brought welcome relief from the burden of Ethiopian rule to the people of the periphery" (ibid, 114). Even, the core of Abyssinia (Tigrayans) rejoiced, 'My big brother, the Italian, with a golden belt, is shepherd of the poor, and only eats what is his' (Gebru, 1991, 92).

In December 1937, Mussolini replaced Governor General Rudolfo Graziani with Amedeo Duca d'Aosta. The 1938 Italian Proclamations formed the federation of *Africa Orientale Italiana* Colony by merging Eritrea, Italian Somaliland, and Ethiopia. This colony was divided into six language based administrative governorates: Eritrea, Amhara, Addis Ababa, Harar, Sidama-Oromo and Somali. A new law empowers the governorates to develop their official language (s) for administration and teaching purposes, promotes the usage the script other than Sabean, and promotes radio broadcasting in the native languages. Historian and linguistics viewed the policy of Italians in various ways. Some described as a colonialist card of divide and rule. Tekeste Negash (1987, 59) is noticeable in this regard with his characterization of the policy as "pacification through apartheid." Van Der Beken (2012, 67) opines similarly; he called it "divide et impera policy, to incite latent ethnic tensions." Be it for a divide and rule agenda or public relations exercise or a genuine attempt to win the hearts and minds of the local peoples aggrieved by the assimilation policy of the Empire; the Italian move was a huge relief from the oppressive imperial language policy.

Mussolini justified his invasion as a Christian civilization mission to save the "savage" Abyssinia, but when he reached Ethiopia, he was all about a "Muslim power" and a liberator from the Abyssinian "Christian" tyranny (Robinson, 2004, 120). He built mosques, instituted Sharia courts and appointed Muslim judges, allowed Arabic teachings and learning, launched radio broadcasts in Arabic, sponsored a pilgrimage to Mecca, and met

Muslim clerics in Rome. Nevertheless, relations with Muslims did not go well. According to Robinson 'The long-term effect of Italian was to intensify the ambiguous relationship that had long existed between Muslim societies and Abyssinia' (2004, 121-2).

Mussolini faced a fierce resistance in the center. He resorted to "pacification through the Reign of Terror," as Tekeste (1987, 56) remarked. The most gruesome measures happened in February 1937 when two Eritreans, Abraha Daboch and Mogus Asgadom, tried to assassinate Graziani. Secretary Guido Cortese instantly proclaimed, "Today is the day when we should show our devotion to our Viceroy by creating and destroying the Ethiopians for three days. For three days, I give you carte blanche to destroy and kill and do what you want to Ethiopians" (Mockler, 1984, 175). Ensued was indiscriminate killing rampage that decimated from a crowd of beggars waiting for distributions of alms to the elites of the country (ibid).

U.S. Responses to the Invasion

Emperor Hayla Sillase pleaded to the League of Nations' collective security; which makes the Italian invasion of Ethiopia *ipso facto* an act of war against all member states (Williams, 1934). His American advisor, John Spencer, played an instrumental role in writing his impassioned, eloquent, and prophetic speech at the League that later shot the emperor to global fame to the extent of becoming the *Time's Person of the Year*.

At the time, the U.S. was digging out of the Greater Depression. Roosevelt was trying to get support of the Congress for his earthshattering domestic reforms, *Second New Deal*. Isolationists were using their vote as a bargaining chip to pass arms-export sanctions on belligerent countries in the event of war break-out. Roosevelt was comfortable with a *quid pro quo* deal as long as they were ready to march with him on domestic agendas. He put international affairs on the back burner for a while. Firstly, he was loath to lose in the court of public opinion by hitting unpopular tone while an election was coming in one year. Secondly, the solution to the Great Depression emanates only from within hence non-interventionism hardly threatened his domestic priorities. Thirdly, he was in a dilemma because of a reticence of European partners to denounce Mussolini. Fourthly, even when Mussolini occupied Ethiopia disregarding his admonition, he still convinced that a peaceful settlement of the conflict was possible (Freidle, 1990; Burns, 1956; Rossini, 1999).

Another factor was the United States policy towards Africa was engineered and road mapped by the European desk at the Department of State. Therefore, it was dominated by the "perspectives and needs of the major European colonial powers," which "had a virtual veto over America's African policy" (Walton Jr., 2010, 25). Furthermore, there were no businesses or national security concerns that necessitate the U.S. to defend Ethiopia. As we discussed earlier, economic bonds between Ethiopia and the U.S. were fragile. The market for American cotton products had gone, and the only viable trade between both nations was the U.S. import of the Ethiopian coffee, which was easily replaceable. For that matter, this trade was below a half million, and U.S. diplomats had a dim view of its future growth. Besides, the concession to build the dam on the Lake Tana had collapsed, and a 75-year mineral concession for the Anglo-American oil companies was a complete fiasco.

To render Roosevelt some justice, it is worth to mention his failed attempt to pass a discretionary arms embargo. The isolationist considered any act of partisanship would drift the U.S. into the war and, therefore, nothing short of full non-interference was agreeable to them. The proposal garnered the support of only three members of the Senate Foreign Relations Committee. The Chairman of the Committee warned "the president is riding for a fall if he insists on designating the aggressor" (Freidle, 1990, 182). In an act of compromise, Roosevelt settled for the Neutrality Act that sanctioned both the wrongdoer and victim. This tremendously victimized Ethiopia vis-à-vis Italy that had armies well-equipped with sophisticated weaponry and that established modern military industries. In effect, it crippled Ethiopia that desperately needed modern weapons for its defense; however, it barely scratched Italy because it only sanctioned the sale of firearms and ammunitions, and it exempted raw materials that Italy needed to produce weapons. When we see the implication of the act against the backdrop of military realities of the belligerent states, it was like disarming the David's sling in a titanic battle with Goliath.

The U.S. declared that it was neither joining the League in imposing a sanction nor enforcing it. This was a tremendous relief for Britain and France. Indeed, the fall of the last African state proves the inevitability of the supremacy of the white race and colonialism. Besides, 'businessmen's government of Britain feared that if the League imposed an oil embargo against Italy, American oilmen would grab the whole Italian market' (ibid, 1990, 181-4). In nutshell, Roosevelt, by succumbing to domestic pressure, failed to throw the diplomatic muscle of the United States behind Ethiopia and eventually let the League pass embargoes with less biting power, what John Spencer called "death sentence" on Ethiopia (see, Spence, 2006, 86). If either the Suez Canal had closed to Mussolini or an oil embargo imposed on Italy, the aggression would have halted effectively and easily as Mussolini admitted later (Philips and Carillet, 2006, 36).

Great Britain, which historically encouraged Italy's foothold in the region as a watchdog to control the expansion of France, fully recognized the Italian annexation in an Italo-Yemen agreement. Disengaging Mussolini by hook or crook from bolstering invincible Hitler was more relevant to Britain than defending Ethiopia. Britain recognition was a big blow to diplomatic efforts of the emperor but a significant diplomatic boost for the Fascists. Britain also gave an asylum for the emperor as part of favor for Mussolini (Spence, 2006, 88-9). France was equally adamant to prevent the two dictators from forming a united front in Europe. It closed the Port of Djibouti for Ethiopian import of weapons. Reciprocally, Rome agreed to abandon its claim on Tunisia.

While Italy exploited the Washington's Neutrality Act to its advantage, the U.S. did not recognize the occupation since it was apprehensive of its ramifications in the Far East where Japan was posing a tremendous threat (ibid, 89). To do justice to the U.S. interest under the nose of Japan and Hayla Sillase, the U.S. closed down its diplomatic mission in Ethiopia in February 1937. It refused to accept the credentials of Italian ambassador, who styled himself as 'Ambassador Extraordinary and Plenipotentiary of His Majesty the King of Italy and Emperor of Ethiopia in Washington'. The Soviet, which softened its anti-colonialist oratory to seek supports of the west against Hitler, followed U.S. footsteps in abandoning Ethiopia. The State Department declined Hayla Sillase's repetitive entreaties to visit the U.S.[1] since it feared to incite violence between African-Americans and Italian-Americans communities.

At this junction, it is worth to remind my readers how United States politicians considered the Abyssinian race a "Caucasian" race during the formation of relations and thereafter. Then, a question automatically arises—where was the "Caucasian" identity of Abyssinian during the invasion? The answer to this question will enable us to understand institutionalized racism in the U.S. foreign policy. Compared to indigenous peoples it conquered, the U.S. politicians considered Abyssinia Caucasian; they considered Abyssinia black in relation to Italians; and they considered Italians closer to black compared to the Northern European race. It was this racial hierarchy and layers of discriminations in the U.S. foreign policy that threw Abyssinia under the bus.[2]

---

[1] In the first place, Britain would have let him go since he was practically placed under the house arrest as a favor for Mussolini. Nor Britain liked the mushrooming of African-Americans' activisms, for it antagonizes its colonial projects in Africa. In fact, various pan-Africanist groups and popular movements in Africa had passed a resolution condemning the occupation of Ethiopia.

[2] Getachew (2009, 23) commented that the U.S. faced in a dilemma on how to address the issue of the "black" African country when it was unable to guarantee equal rights for its black citizens at home. McVety (2011, 209) claimed that the "Caucasian" image of Ethiopia constructed after Adwa and the assumption that Ethiopia 'stretched her hands out to God' changed because this time she turned black, and she stretched her hands to the white man tutelage.

Public Reactions to the Invasion

The Italian invasion garnered such mixed reaction from the American public. Firstly, most Americans wanted to root for underdog Ethiopia. Different religious and civic groups expressed their oppositions to the invasion. On the aftermath of the economic depression, this widespread sympathy barely materialized because of the public nostalgia for the yesteryear of isolationism. At the time, American was deeply embattled by racism. White liberal groups, who strongly opposed fascism, clashed with the African-Americans on the characterization of the conflict since they believed that the aggression was the imperialist agenda than the racial one. Thus, popular activism was mainly confined to the Italian-Americans and the African-Americans for diametrically opposite reasons. For the Italian-Americans, the aggression meant "a renewed pride in Italy's greatness and a desire to aid fatherland" and for the African Americans, it was a transplantation of Jim Crow and the loss of the 'Last of free Africa' (Ross, 1998, 164).

In February 1935, more than twenty Harlem Organizations formed the Provisional Committee for the Defense of Ethiopia (PCDE) to campaign against the Mussolini's preparation for war. On the other hand, in September 1935, the Italian Union of America passed a declaration urging Mussolini to carry out "the final act" of expansion. The PCDE called several meetings to protest Mussolini's bellicosity towards Ethiopia. For example, in April 1935, it mobilized a rally of three thousand people in which Rev. Adam Clayton Powell Jr., the pastor of the Abyssinian Baptist Church, and other prominent black leaders attended. The following resolutions were adopted on the rally: (1) Ethiopia needs money, arms and ammunitions rather than man power, (2) Resolutions of protest to be sent to Mussolini, League of Nations, and Mayor of the New York City, (3) A 50,000 person parade to be held in Harlem soon, (4) Harlemites spend money where it might find its way to Italians fascists to be used "to stab our brothers in the back" (ibid).

African-Americans' activists also established numerous local chapters in different cities to uphold messages of solidarity with Ethiopia. The National Association for the Advancement of Colored People (NAACP) urged America to throw its diplomatic weight into the balance of the world politics and urged the League to condemn Italian behaviors. When its call ignored, it condemned the U.S. and imperialism in its 1936 conference.

When Italy occupied Ethiopia, as historian John Franklin remarked, "Almost overnight even the most provincial among Negro Americans became international-minded." (quoted in Weisbord, 1998, 159). Harold Preece declared that the invasion as the "rape of Ethiopia," and "The rape of Ethiopia is the rape of the Negro race" (Preece, Crisis, 329). Editorial of African-American newspaper called the African-Americans to defend the sovereignty of Ethiopia.

The black activists maintained pickets in front of Italian consulates, engaged in creations of awareness through their publications, rallied in main cities, and organized fund raising events. According to African-American sources, some 17,500 African-Americans volunteers had enlisted to fight the fascists on the side of Ethiopia (Ross, 1998; Skinner, 2003; Scott, 1998). This was unsuccessful as the U.S. opposed to all supports for Ethiopia except humanitarian reliefs. Besides, Malaku Bayyan, a personal representative of the emperor, distanced himself from the enlistments saying "his only mission in the United States was to get an education" (Ross, 1998, 165).

The federal authorities quickly put a lid on the African-Americans' popular activism. The adage goes, 'once the jinn get out of the bottle, it is tough to put it back in it'. The U.S. harassed the African-American activists for fear that their activities might lend itself to the massive movement for equality at home. Likewise, the black activists were harassed at the level of local administrations. One such incident was the Mayor of Chicago, Edward Kelly, who received an award from Mussolini. He condemned the pro-Ethiopian group as a "communist front" (Plummer, 1996, 43-4). On the other hand, the U.S. was accused of condoning the Italian Americans conscription into the Black-shirts (ibid).

In general, spirit of African-Americans was under the roof of the sky, but their political capital was naught. With their limited financial resources and political influences, they hardly changed the trajectory of decisions in Washington. Ironically, informed by church teachings, most African-Americans could not see Ethiopia beyond Whiteman's proverbial image, "Island of Christianity in a sea of black paganism" (Putnam, 2006, 158). That was the overriding theme that reverberated in the pro-Ethiopian articles collection under "the Last Free Africa."

The relation between black activists and Hayla Sillase was not always flowery. To the dissatisfaction of them, he was chanting a mantra of King Solomon race. Foreign Affairs wrote, *"Racially the Ethiopians are a mixture of white and black, with the emphasis distinctly on the former"* [italics added] (quoted in Woolbert, 1935, 340). Some even questioned, "Are Ethiopians colored?" Where do they belong, black or white? This time, whites were denying their whiteness because Italians are whiter than them, and their black brothers in America confused about their double and moving identities.

Moreover, the emperor "feared being too closely identified with Negroes, a universally degraded race, and had therefore rejected the black Americans legionnaires" (Scott, 1993, 90). Thence, they were unable to get a personal audience with him during his exile in Britain. This enraged some of them.

None other than Marcus Garvey, a founder of Rastafarianism, was offended by his idol. He traded the classical Rasta-man chant of Down Babylon for Down Hayla Sillase. He asserted, "When the facts of history are written Haile Selassie of Abyssinia will go down as a great coward who ran away from his country to save his skin and left the millions of his countrymen to struggle through a terrible war that he brought upon them because of his political ignorance and his racial disloyalty" (Hill, 1983, 739). He renounced him for "playing white," running for, and relying on supports of whites (Weisbord, 1998, 162). He questioned Hayla Sillase "mental caliber" and described him as "a cringing, white slave hero worshiper, vision-less and disloyal to his country" (Hill, 1983, 695). Robert Weisbord summarized Garvey's views on the Ethiopian self-abnegation and the Solomonic legend in this style:

> [I]f the 'negro Abyssinian' was ashamed to be a Negro he would be deserted by those Negroes of the world who were unashamed of their race. Referring to the tradition that holds that Ethiopians sovereigns are lineal descendants of Solomon and Sheba, Garvey said: 'The new Negro doesn't give two pence about the line of Solomon. Solomon has been long dead. Solomon was a Jew. The Negro is not a Jew. The Negro has a racial origin running from Sheba to the present, of which he is proud. He is proud of Sheba but he is not proud of Solomon' (Weisbord, 1998, 162).

Garvey, thus, championed the following:

> The future of freedom of Abyssinia must be built upon the highest principles of democracy. That is why it is preferable for the Abyssinian Negroes and the Negroes of the world to work for the restoration and freedom of the country without the assistance of Haile Selassie, because at best he is but a slave master. The Negroes of the Western World whose forefathers suffered for three hundred years under the terrors of slavery ought to be able to appreciate what freedom means. Surely they cannot feel justified in supporting any system that would hold their brothers in slavery in another country whilst they are enjoying the benefits of freedom elsewhere. The Africans who are free can also appreciate the position of slaves in Abyssinia. What right has the Emperor to keep slaves when all the democratic sections of the world were free, when men had the right to live, to develop, to expand, to enjoy all the benefits of human liberty[?] (Hill, 1983, 741)

Garvey also condemned discriminations of the majority of the Ethiopians at the hand of the Amhara elites. The majority of Ethiopians, as he underlined, "are the unfortunate blacks related to other Africans who have always been exploited" (ibid, 695).

The flamboyant Hubert Fauntleroy Julian, also known as "the Black Eagle of Harlem," who resigned from his position of a personal pilot of

Hayla Sillase also reflected similar opinion about the emperor. He said, "Haile Selassie is a monarch without a throne and because he placed a higher value on anything that comes out of a white mouth above anything given to him by his own flesh and blood." Thus, Ethiopians 'held nothing but contempt for American colored people," and 'there was no place in Ethiopia for any black person, whether American, British, or French' (quoted in Scott, 1993, 164).

Malaku Bayyan, a personal representative of the emperor, "took a great pains" to rectify a burden of Ethiopian myths, the myths the Abyssinian elites concocted and westerns amplified to justify their 'manifest destiny' to rule Ethiopia. He explained that Ethiopians opposed the use of a term "Negro," not their skin color or racial affinity to the black race (Weisbord, 1998, 162). His school contact links and his diplomatic passport with African-Americans, i.e., his African-American wife, helped him to make a bridge between Ethiopia and the African-Americans. He had an audience with several influential African-American personalities and groups. Supported with black activists, he established an organization called the *United Aid for Ethiopia* and a periodical called the *Voice of Ethiopia* to organize support movements. The fact that he failed to find an accommodation in downtown because of his skin color made him by default a citizen of Harlem (ibid).

Nonetheless, the split within black activists neither substantially mitigated blacks commitment for defense of Ethiopia nor their identification with Ethiopia, "fatherland" or "motherland" or "our Ethiopian brothers" (ibid, 161-2).

Likewise, the Italian-Americans support for Mussolini was strong. Italian parishioners and wives replicated what happened in Italy; and, they donated their marriage rings for defense of the fatherland. As a certain writer put, "In an age when immigrants were expected to 'Americanize', Italian Americans acted much like Americans in championing Mussolini in the twenties and thirties" (quoted in LaGumina, et al, 2000), 215). "To be against Mussolini would make an Italian American appear "un-Italian" (ibid). The Italian-Americans condemned Roosevelt for sanctioning Italy [Neutrality Act] before Europeans power even acted. In the other hand, they unleashed a tsunami of a propaganda campaign to silence black oppositions. Also, they tried to sell to the African-American that the alleged invasion is, in fact, the civilization mission to change lives of their "savage" brothers. Some argued that the African-American support for Ethiopia bedrock on "hollow groundless form of idealism" and "entirely on misconceptions" since Ethiopians are Caucasians, and the fighting is the Caucasian agenda, which has nothing to do with Negroes (Putnam, 2006, 157). The Italian-Americans also wanted to show that they were more concerned for Ethiopia than the African-Americans by referring to their donations to relief works. Whereas the New York metropolitan area Italians alone donated $500,000 to the

Italian Red Cross, the Africa-Americans nationwide contributed about $15,000 for the defense of Ethiopia (ibid).

It should be indicated that the Italian-Americans' support for Mussolini was not uniform at all. Labor leaders, political immigrants, communists, socialists and anarchist vocally opposed fascism. Most of these groups were, however, disliked by the U.S.

By the end of 1936, the activism of African-Americans had substantially decreased. Roosevelt, however, he offended them, the New Deal had offered them bread. He had won over their stomachs, if not over their hearts and minds. When Mussolini joined the war on the side of Hitler, the African-Americans' supplication heard, and their long neglected voices triumphed, but, the Italian-Americans voices drowned, and their vanity and racist self-delusion came to an abrupt halt. Once America joined the war, the Africa-Americans enlisted enthusiastically; the Italian Americans joined the war on the side of America to show their loyalty to their second country.

In London, the ineffective government of Neville Chamberlain had ceded for the government of national unity led by the Winston Churchill. A new government declared its intention to restore Hayla Sillase to the throne. The emperor broke "his exile culture of complaining in his private journal" (Robinette, 2012, 323). With the Western support, he roared once again as a "Conquering Lion." He "shook 'himself free of melancholia, self-pity, and self-doubt" (ibid, 322). Once he became buoyant enough, he had written off the African-Americans' support. Nature saved Malaku Bayyan, Hayla Sillase's ambassador to the African-Americans, from humiliation. He died in 1940. The father of Rastafarianism, the bombastic Marcus Garvey, also died in the same year before he saw the loathsome emperor transported back to power. In 1941, to sell the imperialist bloodlettings to the African-Americans, Roosevelt extended a Lend-Lease aid to Ethiopia before Hayla Sillase reinstalled. A U.S. diplomat noted, 'American activities in Ethiopia would indicate in a concrete way the interest of the United States in the stake which Negroes have in the war' (quoted in Marcus, 1995, 14). Ironically, when Hayla Sillase enthroned again, he was still the emperor of the Middle Eastern Ethiopia, not the African-Ethiopia. Would Ethiopia be same again? What would be roles of the U.S. in the post-Mussolini Ethiopia? The forth-coming chapter will focus on these questions.

9 The Resumption: Building a Post Mussolini 'Semi-Fascist' Empire

HITLER WAS OVERRUNNING state after state in 1939. Britain declared war on Germany since a tyrannical dictator could be halted only through the barrel of the gun. Mussolini entered the war on the side of Hitler; however, Britain consented to his occupation of Ethiopia. Immediately, Britain labeled Italy from the ally to the enemy state that posed a potential threat to the adjacent British colonial possessions in Africa and the Gulf of Aden, and a security risk to the route to India. It profited from a favor it did for Mussolini, which was keeping Hayla Sillase away from the struggle of his people (Spencer, 2006, 123). In June 1940, it withdrew the *de jure* recognition of the Italian occupation of Ethiopia. In the meantime, Italy drove Britain out of the British Somaliland and incorporated into the Italian East Africa. Encouraged by an initial gain, it was building up army and preparing for the full invasion of the Anglo-Egyptian Sudan.

The Second World War was a wake-up call for Americans. It educated them interconnectedness of the world and the vulnerability of American interest to the event that happens far from its border. As Rossini (1999, 11) said, "A revolution took place in diplomatic and political circles, as well as in the mind of average Americans." Almost in a phenomenon like a dictum about change within a blink of the eye, the United States foreign policy abandoned the golden traditions. The public abandoned worshipping isolationism in favor of en-masse conversion into interventionism (internationalism). After winning the unprecedented third term in 1940, President Roosevelt nickname morphed from "Dr. New Deal" to "Dr. Win the War." Riding on a new wave of mood change, FDR convinced the Congress to abrogate neutrality acts of 1930s and pass "the Lend and Lease Act" to support countries grappling with Nazi aggressions.

Now, the Allied powers were capable to battle the Axis powers anywhere thanks to U.S. supports. The U.S. made 'Great' Britain great again. Britain unleashed a full blown retaliatory measure against Italy. This was a heavenly manna for Hayla Sillase who was at one point pleading, to Mussolini, for abdication negotiation in return for money (see, Spencer, 2006, 84). Britain began to roll the empire of Mussolini from the periphery until the brunt of the battle would be taken to the Hills of Rome. In April 1941, it drove the last nail in the coffin of the Italian East Africa in what was the first victory of the Allied forces against the Axis forces.

Hayla Sillase returned to Addis Ababa under the shadow of the victorious British forces, but he was all about being the "Conquering Lion," once again. In his world, there was no shame for running away from the struggle of his people at the critical time. The man who sat out the war enjoying British life deserves anything but the Croix de Guerre for all the battles brave men/women fallen and wounded.

Albeit the Italian occupation interrupted his power consolidation projects, it benefitted him hugely since it "hastened the centralization of power in the hands of the emperor" (White, 2005, 43). The massive infrastructure improvements such as the expansion of roads, bridges, and modes of communications left behind facilitated his control of provincial dissents without having to negotiate for cooperation of aristocrats (ibid). The ease of transportation also allowed him to exploit the natural resources better, which led to an economic boom at the center and accumulations of more wealth in his hands. Secondly, the occupation had either decimated those patriots who put resistance against occupiers or made those who collaborated with them out of the political equation in the post Mussolini Ethiopia (Van Der Beken, 2012, 68). As White, Jr. (2005, 43) observed, "Ethiopian martial tradition—which compelled combatants to stand and fight, rather than lie on the ground—led to massive slaughter of those" courageous patriots who decided to confront the fascist forces. The lucky ones who miraculously survived Italian death squads were either publicly hanged or arrested for disobeying the rule of the emperor. One such notable case was the public executions of Mammo Haylu, Balay Zallaqa, and 14 of their colleagues. What was shocking was not the fact that the emperor returned his acknowledgment for their bravery by hangings but the barbarity of manners. They watched slow strangulation of their colleagues and killed in a sequence of the degree of challenge they posed to his rule, so that, they would suffer psychological death before the physical one. He made extensive radio announcements for the public watch the killings, so that, it would leave the unforgettable lesson for them, that is, to silence them into submission (see, Lentakis, 2005). Blatta Takla Hawaryat, "the greatest of patriot leaders," was put on the back burner and demised under a murky condition. Likewise, Abdisa Aga, a global anti-fascist hero, was disparaged and died under a dubious condition.

Because of the war, the world changed a lot. Equally, Ethiopia changed a lot. Hayla Sillase was unchanged; however, he stayed in London. Perhaps the only thing he learned was a communication English that helped him to deal with his Anglo-Saxon sponsors without interpreters at times. When he assumed power, his first mission was the restoration of the *status quo ante*. He restored loyal provincial and local governors and resuscitated apparatuses of the predatory state. The empire reinstated the *naftanya* and *balabbat* systems with a new vigor. The gun holders and the land grabbers, the *naftanya* army, who melted away, came back to life swiftly. In persuasive words of Markakis (2011, 114), "All in all, the Italian interlude brought welcome relief from the burden of Ethiopian rule to the people of the periphery, something that made its restoration in 1941 all the more unwelcome."

Hayla Sillase, a man who appealed to compassion and forgiveness during his exile and on his return, was determined to rule by cruelty, and, the Italian fascist left and domestic one returned. Whereas the fascism of Mussolini was known to the world, the fascism of Hayla Sillase was not. For an average person, the emperor 'was the embodiment of the idea of the underdog, the little guy who stood up to the bully, but the world did not have the gumption to come to his help' (Vestal, 2011, 193).

The U.S. had information about his neo-fascist tendency. A U.S. minister in Finfinne described the rule of the emperor "semi-fascist" (Milkias, 2006, 138). Irrespective of that the U.S. decided to bankroll his government militarily and economically so long as he was instrumental in advancing U.S. interests in the region. A chairman of British committee on Ethiopia also pointed to unfairness of the restoration of Amhara tyranny while they were fighting the same tyranny in Europe (Marcus, 1995, 23). Ultimately, Britain decided to be a tool for that tyranny to survive and thrive.

In the era of crumbling of empires, the emperor wanted to form a centralized state with no room for dissent and accommodating diversity. Diversity was the source of inevitable political fragmentation, and he designed a policy of aggressive Amharization. His first decree of 1942 abolished the language-based Italian administrative divisions. In the Berlin Conference style colonial mapping, he reduced the post-occupation Ethiopia into twelve administrative units by squeezing together thirty administrative units in the pre-invasion Ethiopia.[1] He erased the traditional power bases of the nobility, ethnic and regional loyalties so that the "Conquering Lion" would conquer Ethiopia without challenge.

This decree also introduced how these new administrative units should be ruled. The King appointed a lame duck governor general from the center

---

[1] In the new divisions, he enlarged his three feudal power bases. Shawa got a boost by absorbing the entire central areas; Wallo grabbed Tigray and Afar areas, and his birth province of Hararghe became the largest province by engulfing Bale and later the whole Ogaden. The rival Tigray lost its western fertile land to Gondar, the rebellious Raya Azebo divided between Wallo and Tigray, and Muslim majority administrative units of Jimma and Afar were abolished.

with no traditional power base and wholly dependent upon him; with no power to levy tax; and with no power to recruit police officers. As John Markakis demonstrated, 'Provincial officials as a rule had neither modern education nor any other relevant qualifications'. 'The paramount criterion was loyalty to the emperor' (Markakis, 2011, 115). During this time, as John Gunther described that the emperor ruled the country "almost as if it were a kindergarten" (Gunther, 1954, 248).

His restoration also heralded the passage of a proclamation that expressly mandated a monolingual policy [only Amharic] in education for the first time in the history of the nation. The proclamation outlawed teaching, writing, preaching, or broadcasting in any Oromo dialect. Blanketing a language with literary, public, religious, and media embargoes was unprecedented in the entire history of the colonial Africa, even under the apartheid regime (see, Mesthrie, 2002, 450). Besides state machineries and bureaucracies, the emperor changed missionaries into a catalyst of Amharization. He compelled them to use only Amharic for preaching or teaching the non-Amharic speaking populations. Thus, regional and ethnic tension rose in the aftermath of the restoration because of the emperor's fascination and obsession with power consolidation and his zero tolerance for linguistic, religious, and regional diversity.

Hayla Sillase used the biblical language of love of the enemy and non-retaliation to impress the Western upon his return. When his people rose against his unchecked power, he unleashed his evils to crash such oppositions. He publicly executed the patriots of Gojjam, the backbone of anti-fascist movement, because of their opposition to his rule. The way his army crushed the Ogaden uprising of 1942 reminded them the conquests of Minilik. The Oromo peasants in Bale revolted to prevent the restoration of the *gabbar-naftanya* system. He crushed a resistance headed by Mohammad Gada Qallu (as his name shows he claimed to defend Islam, the *Gada* system, and the Qallu institution) in Bale. A contingent of British army from Kenya crushed the rebellion of Borana pastoralists. Similarly, the emperor pacified rebellion in Hararghe, Gojjam and Jimma. In a punitive measure, he wiped out Jimma from the face of Ethiopian map. The Glorious Kingdom of Jimma lost its name and absorbed into Kafa province. The manner his army, in tandem with the British air bombardment, crushed the Wayyane Rebellion, in 1943, reminded many Tigrayans the trauma of victory of Adwa; the victory turned into a political defeat for them. The Tigrayans, who traditionally saw the Amhara in a consanguineal fashion, and who traced their ancestors to the same old Abyssinian kingdom, and who shared ancestral myth of the Queen Sheba and King Solomon, and who shared historical mobility, nobility, and Christianity with Amhara, learned their ethnic distinction and marginalization (see, Joireman& Szayna, 2000, 205). If the core of Ethiopia suffered such unbearable resentment, it is easy to discern the harshness of the system on the peripheral masses.

In addition to this, the emperor passed a law that made the church subordinate to the monarchy based upon the 1931 Constitution while the Constitution was ironically silent on the matter (Keller, 1989, 75). He initiated the law that empowers him to appoint a patriarch for the Church instead of the Alexandrian See. This culminated in the Ethiopian bishoprics establishment; he appointed Abuna Basiliyos as the first Ethiopian archbishop in 1959.

Britain and Ethiopia: Love and Hate Relations of the Empires

Simultaneously, Britain strengthened its hold on Ethiopian soil. It was too early for the emperor to regain the pre-war status. Now, Ethiopia was an occupied enemy territory under the British East African Command consisting of Eritrea, ex-Italian Somaliland, British Somaliland, Kenya, Zanzibar, Tanganyika, Uganda, Nyasaland and Northern Rhodesia. Britain controlled international and war affairs; the emperor was firmly in control of internal matters. The diminutive emperor was incapable of resisting the arm twist of his former harsh criticizer on slavery. Indeed, seeking his foe's aid was a bitter pill to take on the matter than "civilization" mission. Being at the nadir of his power, he had to rubber stamp a decree that abolished slavery. His consolation was slavery in a form of the *gabbar-naftanya* landholding system remained intact until the collapse of his rule. Thus, the "emancipated" slaves were converted into sharecrop peonage (see, Messing, 1972, 96).

On January 31, 1942, an Anglo-Ethiopian convention restored the Ethiopian sovereignty. Britain trained police and armed forces, attached its officers to the Ethiopian army battalions, and appointed advisers to most ministers and regional governors. It provided a good working formula for the rule of the emperor to adopt later. Britain played a lion's share in rehabilitating national bureaucracy, facilitating modernization, and pacifying regional oppositions and disarming the tribal rebels (Ofcansky & Berry, 2004). Irrespective of all these favors, the emperor convinced that the convention was nothing shy of establishing a trusteeship over Ethiopia. In fact, in some areas, Britain effectively clipped the wings of the pompous emperor; he could not help, but he had to sign it. Britain, inter alia, controlled defense, taxations, expenditures, currency, high power radio transmission systems, telecommunications, a railroad system, jurisdiction over matters involving foreigners, and enjoyed exemption of her military personnel from the Ethiopian courts. It placed the emperor under close surveillance and censored his private communication. Most of all, the extravagant emperor tasted austere fiscal disciplines (see, Spencer, 2006).

Britain rejected the emperor's consistent claims of sovereignty over "lost lands" [all Somali speaking territories and Eritrea]. Ethiopia contends that they were "racially, culturally, and economically inseparable from Ethiopia," for Britain, they have distinct political identities (Ofcansky & Berry, 2004, 62-3). Britain maintained Eritrea, and the former Africa Orientale Italiana province of Somalia that incorporated Ogaden. For the emperor, the experimentation with the notion of the "Greater Somalia" was a harbinger to the British clandestine goal of dismembering "a three thousand years old nation." Apprehensions about a British secret agenda of either merging Eritrea with Tigray to form a larger protectorate, or annexing its western part into the Anglo-British Sudan was unseating the emperor who wanted Eritrea for an access to the sea.

British advisers also suggested teaching Arabic in the Muslims dominated areas and indigenous languages for early stages of educations. Suggested was accommodation of the Islamic courts as part of the Ethiopian judiciary on personal matters. Lord Moyne, a chairman of British committee on Ethiopia in Cairo, underscored, 'It could be 'matter of indifference to His Majesty's Government whether Ethiopia is well or ill-governed'. He said, "We have amoral duty to see that the people of [the] country are not oppressed and enslaved. When we are fighting for freedom in Europe, how can we restore Gallas and other subject races to Amharic tyranny?" Therefore, the crucial issue was a choice between a 'good government' and 'no government' (quoted in Marcus, 1995, 23). The emperor accused Englishmen of sowing a seed of divisionism and making his "government hated" (Haile Selassie, 1994, 172).

On the other hand, Britain was dismantling and moving all movable factories to its various colonies to ease "financial burdens" of the war. A "scorched earth policy" of the British looting and plundering was evident from various documents. A telegram of a British officer from Borana says, *'I have with difficulty prevented stripping a hospital roof in Yavello despite occupation by Ethiopians'* (Wrong, 2005, 144).

Goodbye Colonial Empire (Britain), Hello Business Empire (America)

The "Lion of Judah" proclaimed on his return, "As St. George who killed the dragon in the patron saint of our army as well as our allies, let us unite with our allies in everlasting friendship and amity in order to be able to stand against the Godless and cruel dragon which has newly risen and which was oppressing mankind" (Haile Selassie, 1994, 165). Notwithstanding that proclamation and notwithstanding Britain played focal roles in modernizing the otherwise nascent bureaucracy, military, monetary systems, infrastructures of the country, and indispensable in putting down regional oppositions to his rule; he was growing suspicious of the long-run intentions of his ally. Above all, he coveted to find a patron that never interferes in his divine power and his divinely mandated styles of leadership. Hence, the clock started ticking on their bilateral relations.

In the meantime, the U.S. geopolitical interests increased in the area. In April 1941, FDR proclaimed that the Red Sea and Gulf of Aden were free from the combat zone and open to U.S. shipping. To coordinate war effort better, the U.S. used Eritrea as a springboard to facilitate Allied powers war efforts in Africa and the Middle East. It established a naval repair station and an air base in Eritrea under the auspices of Lend Lease act. By August 1942, there were 336 U.S. military personnel guiding projects that employed almost 16,000 workers, out of which 2, 819 were U.S. civilians (Schraeder, 1996, 115).

The emperor sought a new superpower patron to counterbalance the British hegemony. He began a correspondence with FDR who replied with kind words: expressing his satisfaction with Ethiopia regaining independence, appreciating its bravery against a ruthless enemy, conveying the sympathy of the American people, and promising the steadfast friendship during a laborious reconstruction (McVety, 2012; Marcus, 1995). Pursuant to the Lend Lease act, FDR had already determined that the defense of Ethiopia was vital to the defense of the free world before the British army restored the emperor to his throne. Ethiopia was eligible for military assistance, but the emperor sought additional supports to centralize his empire and consolidate his power. Ethiopia's status as the first victim of the aggression and first to liberate from of the Axis powers was a crucial asset for the emperor because the U.S. undertook commitment to Ethiopia's rehabilitation to inspire the peoples under occupations (Spencer, 2006; Marcus, 1995).

When the U.S. was eyeing to reopen its legation in Addis Ababa with enhanced radio communications capability, the hatchet of traditional feud resurfaced between the Trans-Atlantic allies. Britain repudiated the U.S. plan. A rancorous showdown was resolved when the U.S. demoted the sought relationship to a consulate level at Asmara in the fall of 1942. The melodrama landed the U.S. closer to the Radio Marina, the "levitated white elephant" unrecognized by the U.K., which was an ideal place for eavesdropping half of the globe. Rejecting the British opposition, U.S. army's Signal Intelligence Service built a bomb-proof underground concrete bunker to keep the equipment and trained a necessary manpower in Virginia (Wrong, 2005, 199-200). The station proved its potency when it intercepted the top secret Nazi defense strategy cabled to Tokyo by Japanese Ambassador to Germany— Baron Hiroshi Oshima who has been dubbed, "more Nazi than Nazis." Deciphering the Nazi's secret, America masterminded the Normandy landings and the German occupation (Haufler, 2006, 25).

The British legation played interlocutor role between the U.S. Consulate and the Ethiopian government because of British grip on a signal corps.

Shortly, Hayla Sillase first demand was weapon; unbeknownst to him the British control over the signal corps. They replied to him "supplies were no longer available" instead of passing his message to the Consulate (Spencer, 2006, 10).

Gradually, the feud between the U.S. and Britain over Ethiopia grew fat. The U.S. opposed the British "colonial" tendency towards Ethiopia. This antagonism was patent from statements of U.S. Consul in Asmara, E. T. Smith. He harshly criticized the "shame and hypocrisy of British," pushing with the colonialist agendas and pretending to be "the higher mended liberator of concurred people" at the same time. Whereas Ethiopia supposed to be rehabilitated and enabled to stand on its feet, Britain was dismantling industrial infrastructures of its colonization. In his assertion, if the Nazi knew what was happening, "Goebbels could now point to Ethiopia" and say to the occupied people that the Allied victory means degeneration to the level of enemy territory. Accordingly, he concluded that the motivation for British behaviors were Nazi theory, not the Atlantic Charter. He advised Washington to use Ethiopia as a working formula to study a type of administration suitable for the countries under the occupation when they would liberate (Marcus, 1995, 13-16). Mr. Smith boldly attested to the fact that the Conquering Lion "can and does control Ethiopian, and his forces served "as an excellent factor of internal peace." For practical purposes, however, Ethiopia stretches out her hand unto America! Therefore, the time was ripe to send agronomists and agricultural expert to Ethiopia to toy with what it takes to make a country self-reliant (ibid).

His ideas resonated with Washington policy-makers since the U.S. wanted to turn Ethiopia into a food basket for the war efforts in the Middle East and Europe. Italy leaving behind a large quantity of agricultural equipment put the impetus behind the drive. This was a precursor to Ethiopia's invitation to the May 1943 World Food Conference in Virginia.

Beyond U.S. altruistic and idealistic rhetoric deeply embedded was its clandestine goal to expand its sphere of influence at the cost of the British one. In the post war world, while maintaining its colonies ran in the artery of Britain, the U.S. gave primacy for creating a fertile environment for the supremacy of American businesses. When the dust of welfare started to subside, the lenses of U.S. policy makers had begun to see beyond tactical military interests in the region. In short, America business first superseded the assumption of Lend Lease act, that is, the British defense is equal to the defense of the U.S. The discovery of a substantial amount of oil reserve in the Persian Gulf had augmented a geopolitical significance of the region. At this time, this area had surpassed the Gulf of Mexico as the leading oil producing region in the world, and oil had replaced coal as the major source of energy. Located at the juncture of the Indian Ocean and the Red Sea, the world most vital shipping lines, Ethiopia had unrivaled geopolitical significance. In the same way, the U.S. sought to secure dominance of pan American airways in the Middle East by making inroad into the British monopoly of civil aviation in the post war Ethiopia. Along attacking the Nazi and Fascist enemies together, American capital aggressively began attacking the British and French capitalisms to secure its dominance in a postwar global economy (Patman, 1990, 38). Likewise, defending Ethiopia was tantamount with selling war agendas to African-Americans.

Therefore, when Britain was tightening its iron grip on Ethiopia, it was a time for Roosevelt to make Churchill faithful to the Atlantic Charter of August 1941. This Charter was a document which brought Woodrow Wilson in Franklin Roosevelt. It was consonant with the Wilsonian notion of self-determination, which saved Ethiopia's independence in post WWI dealings. Churchill accepted the Charter when he was posturing for U.S. supports against the Nazi, and Roosevelt wanted it to avoid the accusation of defending British colonial interests. They agreed to renounce "aggrandizement of territories" and renounce "territorial changes that do not accord with the freely expressed wishes of the people concerned" (Frost & Sikkenga, 2003, 608).

Hayla Sillase secured broad latitude to deal with Britain confidently. Whereas he was pushing for aids on one hand, he was pushing for the unification of Eritrean and Ogaden with the "motherland," on the other hand. Oddly, Roosevelt was unable to remember the Atlantic Charter this time, and he expressed his support for "restoration" of Eritrea to Ethiopia. The emperor promptly brought that to the attention of a U.S. diplomat in 1943: 'The statement made by Theodore Roosevelt that Ethiopia is an Empire and must remain so is not forgotten by President Roosevelt' (Foreign Relations of the United States: Diplomatic Papers, 1964, 93). He wanted to deal with FDR personally on the matter than to deal with surrogates. Thus, his predilections to visit the White House ensued, but Washington hardly saw a necessity for inviting him over at the time. However, FDR was willing to catch up with him during a tour abroad. Roosevelt passed to Churchill a memorandum in favor of returning Eritrea to the emperor in 1944 (Marcus, 1995).

In June 1943, an Ethiopian delegation led by Yilma Deressa, Vice Minister of Finance, went to the U.S. to attend the United Nations World Food Conference meant for discussing how to provide food for the Allied forces. The delegation found the conference "very interesting and very enjoyable" and "highly pleased with the proceedings and the results of the conference" (Foreign Relations of the United States: Diplomatic Papers, 1964, 97). Along discussing Ethiopia's role in feeding the Anglo-American forces in the Near East, Yilma had discussions with officials at the State Department, Treasury Department, and President Roosevelt himself on bilateral issues. Discussed issues were military assistance, help Ethiopia with revision of the

Anglo-Ethiopian Convention, a new currency, and the banking sector. An overarching theme was nonetheless Ethiopian impatience with the British domination as witnessed during the discussions and from an aide-memoire he handed to the president.

"I think this is extremely interesting," FDR wrote his Secretary of State. He asked him, "Will you talk to me about it?" (ibid, 103). "It is true," wrote the Secretary to FDR, "Ethiopia was administered by the British as enemy occupied territory." "On the face of available evidence the British during this period administered the affairs of the country with a heavy hand." Ethiopians were obnoxious to distortions and vexations of the Anglo-Ethiopian Convention by the local British administrators. "The Ethiopians," he concluded, "are determined to rid the country as soon as possible of British personnel" (ibid, 106-7)

Counting on a new epoch of U.S. hegemony, the emperor was not only pressed for the termination of the convention, but also dreamed to bring Washington and London into a collision course. However, unbeknownst to him, communications between them denied him that opportunity (see, Vestal, 2011, 36). An Anglo-Ethiopian treaty of 19 December 1944 restored the sovereignty of Ethiopia, but Britain maintained Eritrea and Ogaden.

In the summer of 1943, John Spencer was on an active duty in the Navy. At the time, the amphibious command was getting ready to take the fighting to hideouts of Mussolini. The State Department had caught up with him, in North Africa, to fulfill the emperor's dream of acquiring a U.S. legal advisor. Asked about his interest in accepting his pre-war position in Ethiopia, he was initially reluctant but yielded. He took his pre-war position of legal adviser to the Ministry of Foreign Affairs (see, Spencer, 2006, 107). He became an essential asset for both nations. Disguised as scholars, five African-American personnel arrived, in Finfinne, to helm the media, public relations, and propaganda departments. Later, Field Marshal Montgomery assumed the role of Chief of the Imperial General Staff (Marcus, 1995).

Furthermore, in the same year, Ethiopia secured a "the Mutual Aid Agreement," which historian Harold Marcus described as "a watershed in Ethiopian diplomatic, social, and economic history" (Marcus, 1995, 21). A 5,152,000 dollars aid was neither accompanied with a checking mechanism from a potential abuse nor did the U.S. see to it that the public benefited from it. Using the aid the Ethiopian oligarchy launched import-export institutions to exploit the peasants further. The aid morphed the emperor's regime from a feudal exploiter into a tightly controlled corporate family government through its monopoly over the import-export sector. Historian Marcus put the following about proliferating corruption and racketing:

> [The] exchange of goods between the interior and the capital was much quicker than before the war. Peasants were eager to trade their produce for scarce cotton goods that the oligarchy supplied at exorbitant prices

through the Ethiopian National Corporation, the private distributor invariably appointed by the Ministry of Commerce handle the import and distribution of textiles. The Corporation was owned and operated by the imperial family, high government officials, and ranking members of the aristocracy. In 1944, the corporation returned a profit of between £1.2 million and £1.8 million, or 25 percent, approximately double the standard margin for most businesses in Ethiopia. The textiles were supplied through American lend-lease, and U.S. legation officials were horrified at the racket but were powerless to interfere, given the emperor's involvement (Marcus, 1994, 155-6).

At the time, the cotton import constituted 70 percent of the country's total import. An American official, Hickman Price, investigated the behaviors of what he called 'a swarm of sycophants who ruled in the name of Camarilla'. He reported his findings to the U.S., but his superiors tolerated the embezzlement in favor of the harmony to prevail with the new client (see, Marcus, 1995, 47).

In the meantime, both nations cemented the relations further with Washington dispatching of a minister, John Kenneth Caldwell, to Ethiopia. Ethiopia also appointed Blatta Efrem Tawalda Madhin as the first resident minister in Washington, D.C. In 1944, the United States acquired a full title to a ten acre compound in the periphery of Addis Ababa to replace the old legation in the downtown.

In February 1945, FDR was on the way home from the Yalta Conference. He welcomed three old school absolutist sovereigns on board the heavy cruiser Quincy anchored in Greater Bitter Lake in the Suez Canal. They were: the King who gave his name to his country (King *Saud* of *Saudi* Arabia), the King who gave the name of *God* to himself (*Selassie* means *the holy Trinity*]; and profligate Farouk of Egypt. The meeting was social engagement meant to be a mere exchange of pleasantries, gifts, and photo opportunities. Of course, the venue of the event grabbed more attention than the substance of the meeting because of the freshness of the Holocaust in the memory of Americans. The Greater Bitter Lake (known as Mara in biblical times) was iconic for its historical significance since it was a last stop of Moses before fleeing to the Promised Land. This was the same place the Jews were fleeing to after the Holocaust to form a Jewish State (Freidle, 1990, 593). Perhaps, the sympathy Americans felt for Jews might have helped Hayla Sillase because he was anything but the "Lion of Judah" in the wilderness of Africa.

Along with a four inch globe build of 24 carat gold from the Adola mines, the emperor handed a catalogue of requests to Roosevelt. They included access to the sea, the restoration of Ogaden, control of the Djibouti-Addis Ababa railroad, arms and financial assistances, reparations from Italy, and participation in the drafting of the UN Charter (Spencer, 2006, 160-1).

If FDR, who was opposing to European empires, observed properly, the demands of the emperor were exactly seeking the edifice of a stronger empire. This time, he never worried about his "Four Essential Human Freedoms" he endorsed in his State of Union Speech of 1941. These were freedom of speech and expression, freedom of worship, freedom from want, and freedom from fear, and he emphasized the need for the world founded on the right of people to choose their own form of government. The application of these human freedoms universally was underpinned as an antidote for fracturing rampant tyranny and thereby to bring about the prevalence of "a moral order" on its graveyard. He said, "We ourselves shall never be wholly safe at home unless other governments recognize such freedoms" (Forsythe, 1989, 30).

FDR was poised to prop the emperor, the U.S. diplomat called "semi-fascist," because he was a personification of Ethiopia itself and because he was useful to achieve U.S. imperial agendas in the region. As McVety stressed, his abovementioned requests, which were fulfilled over the course of time, turned into a fodder for building centralized, consolidated, and "modernized" empire ruled by "God appointed Monarch" (2011, 76). FDR wanted to correct the guilt of forsaking Ethiopia to the carnage of Fascist Italy. The emperor mastered how to exploit the guilt conscience by noting always that 'we have no one to help us'. Self-interest and sympathy driven diplomacy made the U.S. politicians blind to the countless voiceless victims of his gross human rights violations at home.

The way American flew the emperor was a classic movie plot. Minister Robert Howe of Britain, a guardian of Ethiopian space, awakened by noise of a U.S. air force DC-3 at 5:00 a.m. on February 12, 1945. He passed an urgent message to Churchill. Disturbed by the development, Churchill shortened his visit to Athens, where a mammoth cheering crowd welcomed him, to catch up with the emperor the next day. Robert Howe found a little biplane from Aden to make to a strenuous sequences of short hops across a desert to meet the emperor who suddenly became a big deal. Asked an issue he would like to bring to the attention of the Churchill, the Emperor confidently replied with one word, "none" (Spencer, 2006, 161). When Churchill learned that FDR promised to give four command cars to the King of Kings, he soothed the emperor by a Rolls Royce, and, the latter returned back with naming a main road in Addis Ababa for him, a Churchill road. With Roosevelt's cordiality and Churchill's knee jerk reaction of seeking moderation, the emperor could see the light at the end of the tunnel, regaining his sovereignty over Eritrea and Ogaden through a diplomatic support of the U.S and a British acquiescence.

Notwithstanding the absence of substantive discussion on their bilateral issues with FDR; the rendezvous was an excellent opportunity for a psychological consumption of Hayla Sillase—who lived in his own world of delusion. Now, the "modernizer" monarch could relate himself to a leader of the modern nation.

U.S. Roles in Building the Ethiopian Economy

The U.S.-Ethiopian bilateral cooperation was on the verge of eclipsing bilateral ties with Great Britain. The world newest superpower, to the consternation of its former colonial master, assumed the role of patron over an "ancient nation of three thousand years." The U.S. took a litany of measures to expand, buttress, and accelerate the emerging diplomatic liaisons with Ethiopia to advance U.S. imperialism at the expense of British capitalism (Pateman, 1990, 38).

The U.S. formulated the blue print for the modernization of Ethiopian economy. Accordingly, resuscitating industrial remnants and communication networks of the Italian occupation, establishing the modern educational sector, and enhancing the agricultural productivity were some of the objectives. The U.S. launched an investment worth $11.7 million to create six meat-processing centers and associated tanneries. A textile complex capable to produce ten million of clothes annually was also built. The meat and tannery factories were destined to foreign markets, that is, to earn foreign currency. The textile complex was part of import substitution industrialization to save foreign currency. The surpluses generated would finance other industries such as cement factories, a leather work, tire manufacturing, and coffee-grading and processing facilities. These would be followed by salt refining complex, a potash plant, a chemical company, a soap factory, vegetable oil and sugar refineries, a shoe factory, woodworks…etc (Marcus, 1994, 159-160).

Through the loan arrangement under Lend Lease act, Ethiopia developed a new currency, *the Ethiopian dollar*. The emperor passed the Currency and Legal Proclamation in May 1945; however, he delayed its actual launching to coincide with his birthday, 23 July 1945. The new currency replaced the popular silver bullion of Maria Theresa thalers and the British colonial currency of East African shilling. The thalers were immediately demonetized and called for redemption. Along the gold production of the Oromo country (Adola) and the British gilt-edge bonds and securities, it served as a backing for the new currency notes (see, Luther, 1958; Spencer, 2006).

A United States' nationality helmed the State Bank of Ethiopia by replacing a beleaguered Englishman. In 1950s, the U.S. became a main destination for Ethiopia's coffee and a key player in Ethiopia's national economy. Hayla Sillase bragged of his new currency during his visit to the U.S. in 1954. He noted that *'Ethiopian dollar was the only U.S. dollar based currency in the Middle East,'* and *'Ethiopia's holding of U.S. dollars had increased ten times and the asset of the National Bank of Ethiopia had increased a thousand percent'* (quoted in Nathaniel, 2004, 135). Ethiopia enjoyed a widespread measure of confidence in the new 'paper' money. It changed the mentality of "we accept only what we eat (salt amole)," and "we cannot eat dollars" for good (Luther, 1958, 107).

As we discoursed earlier, the U.S. had the plan to undermine the British stranglehold of airways in the Middle East, India and Far East. Likewise, Hayla Sillase had a desire to launch an airline. His desire was a product of the fact that Ethiopia was a dominion of the British Overseas Airways Corporation (BOAC), which the British Embassy was in charge of approving each and every passenger. The emperor during a meeting with Roosevelt and the Ethiopia delegation to the United Nations inauguration conference were flown by the United States air force. Moreover, the airline was necessary for the throne and country's prestige, for defense purposes, consolidation of power, exploitation of resources from remote areas, and in a nutshell, it was an ultimate symbol of his modernization sham.

In 1945, when Spencer contacted San Francisco based Transcontinental and Western Airlines to develop Ethiopian airline, the U.S. swiftly seized upon to realize its desire to secure the supremacy of pan American airways in the new global economy. The airlines played a key for exploitation of natural resources from the rich areas of the south, for military purposes, for agricultural spraying operations, and for promotion of tourism in the northern part of the country. The Ethiopian Air Line was the most enduring and, relatively, the most successful product of US-Ethiopia relations.

In addition to these, the U.S. allocated $10 million to jump-start road constructions and the education sector. This was welcome news for the emperor to produce a necessary manpower for bureaucratic functions of the empire. He also levied an additional land tax on the peasants to pay for new schools and teachers while he reduced a land tax payable by landlords. Even under the tutelage of the U.S., 'the peasants continued to carry the entire taxation burden' (Ofcansky and Berry, 2004, 63). He reconfigured school system left behind by the Italians to produce an indoctrinated and devoted army of the students for his political purposes than formulating curricula for the benefit of the masses. The funding stimulated momentum of road constructions halted following the withdrawal of the Italians. As the result, old roads were renovated, and new pavements were added. Besides, U.S. companies pioneered in the fields of natural gas and crude oil explorations.

With burgeoning ties, the U.S. upgraded the relations to ambassadorial level. In June, 1949, it appointed George R. Merrell, Ambassador Extraordinary Plenipotentiary. Hayla Sillase appointed his cousin, Ras Immiru Hayla Sillase, as the first ambassador of Ethiopia to the U.S.

Growing Relations in Changing World

The Soviet Union that received assistance under Lend Lease act became assertive. Beyond the ideological antagonisms, it sooner rivaled the U.S. in terms of military capabilities, to the extent of leapfrogging over the U.S. in the areas of space technology. The Iron Curtain Speech of Winston Churchill at Westminster College in Fulton, Missouri, on 5 March 1946, set the tone for the Cold War. The world was undergoing rapid political and economic transformation. Among other things, the formation of satellite people's republics in the Eastern Europe, independence and partition of India and Pakistan [1947], the Berlin Blockade (1948), the creation of the State of Israel (1948), the Chinese Revolution [1949], and the wave of anti-colonialism took place (Weaver, 2011, 43). Particularly, the communist takeover of China augmented the global dimension of the Cold War. The U.S. "lost" China to the communists, and the Chinese communists slammed the Open Door shut in the face of the West (Rossini, 1999, 11). In short, a catalogue of events snowballing one after another nerved U.S. policy makers about the trajectory of future of world politics. As Weaver demonstrated, "U.S. officials feared a world spinning out of control and were compelled to pay more attention to Africa, Asia, and Latin America to offset Soviet inroads" (2011, 43).

George Kennan, a former official at the American Embassy in Moscow came into a prominence after he became a Director of Planning Staff at the State Department in December 1949. He architected a containment doctrine. The doctrine champions that the Soviet was an expansionist empire and the U.S. had to stop it by any means at any cost (see, Miscamble, 1992).

Because of this, human right agendas dreadfully collided with the national security interest, the latter being a primogeniture of American realpolitik. Thenceforth, the discourse of human rights wed to fighting communism, which the U.S perceived "as the gravest threat to liberty and peace in the world" (Petro, 1983, 8). This trajectory enhanced American romanticism with dictatorial regimes that were good at checking the spread of communism at whatever cost, including the sufferance and suffocation of human dignity. Literally, the U.S. passed a death penalty on international human rights agendas.

Harry Truman, who succeeded to the presidency upon sudden demise of FDR, won the election of 1948. He launched a foreign policy based on four cardinal principles crucial for "personal freedom and happiness for all mankind." These were (1) participations in the United Nations, (2) the Marshall Plan, (3) the North Atlantic Treaty Organization (NATO),[1] and (4)

---

[1] The NATO ended the splendid tradition of non-entanglement. Thus, the first principle of isolationism became the last principle to be abrogated (Rossini, 1999, 13).

technical assistance for the underdeveloped world. The fourth priority was geared towards transfer of American science and technology to ameliorate the living conditions of "peace-loving peoples" of the underdeveloped world. This was what implemented in Ethiopia widely and we shall see it in detail.

In his inaugural address, Truman passionately emphasized that more than half of the world's population was "living in conditions approaching misery." They suffered from food shortages, diseases, and a primitive and stagnant economic life. Their poverty was a handicap for the progress of the world and posed a threat to the prosperous areas. Therefore, in his assertion, "For the first time in history, humanity possesses the knowledge and skill to relieve the suffering of these people." He boldly asserted that a new approach "should be to help the free peoples of the world, through their own efforts," and "the old imperialism-exploitation for profit-has no place in our plans." Thus, with democracy and technical assistance, it was possible "to stir the peoples of the world into triumphant action, not only against their human oppressors, but also against their ancient enemies-hunger, misery, and despair" (Truman's Inaugural Address, 1949).

The Point IV Program was not out of altruistic reasons; it was rather a meant to dissuade third world countries from embracing the wave of expanding communism. The U.S. was saying to them, "Join us and you will have more to eat." In a way, a lesson was taken from a book of communist propaganda, to neutralize their gospel of better food security and alleviation of poverty that had strong resonance in the underdeveloped world (Pancoast Jr., 1954, 87). Not only designed to disseminate technical knowhow and help underdeveloped nations to declare "freedom from want," but also to achieve "a host of politically good things—democracy, peace, non-Communist governments, good will, international understanding," according to the architect of the Point IV (McVety, 2008, 372).

In 1950, Act for International Development was passed with strong support of civic organizations and bipartisan congressional support. When Ethiopia requested the technical assistance, U.S. response was positive and fast. Until a request passed through bureaucratic hurdles, the Ethiopian economy received "shot in the arm" from the U.S. worth over 10 million dollars (Marcus, 1994, 159). We should indicate that by 1950, some 52,000 students, 'well taught and thoroughly indoctrinated with loyalty to the throne and patriotism,' were ready for implementation of the Point IV program (ibid, 160).

The U.S. and Ethiopia signed a technical assistance treaty in the summer of 1951. The technical program officially kicked off when Dr. Henry Bennett, director of the Technical Cooperation Administration, came to Ethiopia to explore prospects for establishing a college of agriculture in Ethiopia. A plan was to make the country self-sufficient and net exporter of food. Subsequently, the U.S. played crucial roles in filling administrative positions, in training, in proving funding for the Agricultural College of Haromaya worth $11 million. The Jimma Agricultural Technical School similarly opened with the support of the U.S. The U.S. allocated $1.5 million for establishing a Public Health College in Gondar. Additionally, it undertook comprehensive intervention in the areas of agriculture and natural resources developments, public health, maternal care training, teacher trainings, mapping and national archives, health and sanitations, public administrations, civil aviation and national airlines, water resource development, and so on (Vestal, 2011).

Ethiopia catapulted to the top beneficiaries of the program, and, the U.S. technical aid, by June 1958, was at $29 million (Getachew, 2009, 41). When Ethiopia formed the first national university, the U.S. promised to provide $12 million for its consolidation and expansion over ten years. Also, various U.S. universities helped in developing various faculties and institutions of Hayla Sillase I University (Skinner, 2003, 45). Professor Paulos Milkias (2006) maintains that U.S. investment in the educational sector was designed to create a perpetual triangular partnership between Hayla Sillase, Western-educated elite, and the U.S. against the global communism. We shall explore the triangular axis scrupulously later.

One might be easily carried away if one simply looks at the volumes of U.S. technical supports for Ethiopia. It is pertinent then to ask if those aids transform or democratize the country. Firstly, this trend of economic support did not last long as the cornerstone of the bilateral relations sooner became security assistance. In the security diplomacy, the mutual interest of publics of both countries rarely merited attention. Development oriented packages or trade and investments took a back seat in their bilateral cooperation. For instance, Ethiopia received 80 percent of the U.S. military aid allocated to Africa since 1950s (Skinner, 2003, 43; Lefebvre, 1991, 13-4). However, it only received ten percent of all economic and technical assistances the U.S. donated to the continent (Skinner, 2003, 46).

Secondly, because of corruption, nepotism and discriminations, even the development largesse perpetuated fundamental inequalities in the empire. Hayla Sillase used the aids to further his political agenda and to reward his loyalists and power base. He even changed apolitical American missionaries—for that matter, the western missionaries in general—into the instrument of government assimilation policy. For instance, the most un-egalitarian aspect of the educational system, which the U.S. underwrote, was the survey conducted in 1960s. It showed that more than eighty percent of university students were either Amhara or Tigre, who were below 30 percent of the Ethiopian population (see, Keller, 1989, 35). The majority of the students who benefitted from U.S. scholarship programs were the Amhara-Tigre group (Skinner, 2003, 48). At the time, more than half the Ethiopian students abroad went to the U.S. Primary school enrolment ratio also showed similar imbalance. Addis Ababa had 72 % enrolment rate while Bale was at

16 percent. Educational imbalance foreclosed the non-Amhara-Tigre group from prestigious jobs, political and administrative positions, which resulted in the fundamental power and income inequalities between the Amhara-Tigre group and nations and nationalities of the empire.

Why did the U.S. aids fail to transform Ethiopia? Holcomb and Ibssa emphasized that the U.S. development programs were grafted on the infrastructures of the Ethiopian Empire than introducing new tools of transformations (1990, 229 & ff). According to Teshale Tibebu, the modern Ethiopia is a prototypical predatory state that makes it less of an agent of socioeconomic transformation and more of oppression and exploitation. He argues that a predatory state is "a professional destroyed of productive forces" than to change the means of production as it is a case with its bourgeois counterpart (Tibebu, 1995, 33 & ff).Therefore, the predatory nature of the empire impeded Hayla Sillase's modernist posturing. For example, changing agriculture, which employs more than 80 percent of the population of the country, contravened the exploitative nature of the empire. This was a fulcrum that kept the throne in place and should stay the way it was. According to Marcus, *'the Americans simply worked on the projects defined by Ethiopian policy makers'*. Therefore, insignificant attention was given to change the agriculture beyond producing extension workers, and "the U.S. assistance mission was a simple organization in which technicians were paramount." Also, in line with naftanya system, the Point IV projects assumed that *'towns would be the stage for modernity, whereas the countryside would remain socially traditional'* (Marcus, 1994, 160). As a result, there was no attempt to reform the land policy except making the farmers provide labor for the development (industrialization) of towns.

Asafa Jalata contends that the "U.S. was interested in consolidating the Ethiopian ruling class, which had little knowledge of the modern world in technical and administrative fields." Thus, the American tutelage was the emulation of British hegemonism, and the aids were to assist the Ethiopian Empire in "the development of colonial capitalism mainly in Oromia" (2011, 137). U.S. Ambassador Donald Bliss shares similar views about development unfriendliness of Hayla Sillase rule. "His Imperial Majesty is a master of the type of political intrigue by which he has maintained himself," remarked the ambassador. His objectives were to "maintain his power unchallenged," and fostering "mediocrity," "incompetence," and "sycophantic loyalty." Therefore, he had "has literally no conception of economic and social matter" (quoted in Marcus, 1995, 116). McVety (2008, 374) concurs that the Point Four was the failure, albeit, from a different angle from what Asafa claimed. She states that despite massive investment in Ethiopia, the U.S. capacity to bring change was circumscribed by the emperor's authority. She is partly true.

Undeniably, transformation was acceptable to him to the extent it reinforced his power, and he was unwilling to accept any advice that interfered with his "divinely" mandated paths. Modernization for Hayla Sillase was anything, but "to eliminate once and for all the semi-autonomous strength of the powerful provincial nobles and to centralize power and prestige in his person to a degree never before realized in Ethiopia" (Levine, 1965, 272). As I hinted above, the nature of Abyssinian polity was also one of the bottlenecks for progress. McVety had similar observation on incompatibility of Hayla Sillase rule with progress. She argues that investing in him and expecting transformation, at the expense of his priorities, is 'stretching the scope of human perfectibility beyond reason' (McVety, 2008, 376). Envisioning democratization from the absolutist emperor was similar to an Amharic proverb, *Laam balwalabbat kubat laqama*[Looking for dung where there is no cow].

McVety's contention that leverages of dominant U.S. over the emperor was limited (even to the extent of making him answerable to implementation of its money) is weak, to say the least. However, although the U.S. aids were partly the rent for Kagnew, I argue that the problem was not only the U.S. inability to influence him but also its unwillingness to exercise its limited influence. As Asafa correctly said, the U.S. primary interest was to build and maintain the Ethiopian Empire to advance U.S. national interests than genuinely changing for the benefit of its peoples. The cardinal principle of U.S. foreign policy is national security, and coziness with friendly dictatorial regimes is a norm. Nothing captures this time honored tradition of embracing authoritarian regimes like a powerful expression of FDR with respect to the Nicaraguan dictator Anastasio Samosa, who arrogantly declared that 'Nicaragua is my farm': "He is a son of a bitch, but our son of [a] bitch" (quoted in Coppa, 2006, 287).

Interestingly, however, McVety argues that the Point Four was the disaster from the viewpoint of democratization of Ethiopia; she sees its success from another point of view, revolutionizing Ethiopia. She underlined that the 1974 revolution was the reflection of how the American ideas of revolution inspired the young generation of Ethiopia through its aids. She insists that "[p]oint Four and its descendants certainly did not export the American lifestyle to the people of Ethiopia, but they did export at least a little bit of the American Revolution." "Today," she boldly asserts, "centuries of aristocracy have been replaced by a democracy in progress," and, hence, "Harry S. Truman would be proud" (McVety, 2008, 403).

The U.S., Kagnew, the British Departure, Ogaden and Eritrea

The greatest war trophy of U.S. adventurism into Africa was the former Italian naval radio station of Radio Marina, located in the vicinity of Asmara. This station was first named Asmara barracks and later renamed Kagnew to honor Ethiopian battalion of the Korean War. It was at an ideal location "far from south and north magnetic poles, the Aurora Borealis, and magnetic storms, and in a zone where there was limited seasonal variations between sunrise and sunset" (Lefebvre, 1991, 65). It had a capacity to operate a worldwide military defense communication with a potential to disseminate a radio signal as far as Finland, Australia, Philippines, Brazil, Virginia. Its proximity to the Suez Canal, Red Sea, Indian Ocean, and an oil abundant Middle East was indispensable to guarantee long-term geopolitical interests in the region. Later, the station became a useful tool to listen to the heartbeat of the radicalized Arabic world, because of the formation of the State of Israel through the alleged patronage of the U.S. The strategic preeminence of Kagnew grew to the extent of tracking space satellites and monitoring radio broadcasts from the Communist countries. Additionally, Asmara was a beautiful city known for wide streets and many imposing buildings, ceramics, beer and matches, a large and flourishing market place, municipal buildings, churches, schools, hospitals, cinemas and night clubs that was an ideal place for military personnel to serve during day time and enjoy the nightlife (Schoultz, 2006, 312).

Back in glorious days of British colonialism, when the Union Jack flew in all corners of the earth, Great Britain proudly proclaimed, "The sun never sets on the Union Jack." If the British surely believed that there was no way that the sun sets on their colonialism, there was a way, indeed, the Second World War. The Labor Government of Clement Attlee was consumed with implementing Keynesian economic prescriptions to lift Britain from the ashes of the war, to deflate unemployment, and to stimulate economic growth. In 1947, India, "the brightest jewel in the British Crown," had gone from the jaws of "Great Britain," but sure-to-be the small isles in Europe. While maintaining the already built empire was similar to a famous scriptural allegory of a battle against Goliath, Britain did not see the wisdom of building an empire in the wasteland of the Horn of Africa. When the empire builders were distancing from their very ideas, Hayla Sillase, a Napoleon of the 20th century Africa, had inexorable stamina to build stronger empire with the bankrolling of the U.S.

Hayla Sillase's control over Ogaden became a reality when Britain withdrew in 1948. In the same year, Britain made its intentions clear to the U.S. that it did not want to stay further in Eritrea. Britain refused to entertain options of either staying longer in Eritrea or annexing part of Eritrea, which contains Kagnew, to the Anglo-Egyptian Sudan because of the financial burdens of such trusteeship. The U.S. intelligence sources underlined that the former Italian colonies would serve as a Trojan horse for communist penetration of the Horn of Africa because of their economic vulnerabilities (Schraeder, 1996, 117). In the same year, Admiral William Leahy, the then Chairman of the Joint Chiefs of Staff, presented this report to the Secretary of State: "The Joint Chiefs of Staff would state categorically that the benefits now resulting from [the] operation of our telecommunications center at

Asmara can be obtained from no other location in the entire Middle East-Eastern Mediterranean area. Therefore, United States rights in Eritrea should not be compromised" (in Wrong, 2005, 200).

The U.S. decided to maintain the irreplaceable listening post in the hands of the friendly nation. The right of the Eritrean people to have a say over their future became a sacrificial lamb for the U.S. national security. Secretary of State Foster Dulles blatantly said: "From the point of view of justice, the Eritrean people must receive consideration. *Nevertheless, the strategic interest of U.S. in the Red Sea basin and consideration of security and world peace make it necessary that the country has to be linked with our ally, Ethiopia*" [Italics added] (quoted in Patman, 1990, 37).

The logical conclusion for defending the national security of the U.S. was encouraging Hayla Sillase to claim Eritrea. He was more than willing to do that since he had the ready-made discourse, at his disposal, to drive his *irredenta* home. His government underscored, "For 4,000 years Eritrea and Ethiopia have been identical: identical in their origins, identical in their historical developments, identical in their defense of the Ethiopian and Eritrean region" (quoted in Wrong, 2005, 112).

In the interim, Britain referred Eritrea's status to the United Nations in 1949. The UN established a Commission to oversee Eritrean case, and it passed a resolution advising Britain to depart Eritrea by September 1952. The Eritrean Assembly approved the U.N. Commission mandated progressive constitution. Eritrea, with a capital city, flag, official languages, and liberal constitution, was nothing short of an independent state. But the political forces in Eritrea were weak. More than a common vision for nationhood, Eritreans were divided and united along religious and tribal lines.

Three principal groups with three different visions were vying for its future. The Christian highlanders—constituting mainly the Tigrinya speaking population of Eritrea that shares a similar history, language, and religion with their Ethiopian counterpart of Tigray people—were favoring unification with Ethiopia. The Muslim lowlanders were demanding formation of an independent state or unification with Anglo-Egyptian Sudan. Whereas Muslims were campaigning to form the independent nation in opposition to the Christian Ethiopia, the Christian Eritreans' zealotry to join the intolerant Christian Kingdom towards their culture was because of anticipated fear of Islam domination in an independent Eritrea (see, Tekeste, 1997, 47). The Christian plateau overwhelming support for union with Ethiopia on the aftermath of harsh treatment of their Tigre kinsmen, during the 1943 Wayyane rebellion, showed how religious motivation transcended other considerations during decision makings. The profound impact of religion on shaping the narrative of Eritrean future coupled with the lack of vibrant neutral choice, which was capable to jettison the fervor of sectarianism in favor of putting the Eritrean quest for independence along nationalistic course in the society that straddles proportionally along the religious fault lines jeopardized consensus formation. In between these two conflicting groups, there were Eritreans who favored Italy's demand for the restoration of Italian rule.

Diversity of opinion over the future of Eritrea was also common among superpowers and stakeholders. Italy was requesting the restoration of the colonial status (or trusteeship) which the Soviet supported, at the beginning, anticipating communist triumph at polls in Italy. France was also backing this idea. The return of democratic or undemocratic Italy to the region was nightmarish scenario that Hayla Sillase was not ready to consider (Schraeder, 1996). To his dismay, the great powers had already restored the Italian rule to Somalia in the form of the UN trusteeship. This time, Britain was adamant to allow "Italian rule with British bayonets" (Vestal, 2011, 42). Considering Eritrea an extension of the Arab world, the Arabs also showed keen interest to either absorb Eritrea into their territory or the creation of an independent nation. Yearning for access to the sea and counting on the U.S. unwavering patronage, Ethiopia strongly pushed to assert control over Eritrea.

Amidst schism on the future of Eritrea, the foreign ministers of Britain and Italy jointly presented the disposition plan of Eritrea that involved Eritrea's partitioning between Ethiopia and Sudan. While part of the United Nations disposition plan of uniting the southern and Eastern Coastal areas of Eritrea with Ethiopia was approved, the Western Eritrea merger into Sudan was rejected. Ethiopia that primarily interested in having access to the Red Sea ports voted for the partition of Eritrea (see, Tekeste, 1997, 46-47). Nevertheless, the question of disposition of Eritrea was postponed until the United Nations' Inquiry Commission consisting of Burma, Pakistan, Guatemala, South Africa, and Norway presented its final reports. The Inquiry Commission failed to reach a unanimous decision. While Burma, South Africa, and Norway favored union with Ethiopia because "Eritrea lacked national consciousness and an economy that could sustain the independence" (McKenna, 2011, 131), Pakistan and Guatemala recommended the formation of an independent Eritrea. The United Nations General Assembly did not endorse a referendum (plebiscite) to determine the wishes of the Eritrean people. For the UN, wishes of Eritrean people were expressed by political parties [associations] that claimed to represent the people and a handful of "hearings of the local populations" (Cassese, 1995, 220).

In the middle of this, the United Nations Security Council—in the absence of the Soviet Union representative from the Security Council—adopted Resolution 82 on June 25, 1950 to prevent a communist takeover of the Korean peninsula. Hayla Sillase promptly expressed his unequivocal support to protect the Korean people since it reminded him of the Italian invasion. To support the reliable ally, the U.S. engineered the third option, federation of Eritrea with Ethiopia while U.N. was debating options presented by the Inquiry Commission. Thanks U.S. diplomacy, the U.N. General Assembly Resolution 390 (V) overwhelmingly sanctioned federation of Eritrea with Ethiopia on December 2, 1950. Under this loose federal structure, Ethiopia controlled foreign affairs, defense, and currency; Eritrea maintained its democratic internal self-administration.

The festivities were in full swing in Addis Ababa for a motherland acquiring an access to the sea and her head, becoming a full-fledged person. The Eritreans had a little of the raptures since the "motherland" decided to move to Shawa the remnants of its industrial infrastructures from the British plundering (see, Lefort, 1983, 41).

The emperor kept his promise of defending Korea. He deployed his Imperial Bodyguard, making Ethiopia the only non-NATO member state to participate in the campaign. He used it as a masterstroke of diplomacy and to show the vitality of his empire in the era of the Cold War. As Wrong emphatically expounded, his involvement provided the U.S. "with a glorious propaganda coup" as it fits the narrative of black people fighting for freedom along the Western nations (2005, 204).

The Era of Military Supports without Accountability

Following the U.N. Resolution, the last British contingent left Eritrea. With this, the British role as the chief weapons provider to Ethiopia ended. The U.S. was ready to feed the emperor in exchange for the Kagnew base agreement. In return for granting the base usage, Ethiopia insisted for a long term grant aid. The U.S. was offering Ethiopia reimbursable military aid since it hardly met the eligibility requirements for grant aid. Neither Ethiopia's military was crucial in Cold War conflicts nor did she have abundant natural resources. Nor, Kagnew was more than a communication center. Nonetheless, the Ethiopian Mutual Defense Assistance Agreement was signed along a Defense Installations within the Empire of Ethiopia agreement on 22 May 1953. This landmark base rights agreement was in a quid pro quo for warranting a comprehensive defense strategy for Ethiopia, which implied modernizing, training, and equipping Ethiopian military and paying a nominal land rent up to $7 million. Whereas the IEG was solely responsible for the external security of Kagnew, the U.S. assumed responsibility for its internal security. The U.S. refused to provide external security for the base against attack from the socialist or Arab countries since it was not a military base. The treaty was valid for twenty five years, until 1978, and subject to one year's termination notice by either side (Lefebvre, 1991; Spencer, 2006; Marcus, 1995).

In the summer of 1952, Ethiopia formally petitioned for arms supply under Section 408 (e) of the Mutual Security Pact. Excited by the strategic prize offered by the station and roles Ethiopian army played in Korea,

Washington accelerated arming and bankrolling the Ethiopian Empire. The U.S. armed the imperial defense forces with M-41 medium tanks and M-24 tanks (Mott, 2002, 259). Also, Ethiopia received a wholesale supply of the armed combat vehicles; naval vessels and aircrafts either through grants or zero interest loans. It benefitted from the expertise of U.S Military Assistance Advisory Group (MAAG), which helped his military down to the battalion level (Keller, 1989, 80). For the Ethiopian internal defense purposes, U.S. military personnel took charge of training three divisions of 6,000 armies at Holata and Hayla Sillase military academies. The U.S. became a leading weapon supplier to the Empire by eclipsing Sweden, which was instrumental in establishing, equipping, and training the Imperial Ethiopian Air-force with Saab-91 and Safir aircraft, and B-17 Bombers (Mott, 2002, 259).

The U.S. provided $279 million in military aid to the Empire until the mutual defense pact collapsed in 1977 (Yohannes, 1991, 225). On top of this, Ethiopia purchased $80 million military hardware from the U.S. (Mott, 2002, 260). During this time, the U.S. economic aid to Ethiopia was around $1 billion (ibid). Additionally, Ethiopia received $532 million loan from the U.S. most of them in the form of weapons supply (see, Yohannes, 1991, 225). As we shall see, Ethiopia used part of cash flow to buy weapons from other nations, including from the communist ones. During this time, 3,900 military cadets went to the U.S. for advanced trainings (Mott, 2002, 260).

At this time, the Ethiopian economy flourished thanks to the U.S. technical aids, improved transportation system, high world demand of Ethiopian coffee, and crop failures in Brazil. In 1953 and 1954, the economy showed net surpluses of about $50 million (Marcus, 1994, 160-1). Hayla Sillase used the surpluses for purchasing weapons. Ethiopia had among the highest military expenditure ratios in the world, and a third of the country budget went to arms purchase (Lefebvre, 1991, 32). In ten years alone, Ethiopia spent $562 million on arms purchase (ibid, 42).

A host of U.S.' Western allies also provided the Ethiopian army with modern weaponries and trainings. Whereas Norway undertook commitment to modernize Ethiopian navy, Britain provided Ethiopia with modern fighter aircrafts and heavy weapons. West Germany provided materials for equipping and training the navy as well as equipment for training and arming paramilitary forces for the internal defense of Ethiopia. Later, Israel also became a major player in arming the Ethiopian defense forces and providing counter-insurgency trainings (Agyeman-Duah, 1994).

Indeed, Hayla Sillase established powerful military diplomacy with Asia and the Eastern Europe, as well. Whereas India trained the Ethiopian army and air force on how to use modern weapons efficiently and effectively, Yugoslavia furnished Ethiopia with weapons and training for the navy (ibid). The Communist Czechoslovakia built an ammunition factory. To the consternation of the U.S., Hayla Sillase purchased twenty tanks from the

Communist Czechoslovakia. A diplomat said this, "Ethiopian government is prepared to waste a large sum of American dollars on buying these tanks reveals the extent of their irresponsibility and of their desire to maintain at all costs their façade of modern technical development in the military as in other spheres" (quoted in Marcus, 1995, 77).

However, the U.S. and its allies opened a floodgate of modern firearms to feed the rapacity of the violent king; there was no instrument in place or even a concern to check his abuse of them. Requirements such as regulating a use of them against the civilian populations (peasants) were not envisaged. When Ambassador Edward Korry asked about Hayla Sillase abuse of them, a Pentagon officer responded in a negative fashion: 'There wasn't much we could do with Ethiopians, and it was really Kagnew rent money. If the Emperor wanted it in *solid gold Cadillacs*, he could have it that way' (cited in Wrong, 2005, 201). At the time, all Ethiopian neighbors were under colony. An observer asked, "Who was the Ethiopian army supposed to fight?" (quoted in Lefebvre, 1991, 117).

When Ethiopian neighbors liberated, the militarization of Ethiopia fueled a fierce arms race in the Horn of Africa (ibid). The U.S. bureaucrats acquired an easy rationale for weapons supply to Ethiopia. She had 'five thousand miles border to defend bordering five different territories, and a seacoast of seven hundred miles on one of the most important and strategic bodies of water on the globe' (White, 2005, 56). Unbeknownst to them, Ethiopia wanted the guns for the domestic rule. As William Mott fittingly said, "Ethiopia, found its problems and aims almost wholly within its own borders" (Mott, 2002, 260).

In a traditional Ethiopian polity, regional nobilities used to play crucial roles in supplying militias to defend the throne during the turbulent times. In the nation where institutions for checking and balancing were missing, this was a traditional means of checking and balancing the absolute power of the emperor. With the modernization of military and supply of sophisticated weapons, a single person for the first time in the history of the violent empire monopolized the means of violence. The emperor totally ruled Ethiopia without the need for cooperation of feudal knights. His antagonists fell before his firepower easily; he controlled the peasant more effectively, and he got the opportunity to consolidate his power with much vigor (Wrong, 2005; Keller, 1989; White, 2005). In general, he single-handedly ruled the nation of the "King of Kings" where no king left but him. He established four military divisions. The first division, the Imperial Guard, safeguarded his throne; the second one battled insurgency in Eritrea, the third division in Hararghe suppressed Somali and Oromo rebellions; and the fourth division in Nagelle monitored the Oromo peasants in Bale and Borana.

Militarization or military expansionism leads to "an increasing role for military institutions both in national affairs, including the economic, social and political spheres, and in international affairs" (Agyeman-Duah, 1994, xxvii). This comes most of the time, and if not always, at the cost of good governance, economic development, and rule of law. As Nicole Ball aptly noted, in this scenario the "security forces play an active role in politics; a large share of government resources is devoted to the security sector; [and] the government seeks military, rather than political, solutions to domestic and inter-state disputes" (quoted in Agyeman-Duah, 1994, xxvii). This was what happened in Ethiopia. Marina Ottaway had correctly observed it: "In Hayla Sillase's Ethiopia the army was the only institution that functioned" (quoted in Wrong, 2005, 215). Because the political elites maintain power through the threat or actual use of force, this process instead of making them self-reliant, it increases their parasitic propensities on the patron for steady economic and military supports. Once the patron withdraws its hands, the client's rule deflates like a balloon. As Marina Ottaway well-said, 'by investing in the military buildup, the US made Hayla Sillase's departure a matter of time' (quoted in Wrong, 2005, 215).

What was Hayla Sillase's worth? The thorns on the side of U.S.-Ethiopia relations were Hayla Sillase's high self-projected image as a crucial player in the Cold War, and a high price tag—in the form of endless demand for weapons—he placed on the Kagnew base. The U.S. appeal was nothing more than the base, and hence, Ethiopia's importance in global security was marginal. Hence, it placed quantitative and qualitative ceilings on types and technological sophistication of weapons given to Ethiopia *vis-à-vis* resource-rich U.S. Middle Eastern allies. The fact that Washington treated the state of art firepower voracious emperor inferior to states such as Iran, Saudi Arabia and Israel was contemptuous to his prestige. Whereas Hayla Sillase wanted to build a strong national army of 40,000 men, out of his 77,000 standing army, Washington was insisting to build small, highly equipped, and qualified mobile force capable to quell regional turmoil quickly. Besides, the U.S. was not ready to make indefinite commitment to him on three grounds. Firstly, the U.S. had already bankrolled the emperor to build unrivaled army in the continent, it was reluctant to increase U.S. commitment beyond the worth of the base right. Secondly, it was unnecessary in light of absence of a foreseeable external threat to Ethiopia. Thirdly, Ethiopia economy was incapable to support such large standing army (Wrong, 2005; see also, Lefebvre, 1991; Marcus, 1994; Marcus, 1995).

Nonetheless, Hayla Sillase had obsession to build unrivaled army in the "Middle East" since Ethiopia is naturally enclosed by enemies that exacerbated by the presence of the base on his soil. He argues, "By allowing Kagnew Station, Ethiopia was putting herself at enormous risk, laying herself open to the threat of punitive action by anti-Western Arab neighbors" (Wrong, 2005, 209). Washington rejected his imagined threat and refused to enter an open-ended assurance. For the U.S. policy makers, the emperor was positing himself too much for his worth. In his book, *Holding the Line, Race, Racism, and American Foreign Policy towards Africa*, George White argued that the emperor's constant demands reinforced the image of blacks' dependency and "insatiability" of their demands (White Jr, 2005, 42). Whereas Hayla Sillase was asking how long the U.S. was willing to bankroll his absolutism, the U.S. was asking, how long it takes for him to help himself, but none of them concerned to ask how best to help the Ethiopian peoples.

Forgetting a gigantic U.S. role in the acquisition of Eritrea, the emperor unleashed his Prime Minister Aklilu Habtawald to blackmail the U.S. for more quantitative and quantitative supply of weapons. He played a psychological game with U.S. policy makers. Should the U.S. failed to meet *quid pro quo* obligation, "Ethiopia must ask itself again, just what place does Ethiopia actually hold in the eyes of the US." He warned, "Many European bees will want an equal right to sip the Ethiopian honey." Fearing the strategic disaster of Ethiopia's defection, the U.S. succumbed to the pressure. Ethiopia garnered a weapon worth 3.8 million dollars by March 1954. As a certain American bureaucrat noted, "Military aid would save the American position in Ethiopia, a country whose worth more in propaganda than in value" (Marcus, 1995, 92).

This was far from satiating the demands of the emperor since Britain handed the Haud and the Reserved Grazing Areas of Ogaden over to Ethiopia, which Hayla Sillase was considering to trade for the corridor to the sea at Zayla (see, Spencer, 2006, 271). The British decision inflamed anti-Ethiopian feeling among Somalis because "the transfer took place at a time when seven Ethiopian Somalis were executed by slow strangulation in front of their families" for opposing the Ethiopian rule (Gilkes, 1975, 219-220). The emperor continued to pacify Ogaden through violence since notions such as self-government, and cultural autonomy were thinkable in his world. The Ogadenis were ruled by the unfriendly Amhara governors that had utter disrespect and contempt for the local culture. Educated in Amharic, the only vacancy available for them were serving as interpreters for Amhara rulers. Even if, they secure posts; "the lowest Abyssinian official had more authority than the highest ranking Somali" (quoted in Markakis, 2011, 142).

Hayla Sillase worried that he compromised his prestige by sanctioning the Kagnew spy center, a sovereign within a sovereign, for the aid below his expectation. Not only he was disenchanted with Washington, but also he was fed-up dealing with the surrogates. He obsessed with having a face-to-face diplomacy with the leader of the free world. Thus, he pushed to get an invitation to the White House to see for himself how the White House works. His request came at the time when hostilities of the Cold War were spreading like epidemic, and, at the time when Washington was embroiled in the global fight against communism. Domestically, the U.S. was consumed with colossal communist witch-hunts (McCarthyism and red-baiting). Besides, discriminations against its black minority were undermining the rhetoric of the free world leader. Welcoming the "black" emperor, who epitomized collective security and who fought communism along the U.S., served U.S. propaganda perfect. On the aftermath of Supreme Court landmark case of Brown vs. Board of Education, Hayla Sillase came for a state visit.

On first June 1954, Hayla Sillase received a rock star welcome by a huge crowd of people in the New York City. A Mayor of the New York City welcomed the absolutist monarch as a quintessential icon of modernization and democracy as follows:

> We pay honor today a very great man, a man who represented one of the ancient governments and cultures in the world, and who, with progressive thinking and constructive planning, has brought his nation to the forefront of modern civilization. The heritage and the tradition of 3,000 years of royal lineage encouraged our most distinguished guest of honor to ever greater efforts on behalf his people and thereby enormous contribution to the welfare of the world. We honor today, an emperor, a king, the royal leader of the royal country. But his Imperial Majesty, Haile Selassie I, more than emperor, more than a king, proved himself to be a man, a great man with courage; with vision; with determination; with humanity; and with humility. He gave his ancient nation its first written constitution, relinquishing much of his authority to a parliament and a judicial system, and thereby encouraging the greater development of democracy in his country (quoted in Nathaniel, 2004, 140-1).

The emperor addressed the U.N. and became the first and the only head of state to address both the League of Nations and the U.N. According to the United Nations Secretary General Dag Hammarskjold, "The Emperor of Ethiopia stands in the perspectives of the history of our time as a symbolic trademark, a prophetic figure of the path of man's struggle to achieve international peace and security through concerted international actions" (ibid, 141-142). He received honorary degrees from the Harvard University, Colombia University, McGill University, Laval University, and the University of Michigan. He was welcomed by the governors, mayors, and public officials and visited, inter alia, a Michigan automobile, the Chicago stockyards, a U.S steel plant, and the Grand Coulee Dam, and Hollywood. Major newspapers applauded the emperor in their editorials (Vestal, 2011).

"Never before or since had one man been accorded so much honor and respect by America's government, business, religious, educational, civic, and military institutions. It was no overstatement to say, therefore, that His Imperial Majesty was the greatest human being to set foot in the United States," wrote Nathaniel (2004, 142). During Hayla Sillase's second visit to the White House, his host President Kennedy alluded to his first visit as "one of the most extraordinary revolutions in history" (Vestal, 2011, 113). For

Donald Levine, the visit was not only a 'historic' but also a 'prophetic' one (quoted in Nathaniel, 2004, 112). President Eisenhower praised the emperor as "a defender of freedom and a supporter of progress" (Vestal, 2011, 52). What were the impacts of all these fanfares?

Nathaniel (2004), writing from the vantage point of Rasta man, upholds that milestone decision of *Brown vs. Board of Education* was the U.S. good gesture of welcoming the "Lion of Judah." For him, he was anything but the liberator who destroyed racism of the U.S. by the magic of his visit. Professor Vestal contends that the emperor's reputation changed Americans' perception of race relations and the image of blacks, and thus, he indirectly contributed for the election of the first black president, Barack Obama (Vestal, 2011). It is true that American media had popularized him, even mystified him, which might have broken the racial barrier, but, his cruelties at home yet got no traction. The tsunami of sympathy he generated, his reception and portrayal emboldened him to push with his notorious brutalities and inhumane dictatorship.

In his speech to the joint session of the Congress, reading a fever of radical Arabism running high in U.S. politics, the opportunist Emperor took no time to jockey his empire as a force to be reckoned with in the Christian-Islam fault lines. He lectured the Congress on the geographic distribution of Christianity: "The two Americas and the continent of Europe together constitute exactly one-third of the land mass of the world," which are populated by "the peoples of the Christian faith." "Christianity does not extend beyond the confines of the Mediterranean," and, the remaining two-thirds of the earth's surface, according to Hayla Sillase, is a land of infidels and/or heathens. Thus, in the nucleus of heathens-infidels, Ethiopia is the "largest Christian State in the Middle East." In the world of the emperor, Muslims Ethiopians or the Christian Sub-Saharan Africans were irrelevant. Therefore, "It is this force which gives us, among the other countries of the Middle East a profound orientation to the West." He added; "We read the same bible. We speak a common spiritual tongue" (quoted in Nathaniel, 2004, 25-29).

The logic was straightforward, religious affinity justified strategic alliance with his empire against infidels and heathens. Thus, he needed more-and-more aids and weaponries. He underlined, "So great are your power and wealth that the budget of a single American city often equals that of an entire nation (…) [Y]ou gave us lend-lease assistance during the war, and at present, both mutual security and technical assistance. Yet, so vast are your power and resources that even after deducting all expenses of the Federal Government, you have met the costs of this assistance in one quarter of an hour and fifteen minutes—of your production" (ibid).

His incessant request for aid, military hardware, and long-term military commitment unheeded except the promise, we should see what we could do.

Why did he fail to secure the aid he needed so much? "Washington's bureaucrats might listen intently to Hayla Sillase's request for a whooping hundred million dollar aid package," reasons Marcus, "but they were Yankee traders who wanted fair returns and they believed that they already had bought Ethiopia" (Marcus, 1995, 92) George White. had similar observation: "Ethiopians were simply an asset over which the United States exercised control, a pawn in this contest with the Soviet Union" (White, 2005, 63). They expected from him a thank you speech. That was what Hayla Sillase indicated during his arrival at the New York City; "We have come solely to express to the American people our sincere and profound gratitude and our admiration" (ibid, 12). Came back home empty handed; Hayla Sillase used the same blackmailing strategy for more weapons as often.

Hayla Sillase's Ethiopia, Nasser's Egypt, Eisenhower's America

In 1952, the demise of King Farouk of Muhammad Ali Dynasty of Egypt brought a firebrand nationalist Gamal Abdel Nasser to the helm of power. Nasser was not only a popular Arab hero; he was also a heartthrob of progressivism all over the world since he turned one of the rotten systems into a system full of life. Beyond his victories over ancien regime and imperialism, there was something magnetic about the man even in the nation where chemistry was lacking for his rhetoric. Thus, the young intellectuals and officers in Ethiopia admired him for his model of leadership, answerability to masses, and for being playing representative politics; although, they dreaded him for his bullish Arab agenda (see, Erlick, 2002, 149). His Arab nationalism became a regional phenomenon and a challenge for U.S. national security.

Under Farouk, Egypt was an American client and amongst the largest beneficiaries of its largesse. This trajectory was unchanged as Egypt continued to receive increased aid during initial years of the revolution. In 1953, Secretary Dulles made a visit to Egypt taking a gift of President Eisenhower to Muhammad Naguib, as a symbol to convey a message to "statesmen in the uncommitted nations that militant vigilance against designing communists was the price of American friendship" (Matthews, 2012 63). The gift was a 38 caliber silver-plated automatic pistol upon which the following words were inscribed, "To General Mohammed Naguib from his friend Dwight D. Eisenhower" (ibid; Alteras, 1993, 58). Dulles assured Naguib that "the US would be prepared to consider making the Egyptian Army a real force in the world" (Hart, 1998, 70). Even sidelining the opposition of Jewish community, the Eisenhower administration provided funding for the construction of the Aswan dam (Ahrari, 1987, 34).

By the end of 1954, the bombastic Colonel Gamal Abdel Nasser had effectively cornered a symbolic head of the revolution, General Muhammad

Naguib, and the Muslim Brotherhood and the Wafd party. Washington attempt to woo Nasser, and secure the Suez Canal in the hands of friendly Great Britain floundered as he chose to play neutral position. Egypt declared that it would "take a hostile attitude towards and refuse to cooperate in any way with anyone who stands against our dignity and our freedom, while we cooperate and support anyone who helps and supports us" (Holland, 1996, 56). Underlying his orientation towards Soviet, Nasser said, "We have not rejected the Soviet offer, it was still 'in my pockets'. His move nerved pro-Israel groups in the U.S. despite he gave assurances, "We have no intentions to attack Israel" and clarified his defensive positions; "Our whole thought is on the preparedness against an attack from the Israelis" after his alleged bellicosity dominated headlines of America's press (Nichols, 2012, 93). Sooner, he signed arms deal with the Communist Czechoslovakia, and, he recognized the then diplomatic pariah state of the People's Republic of China. These sent a cacophony of diplomatic sirens to the United States, Israel, and Western Europe. Egyptian Minister of National Guidance Major Salah Salem was portrayed as a "Goebbels-like figure" (Cull, Culbert & Welch, 2003, 16) or "Egyptian version of Joseph Goebbels" (Holland, 1996, 56) and "Nasser as another dictatorial tyrant, as a potential Hitler" (Hopwood, 2002, 49). Eisenhower administration took the series of rush measures to fill the diplomatic vacuum created in the region. By now, Nasser defection was manifest to Washington.

The U.S. cash-cow weaned off funding the Aswan dam construction when a skirmish breakout between Israel and Egypt in 1956 (Boyle 2006, 105). Britain also followed the footsteps of the U.S. on the next day (ibid). Nasser's knee jerk reaction was a nationalization of the Suez Canal to fund it. This was nothing short of a declaration of independence from imperialists' domination of Egypt since the opening of the Suez Canal in 1869.

Under the auspices of the State Department, Ethiopia along Australia, Iran and Sweden pressured Nasser to set aside his plan in favor of an international regime (see, Spencer 1977, 24). The initiative failed, but it brought Ethiopia into the collision course with Egypt. Britain and France barely tolerated the defeat of their "veiled" imperialism; they overcame their historical animosity to invade Egypt together. Israel also jumped, on the board, to punish her sworn enemy, Nasser. Eisenhower was apathetic to intervene in the Suez Crisis; England and France withdrew from Egypt with egg on their face. Of course, the position of America was the hair-raising moment for Hayla Sillase, who expected an aggressive reaction from the Eisenhower administration.

Hayla Sillase had cordial relations with Egypt. Cairo was his stop during his visit to Europe in 1924 and during his exile in 1935. As a matter of the fact, during the Italian invasion, Egypt sent doctors and ambulances to Ethiopia. In 1941, the then young officer Nasser, in Sudan, warmly welcomed the emperor when he was following the footsteps of the British army to reclaim his throne. The emperor rejected Nasser overtures and a call for unification of the Nile Valley. He was already disgruntled by a U.S. decision of sponsoring the construction of the Aswan Dam. Therefore, the U.S. and Egypt diplomatic row was a welcome development for the emperor. The leader of the "largest Christian State in the Middle East" felt like he owned American cash cow without a rival. Along the U.S., he championed the notion of placing the Suez Canal under the control of an international body. This was a Hayla Sillase version of revenging Egypt for supporting the independence of Eritrea.

The emperor did not learn an iota of lesson from the disgrace of his friend Farouk, and, he was too fast to take advantage of the crisis for building an oppressive empire. He was ready to purge supporters of Nasser from Eritrea. He banned public education in Arabic and eliminated Muslims from public sectors in Eritrea in violation of the Eritrean Constitution and the federation act. Whoever disgruntled by his rule [especially for Eritreans], Cairo was a safe-haven to launch a propaganda campaigns against the emperor. In 1958, the Eritrean exiles headed by Hamid Idris Awate founded the short-lived Eritrean Liberation Movement (ELM) in Cairo. In July 1960, Secretary Osman Saleh Sabbe declared a formation of the Eritrean Liberation Front (ELF) in Cairo, under the patronage of Nasser, with the objective of forming an independent "Arab Eritrea" (Carol, 2012, 205). The ELF took advantage of the growing Arab nationalism by characterizing itself as an Arab-Muslim movement (Spencer, 2006, 318).

The defection of Nasser was a serious setback for the Eisenhower doctrine of shielding Middle Eastern allies from advance of the Soviets. The pledge of this doctrine went beyond pumping military and financial aids, but also to the extent of the Congress endorsing unilateral intervention to halt aggression of communism on any friendly Middle Eastern State (Yaqub, 2004, 76). Now, not only the strategy of defending the Middle Eastern allies should move forward without Nasser but also containing his fervent Arab nationalism became among the priority of Washington. In 1955, the State Department facilitated signing of a Baghdad pact by Iran, Iraq, Pakistan, the United Kingdom, and Turkey to defend one another in the event of aggression from the Soviet Union. Hayla Sillase campaigned for the formation of a "southern tier" against the expansion of communism in the Middle East (Spencer, 1977, 22). The U.S. rejected his plan because it did not see the need for an Ethiopia-centered pact against communism. Nevertheless, when the U.S. considered replacing a Baghdad Pact with the broad-based and comprehensive "Middle East Charter;" Ethiopia was among some of the U.S. endorsed countries to join (Yaqub, 2004, 77).

The "Lion of Judah" also showed his diplomatic weight by inviting Israel to have a permanent consulate in Ethiopia, which came as welcome news for Israel's triangular periphery strategy, which incorporates Turkey and Iran (Beit-Hallahmi, 1987, 50). In 1956, the Israel diplomats came to Addis Ababa to discuss on how to 'stop radicalization' and 'pan-Arabism' in the region (ibid). In 1958, they corroborated their ties with signing a "secret military pact." Ethiopia and Israel strategies had a similar ideological rationale. Whereas Israelis perceive themselves "as a brave people surrounded by hostile Muslim forces that seek to seize historic homeland" (Beit-Hallahmi, 1987, 50), Ethiopia perceives itself as "a beleaguered country surrounded mostly by hostile or potentially hostile countries with no natural friends in its immediate vicinity" (Negussay, 1977, 50).

With the deterioration of diplomatic relations between Nasser and Washington, the shunned emperor found a new relevance. Abyssinia, a natural fortress against Islam and Negroes takeover of Africa, would serve as an iron wall against epidemic of communism! Various U.S. delegations visited Ethiopia to emphasize its importance in checking the spread of communism and foiling Nasser's call for the formation of regional unity. On 12 March 1957, Vice President Richard Nixon came to Addis Ababa to promote the Eisenhower Doctrine. The emperor informed him that U.S. responses for his extreme urgency for military equipment had been rather discouraging (White, 2005, 55). To an embarrassment of the trusted ally, the Ethiopian army marched with Czechoslovakian weapons during the Jubilee celebrations!

In the same year, Ambassador James P. Richards came for the same purpose. Prime Minister Aklilu unleashed a barrage of criticisms on the U.S, and asked, "Do you throw us into the arms of others [the Soviet]?" The Ambassador hit back with a harsh tone, "To listen to you, Mr. Minister, I ought to be ashamed to be an American. But let me tell you this, were it not for the United States, Ethiopia would even be on the map today" (Spencer, 2006, 292). However, mutual interests prevailed; the U.S. and Ethiopia signed a new eight point mutual understanding in Addis Ababa on December 26, 1957. The purpose of this understanding was "to increase the capacity of Ethiopia to produce, maintain, repair or overhaul military equipment and materials used for the purpose of common defense (...) of the free world" (United States Treaties and Other International Agreements, 1958, 2483). In return, the U.S. increased military aid for Ethiopia.

When Nasser engineered the United Arab Republic (UAR) by uniting Egypt and Syria as a single political entity in 1958, Hayla Sillase's stature rose in the eyes of the Eisenhower administration further. The emperor "offered to take the lead in establishing close collaboration with Sudan and Somalia to deter the southward expansion of UAR influence" (White, 2005, 53). The U.S. determined to deny the Horn of Africa to Soviet and UAR influences so that it would ensure 'unhampered use of important Western sea and air communications in area' (Note from the executive secretary to the National Security Council on US policy toward the Horn of Africa, 1959). 'Providing

Ethiopia with technical assistance, economic assistance, military equipment and training' were the policy recommendations to "strengthen Ethiopia's orientation toward the West" and halt the expansion of Nasserism southward (ibid). The U.S. intensified modernizing, training, equipping the Ethiopian national army; besides training 4,000 support troops and purchasing ten vessels for strengthening Ethiopia's fleet. The annual military aid reached 20.9 million dollars from 1957 to1960 (Schraeder, 1996, 121).

The Revised Constitution and Consolidation of Aristocracy

Ethiopia underwent a rapid transformation, which literally touched all aspects of Ethiopian lives. The Italian conquest (1935-1941) with the cultural diffusion and expansion of communication infrastructure, the British occupation and development of bureaucracies (1941-1948), the creation of the United Nations (1945), the passage of the Universal Declaration of Human Rights (1948), the federation of Eritrea with Ethiopia (1952), and the rise of Africanpeoples against colonial shackles were among notable developments (see, Keller, 1989).

Fasil Nahum, a prominent scholar of the Ethiopian Constitution argues that the federation of Eritrea with Ethiopia was the first and foremost factor that necessitated a new constitution to harmonize "the jurisprudential marriage between un-equals" (Fasil, 1997, 25). Whereas the progressive Eritrean constitution incorporated "the enlightened values of an ideal democratic society" (ibid), the Ethiopia's constitution espoused the power of the emperor given from heaven. Whereas the Eritrean assembly acquired legitimacy from the popular vote, both chambers of the Ethiopian assembly were symbolic appointees of the emperor.

On the other hand, the emperor wanted to address the pressure that African countries, under colonial rule, were surpassing Ethiopia economically. Unlike elsewhere in Africa, there was no external colonizer to be blamed for Ethiopia's "backwardness," and the budding intelligentsia was ready to rise against the ruling class unless it destroys poverty. His American advisors were ready to give a legal facelift for the rotten imperial body politic, but the emperor was loath to make any meaningful concession. Whereas the transformation Ethiopia experienced, in a quarter of the century after the benevolent emperor granted the constitution to his subjects, was nothing short of a revolution, the philosophy that underpinned the revised constitution was the same old view of the generous emperor giving a gift to his subjects. Therefore, all he wanted was giving the same old gift wrapped with a brand new gift wrapping.

The first two chapters of the constitution, 36 articles out of 131 articles of the constitution, tasted like the same old wine in a brand new bottle. They were dedicated for the solemnizing the power of the monarchy and reaffirmed the myth of a divine ordainment of Solomon dynasty to rule. Article 4 underlined the 'inviolability of the emperor's dignity, the sacredness of his personality, and the indisputability of his powers'. According to Article 26, the Hayla Sillase is "the supreme authority over all the affairs of the Empire." He "determines the organization, powers and duties of all ministries, executive departments and the administration of the government and appoints, promotes, transfers, suspends and dismisses the officials of the same" (art. 27). He is the commander in chief of the army (art. 29); he exercises the supreme direction of the foreign relations of the Empire (art. 30); he has the right to coin, print and issue money (art. 32). He is appointer of the parliament members, and "all members of parliament shall individually take an oath of homage and fidelity to the Emperor" (art. 22); he has the right to dissolve the parliament (art. 33). In the words of Bahru Zewde (2001, 206), "*Even more than its 1931 predecessor, the Revised Constitution of 1955 was a legal charter for the consolidation of absolutism*" (italics added).

In short, origins of his authority and his powers and prerogatives stipulated in the Constitution morphed him into "the earthly God" of the Empire. The government and the state itself was none other than him, according to the constitution. "L'État c'est moi [I am the state]" of Louis XIV was perhaps less expressive to denote the Hayla Sillase's hubris in the 20th century. He infamously admonished an aristocrat, who buttressed him to ascend to the throne, about his patriotic intonations: "You keep on chanting the mantra 'Ethiopia, Ethiopia!' but Ethiopia without me means virtually nothing" (quoted in Paulos, 2006, 189). Fascinatingly, as Louis XIV styled himself Le Roi Soleil [the Sun King], Hayla Sillase's called himself the light of the world and sponsored royal chronicle for himself entitled, An African Sun on the Ethiopian Sky (see, Rubinkowska, 2004).

Whereas the 1931 Constitution was silent about a relationship between the church and the monarchy, the revised constitution explicitly assures the monarch supremacy over the church. Accordingly, the emperor was 'the protector of the Ethiopian Orthodox Church and his name "shall be mentioned in all religious services" (art. 126).

The notion of the popular sovereignty and parliamentary regime were taboo to be addressed. He equated multiparty elections with "dangerous regionalism" (Spencer, 2006, 258 & 277). For the sake of window dressing, there were separations of power, and twenty eight articles (from 37-65) dedicated for "rights and duties of the people." It recognizes, in principle, personal freedoms and liberties, such as freedom of assembly, movement, speech, religion, and the due process of law. Most of these "rights" were enjoyed "in accordance with the law" or "subject to the law." The emperor enjoyed the power to suspend those rights during the state of emergency (articles 29, 42, 92). The constitution warrants the rights of individuals to sue the government, but not the emperor (art. 62). This endorsed the immunity and impunity of the imperial tradition: *Nigus ayikasas samay ayitaras* [It is impossible to plough sky, it is impossible sue the king].

However, the constitution came into existence on the aftermath of the emergence of self-determination as political vocabulary; it was silent about the cultural self-determination of various entities of the empire. Contrarily, it solemnized and reaffirmed Amharic monopoly. Article 125 stated Amharic the official language of Ethiopia. The constitution's silence about the status of other languages in the nation of more than 80 languages made them mutatis mutandis a legal outcast. Moreover, a conspicuous phenomenon of cultural genocide and ethnocide was the tabula rasa repeal provision enshrined in the Civil Code of 1960. Article 3347 stipulates, "All rules whether written or customary previously in force concerning matters provided for in this code shall be replaced by this code and thereby repealed."

One of the drafters of the constitution put a motif the emperor in this way, "[B]ehind the screen of this pretext [liberalization] he was pursuing his longstanding policies of centralization and of constructive check-valves against the mounting pressure of liberalization. The end result—the opposite of what he expected—was accelerated demands for further liberalization" (Spencer, 2006, 257). He also noted, "[T]he emperor was in reality opposed to any thing suggestive of a parliamentary regime.... it [was] clear that concentration of power and form rather than reform and liberalization remained at the center of Haile Selassie's interests" (ibid, 277).

Whereas the federation of Eritrea with Ethiopia was the main reason for the birth of the new constitution, Hayla Sillase wanted nothing more than a formality framework to tighten his control over Eritrea. Hence, the first victim of absolutism consolidated under the guise of the revised constitution was a political progress in Eritrea. He banned the Eritrean constitution, assembly, and the multiparty system. He arrested the leaders of political parties, sacked even the Christian governor of Eritrea [Tadla Bahru], and abolished the principle of equality between Muslims and Christians in the public sector and governance. Furthermore, he changed the name of "Eritrean government" into Eritrean administration and brought Eritrea under direct financial control of Addis Ababa. In general, he made the federation act dead letters (Spencer, 2006; Shinn and Ofcansky, 2004; Keller, 1989).

With the consolidation of absolutism, dissatisfactions with the monarchy grew fat among all sectors of society. As Ofcansky and Berry (2004, 64) noted, "In 1950s, despite his many years as emperor and his international stature, there was almost no significant section of the Ethiopian population on which Hayla Sillase could rely to support him." Therefore, domestic oppositions to the emperor's rule, independence of neighboring countries, and communism took the U.S. Ethiopian relations into a new chapter. The following chapter deals with these challenges and their responses.

10 Challenges and Responses

IN THE ERA WHEN COLONIALISM flew off into the sunset and colonial empires were falling like the house of cards in Africa, Hayla Sillase coveted for anything but building a bigger empire. There was a precedent for this, Eritrea. He drove this point home in his 1954 Congress address: "Ethiopia has been one of the few states in the post-war world to have gained lost territory pursuant to post-war treaties and in the application of peaceful means" (quoted in Nathaniel, 2004, 27). He credited the U.S. for that: "If, today, the brother territory Eritrea stands finally united under the Crown, and if Ethiopia has regained her shorelines on the Red Sea, it has been due, in no small measure to the contribution of the United States" (quoted in Wrong, 2005, 204). The Emperor not only wanted to build the empire, but his dream was far-fetching; he wanted to recover all the fictional Ethiopia of the Minilik's circular letter of 1891, from Khartoum to Lake Nyasa. To be the "Conquering Lion" of the whole Northeast Africa, he proposed his dominion over the entire Somali speaking territories and the Anglo-Egyptian Sudan (see, Lefebvre, 1991, 96). He called for U.S. supports so that Ethiopia would regain lost territories and it would ensure the Horn of Africa from the influence of Nasser and Communists.

Egyptian revolutionaries' withdrawal of sovereignty over Sudan culminated in the collapse of the Anglo-Egyptian Condominium. Britain could not help but had to recognize the independence of Sudan. Sudan became a free nation on January 1, 1956. Hayla Sillase suddenly changed his mind and recognized Sudan; he signed a friendship and border closure agreement (to control Eritrean rebels) with the military rule of General Ibrahim Abboud. By default, Somalia was his last diplomatic gambling to recover *lost territories*. Acquired Eritrea through the patronage of the U.S.,

Hayla Sillase's had strong confidence to acquire British and Italian Somalilands with the blessing of the U.S.

The restoration of Haud and the Reserved Grazing Areas to Ethiopia, not only inflamed the region with tension, but it also increased the resolve of the Somali Youth League to campaign for the formation of an independent, unified, and non-clannish pan-Somali state. Whereas Somalis perceived Ethiopian demand for sovereignty as part of Ethiopian colonial expansionism, Ethiopia perceived Somalis' unification/independence bid as a danger to its territorial integrity.

Like, elsewhere in Africa, there was a paucity of knowledge about Somalia, and it did not escape from stereotypical attitudes of U.S. politicians. During a discussion of National Security Council in 1959, a puzzled President Eisenhower inquired, "Did Somalia consist of wild jungle?" He wanted to know the identity of the Somali people, "whether ...they were primitive and aborigines" (quoted in Grubbs, 2009, 19). Director of CIA Allen Dulles highlighted that the topography of the country is mainly arid and desert. Director of the Bureau of the Budget, Maurice Stance, noted that he saw some Somalis in Kenya: "[They] were probably much the same as their brethren in the actual Somalia areas. They were certainly primitive. On the other hand, Somali women were said to be the most beautiful in Africa" (quoted in Vestal, 2011, 96). Then, the president expressed his doubts about "how the native of Somalia could expect to run an independent nation and why they were so possessed as to try to do so." Dulles also wandered if the Somalis were ready to "organized and administer a modern civilized state" (quoted in Grubbs, 2009, 19).

Britain and Italy favored the emergence of Somalia as an independent nation instead of merger with Ethiopia. With more African countries poised for independence, the U.S. perception of the indigenous peoples' incompetence to govern their affairs began to change. So did the nature of Somalia-Ethiopian dispute. Washington interprets the dispute as 'an old blood feud reminiscent of India and Pakistan problem'. It decided to recognize the independence of Somalia to avoid regional tension, curb further financial commitment from Ethiopia and deny an opportunity for the Soviet to exploit (Memorandum from the President's Special Assistant (Rostow) to President Johnson, October 12, 1966).

In 1959, Hayla Sillase was informed that Washington supports the unification of the British Somaliland and the Italian Somaliland to form an independent nation. This came as a thunderbolt to him. Firstly, as the result of U.S. reluctance to uphold his sovereignty over Somalia the Indian Ocean region would be exposed to the influence of communism and Arab nationalism. Secondly, the U.S. decision was tantamount to endorsing the British-Italian project of "Greater Somalia," which implied not only the secession of Ogaden (a quarter of Ethiopia), but also implied the opening of a Pandora's box of secessions for other ethnic groups (see, Schraeder, 1996, 122). Ethiopia threatened to abrogate the Anglo-Ethiopian border treaty of 1954, should Somalia choose to declare its independence.

Despite trepidations of Hayla Sillase, the U.S. and Italy had the accord that the 'overriding importance was a need to keep Ethiopia that is firmly linked with West' in post-independence of Somalia. Italy "pointed out that Ethiopia was the only independent Christian country in North Africa (sic)," and it "would try [to] impede Greater Somalia, for which no natural reason exists." The U.S. agreed with Italy (Telegram from the Department of State to the Embassy in Italy, April 15, 1960).

In 1959, the U.S. had officially communicated to Ethiopia that it would reject the "Greater Somalia." It also tried to placate the emperor with the provision of F-86 fighter aircraft, "the most technologically advanced fighter aircraft in the U.S. arsenal," which it refused to donate to Ethiopia in 1957 (Schraeder, 1996, 122-123). This failed to appease him since he imagined Nasser in Ogaden and communists in his backyard. Moreover, he was dissatisfied with the quantity of the military aid he received; although, there were significant increments from 1957 to 1960 as we discussed earlier.

At this time, the tide of anti-colonialism shifted from the Middle East to Africa. Observing a fundamental incompatibility of Arab movements with communism and inter-Arab rivalry, the Eisenhower administration sought rapprochement with Nasser. The United States recognized the contentious Egyptian nationalization of the Suez Canal. Likewise, Nasser had recognized overplaying his hand badly. He faced a challenge from Qassim, who overthrew the pro-Western Hashemite regime in Iraq and who appeared more communist than Nasser. Thus, Nasser sought a rapprochement with the U.S. (Holland, 1996, 171).

Because of his closeness to the U.S. and his stance against Arab nationalism, the neighboring Arab countries had shunned the emperor. This amplified his besieged mentality syndrome. He was sinister of Nasser's retaliation either militarily or by revivifying Egyptian dream of controlling the Nile on the face of dwindling military commitment from the patron. In the mind of the emperor, thus, a traditional image of Ethiopia as the nation closed in by the sea of Muslims loomed larger more than ever. He lost his cool; he suffered sense of isolation that accelerated his withdrawal from the west (see, Spencer, 2006, 261). Instead of facing a chest-beating Nasser single-handedly, he chose to pursue a rapprochement with him.

He went to Cairo in June 1959. The adjustment was too quick and too clever; the emperor "embraced Nasser and even Nasserist terminology." Even, he praised his arch-nemesis "as one of the world's great leaders" (Erlick, 2002, 149). The Ethiopian Herald echoed the rapprochement with Arabs in this fashion: "Ethiopia's relations with Arab countries go back for centuries. But owing to certain misunderstandings, fears and suspicions, the contact between the Arab world and Ethiopia has fared badly from time to time. During his visit, His Imperial Majesty carried the message of goodwill, harmony and fraternity. As the result, prejudices have been removed, misinterpretations rectified and fears and suspicion dispelled" (ibid). Through the visits, the emperor also familiarized himself with the rhythm of non-aligned movement. In 1961, he took part in the meeting of non-aligned countries, in Belgrade, as the official guest of President Tito of Yugoslavia. He bestowed the Collar of Saba, an Ethiopian order, on Tito; the latter in return gave him a yacht for his 62 birthday gift.

Bracing for conflict over Ogaden with independence of Somalia, the emperor wanted additional armaments from the Communist bloc. As a matter of the fact, the Eastern bloc was trying to get a foothold on strategically vital and mineral rich African continent. During this time, the Soviet showed readiness to provide weapons to attract any nation [guerilla] to their side. Besides the formation of the Warsaw Pact of 1955, the Soviet had carried out a propaganda coup against the West by sending Sputnik to orbit in 1957. Some considered this as a "proof of Soviet military and technological supremacy over the United States" that might attract developing countries towards the communist bloc (Brzezinski, 2008, 184-5).

Emperor Hayla Sillase wanted these modern weapons from the Soviet. The assertive Soviet had already made overtures to him that it would be ready to give him military supports if he desired so. It also cautioned him about fallout of nuclear on Ethiopian soil if and when a war breakout between them and the U.S. because of the high value target of Kagnew (see, Spencer, 2006, 291). This brought to him the flash back of U.S. refusal to defend Kagnew should it be attacked by an enemy. The emperor made a highly publicized two weeks tour to Moscow in 1959. He became the first African head of state to do so and secured the highest loan the Soviet committed to a Third World country, a hundred million dollar credit line (Porter, 1984, 191). He also secured a loan from Czechoslovakia.

Although the communist ideology of Godless state was repugnant to "the Elect of God," and although the communist ideology of kingless state was unacceptable to him since he could be anything, but a totalitarian king; his visit was a pragmatic move to play a Cold War Card and to create additional venues for military hardware to silence his "subjects" at home. For that reason, more than ideology, the visit was necessitated to protest against the patron's behavior with the threat of defection.

The U.S. was staunchly inimical with his rapprochements with both Moscow and Cairo since the raison d'être for favoring him was to bulwark the expansions of Arab fundamentalism and communism. The U.S. was apprehensive of his motives for shopping around and his commitment to deliver its mission in the region. In his 1959 visit to Washington, the Italian Foreign Minister Segni presented "alarming reports" about the "vast communist expansion in Africa" and "that Emperor Haile Selassie [...] had turned for help to the Soviet Union." "He compared this situation with that of President Nasser" who "condemned internal communism ... nevertheless brought military as well as civilian technicians into Egypt." Segni underlined, "Italy was deeply concerned lest Ethiopia might be transformed from a center of resistance to communism to a Communist stronghold." In relation to this development, Italy asked to have four powers (US, UK, France and Italy) ambassadorial level talk on this issue and the issue of Ethiopia-Somali dispute. The U.S. agreed to the idea but it underlined that it "should be held without publicity since Ethiopia would be irritated at being the subject of Four Power conversations" (Memorandum of Conversation, PSV/MC/16, Segni Visit, 1959).

The emperor visit to Moscow was talking memo at the 414th meeting of the National Security Council, on July 23, during the discussions of significant world developments. Director of the Central Intelligence, Allen Dulles, remarked that this was "the first major attempt of the Communist bloc to penetrate into the deeper parts of Africa" and "warned that this was a situation which must be followed very carefully." On the other hand, he dismissed the emperor's visit as an attempt to "blackmail the U.S.," and hence, he refrained from endorsing the unpopular "idea of putting the Crown Prince on the throne." They also discussed an unconfirmed report that the Soviet ordered the emperor to repeal the Kagnew base agreement, which they agreed "extremely serious" should it proved true. Secretary Gates pressed the base importance, and, the Chief of Naval Operations Admiral Burke buttressed its extra importance if America denied base rights in a Muslim Morocco (Editorial Note of the 414th meeting of the National Security Council, 1959).

The strategy of the emperor to impact changes in the patron's behavior worked, indeed. The report of National Security Council (NSC-5903) recommended the U.S. and its allies to show their interest in Ethiopia and its problems to prevent the Soviet penetration (see, Schraeder, 1996, 123). The Operations Coordinating Board (OCB), which followed up on NSC-5903, passed the resolution "to increased military assistance to Ethiopia in an effort to improve Ethiopian attitudes, limit Soviet penetration and obtain agreement to additional military facilities" (Memorandum from the Assistant Secretary of State for African Affairs (Satterthwaite) to Secretary of State Herter, 1960). 'The Eisenhower administration had secretly assured Haile Selassie of the 'continuing interest' of the United States in securing the territorial integrity of Ethiopia' (Schlesinger, 2004, 203). Therefore, the U.S. agreed to train 40,000 Ethiopian armed forces in return for garnering an additional 1,500 acres of land at Kagnew(Schraeder, 1996; Wrong, 2005). Somalia only had 2,000 troops, at the time (Schlesinger, 2004, 203).

In December 1959, the U.N. General Assembly Resolution 1418 (XIV) declared termination of a U.N. Italian trusteeship in Somalia. Hayla Sillase announced the nullity of the London-Addis Ababa treaty of 1954. So did Somalia nullify it since it violated a prior treaty of London with Somali tribes. The Somalia Republic, a nation with undefined and contested boundary, came out of a union of Italian and British Somali-lands on July 1, 1960. A new republic chose the path of democracy and parity of positions between the united territories. Adan Abdullah Osman of the Italian Somaliland and Abdirashid Ali Sharmarke of the British Somaliland elected President and Prime Minister respectively. The U.S. recognized Somalia on the same day and diplomatic relations upgraded from a consular to an embassy level.

Somalia adopted a manifesto calling for the formation of the "Greater Somalia" to end a colonial legacy of Somali people, who share a common language, a common religion, a common culture, and a common understanding of themselves as a political community, but under the occupation of various sovereigns (Patman, 1990, 46). On the UN flag inspired blue background, it adopted a "five-pointed star" as a manifestation of "unity" of Somalis of Djibouti, Ogaden, Kenya, British Somaliland, and Italian Somaliland. Of course, a star is five pointed figure except the Star of David and a few others, but more explicit claims to the ideology of pan-Somalia were enshrined in the Constitution of 1961. Whereas its preamble referred to "sacred right of self-determination of peoples enshrined in the Charter of the United Nations," and a mandate "to consolidate and protect the independence of the Somali nation;" article I underscores the 'indivisibility of Somali people' and their aspirations to achieve unification through "legal and peaceful means" (Lefebvre, 1992, 97-8). The Somalia issue became the thorn on the side of U.S.-Ethiopian relations and a factor for regional destabilization as we shall see in extended fashion later.

While Hayla Sillase consumed with the Somalia issue, at home, he was found himself in a dilemma of his cosmetic reforms. His attempt to use modern means to enhance his archaic rule started to backlash. During this period, "the emperor began a period of personal rule" (Marcus, 1994, 166). He effectively tightened his grip on the central administration by building bureaucracy based on "a master-servant relationship" (Tibebu, 1995, 131). A new generation of educated class and returnees from abroad were crucial to build this bureaucracy. As opposed to making them work for a common goal of developing the country, he inculcated "a competing power faction" among them (Marcus, 1994, 166). He controlled them through favoritisms, nepotisms, and endless process of demotions and promotions (shum-shir). In these fast processes of demotion and promotion, an appointee had to exploit the peasant as much as he could before his demotion since the culture of plunder had changed into the national culture of corruption in the age of the civil service. The adage goes: Sishomut yalballa sishirut yiqochal [An appointee who fails to benefit will regret when he leaves].

The emperor created unnecessary and redundant positions for his sycophants at the upper echelons of powers that reduced their productivity and wasted the meager resources of the country. More than working for common good, the intelligentsia engaged in a futile "barrages of competitions" and battled over showing loyalty to the emperor, and, the latter got a chance to shop for a policy based on his taste than what was good for the country (ibid). Besides the obstructionism of the emperor, the newly graduated students had to wrestle with the establishment altogether and with their colleagues who were already deeply fortified in the system (Paulos, 2006, 20). For the young generation of elite, even the earlier reformist elite, was conservative and wanted to maintain the *status quo*. Thus, a gigantic rift created between the intellectuals since beneficiaries of the system wanted to maintain the *status quo* and the disgruntled ones wanted to destroy it (ibid).

The students "became disenchanted working for a regime in which personal loyalty to the emperor was the paramount consideration" (Marcus, 1994, 166-7). Thus, it became commonplace, perhaps weird phenomena, to find unemployed intellectuals in the nation of a handful educated people. This was among the factors that culminated in the mushrooming of educated guerrilla fighters later (Paulos, 2006).

The neglect of the people, who considered themselves an agent of change, by the system they wanted to change, fermented a dangerous resentment. In his acclaimed work, *Political Order in Changing Societies*, Professor Huntington (2006) argues that a *fundamental dilemma* of changing state is a clash between the traditional and the modern authority. He argues that centralization of power was necessary to promote reform, but at the same time, the centralization makes impossible for the absorption of an elite class hatched out of modernization into the old power structure. Thus, reforms, instead of strengthening, would eventually destroy traditional sources of political authority institutions. In the same way, the fruit of Hayla Sillase's modernization programs wanted to change the very system that created them.

There was no venue for this progressive group to nurture and advance their agenda peacefully since neither election nor civic forum was permissible in the empire. Nor did they know the degree of popular support for their idea to incite a popular uprising. Nor did they even know their backing within the military because of the culture of mistrusts and secrecy that permeates military structures and leadership positions, and the divide and rule employed by the regime. Informed by bitter dissatisfactions, their logical conclusion was destroying the system to change it. Therefore, a coup was a necessary evil. The ensuing subject will deal with that coup.

The Aborted Coup

On 13 December 1960, Brigadier General Mangistu Naway, a commander-in-chief of the Imperial Body Guard, and his brother Girmame Naway, a political science graduate of the prestigious Columbia University, staged a coup while the Emperor was in Brazil as part of his mundane tour of relishing his status of international statesmanship. The coup was defined by the experience of Girmame, a person of high intellectual rigor, who was preoccupied with prevalent mood of transformation and his rejection by the oligarchy (Marcus, 2002, 167). On his return from the U.S., he was appointed under the tutelage of Dajjazmach Masfin Silashi, "the archetypal Ethiopian oligarch," as Harold Marcus nicknamed him, to immerse him in the art of governance. It rather opened his eyes to their embezzlement, exploitation, and oppression of the local populace (ibid).

On oppositions of nobilities, the emperor appointed him the governor of Walayta province. He distributed land among the landless peasants, and still, 'his period is remembered locally with enthusiasm' (Vaughan, 2003, 254). Contrarily, the vehement opposition of the local aristocrats culminated in his recall. The emperor, who had authored his biography My Life and Ethiopia's Progress, which gave the impression that his life was intrinsically intertwined with the progress of Ethiopia, was not ready to tolerate the reforms of the archaic system. As Edmond Keller noted, "In spite of his modernist pretentions, it became clear that Haile Selassie was not prepared to undermine feudalism completely in the 1950s" (Keller, 1989, 133). Instead of praising the young leader for his progressive ideas, he demoted him to the governorship of barren land of Jijiga, "where he couldn't give away land because the only inhabitants were nomads" (Kapuscinski, 1984, 67). The disappointed young leader left for Jijiga without seeking the blessing of his Majesty, i.e., kissing his hands and knee (ibid). The neglect, poverty and underdevelopment he saw appalled him. Once again, he ended up recalled owing to his innovative approach to local problems.

The enlightened man had intense enthusiasm for transformation of his battered country out of shackles of poverty. It was an embarrassing situation to see a lack of economic progress in his country, which newly born African countries easily surpassed. The repudiation and obstructionism of the imperial system symbiotically interwoven with nobilities made clear to him lack of space for his progressive ideas. The staunch believer in change from below learned impossibility of reforms unless the system dismantled from top and hence, initiation and masterminding of the coup was in progress. As Kapuscinski noted, "There was something about him that drew people to him. [He had a] burning faith, a gift of persuasion, courage, decisiveness, keenness. Thanks to these characteristics he stood out against the gray, servile, fearful mass of yes-men and flatterers that filled the palace" (ibid, 68). His vision had tempted his otherwise loyalist brother, who was entrusted with safeguarding the emperor, to a tendency of the coup.

On the first day, December 14, 1960, the coup leaders announced a successful coup on the national radio. They pledged to form the government that lifts the people out of the economic inertia, and thereby to change the economic, social, and political conditions of the population and to improve global images of the country, which became synonymous with hunger and poverty. They appealed to the traditional authority by enthroning the Crown Prince Asfaw Wassan as Emperor Amha Selassie. The new emperor, on his radio speech, remarked that the "Ethiopian people have a history of more than 3,000 years, but in that long history no progress was made in agriculture, commerce or industry" and "the newly formed independent African nations are making progress, [while] Ethiopia is lagging behind, and this fact is now realized." He indicated that "there is no nation which, in time, would not extirpate ignorance from among its people and not aim, at improving the standard of living," but, "Ethiopia has always been lulled by vain promises." He justified the coup as a national salvation from a minority clique that exploited the Ethiopian people, who "manifested patience, such patience as is unknown in any other nation" and who "waited in the hope that betterment would come from day to day" (quoted in Balsvik, 1985, 94).

On the second day, the coup plotters summoned U.S. Ambassador Arthur Richard to the palace to explain why they carried out the coup. Girmame unequivocally informed him that what inspired the bloodless transition was exactly the liberalism and modernization of the U.S. Declared to the ambassador was a new administration's commitment to observe all international obligations and protect U.S. citizens and their property. Guaranteed was also their desire to maintain bilateral security cooperation with the U.S. on the friendliest basis, "a thousand percent better than in the past." They sought recognition from the U.S. as a legitimate government of the Ethiopian people (Marcus, 1995, 130).

Learning that the coup plotters were disillusioned officers, not rogue communists, Washington waited until the dust settled and a winner emerged. Therefore, it assumed "neutrality," but it facilitated the loyalists to pass a message to the monarch. For the first time in history the students of the sole higher educational institution in the nation demonstrated in support of the coup chanting "liberty, equality, and fraternity" (Donham, 1999, 125).

The coup plotters felicitations lasted not long. It only survived two days. They won a support of the police chief, Warqinah Gabayyahu. They gambled on the support of the army and air force. As a result, an outcome of the coup was dependent on which side of the equation they align with, either on the side of maintaining the *status quo* or demolishing it. Taking the support of the army, air force, and the public on the simple declaration that an "evil" emperor had dethroned for the sake of progress happened to be a political miscalculation as the brothers hardly moved them on their side.

At the same time, loyalists were designing a strategy to dislodge them. Seeing loyalists' superior force, America, which inspired the brothers with its modernity, disowned them in favor of preserving the *status quo*. United States embassy ruled that the coup was "an attack against Ethiopia" and saving the emperor was tantamount with saving Ethiopia. That was what all it meant to be a mutual defense agreement with the Ethiopian Empire (Schraeder, 1996, 125). While engaging the coup plotters in a vain cease fire attempt, which halted their momentum, the U.S. played a crucial role in drawing a roadmap for loyalists, providing logistic support, flying reinforcements from provinces, providing aerial photography, and scarring the plotters with over flights that broke the sonic booms and the sound barrier (ibid; Marcus, 1994, 171). The U.S. flew Hayla Sillase from Brazil to Liberia; then took him to Kagnew to facilitate communication with loyalists.

On the third day, the loyalists stormed the palace, aborted the coup, killed 474 and arrested 2,000 members of the Imperial Guard. The fatalities on the side of loyalist soldiers stood at 72 (Keller, 1989, 134-5). Ambassador Richards barely survived the bloodbath jumping through the window (Vestal, 2011, 110). The desperate coup-plotters decimated fifteen of twenty-one high ranking officials they kept hostage so that the face of the country would be forever changed. Girmame committed suicide; Mangistu was captured, court martialed, and hanged at market place. The dead body of Girmame and other renegades were "hanged to show Hayla Sillase's resolve that he would not tolerate any such rebellion in the future" (Paulos, 2006, 106). He pardoned his son, Crown Prince Asfaw Wassan.

On 17 December, dignitaries, the patriarch, Ambassador Richards and his military attachés greeted the emperor at the airport. He sincerely expressed thanks to the ambassador, the people of the United States and President Eisenhower for saving his throne.

Why did the coup fail? As Gebru highlighted, it was spontaneous; it lacked a proper planning, executions, and coordination, which eventually pitted the coup plotters against each other. Because of "cleavages within the army" and rampant culture of secrecy and suspicion, the plotters staged it without consulting their own rank and file soldiers let alone seeking the support of the army, air force, and key government ministers (Gebru, 2009, 12). They lacked a plan beyond controlling Addis Ababa and naively expected the rise of disenchanted mass with depressing system. Contrarily, the mob stoned and stabbed to death the "infidels" who were running in disarray when the loyalists stormed the palace. There was neither calculations nor deals in place to neutralize the robust support of the emperor from provincial nobilities. In one of the most religious nation on earth, their failure to mention a name of "God" at least once in their official dethronement

Communique ruined their chance of legitimacy in the eyes of the public, as Greenfield (1965) surmised. The coup lacked a radical solution to bottle necks of the empire and failed to gain support from non-Amhara [peripheral peoples] as it was wrath of centrists on the center. *It neither said anything about the land reform nor did they say anything about addressing religious discriminations nor did they utter a word about nationality issues.*

What was the importance of the coup? The protagonists of the coup were not abolitionist. The monarchy abhorred a wake-up-call for reform to hinder reoccurrence of a similar situation and, therefore, opted for rottenness and implosion. The emperor shocked upon learning the coup. He exclaimed, "NOW I am reaping the crop I have sown" [capitalization original] (Pearson, 1965). Upon his return, he declared that he would push with his divinely guided path without a "slightest deviation" (Wrong, 2005, 214). In his philosophy, thus, the coup was the failure of sporadic experimentations with recruiting capable outsiders. Thence, he relied more on blood relations as an acid test for appointments of military officers and civil servants. "A researcher has able to place on a single genealogical tree 70% of the ministers making up the various successive cabinets from the end of the Emperor's exile to 1966" (Lefort, 1983, 17). The emperor won the battle temporarily. However, he was losing the war since he leaped forward with his single-handed rule. According to his simplistic assumptions, reshuffling ministerial posts, bolstering security apparatus, and buying loyalty of the army and police by land-grant and the peasants' labor sufficed to rest the issue.

Albeit it was impromptu and doomed to failure, the underlying message of the coup never failed. The relay for change had begun, and a torch had been passed to the students. The brothers had stirred intellectuals' rancorous stance against the incompetent administration.

Empress Menen complained of recurrent nightmares and expressed her discomfort of staying in the bloodstained palace (Paulos, 2006, 52). To delight of his wife, the Emperor abandoned this palace since he had three official palaces in Addis Ababa. "It was to be an example that We donated Our personal property to be a site for the University," said the emperor (Haile Selassie, 1972, 228). The U.S. pledged $12 million for its expansion, curriculum development, library and laboratory constructions, staffing, and so on (Skinner, 2003; Paulos, 2006). A U.S. citizen became acting president of the university. The radicalized students used the university as a brewing ground for their left-leaning ideologies crucial in advancing the messages of the coup and toppling the totalitarian rule of the emperor eventually. A prominent historian expresses the role of the students in these words: "As impassioned advocates of change, more than any other sector of the society, they proved to be the grave-diggers of the old regime and the generators of the Ethiopian revolution" (Bahru, 2001, 220).

The coup openly challenged the myth of the divinity and infallibility of the King and power given from Heavenly God (see, Greenfield, 1965). The "Elect of God" learned that he was not even an elect of his best-bribed palace guard, let alone of the people. It debunked the image of emperor, whose office is sacred, whose dignity inviolable, and whose power indisputable. Had he understood, it would have taught him that no matter how strong the external support he garnered, he could hardly govern in splendid isolation from the consent of the people. A new chapter in Ethiopian politics had ensued, the chapter of a new political consciousness, a decade of social activism, and dichotomization of the rhetoric of the "masses" versus the "aristocrats" (Gebru Tareke, 2009, 13). A newly found orator of populism was potent, undermined, and challenged the grip of the autocracy on power. As Gerbu Tareke eloquently stated, "[The] challenge to autocracy shifted from the palace to the open space of the society, from clandestine to overt, from parochial to popular, from peaceful to violent opposition, from sectional conspiracies to mass-based insurgencies, and from the center to the periphery" (ibid, 13).

U.S. Assessments of the Coup

Unabashedly played a pivotal role in foiling the coup, the U.S. bought itself one staunch supporter but gave itself a lot more enemies. It made an ineffectual, inadequate and misguided effort to reassess its policy toward Ethiopia on the aftermath of the coup. The CIA produced a report entitled, "Ethiopian Prospects after the Abortive Coup" to evaluate "the significance of the abortive coup" and its ramifications for the Ethiopian internal stability. Underlying that the coup had been intramural palace revolt solely driven by small Amhara elites, the decimation of leading protagonists, and the incompetence of the Crown Prince, the report concluded that "the abortive coup has served to underscore the personal importance of Haile Selassie as the dominant force in a far from united Empire." What was a mockery of analysis when the nadir of almost eclipsed emperor played to his advantage! While the report assured about the unchallenged dominance of the monarch during his life time, it predicted chaos and disintegration on the event of his departure from the scene since "the ineffectual performance of the Crown Prince has almost certainly reinforced the Emperor's grave doubts about him as a successor" and since "there are no clearly qualified alternative candidates." The assessment was unable to foresee the possibility of the storm consuming the emperor himself. Stating the assassinations of many of his most trusted men and the unreliable nature of his security services, predicting "his penchant for a constant shuffling of top government officials," it determined that the emperor would "reinforce his customary practice of using a variety of foreign advisers." Thus, the mistrustful emperor about U.S. intentions to defend his throne had been "reassured by the assistance rendered by the US" and above all, he would look more towards America than to the Communist bloc (Ethiopian Prospects after the Abortive Coup, 1961).

Contrarily, the U.S. ambassador remarked that grievances of the bodyguards were emblematic of a profound frustration in the entire system. "If the emperor does nothing," he warned that "it is not unlikely that a similar recourse to violence to reoccur at some future date, possibility with great success"(quoted in Wrong, 2005, 214). Similarly, an economic analyst at the U.S. embassy predicted, "Our assistance Programs especially military assistance, have identified us to a disturbing degree as a supporter of an archaic regime" (ibid). Unfortunately, these token assessments lacked backing of necessary foreign policy tools to press the regime to expedite a reform process.

In the same way, an American advisor of the emperor, Don Paradis, had foreseen the coming of greater danger. He advised him about the necessity to form "a truly responsible government" to avert a looming "danger and catastrophe" on his throne. "[T]he forces of history are in motion, and while they may be halted temporarily, and they can never be repulsed permanently." He told him the choices in the black and white, i.e., "either move with them or be overwhelmed by them." For that reason, a real reform was a bitter pill to take. He noted, "unless Ethiopia changed fundamentally the educated classes inevitably would turn to revolution against a system which has created obstacles and frustrations at every turn, which has inhibited and prevented progress" (quoted in Gebru, 2009, 12-3). As Gebru Tareke pertinently put, "It was eloquent and grimly prophetic exhortation. But the Emperor did not see the threat in such apocalyptic terms and loath to yield his autocratic power" (ibid, 13). From the political theater that almost shattered his power, "Haile Selassie had neither forgotten anything nor learned anything new," like the Bourbon kings" (Marcus, 1995, 164).

The U.S.-Ethiopian Relations in the Post-Independence Africa

In 1957, Nixon visited Accra leading the American delegation on the inauguration of the independence of Ghana, the first black nation in the sub-Saharan Africa to emerge from colonial rule. A Ghanaian newspaper wrote that 'Martin Luther King finally caught up with the Vice President, Richard Nixon in Ghana' to talk on Montgomery, not Ghana (quoted in Von Eschen, 1997, 183). Unlike the Empire of Hayla Sillase, a new Africa followed America's racial politics with an interest. The U.S. had to put its house to have healthy relations with them. Ghana was independent, assertive and pan-Africanist nation. Kwame Nkrumah was neither a sidekick to imperialists' agendas nor a sycophant, but wanted to play a role in global affairs based on mutual benefits. He made, to the dismay of U.S., the pan-Africanist W.E.B.

Du Bois a citizen of Ghana after the U.S. denied renewing his passport because of his political views, joining communism (Von Eschen, 1997, 183). Thompson (1969, 270) opined, "Nkrumah increasingly perceived himself as Africa's Castro, and Ghana as Africa's Cuba, genuinely threatened by a great power and with a mission to liberate the rest of a continent."

Nixon had noted assertiveness of the new Africa, and American neglect of the continent. He warned that the U.S. race politics would determine if Africa "will go communist or not,"and, the 'right amount of aid in the right places will tip the ideological scales to the side of the free world' (Von Eschen, 1997, 183). He underscored that "Africa in the mind of many Americans has been regarded as a remote and mysterious continent which was the special province of big game hunters, explorers and motion picture makers" (quoted in Schraeder, 1996, 1). Thanks to his lobbying, mineral resources of the continent, and communist threats, Africa could be hardly ignored anymore. In 1960, a year 17 African countries gained independence, an African desk created at the Department of State. Theoretically, for the first time the U.S. foreign policy on Africa liberated from the agenda of European colonial powers (Walton, 2010, 25).

In 1961, President John F. Kennedy (JFK), a Catholic icon, who made Africa a campaign agenda, inherited America with a lot of issues. The shock of Sputnik launch, mushrooming of free nations in Africa, communism penetrating the heartland of Africa, and above all, the power grab of Castro under the nose of the U.S. were worth mentioning ones. JFK remarked that "only real question is whether these new nations [of Africa] will look West or East—to Moscow or Washington—for sympathy, help and guidance in their effort to recapitulate, in a few decades, the entire history of modern Europe and America(quoted in Schraeder, 1996, 1). He appointed G. Mennen Williams, a liberal minded Governor of Michigan, as an Assistant Secretary of State for African Affairs. Williams underscored that a "danger in Africa was not 'what the Communists are doing' but 'what we are not doing.'" He criticized racial segregation (especially of African diplomats) as a handicap for the U.S. policy in Africa since it gives "Communists a source of propaganda [and makes] the nation appear hypocritical in its rhetoric about freedom" (Noer, 2009; 243).

Confronted with the expansion of communism in the developing world, JFK resorted to American idealism to check it. This was evident from his inaugural speech of January 20, 1961. "The world is very different now," pronounced JFK; "for man holds in his mortal hand the power to abolish all forms of human poverty and all forms of human life." "The torch has been passed to a new generation of Americans [who are...] *proud of our ancient heritage and unwilling to witness or permit the slow undoing of those human rights to which this nation has always been committed, and to which we are committed today at home and around the world*" (italics added). "Now the trumpet summons us again; not as a call to bear arms… but against the common enemies of man: tyranny, poverty, disease, and war itself," said JFK. "My fellow Americans," he proclaimed, "ask not what your country can do for you, ask what you can do for your country." He had a similar message for the world: "My fellow citizens of the world ask not what America will do for you, but what together we can do for the Freedom of Man" (JFK, Inaugural address, 1961).

The immediate outcome of the speech was a creation of Peace Corps by the Executive Order of March 1, 1961 to send American volunteers to underdeveloped countries to help them with their development programs. JFK convinced that his "Peace Corps would be the West's answer to the atheism and socialism extolled by Soviet apparatchiks in the countryside" (Maier, 2009, 366). He chose young generations of American to "serve the cause of freedom as servants of peace around the world" to silence communist propaganda of portraying U.S. volunteers as "a nest of spies" of the CIA and agents of corporate America (ibid). Everybody was not a fun of the Peace Corps even at home. Detractors lampooned as "Kennedy's Kiddie Korps," "the children's crusade," and "a haven for draft dodgers" (Vestal, 2011). The ex-President Eisenhower mocked it as a "juvenile experiment." He also took a jibe at JFK's moon mission, "If you want to take a trip to the moon, why not send a Peace Corps up there? It is an undeveloped country" (Hadden & Luce, 1961, 16).

In November 1961, President Kennedy signed the Foreign Assistance Act (FCA) that gave birth to the United States International Development Aid (USAID), a successor to the Point IV. In his speech to the Congress, he said, "Existing foreign aid programs and concepts are largely unsatisfactory and unsuited for our needs and for the needs of the underdeveloped world as it enters the Sixties." "There exists, in the 1960's, a historic opportunity for a major economic assistance effort by the free industrialized nations to move more than half the people of the less-developed nations into self-sustained economic growth." "[It is] our moral obligations as a wise leader and good neighbor in the interdependent community of free nations" and *our political obligations as the single largest counter to the adversaries of freedom*" [italics added] (JFK, Special Message to the Congress, 1961).

Ethiopia was among the first and largest recipient of Peace Corps in Africa. The first dispatch of 300 volunteers arrived, in 1962, under the leadership of Harris Wofford. A number of the Peace Corps volunteers increased to 582 in 1965. Most of these volunteers taught in secondary schools and helped Ethiopia to develop American style of teachings. At its heyday, the volunteers covered a half of teaching positions of the secondary schools in the country (Skinner, 2003, 44).[1]

---

[1]Americanization of the educational system coupled with the British occupation ushered in the era of English as the medium of instructions for the

There are differing views on the achievements and successes of the Peace Corps and their relations with the Ethiopian students. Some characterizes the relations between the Peace Corps and the Ethiopian students rosy; others contend otherwise. As we shall discuss in due course, the relationship between the Peace Corps and Ethiopian students was a mixed bag of friendliness at the beginning and of total antagonism at the end.

In 1961, the Soviet had another successful psychological coup against the USA when the Cosmonaut Yuri Gagarin orbited the earth. JFK offered his famous moon landing mission to use it as the modern form of the ancient practice of 'single combat' (Harland, 2008, xx). Above all, he was ready to confront Khrushchev be it in Africa or the space race.

His administration inherited Congo-Kinshasa that descended into chaos. When Moise Tshombe declared the secession of Katanga, Belgium intervened to defend interests of its white settlers. Prime Minister Patrice Lumumba clashed with President Kasavubu. When the former sought an aid from the Soviet, it was handy. Lumumba's flirtation with the Soviet hardly escaped U.S. eavesdroppers at Kagnew (Wrong, 2005, 221). By the summer of 1960, the Eisenhower administration had concluded that Congolese Premier Patrice Lumumba was an "African Castro," a Soviet client, and thus an enemy of the most dangerous type" (Whiteman & Yates, 2004, 359). Thus, "he would have to be eliminated" (Gleijeses, 2004, 61). Kennedy masterminded an intervention to foil the communist takeover of Congo and help its NATO-ally, Belgium. Therefore, the Congo crisis became the proxy war between the United States and the Soviet Union. The pro-American group won the conflict decisively, but Congo was far from enjoying peace since the victorious group was neither capable to bring peace nor unify the country.

Dismayed by the defeat and death of Lumumba, the Soviet vetoed the Security Council Resolution proposal by the west to send the UN peacekeeping force to Congo. The General Assembly mandated the operation on an *ad hoc* voluntary basis. The emperor stood by Belgium, the former trainers of the Imperial Bodyguard, and the U.S. He sent the Ethiopian battalion to Congo. His involvement paid off as America promoted him as a voice of moderation and role model for the newly emerging African states. The UN forces crushed the Katangese opposition and unified Congo. JFK welcomed Mobutu Sese Seko, a dictator in a pipeline,

---

secondary/tertiary level educations and a second working language. "The sun had set on the British Empire, but it never set on the English language." Au revoir à la langue de la civilisation et la langue d'amour! French of the olden days of the Minilik-Skinner's treaty had gone, but its legacy of making a homogeneous state (nation-state) had stayed in the patched-together-Empire because of only-Amharic policy.

at the White House and showered him with praises, 'If it had not been for you, the Communist would have taken over' (ibid, 62)

The Soviet defeat in Congo had increased the resolve of Nikita Khrushchev to push with anti-imperialistic foreign policy. As a consequence, supporting liberation movements was a fundamental approach to entrench communism on African soil, a fertile ground for expanding Soviet influence (Walton, 2009, 32). Africa became the center of Cold War conflicts.

Meanwhile, in a significant regional development, Nasser suffered a colossal backlash. Syria withdrew from the United Arab Republic in 1961. When Yemeni civil war broke out in 1962, he was ready to spread the Egyptian revolution. He sent his military into Yemen. As a result, not only he created "his Vietnam," as he later admitted, but also he opened a door for the rise of Saudi Arabia and political Islam (Ferris, 2012; Madkhli, 2003).

Exploiting Nasser's adventure into Yemen and counting on steadfast support of the U.S, Hayla Sillase annexed Eritrea in contravention with the U.N. mandate in 1962. None other than Don Paradis, his American legal advisor, engineered the proclamation for annexation (Vestal, 2011, 43). Eritrea became the 14th province of Ethiopia; he substituted locally elected leaders with the centrally appointed Amhara nobilities. Measures put in place were a *coup de grace* against the civility of Eritrea. The authoritarian emperor reversed a clock on the progress of Eritrea by "re-feudalizing" the country that had already developed a nascent bourgeois stratum, multiparty democracy, and the parliament.

A mood of the Christian Eritreans was of bafflement and betrayal for the Christian kingdom they counted on had thrown cold water on their identity. Lost their language, they had to learn Amharic from scratch to compete against the Amharas for academic excellence and/or jobs. This crippled their upward mobility. For the Muslim Eritreans, it vindicated their demands for independence. Thanks to unintelligent decision of the emperor; the call for independence was no longer the dream of Muslims yearning for the triumph of "Pan-Arabism" or "Pan-Islamism;" it was the cause of the Christian plateau, as well.

Following the annexation of Eritrea and harassment of pro-independence groups, an influx of Eritrean refugees became a part of landscape of eastern Sudan. Egypt was ready to support the Eritrean movement for liberation. In 1964, the military rule of General Abboud of Sudan collapsed. This removed the border closure Hayla Sillase negotiated with Sudan, to end cross-border sanctuary for the Eritrean insurgents, in return for stopping Anya-nya rebellion from using Ethiopia as a spring board to assault Sudan. Came under the pressure of Eritrean sympathizers, the nationalist government of Sudan opened the border for Eritrean insurgents. Somalia, with its meager resources, was also willing to support the 'Muslim' movement in Eritrea. By 1966, the insurgents had changed Eritrea into the battle ground, and, above all, they managed to control most of the barren lowlands and coastal areas of the northern and western Eritrea.

The U.S., Ethiopia, Somalia, the OAU

Ethiopia and Somalia were typical examples of the cat's paws of Cold War superpowers in Africa. Somalia had already tried to claim Ogaden by force in December 1960, following the aborted coup in Addis Ababa. Although Ethiopia defeated Somalia with U.S. armaments, the U.S. maintained neutrality.

Somalia leaders blamed the U.S. favoring its Christian ally, Ethiopia. Out of concern for the emperor, the U.S. was unwilling to arm Somalia, but it provided half a million dollars aid program to Somalia police, limited economic aid and the Peace Corps to Somalia (Memorandum from William H. Brubeck, 1963). Somalia leaders lobbied for a White House visit to campaign for the cause of pan-Somalia and get additional aids. Otherwise, they threatened to seek from the Soviet, which condemned the colonial legacy of Somalia and signaled readiness to help.

From the Bay of Pigs Invasion and the Cuba Missile Crisis, JFK learned a danger of declining the request of assistance by small nations. A Somalia delegation received an invitation to visit Washington. Robert Komer of the National Security Council produced this memorandum for JFK on the visit:

> Nothing you can say will be of more benefit to US policy than urging Abdirascid to lay off Somali-Ethiopian disputes. Unless the trend is reversed, things are heading toward an eventual clash in which we will end up backing Ethiopia [...] There is no point in debating the specifics. We understand Somali's ethnic claims. But the overriding fact is that Ethiopia is so much bigger than Somali that Somalis can't win. You could drive this home by warning Abdirascid that if the issue is pressed to a confrontation, we may be forced to take the Ethiop [sic] side. [...] But we cannot resist Ethiopian pleas if the Somalis get a lot of equipment from Moscow and Cairo. Therefore, we're happy to hear that Somalis aren't seeking arms from the Soviets (Memorandum from Robert W. Komer of the National Security Council Staff to President Kennedy, 1962).

On November 27, 1962, a Somali high delegation led by Prime Minister Abdirashid Sharmarke met President Kennedy, during which, as anticipated, the dispute of Ethiopia-Somalia dominated the discussion. The premiere described the "artificial and unjust" division of the Somali peoples during the colonial period, and the "greatest hope of the Somali people was for reunification, but the Somali Constitution condemns all manifestations of violence." He then indicated that "Ethiopia toward the end of the last century had incorporated a large part of Somali territory." Ethiopia oppressed the Somali people using troops who "were equipped with arms furnished by the United States" and the "U.S. should stop the moral and material aid it was providing Ethiopia against the defenseless Somali people." JFK compared Ethiopian Somalia problem to the problems of the Pakistan-India and Cuba-U.S. disputes. Remarking Ethiopia's allegation that Somalia was getting weapons from Egypt and the Soviet, he then said, "we would attempt to prevent the wrong use of the arms we were giving Ethiopia" (Memorandum of Conversation, 1962).

The Somalia delegation returned to Mogadishu without support. Washington had already decided that the notion of pan Somalia was "illegitimate" and "counterproductive" to the U.S. national interest (Schraeder, 1996, 126).

Meanwhile, Somalia leaders learned that Britain was grooming Kenya for independence. Despite the fact that the majority of Northern Frontier District population voted to join Somalia, Britain decided to maintain it within the map of sure-to-be independent Republic of Kenya. When Britain disregarded the referendum it organized, the Somalia leaders decided to face two formidable enemies at a time, Ethiopia and Britain. Somalia lost the irredentist war against Kenya thanks to British counter insurgency campaigns.

Still, Somalia counted on pan-African ideology that condemned the Berlin Conference style artificial boundary. Both the All-African People's Solidarity Organization Conference of January 1960 and the Afro-Asian People's Solidarity Organizations Conference of April 1960 overwhelmingly supported the Somali people's right of self-determination.

In early 1960s, the anti-colonial atmosphere and solidarity of colonized peoples in lending hands for one another gave a strong boost for the Pan-African movement. Observing the fashion of pan Africanism, Hayla Sillase, who once declared that Ethiopians are not Africans, was ready to dance to the tunes of anti-colonialism and pan-Africanism. For the melody of rhythm, there was this grandiose image of Ethiopia as the trailblazer for the colonized people by entombing the Whiteman's jingoism at Adwa and holding ground to the fascist scourge. By "supporting" Pan-Africanism, the imperialist Hayla Sillase in the garb of pan-Africanism had stolen the stage from protagonists of the movement such as Kwame Nkrumah, Sekou Toure, and Jomo Kenyatta. He carried out a coup on the pan-Africanist "sacred" idea of self-determination in favor of principle of uti possidetis, maintaining a colonial border. A golden rule of pan-Africanism becomes territorial integrity, not self-determination any more. An Assistant Secretary of State for African, Chester Crocker, remarked, *"There was no messing with inherited boundaries. The Latin doctrine of uti possiditis was very Ethiopia in its conception. But it also served the conservative interests of a number of leaders who were desperately insecure about how they were going to keep the new states together"* [italics added] (Wrong, 2005, 205-6). As a consequence, Ethiopia had stolen impetus from Somalis push for the formation of Pan-Somali State.

The OAU came at the crescendo of civil right movement, when the U.S. had a global image problem with its black people. The U.S. caught in a quagmire between two competing goals. On one hand, launching the pan-African body would fuel anti-colonialism wave and destabilize the continent, not to mention raising the temperature at home. On the other hand, it was reluctant to sit idle and watch while the newly emerging states were gravitating towards communism. In all these theaters, a consolation for the U.S. was the idea of its trusted ally, Hayla Sillase, triumphed over "a dangerous radical" [Nkrumah] calling for a "United States of Africa" (Wrong, 2005, 205).

Conjecturing the inevitability of pan-Africanism triumph, the U.S. was already insisting the Emperor to jump on the bandwagon when he was loath to the buoyancy of the movement, and when he was ambivalent about the African-ness of Ethiopia. The U.S. encouraged him to have an interest in Pan-African affairs to moderate its influence (Note by the Executive Secretary to the National Security Council on U.S. Policy toward the Horn of Africa, 1959). Hayla Sillase boosted his image as the pan Africanist and acquired leverage to deal with the West on African matters. His stature and his empire becoming a "capital of Africa" would help the U.S. to carry out its missions in the continent through him.

In 1963, Ambassador Edward Korry, a man who had a reach journalistic background replaced Ambassador Richards. Ambassador Korry was admired for his "dynamic, imaginative and purposeful leadership" (Vestal, 2011, 144). Professor Vestal described him as "intrepid watcher, surpassed commentator, and knowledgeable (ibid). Ambassador Shinn says, "More than any other American chief of mission in Addis Ababa either before or since, he had the greatest impact on U.S. policy towards Ethiopia. He was not only capable ambassador but served there during the high water mark in the relations and at a time when there was frequent tension in the relationship" (Skinner, 2003, 47). He had a strong influence in shaping the policy of the African Bureau. His counter proposal to a G. Mennen Williams report of 1965 might have contributed in the latter's resignation (Noer, 2009, 286 & ff).

Ambassador Korry never had such a terrific personal chemistry with Hayla Sillase. As soon as he assumed his post, two things tested his diplomatic qualities, the Somalia issue and recurrent famines.

While the Emperor was scratching his head over the amount of military aid, there was a famine problem [1963-64] that was making a significant number of Ethiopians scratch their heads. Behind curtains, the ambassador tried to persuade him to reform the exploitative landholding system to alleviate the problem of famine sustainably. Ambassador Shinn wrote Korry's observation in this way, "The U.S. has long been uneasy with Ethiopian land policy. During the imperial period control over the land by large land owners, the Ethiopian Orthodox Church and the government led to exploitative relation between land owners and peasant farmers. The U.S. urged land reform while the emperor refused to change policies" (ibid, 46). His suggestion to make relief aids conditional upon the land reform failed to yield any tangible outcome.

A dilemma was when Washington made food donations contingent upon the agricultural reform; it never pinched the emperor as he was callous about the plight of his people; not to mention that he knew that it was unethical for Washington to indefinitely withhold humanitarian aid from the dying people. If the U.S. applied military aid that had a tooth, there was a fear that the landlord of Kagnew would defect.

Whereas Hayla Sillase refused to listen to the U.S. on famine and land reform issues, on the other hand, he launched a media campaign against the U.S. because of its alleged support for Somalia and his dissatisfaction with the amount of military aid.

After JFK received the Somalia delegation, Hayla Sillase's mood was nothing short of mourning because their reception was ipso facto a betrayal of Ethiopia. The emperor, who despised diplomatic memo except a face-to-face diplomacy, commenced lobbying for a White House visit to restore the status quo ante of diplomatic confidence and military supply. Securing the invitation, he invited Ambassador Korry at his retreat in Dirre Dawa. The rendezvous was not for a civil discussion, but the emperor was loaded for a tongue-lashing. He exploded: "What had the Ethiopian people done to deserve such treatment at the hands of the U.S. Government? It fills our hearts with sorrow" (quoted in Vestal, 2011, 123). Flabbergasted by his undiplomatic tone, some of his advisors tried to cancel the visit, but, as Vestal noted, "Cooler heads prevailed ... and the state visit occurred as scheduled" (ibid). Korry dispatched his assessments of the regime to Washington. He described it as "repressive" and "police state" that disillusioned "increasing numbers of Ethiopians from all classes"(ibid, 121).

Hayla Sillase arrived on October 1, 1963. His host showered him with kind words. The emperor made his trademark dramatic speeches at the White House and the United Nations in his native Amharic language. Then came was discussion on the bilateral security issues. JFK tried to bring up the thorny issues of domestic reforms, which the emperor killed with one word, 'no'. Whichever ways he ruled were divinely mandated; however, he was willing to talk about the weapon he wanted for his rule. Thence, the arms issue and the Somali agenda dominated the talk. The "arms assistance to Somalia," said the emperor, "encouraged Somali irredentism, had caused bloodshed and unrest within Ethiopia, had been particularly harmful because of its timing, and had not precluded communist assistance." President Kennedy responded that aid to Somalia was very small; it was for "civic actions;" and the policy objectives of the aid were "exactly the same as Ethiopian objectives." He indicated that "responding with some assistance; it is possible to increase influence and promote stability," and the U.S. had learned some harsh experiences when it has rejected requests for assistance in such situations." It would reconsider its arms aid to Somalia should either China or the Soviet gave considerable military support for it. Hayla Sillase underscored that "a modus vivendi was necessary between Somalia and Ethiopia and the U.S. must support this." JFK replied, "Ethiopia was the key country in that part of the world and that it was with that in mind that we made our policies" (Memorandum of Conversation, 1963).

Washington goal was striking a golden average between appeasing the landlord of Kagnew without alienating the fragile government of Somalia. The logic was if they offended Somalia, it would invite the influence of the Soviet in the region, which was the nightmarish scenario for the emperor, as well.

This mission of precluding the influence of Communists from the Horn was utter fiasco for Somalia was trapped in a Soviet net. In November 1963, Somalia had decided to take $35 million military support from the Soviet, which was the largest per-capita credit it had given to a foreign country. The U.S. refused to give $9 million Somalia requested (Patman, 1990, 48-49).

Forgetting his mammoth 100 million dollars from the Soviet, Hayla Sillase panicked for Somalia getting a third of what he got and started to press the U.S. to either cancel aid for Somalia or provide him with more aid. Washington was prompt to express "deep regrets and concern of the U.S. government at the reported decision of the Somali Council of Ministers to accept an offer of large-scale Soviet military aid." The U.S. and its allies terminated all the military aid for Somalia to "make the Ethiopians happy" (Memorandum from William H. Brubeck, 1963).

On November 22, 1963, JFK was assassinated. President Lyndon B. Johnson (LBJ), a Texan, who was seen suspiciously by the civil rights advocates, rose to prominence when he pledged to honor a life-passion of Kennedy and signed the Civil Rights Act into law in 1964. LBJ made a name for himself in American history despite his Vietnam chaos tarnished it.

Hayla Sillase was the only African head of state to attend JFK's funeral. He knew how to use every window of opportunity he found to press for additional weapons. The U.S. said no. He unleashed his surrogate for blackmailing. "The United States must either give us the assistance we require," said Defense Minister Marid Mangasha. Otherwise, "we might have to deal with the Devil (the Soviet) himself to save our country" (quoted in Wrong, 2005, 214).

Once again, Hayla Sillase decided to play the Cold War card. In 1964, the first Premier of the People's Republic of China Zhou Enlai came to Africa declaring the continent "ripe for revolution" (Lyons, 1994, 247). To dismay of the U.S., he received a warm welcome in Addis Ababa. The emperor also went to Moscow to seek military assistance. The Soviet was reluctant to give him more aids otherwise he would cancel Kagnew agreement with the U.S. Not only it refused to cancel the support for Somalia, but also it began to build radar installations and a naval base in Somalia to boost its military presence in the region.

Because of the diplomatic reorientation of the emperor, a certain influential journalist had predicted an apocalypse of communist takeover of the continent:

> One of the most important showdowns between East and West is in the making of Ethiopia and adjacent East Africa. Upon its outcome may depend whether the United States must stand behind those who have supported it in the past—in this case Emperor Haile Selassie. It cannot ride two horses going in opposite directions by also trying to appease Nasser's Arab friends in East Africa. This issue is immediate, and decisions in the nature of more military support for Ethiopia will have to be made now. Otherwise we may well find Africa starting to go the way of the Far East. Haile Selassie has great prestige in Africa. (Pearson, 1964).

Following the Soviet military investments in Somalia, U.S. interests in the Kagnew station had enlarged considerably. So did the level of cooperation between the U.S. and Ethiopia.

Thanks to Cold War rivalries, the Soviet armed Somalia to teeth. So did the U.S. for Ethiopia. Therefore, the 1964 border conflict between Somalia and Ethiopia transformed from an insurgency (counterinsurgency) to a conventional war. Ethiopia's reaction to a military attack from Somalia was fierce. Somalia declared the state of emergency throughout the country. Ethiopia also launched a clandestine Somali-language radio making her among the first African states to use such a radio (see, Hydén et al., 2003, 87). The scale of retaliation created a fear that Ethiopia might seize the entire Somalia to achieve historic claim (Schraeder, 1996, 128). The fear was palpable in light of an Ethiopian ambassador to the U.S. declaration, "Somalia never existed as a nation… Somalia is a creation as recent as four years ago. It is also a matter of history that the area was part and parcel of Ethiopia" (Berhanou, 1964).

The national security analysis noted, "The basic problem for the US is to maintain our strategic interests in Ethiopia while preventing a substantial Soviet foothold in Somalia." Proving unconditional support for Ethiopia in a conflict with a Soviet-armed Somalia only aggravates the basic ethnic and tribal tensions in the area. The U.S. even lacked the gumption to facilitate a dialogue between the belligerents as it wanted to pass the burden of finding a solution to Africans. A telegram from the State Department says, "We differentiate between two problems, primarily African one of Ethiopian-

Somali crisis for which burden should be shifted to Africans" (Telegram from the Department of State to the Embassy in Somalia, February 20, 1964). Professor Lyons (1994, 245) explains Johnson's administration policy of "keeping Africa off the agenda" in this manner.

> Africa occupied a peripheral position on Johnson's list of priorities, and the president sought to avoid the diversion of attention or resources to the continent. […] From Johnson's perspective, Africa was best kept on the back burner, handled by the State Department bureaucracy or ignored as much as possible. Africa was the farthest corner of the world to Johnson, the place to threaten to send indiscreet officials who drew his ire.

By threatening to withhold the military assistance, the U.S. forced Ethiopia to stop the air raids (Schraeder, 1996, 128). However, it neither advised the emperor to scale down his counter insurgency measures nor did it advise him to ameliorate the socio-economic condition of Ogaden-Somalis. A Telegram from the Department of State to the Embassy in Somalia, on January 21, 1964, said, 'we have been trying to persuade His Imperial Majesty that purely military solution not answer Ogaden question and encourage him to embark on economic and on social measures to improve the conditions of Ogaden Somalis'. Contrarily, the United States sent four, twelve team member mobile training teams (MTTs) to Ogaden to train the Ethiopian army in a successful counterinsurgency strategy. The motivation for the training was the U.S. "desire to reassure the Emperor that we [the U.S.] appreciate the seriousness of his internal security problem posed by the Ogaden Somalis" (Agyeman-Duah, 1994, 161).

No matter how it locked in the incessant wars with its neighbors, a democratic vibrancy was highly visible in Somalia. In 1964, it conducted a parliamentary election that featured 18 parties.

Expansion of Kagnew and Escalations of Turmoil in Ethiopia

As I mentioned earlier, the escalations of Cold War antagonisms in the region, the U.S. interests in the Kagnew station had grown exponentially. To enhance U.S. defense in the area, the U.S. was planning to build a highly clandestine project called Stonehouse project at the station, which meant erecting of two monumental parabolic antennas, an equivalent of fifteen stories high (Lefebvre, 1991, 122). 'The biggest dish, 150 feet wide, 6,000 tons and worth $600,000, was estimated, at the time, to be largest movable object ever built" (Wrong, 2005, 218). The Project contained 185 buildings, 700 antennae, spread on 3,400 acres of land, and visible from 30 miles away (ibid). The official version of the project was "to conduct research in satellite communication" but the hidden goal was "to intercept Soviet space telemetry and aid in the development of U.S. ballistic missiles" (Lefebvre, 1991, 122).

Located at the same longitude with a Soviet base in Crimean, the Stonehouse project offered the chance to monitor and intercept Soviet spacecraft (Wrong, 2005, 220).

Consenting to the known unknown with all its risks and oppositions, the generous hand of America unfolded to Hayla Sillase further. The benefits trickled down immediately one after another. The military aid jumped by more than two folds, from 8.9 million dollars to 18.2 million, and economic aid increased from $9.2 to $19 million (Schraeder, 1996, 130). The U.S. donated to Ethiopia 12 supersonic jet fighter called F-5 Freedom aircrafts, which made Ethiopia the first in the sub-Saharan Africa and among a handful of the third world nations to acquire them. The operation at Kagnew reached all-time high. At its heyday, there were about 7,000 U.S. civilians and military personnel in Ethiopia, including 3,500 at Kagnew station by May 1964 (Schraeder, 1996; Lefebvre, 1991; Wrong, 2005).

The growth of aid took place when Ethiopia was fighting with Somalia and suffering from lack of human rights protections. The U.S. knew all these. Its ambassador called Hayla Sillase's rule 'repressive' and 'police state' and disliked by 'all classes of citizens'. In 1965, Ethiopian ambassador to the U.S. Berhanu Dinqa, who was among a handful of 1960 bloody coup survivors and who related to the emperor by marriage, resigned his post in opposition to his one-man rule and to lead a "struggle for freedom." He said this for his resignation:

> I am in a free country where I can breathe, speak and write freely while my people, haunted by fear of arrest or punishment, impose upon themselves the limitation to express their human rights. This limitation and their hunger for freedom cannot be eternal. Herbert Hoover once made this living observation: 'The spark of liberty in the mind and spirit of man cannot be long extinguished; it will break into flames that will destroy every coercion which seems to limit it.' To this end, I appeal to all freedom-loving people to write to the emperor urging him NOT to deny the right of the people to air their grievances, and to respect the constitution which he himself claimed to have granted of his own free will and accord (Pearson, 1965).

"The country is full of criticism and bitterness," said Berhanu, "The veil is too thin to shield this fraud." "This is the time to test its sincerity" (ibid). His resignation generated a widespread, almost universal support, from Ethiopian students abroad. Conversely, this never discouraged the emperor from pushing with his single-handed style of rule. Instead, he escalated his over-centralization and over-consolidation power amidst an outcry for the political and cultural space thanks to the U.S. benefactions. The subsequent commentary will try to highlight some of the burning domestic problems.

Abolishing of *Macha-Tulama* Association

Frustrations had also reached a boiling point in all corners of Ethiopia. Hayla Sillase decided to close the door on, all types of, peaceful political organizations and movements. The best case to demonstrate a lack of political space was a case of *Macha-Tulama* Self-help Association. Before I begin commenting on this, it is a matter of utter necessity to shed some light on conditions of the Oromo people, at the time, in a piecemeal fashion to have a good picture of the matter.

The Oromos are the single largest ethnic group, and a "minoritized majority" par excellence in the empire. They inhabit in all but two provinces of the country. They extend from the Kenyan border in the south to Tigray province in the north, to the Ogaden border in the east to the Sudan border in the west, and, they occupy the fertile areas in the country. The Oromo country, Oromiya, is the skeleton and flesh of the Ethiopian economy. The Oromos are among the most victimized, neglected, and exploited people since the creation of the empire. They were the only nation the empire prohibited their language. In short, Oromos were-and-are a living witness of the burden of the Ethiopian rule.

Hayla Sillase pursued total assimilation of the Oromo people. This went to the extent of rechristening indigenous names of Oromo towns and urban centers.[1] An economic, a geographic, and a linguistic centrality of Oromo to the empire justify herculean assimilation policy towards them. Thus, first and foremost, the Abyssinians considered the Oromos a threat, an existential threat, to their hegemony because of their sheer numbers. Secondly, an imperative of making Amharic a majority language militated the minoritizing of the Oromo language and Amharization (Ethiopianization) necessitated the de-Oromization.

Even for those Oromos who fully assimilated to achieve the Abyssinian dream, their chance was like a camel passing through the eye of a needle. Unlike the empire wished, the Oromos were not complacent with second class citizenship forever. In this context, the *Macha-Tulama* Self-help Association came into being, in 1963, to promote development and education of the Oromo people so that they would be self-reliant and free from government debilitating system. It was formed in "reaction to an unbridled policy of Amharization" and the "realization of the legal, economic, political,

---

[1] Adama was christened Nazareth (of Jesus); Bishoftu was christened Dabra Zayt, an equilibrium of Orthodox fasting; Kuku was christened Hagara Maryam [a land of Mary]; Adola was christened Kibra Mangist [the Glory of Kings]; Ambo named Hagara Hiwot, Waliso was named Tsiyon (Zion), Chiro named Asaba-Tafari, and so many countless cases of renaming.

social and cultural policies," which crippled the upward mobility of the educated and assimilated Oromos (Mohammed, 1999, 239).

Despite a myriad of hurdles, it became a model for an overnight success because the educated urbanites, private soldiers, civilian officials, business and religious leaders flocked to it. This "provided the association with their skills, knowledge, organizational capacities, and leadership qualities, and in the process they transformed what started as self-help organizations into a pan-Oromo movement with huge membership and branch offices all over Oromia" (ibid).

The awakening of Oromos sent a shock wave of fear in the imperial inner circle. They knew a critical failure of their ambitious assimilation policy. One of such incident was a case of General Taddasa Birru, a decorated anti-fascist hero, a man who played a leading role in foiling the 1960 coup[1], a man who trained an icon of black race (Nelson Mandela)[2], and a man who was an Oromo by blood but an Amhara by psychology. Because of his ardent Amhara nationalism, he was adamant to join the education of his native people even in a language of the ruling class until he yielded after several entreaties from Oromo elders, who wanted to use him as a symbol of inspiration.[3] Symbolism of opting for the most assimilated man speaks for itself; they were not anti-Ethiopian, in essence.

---

[1] Taddasa Birru was a commander of the mobile Ethiopian Special Police Force, an equivalent of Hayla Sillase's Kamikaze, who, upon learning the coup of 1960, marched into Addis Ababa under the slogan, 'Let us sacrifice ourselves for our beloved emperor!'

[2] Mandela wrote this about a piece of advice he got from Taddasa while he was in Ethiopia in 1960s. "I was lectured on military science by colonel Tadesse, who was also assistant commissioner of police and had been instrumental in foiling a recent coup against the emperor." He also says, "In my study sessions, Colonel Tadesse discussed matters such as how to create a guerilla force, how to command an army, and how to enforce discipline. One evening, during supper, Colonel Tadesse said to me, 'Now Mandela you are creating a liberation army not a conventional capitalist army. A liberation army is an egalitarian army. You must treat your men entirely differently than you would in a capitalist army. When you are on duty, you must exercise your authority with assurance and control. This is no different from a capitalist command. But when you are off duty, you must conduct yourself on the basis of perfect equality, even with the lowliest soldier. You must eat what they eat; you must not take your food in your office, but eat with them, drink with them, not isolate yourself.'" Nelson Mandela, Long Walk to Freedom: The Autobiography of Nelson Mandela (New York: Little, Brown and Company, 1995).

[3] Taddasa was an assistant police commissioner and the chairman of the national literacy campaign at the time

But, what Taddasa heard from the Prime Minister of Hayla Sillase, Aklilu Habtawald, was a rude awakening for him, a life changing experience, which changed him from the wholeheartedly assimilated Ethiopian patriot into the father of modern Oromo nationalism. Assuming that the indistinguishable General was his fellow Amhara personage, he earnestly advised him that 'teaching the Oromos [in Amharic] is an ocean whose wave could flood them' (Mohammed, 1999, 240).

General Taddasa Birru (left) and Nelson Mandala. Author: Unknown.

This turned his worldview upside down, for the nation he loved so much, never loved him back, and for the throne he almost vanished for wanted to keep his people under literacy embargo. He shaded his Amhara mask, a transition from pseudo persona (camouflage) to real self, from self-despise to self-respect, from subservience to assertiveness, and from accepting second class status to yearning for equality and freedom. For choosing to educate his people, the empire dealt a *coup de grace* to his colorful military career. He was fired. The decision embittered him. He was more committed than ever to become the mouthpiece of his unhappy people. Thus, the association became a popular movement and a semblance of political party in the party-less imperial system.

Though the association came into existence in accordance with law of the land, it violated the Hayla Sillase's linguicide policy since the members held their first public meeting in a prohibited language. The regime accused the proponents of the association of inciting tribal tensions, endangering the unity of the country and promoting disloyalty to the throne. Under the pretext of a bomb detonation in an Addis Ababa cinema, which government agents choreographed, the government outlawed the association. In a trial, which was described as a mockery of justice, a court martial found more than 100 of its prominent members, guilty based on the dubious evidences and confessions that the police extorted through torture and duress. Norma J. Singer demonstrated the trial in this condition:

> In a trial (from 1967-8), which was partly observed by the representatives of the International Commission of Jurists, judge attempted to dismiss the case, but he was himself dismissed from his post. Two defense lawyers were fined by a new judge (military Colonel with no legal experience) and severely warned. Defendants were not allowed choose their own lawyers and were kept in solitary confinement without access to lawyers until the trial, which was mainly in the closed court. Several witnesses, claiming that they had been tortured, tried without access to withdraw their statement against the accused. They alleged they had been deprived of food for three days, then interrogated continuously for a week without being allowed to keep sleep or go to the toilet. They stated that thy were put in separate lice infested cells, bound hand and foot, beaten and forced to drink boiling hot drinks, swung from their arms until blood dripped, tortured by electric shock and other means (quoted in Holcomb and Ibssa, 1990, 297-298.).

Due to the severity of torture, some of the accused men were unable to attend the trial and tried in absentia. Mammo Mazammir, a law student at Hayla Sillase I University, was executed; and Taddasa Birru was imprisoned to life sentence; and Hayla Maryam Gammada, a chief ideologue and initiator of the association was condemned to long-term imprisonment. Ironically, the government also imprisoned witnesses for the prosecution and the defense after the trial (Gilkes, 1975, 226). Contrary to wishes of the Empire, this placed the Oromo nationalism on the Ethiopian political map.

In all these, one would wonder U.S. response to a shrinking of the already slim political space in Ethiopia. Came at a heyday of cooperation between Addis Ababa and the U.S, Washington chose silence. Contrarily, it increased military and economic assistances to the regime once the peaceful resistance metastasized into violence.

As Donham and James (1986, 37) said, "The nature of Ethiopian States provided almost no means for demands at the periphery to be translated into action at the center. Instead, the center principally relied upon force, and peoples in the periphery faced a limited set of options—'quietism, partial assimilation through the few inadequate available channels, or revolt'." For a while, the association tried to operate clandestinely. But an attempted to operate underground was like a dictum about an elephant passing through the eye of a needle because of the police-state nature of the Ethiopian Empire. When these efforts proved fruitless, some of its protagonists opted for belligerency. Such an instance was a man called Sheikh Hussein, the former associate of Taddasa Birru, who established a rebel group called an Oromo Liberation Front in mid-1960s in Hararghe area (De Waal, 1991, 69). The prohibition was fermentation for a Bale peasant rebellion that rattled Hayla Sillase's government for a decade in Bale and Borana areas.

In the meantime, Somalia launched an Oromo language Radio from Mogadishu to counter the Ethiopian clandestine radio. It was destined to galvanize the support of the Muslim Oromos against the Ethiopian rule within the framework of the Somali nationalism (Marcus, 1994, 179). Came at the time when Ethiopia ridicules that broadcast in Oromo breaks radio, and when the Ethiopian government banned the Oromo language, the radio program catered for the Muslim Oromos even turned out to be popular among protestant Oromos in the Western Oromiya (Leenco, 1999, 176). Hayla Sillase, in contravention of his linguicide policy, forced to launch a radio broadcast in Afaan Oromoo from Harar, in 1967, to counter the Somali propaganda. Contrarily, this emboldened the mass who felt they were reaping of the fruit of their resistance. It also increased their self-awareness and identifications with their culture as opposed to with an alien culture.

Amidst this, Hayla Sillase tried to tighten his hold on regional incomes by passing a modern tax system [land registration and measurement] to finish off the power of the landed nobility. His house of nobilities, a rubberstamp parliament, shifted their burden to peasants (Ofcansky and Berry, 2004, 72). Bale peasants of the southern Oromiya, under the leadership of Waqo Gutu, revolted rejecting harsh taxation of their lands and live stocks, and restriction of their free movements in search of pasture and water. A new law poured salt on their gaping wounds created by harsh landholding system in place. Bale became a leader, among all provinces, for the land confiscated on the ground of tax default and political crimes while it was the least developed and the worst served of all the provinces (Markakis, 2011, 150). There was neither a hospital nor single doctor in the province, a second largest in the country. As Gebru (1991, 133) noted, "Without roads and telecommunication facilities until the late 1960s, Bale was regarded as a hardship post where tax collectors, custom officers, judges and inspectors could live on their prerequisite, using methods closely approaching those of highway robbers."

The government confiscated almost five million hectares of arable land and granted "to dignitaries from the civil and military services" (ibid, 132). Resentments at the close-fisted Amhara rule that robbed their resources to the advantage of the Amhara elites and enrich their regions were intensifying. A peasants' leader spoke of the fermentation of rebellion turmoil in such melancholy words:

> Our history has been of deprivation and misery, story of endless tragedy. In our country, we have lived as aliens and slaves, deprived of our lands and discriminated against on the grounds of our tribal and religious identities (ibid, 134).

A certain peasants' leader lamented,

> Innumerable crimes that have not been committed by the European colonialists on the African peoples have been perpetuated upon us (ibid, 131).

Outright rejections of their Islamic faith and cultures, punitive land and taxation laws, spilling effect of the whirlwind of conflict between Israel and Arabs, abolishing of the *Macha-Tulama* association, the assertive Somalia foreign policy threw an impetus behind the revolt.

The emperor sought no compromise to address their legitimate grievances. Thus, violence was a weapon of choice to crash the rebellion (Marcus, 1994). At this junction, the highly trained segment of Ethiopian army was busy with countering insurgents in Eritrea, which controlled most of the barren lowlands and coastal areas of Eritrea. An Amhara governor of Bale, Warku Inqwa Selassie, marched police, Territorial Army, and local guards, and unpaid volunteers from local naftanya populace, who counted on enriching themselves by plundering the rebelled areas (Markakis, 2011, 151). He vowed to inflict the harshest punishment on "thoughtless nomads" (Gebru Tareke, 1991, 137). Contrarily, they repelled a series of onslaughts and controlled more areas. The crisis continued unabated.

Similarly, the northern part of the country, which was immune to the draconian landholding system, unlike the peripheral areas, felt for the first time their excruciating pain. This was particularly so in Gojjam, where the reform proved to be a fiasco. Unlike the Bale case, the emperor pulled out his troops; stopped the implementation of the law, and dropped all arrears of taxation going back to 1940 (Ofcansky & Berry, 2004, 72).

General Waqo Gutu Usu (left). Waqo was born in 1942 from the Rayitu clan of Arsi in Madda Walabu, Bale. He led the struggle of his people until his death in 2006. He also lived as a refuge in Somalia and Kenya. A picture to the right was taken while he was in Malindi, Kenya, with his colleague, Abba Nagesso (right), in 1998. Image courtesy of General Waqo Gutu family and Hassan Kilisi.

Religious Oppressions

"Hagar yagara naw, haymanot yagill naw" [A country belongs to all and religion is a personal matter]. This is a classical adage embodying tolerance and coexistence between various religions attributed to the repertoire of the emperor. Beyond this superficial rhetoric of Ethiopian semantic gymnastics (of hidden meanings) laid deeper contradictions and flaws within the Ethiopian polity, and there were bitter realities for religious adherents other than the Orthodox Christians. To establish the historical record straight, Hayla Sillase neither proscribed the worship of Islam nor imposed the conversion of Islam, unlike his predecessors, but he "undermined Islam and Muslims through purposeful and systematic disregard" (Levtzion, 2012, 240). He neglected Muslims since his empire, as he told to the U.S. Congress, was all about the "largest Christian State in the Middle East."

As we discussed in previous chapters, the Ethiopian Orthodox Church was the only religion recognized in the constitution, and it used to manufacture a legitimacy fiction for the ruling class. It was an official state church, a possessor of massive asset, and a recipient of the state largesse. Among other things, it controlled a third of the empire arable land; it had legal personality under the Ethiopian Civil Code; it had the status of tax exemption for its property and income, and, it received the educational subsidies (Markakis, 2011).

Religion is the dominant and constant factor in life and culture of Abyssinia. Asked to define himself, he goes by the boundary of his parish, and his church is the center of his universe. Contrarily, followers of other religions hardly enjoyed the right to identify themselves with their religions. In fact, when people clashed and severed ties, the analogy is straightforward, and the dichotomy is black and white: 'They became Muslim and Christian' (ibid, 33).

Hence, the Muslims, a half of the population of the Empire, were unrecognized. They were considered as invaders, the people who followed footsteps of the Conqueror, Ahmad Grany, and stayed behind after he lost battles. As Hagai Erlikh captured, they were treated as 'aliens who are only tolerated thanks to the altruism and hospitality of Ethiopians' (Erlikh, 2007, 215). Thus, the empire characterized Muslims as foreigners residing in Ethiopia, and, Islamic festivals as alien holidays, not the official holidays of the country (Levtzion, 2012; Markakis, 2011; Leenco, 1999; Østebø, 2011; Teshale, 1995). The Muslims had to work on Friday and observed Sunday as a holiday. Besides, the empire discouraged promotion of Islam and assigned foreign missionaries to proselytize in their areas (Levtzion, 2012, 240). They were denied the right to build religious gatherings and burial places. Asked to identify a business or a professional opportunity, Muslim entrepreneurs had to come up with commerce or crafts or tax collection since they were unwelcome in the administration, civil service, schools, media, justice, military, and so on. Nor they think of farming since they were foreclosed from land ownership, the main means of livelihood. An Abyssinian proverb goes: "The sky has no pillar, the Muslim has no land" (Markakis, 2011, 33). Even they did not have the right to use land. A proverb says, "The sky has no pillar. The Muslim has no rist [land use]" (Donham and James, 1986, 254).

Because they were denied the right to teach their children in Arabic, the language of their faith, they had to send their children to clergy-run-schools or public schools that they feared to compromise their religious identity. Some families refused to send their children to these schools lest they would be proselytized or converted. To save their religious identity from assimilation and domination, they retreated from the world of literacy, public squares and politics. To this day, Muslims are disengaged from the political process in Ethiopia.

The massive codifications of 1960s neither accommodated the values of Muslim populations nor did the government consult them on reconciling the Western imported values with their cultures. According to Réne David, the main drafter of the Civil Code, "the Civil Code was made for the more advanced populations of Ethiopia and Eritrea" (quoted in Markakis, 2011, 117). In other words, it was codified for Christians. Indeed, Muslims' customs were victims of wholesale abrogation encapsulated in the Civil Code and Criminal Code. Tacitly, a new law abolished the Muslim court established by Mussolini and recognized by the emperor after his restoration. Muslims repetitive entreaties to the monarch for the religious and cultural rights produced no fruition (ibid). In a nutshell, a certain observer noted, "apart from the Muslims of Spain no other Muslim people has [sic] suffered over the centuries such atrocities as the Muslim of Ethiopia" (quoted in Robinson, 2004, 121).

Unlike the quote of "a country belongs to all and religion is a personal matter," it was a fear mongering about Muslims that Hayla Sillase used to galvanize his traditional support base and secure external legitimacy for the existence of his throne. Islam was associated with pan-Arabism (Nasserism), Ahmad Grany, Eritrean secessionists, the irredentist Somalia, the Bale rebellion, and even to Communism. To that effect U.S. national intelligence commentary wrote the rationale of Ethiopia alliance with the U.S. in this way: "The dominant group in the country would still see itself as defending a Christian bastion against Moslems whose support from the Communist powers could only be balanced by aid for Ethiopia from the West" (National Intelligence Estimate 75/76-70, 1970).

Let alone Islam, in the empire had never been cordial with protestant followers that spread in peripheral areas. A "secondhand religion," a "wheat imported religion," "an alien religion" were some of scornful appellations given to them (Mersha, 2005, 204). As a consequence, they neither had a privilege to participate in the politics of the empire, nor did they enjoy equal rights with their fellow Orthodox Christians.

Indigenous beliefs were totally unwanted and unacknowledged part of national persona. Their followers were excoriated as "heathens" who had to be civilized to be Ethiopians. It was imperative for their educated sons to embrace "Orthodox Christianity" to claim that he is 'modern (zamanawi)', 'civilized (yasalatane)', 'educated (yatamare)' (Donham, 1986, 128). An account of a certain Oromo man was emblematic of that cultural milieu:

> I was baptized as a young man in the Ethiopian Orthodox Church. It was not because I believed in Jesus. Many people were baptized at the time. It was modern or should we say civilized. The Amhara were Christians and civilized. We were pagans and uncivilized. We wanted to be like Amhara. They were the rulers. We were peasants. We tried to look like them (ibid).

The Empire (the Orthodox Christianity), protestant missioners, and Muslims demonized and bullied these non-institutionalized, pacific, and harmonious religions with nature. Their land was as religious no-man's land for the Orthodox, Muslim, Protestant missionaries. They were allowed to proselytize them at liberty, which was often orchestrated by abuses such as despising their culture, witch-hunting, and attacking people possessed with spirits. The government converted the herculean protestant missioners, at proselyting, into being the catalyst of the assimilation policy since it instructed them to conduct preaching and teaching only in Amharic. Thus, they colonized the mind of indigenous believers at two levels: firstly, at the spiritual level, to the alien religion; and secondly, at the national level, to "the Ethiopian colonial system" through their curricula.

The subsequent altercation between the Borana ruler and the emperor was emblematic of a bulling of worshippers of indigenous faith:

> In the mid-1950s, Emperor Haile Sellassie summoned the then Boorana Abbaa Gadaa Madha Galma (1952-60) to consult on ways of fully integrating the Boorana into the modern Ethiopian government. The men discussed the allegiance of the Boorana to the qaalluu and Oromo traditional religion. The emperor told Madha Galma that every Ethiopian has religious freedom but that the Boorana should consider abandoning the Oromo indigenous religion, which he described as a sign of backwardness, and converting either to Christianity or Islam.

The Borana leader responded:

> I am not bestowed with authority to direct the Boorana to become [Orthodox] Christians or Muslims. Please don't pretend that you

summoned me here for consultation. Tell me the truth that you called me to your palace to kill me. Accepting death for truth is to be immortalized; let history be made (quoted in Gebissa, 2012).

It was this pressure by the state that pushed Borana to embrace Islam, a religion of their Somali neighbor. There is a Borana "prophecy that Borana people should prefer Islam to other religion when the worst days come." The logic for the preference of Islam was easy; thanks to the Sufism doctrine, there was a room for accommodating Borana culture.[1]

Beta Israel (House of Israel), who practiced early variants of Judaism, went through similar discriminations on account of their faith. They neither had a right to hold office nor own land because they were the "exiles," Falasha. However, the emperor styled himself 'Lion of Judah; they extremely suffered under his administration. Andrea Stanton indicated, "The Falasha made a special appeal to Emperor Haile Selassie in late 1950s, enumerating 13 cases of murder of Jews accused of sorcery and numerous examples of arson, degradation of cemeteries, evictions, extreme rent charges and similar abuses. No real help was provided" (Stanton, 2012, 275-276). The emperor neither stopped their persecutions nor did permit, as a matter of pride, their exodus to Israel.

What was the response of the United States to the religious oppression in Ethiopia? Firstly, the U.S. had a clear picture about the problem. The U.S. intelligence report says this on the issue: "The Moslem and animist peoples, who together constitute a majority of the population, dislike the ruling Amharas and feel little allegiance to the Empire. They have failed to gain much materially from incorporation in Ethiopia." The same report concluded that Christian Ethiopians would seek the support of the West against the Communist supported Muslims (National Intelligence Estimate 75/76-70, 1970). Similarly, most of the National Security reports were obsessed with and 'disturbed by the Egyptian propaganda directed at the Muslim populations of Ethiopia'. In consequence, the fears that Muslims might "make common cause with Muslims worldwide" got more attention than their plights in Ethiopia (White, 2005, 56).

---

[1] The Borana saying goes: 'Yoo Islaantee, Boorantiittiin akkuma ofiiti' [When one converts to Islam, the Borana identity remains intact] (Ibrahim, 2006, 69). Günther Schlee says, "Borana define their (non-Islamic) gada system and the whole of customary law with a reference to Islam." He had similar observation with the Gabra Oromos who espouse that gada is the system established upon the foundation of "the orders of the Muslim Sheikh." Thus, they maintained their Oromo identity since gada is the most marvelous thing next to the Qur'an, a basis of Islamic law (Schlee, 1998, 144).

Washington Insiders' Whispers and a Secret Plan

So far, we saw how the peasant upheavals rocked the authority of the monarch and how he pacified through vindictive measures. We also had a glimpse at how the communist expansion in the Horn alarmed the United States. We also touched how the amount of interdependence and cooperation between the U.S. and Ethiopia grew significantly following the Stonehouse project. Above all, we analyzed how the U.S. saved the throne of its staunch ally during the palace coup of 1960.

Although Washington shepherded Hayla Sillase from domestic upheavals, its dissatisfaction with his recalcitrance to address domestic problems was evident. According to my review of the national security papers, "rigid," "unchangeable," "obstacle for change," "old school," "incompetent," "difficult," "embarrassing" and "repressive" were some of the adjectives used to describe his leadership. From the very resumption of diplomatic relationship during the Second World War, United States diplomats did not like his government record on tackling the issues of the people. In 1944, a U.S. representative criticized his administration as an administration of 'corrupt go getters' (Paulos, 2006, 138). In 1956, Ambassador Joseph Simonson described it as a 'virtual feudal' that thrived on the 'ruthless exploitation of peasant' (ibid). A United States representative in Addis Ababa had the audacity to equate the nature of his administration to nothing but 'semi-fascist (ibid). Despite the clear understanding of weaknesses of his rule, the U.S. was unwilling or unable to address it. Paulos Milkias articulates this matter follows: "U.S. interests outweighed the plights of the Ethiopian people. Thus, no matter what kind of regime ruled the country, the United States was determined to insulate Ethiopia 'against international communism' and any 'subversive efforts to overthrow' it. Ethiopia was also 'to be prevented from any kind of connection, relationship (or) dependency on the Sino-Soviet bloc' (ibid).

Assurance against the expansion of communism and subversion from within to topple the regime came without any string attached to it. Hence, Ethiopia enjoyed considerable diplomatic and military support regardless of the regime's engagement in egregious and widespread violations of human rights with impunity.

Coincided with upheavals in Ethiopia were the escalations of the Cold War rivalry in the region because of the Soviet increased visibility in the region, not to mention the psychological impact of Moscow's first spacecraft soft landing on the Moon in 1966. To enhance U.S. defense in the area, Washington was considering making additional investments in the Stonehouse project at Kagnew meant to intercept Soviet satellites and develop ballistic missiles. The growth of uncertainties in Ethiopia stood as a stumbling block for the U.S. to make further investment in the station.

Thence, the tranquility of the throne of the emperor was to the best interest of the U.S. The erstwhile reluctant patron [to press the emperor for moderation and accommodations over his domestic demands] got a reason to worry when its national security interest was at stake. Realizing a recipe for another coup, some Washington policy makers were asking the possibility of the monarchy to reform itself to thwart another coup.

On February 8, 1966, Robert Komer, the President's Deputy Special Assistant for National Security Affairs noted "that the rule of the Emperor in Ethiopia is in growing jeopardy" because of widespread 'criticism at all levels—even from hitherto loyal sources.' He pondered, "Don't we have some of the essential ingredients of another coup?" He asked the Assistance Secretary for African Affairs G. Mennen Williams, "Would there be any merit in a quite U.S. campaign to convince the emperor of the need for some quick domestic reforms designed to eliminate the most threatening complaints?" In essence, he was considering the possibility of making the emperor a 'modern reformist monarch'. His goal was starting from a small since a quick domestic reform would provide an opportunity to buy an extra time for fundamental reforms. He expressed his interest to bring the matter to the attention of the president so that he would give advice to the emperor, as a message from one statesman to another. Considered was also the possibility of giving "a frank appraisal of the situation" to the Ethiopian Ambassador "if he has the Emperor's confidence." Komer closed his letter saying, "I'm sure you'd agree that political stability in Ethiopia is most important to us. I'd be happy to join you in finding ways to help maintain it." (Memorandum from the President's Deputy Special Assistant for National Security Affairs (Komer) to the Assistant Secretary of State for African Affairs (Williams), February 8, 1966).

A response of Williams came on February 11, 1966. He came with a pessimistic response; even though, he could not agree more with him on 'certainty of reasons to worry about the coup possibilities'. He indicated, "It is becoming increasingly difficult to believe that anything or anyone can persuade the Emperor at this stage of his career to anything against his 'better' judgment." He was of mind that there was no room for change in the emperor's world if it would not help him to reinforce his power. In his words, "[The] Emperor belongs to a much older generation and the underlying feel that domestic reforms, instead of strengthening his own position, would strike at the heart of the personal power, as indeed they probably would." Williams also rejected the idea of using "the trump of a Presidential message" to urge the monarch on domestic reforms.

He underlined that Ambassador Korry held talks with the emperor, who dismissed the suggested reforms as unviable propositions. "[I] heard this song before," the emperor insisted, "time and experience were essentials to all sure progress." Williams concluded that "his net impression was clearly of a man who after almost 50 years in power was confident he knew how to deal with the present crisis." In the same way, disregarding the palpable dangers, Ambassador Ed, who consistently underscored the need for reforms, infamously determined that "the Emperor will probably stay on top" (Memorandum from the Assistant Secretary of State for African Affairs (Williams) to the President's Deputy Special Assistant for National Security Affairs (Komer), February 11, 1966.)

On February 18, 1966, Komer wrote a second memorandum to the Williams. He stressed, "I appreciate your reply of February 11, but feel that our dilemma in Ethiopia is that if we don't take a few risks now we'll risk a lot more trouble later." He expounded: "True, past experience tends to indicate that the Emperor 'will probably stay on top' over the short-term. But how long is he likely to be around?" He underlined, "our interest would certainly be better served by a controlled evolution than chaotic political upheavals when HIM [His Imperial Majesty] dies, or even before" because "the situation calls for an effort now to try and influence events and the risks of moving now seem to me less than those in doing nothing." Komer asked Williams, 'Why not at least come up with a package of reforms designed (a) to reduce the current widespread disaffection among key elements of the population and (b) to increase the likelihood of gradual rather than violent change?' He stressed reaching out to the emperor through "some high-level personage" to convince him on the need for reforming his embattled government. He came up with Governor W. A. Harriman, Under Secretary of State for Political Affairs. In his claim, they were co-equal in statesmanship, and they belonged to the same generation. Thus, the emperor would be impressed if they make a number one trouble-shooter to see him. Komer also mentioned the success of the governor in convincing him to deny recognition to the People's Republic of China. He prophesized, "If the present pattern continues in Ethiopia, our stake there will be in serious jeopardy." "The lack of alternatives suggests that a timely effort to stave of trouble would be worth taking, even if its chances of success are slight," concluded Komer (Memorandum from the President's Deputy Special Assistant for National Security Affairs (Komer) to the Assistant Secretary of State for African Affairs (Williams), February 18, 1966).

A National Security Council specialist on the Sub-Saharan African Affairs Ulric Haynes also bolstered his concerns. He clearly underlined a ticking time bomb for U.S. security unless the domestic crisis in Ethiopia addressed. Criticizing a "short-sighted approach," he predicted that the "explosion in Ethiopia" was not 'the question of "whether" but the question of "when." "Therefore, an immediate effort to convince the Emperor to make necessary reforms had to be made, no matter how slim the chances" (quoted in Memorandum from the Assistant Secretary of State for African Affairs (Williams) to the President's Deputy Special Assistant for National Security Affairs (Komer), February 11, 1966).

However, these heated debates hardly translated into a concrete policy action. On the other side, a CIA's memorandum of March 31, 1966 said, "Haile Selassie still reigns as [the] supreme authority in Ethiopia, but his declining vigor, his absorption in external affairs, and the growing complexity of government are leading to general immobility of the Imperial system." Noticing Emperor's disinterest "to change the system in any meaningful way," it predicted the growth of "internal discontent, continued insurgency in the provinces, and demands on the US for more military aid." As always, it predicted the crisis after the death of the emperor and failed to foresee dangers that would consume his throne (Prospects for Ethiopia, March 31, 1966).

For the U.S. that strongly obsessed with crisis on the death of the emperor, the fact that he was adamant to name the successor was particularly disappointing. In the words of Spencer, 'The emperor immobilism finally turned him into a 20th Louis XV—*Après moi le déluge*' (1977, 34). Frustrated dealing with the unchangeable emperor, Ambassador Korry vociferously and relentlessly urged U.S. bureaucrats to have a second look at Ethiopia's significance to the U.S. interests.

Therefore, the U.S. began to covertly explore alternatives to withdraw from the Kagnew station and thereby to end entrapment in the Ethiopian turmoil. In 1966, the revolution in the satellite technology eclipsed the relevance of land-based traditional information gathering systems. Subsequently, intelligence collection services at Kagnew became obsolete, redundant and unnecessary as the satellite technology got an upper hand in this field. In a successful demonstration of superiority of its satellites technology to the world, a U.S. manned spacecraft landed on the moon in 1969. This made the cliché of Kagnew as "irreplaceable" communication center for the U.S. security a matter of history. Hereafter, Kagnew primarily destined for relaying radio-communication messages for Polaris submarines in the Indian Ocean.

In 1966, the U.S. garnered permission from Britain to develop its Indian Ocean island of Diego Garcia for a naval facility. The island has similar whether to the Red Sea area and mainly free from tropical storms and typhoons. The U.S. depopulated a few thousand residents of the island. Therefore, there would be no inhabitants, no internal political instability that would invite communists. It was a potent addition for the navy since it would have a permanent naval base in the middle of the ocean, more than 1,000 miles from the tip of India (Rais, 1987). Whilst the Senate Appropriations Committee repeatedly rejected building the facility, the political uncertainty in Ethiopia compelled them to fund it (ibid, 80-1). The navy immediately embarked on building a naval communication center.

Ethiopia knew nothing about the U.S. intention to depart the base. As always, he was prepared to use Kagnew as bargain chip to obtain a large quantity of military supply. He requested five years military reserve estimated at $150 million. A catalogue of lists included tanks, armored personnel carriers, antitank and anti-aircraft guns, C-130 Hercules aircraft, more F-5 fighter, and helicopters (Vestal, 2011, 146). During this time, the tension with Somalia had rescinded, but the peasants' resistance in Bale was intensifying. Ethiopia faced serious crop failures for consecutive two years [1966-67]. Once again, Ambassador Korry advised him to deal with the drought issue first by overhauling the exploitative landholding system. Ethiopia rejected the suggestion out rightly. Ambassador Korry's attempt to convince the Emperor from moving forward with his insatiable appetite for military hardware was, of course, exercise in futility as often. He was as determined, as ever, to get a rent increase for Kagnew at the time when the Washington was going through the hard school of financial/military discipline because of the dirty Vietnam War (ibid).

When President Johnson received the request of the emperor to see him, the Undersecretary of State Nicholas deBelleville Katzenbach recommended him to 'politely decline' it. He gave three reasons why he had to reject it: (a) to avoid inflaming tension with Somalia; (b) to push the emperor "to a less bellicose position;" and (c) to promote regional disarmament plan for Africa (Memorandum from the President's Special Assistant (Rostow) to President Johnson, October 12, 1966). Finally, Washington caved in after his entreaties for six months, and he came to the White House on February 14, 1967).

On February 11, 1967, the President's Special Assistant, W. W. Rostow, wrote a memo for President Johnson regarding upcoming state visit of the emperor. He advised the president to ensure the emperor that the "strong and continuing U.S. interest in Ethiopia [that] is reflected in the very substantial economic and military aid we have provided her for many years (A total of more than $60 million in 1966, more than $300 million overall)." This is because the emperor "is extremely proud of his stature as a world leader and a spokesman for Africa." Therefore, "butter, strategically applied, can make up for many tons of undelivered guns." Otherwise, he concluded:

> The Emperor will be taking a careful reading of the temperature of U.S.-Ethiopian relations. In particular, he will be trying to get us to increase our military assistance to Ethiopia, now running at about $14 million per year. Though he probably won't say so, his bargaining leverage flows from his knowledge that our communications base—Kagnew Station—in his country is very important to us. (It is our chief listening post for Europe, the Middle East, and much of the Soviet Union. It contains equipment which could not be effectively operated from any other available location.)
>
> Your advisers are agreed that we should not agree to any major increase in military aid to Ethiopia. The Emperor's real security

problems are internal. Moreover, any substantial rise in our arms shipments would put pressure on the Soviets to enlarge their deliveries to the neighboring, arch-enemy Somali Republic, thus adding fuel to an already simmering arms race. Finally, an increase would be next to impossible to finance from [a] current MAP appropriations and very unpopular on the Hill.

We do not believe that the Emperor will react to this position by giving Kagnew Station a hard time. He is too dependent on the present flow of aid. We have, however, put together a small package of about $2 million in counter-insurgency help over the next two years which will save him the embarrassment of returning empty-handed (Memorandum From the President's Special Assistant (Rostow) to President Johnson, February, 11, 1967).

In parallel development, the Red Sea Basin was undergoing a rapid change. On one hand, Nasser was grappling with his involvement in Yemen; on the other hand, he expelled a U.N. peacekeeping force from Egypt's border with Israel. Israeli politicians were criticizing Levi Eshkol's government approach of "wait-and-see" towards him. The Soviet openly threatened to respond to any Israeli aggression militarily, and it moved its naval fleet within miles from the US's naval fleet in the Mediterranean Sea. Deep in the Vietnam crisis, President Johnson feared that a preemptive strike of Israel would lead to the Third World War, and, he tried to soothe Israel with financial incentives (Broyles, 2004, 27-30).

To monitor the situation closely, the U.S. sent a spy ship, USS Liberty, into the waters off Israel's cost. Israel was undeterred. It launched six days surprise bombing raids against Arabs. To disable a communication system of the U.S. spy ship, its amphibious and air force attacked the ship killing 34 service men on board. Kagnew eavesdroppers heard the attacks, the cries of service men for help, but they were of no help (Wrong, 2005, 218). Israel occupied the Sinai Peninsula, the Golan Heights, the West Bank, the Gaza the strip, and East Jerusalem. Nasser's impromptu responses were the closure of the Suez Canal and ephemeral theatrical resignation, which a popular referendum reversed. The closure of the Suez Canal caused inflation, and less revenue generation from the tariff and duties in Ethiopia.

The Israel action led to deterioration of diplomatic relations with the Sub-Saharan Africa. It was none other than the "Lion of Judah" who made the most benefit out of the crisis. Firstly, it crippled the ELF momentum since it lost strong support from Arab nations that were licking their wounds from the debacle of the war. Secondly, the Israel's strategic interest in Ethiopia grew exponentially. According to Shimon Peres, the then foreign minister of Israel, a cardinal principle and the most important course of action of Israel's foreign policy was 'to build a second Egypt in Africa, that is, to help convert Ethiopia's economic and military strength into a counterforce to Egypt, thereby giving Africans another focus' (Beit-Hallahmi, 1987, 51). Ethiopia morphed into a "nerve center" for Israeli clandestine political activities in African. Israel also wanted to explore petroleum in a friendly Ethiopia to secure oil independence, i.e., to deny Arabs a chance to use oil as a weapon. Emperor Hayla Sillase asked "the Israelis to organize counterinsurgency commandos composed of Christian peasants" to destroy "Arab sycophants" in Eritrea (Marcus, 1994, 178). Therefore, turning Ethiopia into the 'Second Egypt' did not move beyond simply building Ethiopia's military power to crash the ELF.

Nasser's foray into Yemen was a strategic blunder. The fact that he committed enormous resources for this futile attempt of exporting his brand of Arab nationalism perhaps had a role in his humiliating defeat by Israel. He withdrew his forces from Yemen, which broke into South Yemen and North Yemen. Subsequently, South Yemen declared a formation of People's Republic of South Yemen in November 1967. For the first time, the Soviet Union controlled vital piece of the Red Sea that increased the importance of Ethiopia. Because of this new threat, the United States donated to Ethiopia seventeen M-41 tanks, four helicopters, additional F-5 fighter jets, and MAAG trainings for additional one year (see, Vestal, 2011, 152). In general, Ethiopia received 19 million dollars aids in 1967(McVety, 2012, 185). In the same year, William O. Hall replaced the prolific and prodigious Ambassador Korry.

Neither Ethiopia was willing to abandon her imperialistic desire towards Somalia, nor was Somalia willing to abandon its irredentist claim towards Ogaden. For the U.S. that was alarmed by the Communist takeover of South Yemen, the ongoing tension between these two nations was an ominous ring. As I have already pointed out, the U.S. foreign policy towards the Horn was in a dilemma. On one hand, the U.S. wanted to promote the Somali experiment with liberal democracy as an example for the long term stability of the region. On the other hand, it did not want to give an impression that it preferred Somalia lest it would offend the landlord of Kagnew. This was a classic example of the tensions between American idealism and political realism in the U.S. foreign policy. Thus, to counterbalance these competing goals, Washington wanted to promote at least a détente between these two nations. It is against this background that the discussion of the 1967's elections of Somalia becomes among the most appealing phenomena that happened in the Horn in shaping the US-Ethiopian relations.

During this period, the Somalia Youth League, with its advocacy for the Greater Somalia or nothing, dominated the Somali politics. Igal Ibrahim, an ardent opponent of the Somalia Youth League, was handpicked, groomed and promoted by the CIA to pivot Somalia towards the Free World [Anglophone] countries (Schraeder, 1996, 292). He was the underdog who hardly stood against the heavyweight champions of the "sacred" cause of the unity of Somali peoples. He helped Prime Minister Abdirashid Sharmarke [from Majarteen clan] to defeat the seating President, Adan Abdullah Osman Daar [from Hawiye clan], who graciously accepted the defeat. His election brought an ascendancy of Igal [from Isaaq clan] of the ex-British Somali to helm the office of prime minister. Thus, the two influential powers of the President and Prime Minister fell in the hands of the northerners (Isaaq-Darod clans) to the dismay of the southern Somali influential tribe of Hawiye. This arrangement debased parity of positions between the south and the north and tribal power equilibrium. Whereas this election ended the alienation of the Northern Somalis, it moved a Somalia issues from the North-South split to the clan politics (see, Abdullahi, 2001, 29).

As planned, a new Prime Minister pursued reconciliation with Ethiopia, French Somaliland, and Kenya to promote regional peace and economic development at the expense of Somali's *irredentist* claims. In no time, an English speaking politician became a heartthrob in Washington. In a memo for President Johnson, the Undersecretary of State Katzenbach wrote, "He speaks English fluently and, though a Muslim, [he] enjoys a drink. He is a pragmatic African moderate and is pro-West" (Memorandum from the Under Secretary of State (Katzenbach) to President Johnson, March 12, 1968). His popularity within Washington circles skyrocketed to the extent of being called "our man" in Somalia (Schraeder, 1996, 132). In 1968, to encourage his initiatives, Vice President Hubert Humphrey went to Somalia. He praised his leadership style for the country that he described as "the most democratic country in Africa" (Vestal, 2011, 154). His popularity was discernible from what the First Lady Bird Johnson wrote about him:

> The Prime Minister of Somalia, a youngish, round faced, pleasant, and able-looking man wearing a white embroidered Muslim cap, and accompanied by a delicate, pretty wife, whose soft-spoken English was excellent. I was impressed with the simplicity and straightforwardness of the Prime Minister's Speech" (Johnson, 2007, 63).

One of the justifications of the détente was to help Ethiopia to focus on domestic issues. This means Ethiopia would crush insurgencies in Bale and Eritrea. Hayla Sillase cornered ELF through pyrrhic victories using the firepower and counter insurgency trainings given by the United States and Israel experts. The ELF was rocked by high level defections and handicapped by a shortage of arms and ammunitions. He stepped up military and paramilitary offensive against it; he waged a propaganda campaign against it as a foreign-directed subversive organization with pan-Arab aims, and he gave arms for self-defense to loyalist villagers (Airgram A-194 from the Embassy in Ethiopia to the Department of State, 1969). Whereas Ethiopia was winning the battles temporarily; there were no genuine signs to address issues of the Eritrean people.

He was quick to write the obituary of ELF, "the beginning of the end as an organized armed struggle." Washington was ready to high-five him. On June 18, 1969, a telegram from the the U.S. Embassy in Addis Ababa says, "We do not expect that the ELF can attain power in Eritrea." The embassy thought that it had clearly seen the victorious party and decided to take the side. It recommended Washington to "stand fast" with Kagnew Station because "the IEG [Imperial Ethiopia Government] can weather the storms of insurgency and give adequate protection to the station" and to "continue a military assistance program to Ethiopia as a whole, the benefits of which improve the Ethiopian ability to cope with the insurgency without running serious risks." Ironically, this analysis suggested 'reductions in U.S. profile at Kagnew as technology permits' while at the same time recommending 'continuation or increased level of military assistance to the Ethiopian armed forces' (ibid).

Now, it was time to focus on Bale. It was assumed that the detente between Ethiopia and Somalia would instantaneously eliminate the insurgency in Bale. According to the U.S. intelligence report, Bale revolts were anything but simply an outgrowth of Somalia irredentism. The U.S. described them as "bands of Arussi Gallas with only vague ideological or political aims, but with some support from Somalia" (National Intelligence Estimate No. 75/76-70, 1970).

As we mentioned earlier, the Bale peasants had repelled repetitive attacks from the police, Territorial Army, and local guards, the *naftanya* volunteers. Ethiopia was ready to use supremely sophisticated war machines on the peasant armies. The military employed scorched-earth tactics such as indiscriminate air-raids, destroying flocks, denying water holes and food supplies to the peasants, and controlling over people's movements severely (Marcus, 1994; Gilkes, 1975). Here is an account of my informant:

> One morning we were about to milk our cows. We saw a jet hovering around. Some wise men advised us to run away from the village. In about half an hour, we heard a powerful explosion. It shook the earth. A black smoke covered the entire area. We were shocked. Everybody was crying. We never heard such a big noise in our life. Later, we went back to see what happened. The jet dropped its bombs. It destroyed all our animals: cows, goats, sheep, hens, no living thing survived. Some 350 cattle of our family alone perished. Instead of being a destitute in our land, we decided to flee to Somalia (personal interview, Minnesota, 17 April, 2013).[1]

---

[1] My interviewee is an Oromo from Bale, currently living in Minnesota.

Notwithstanding the military imbalance, the Bale fighters were invincible and made the province ungovernable for the *naftanyas*. Ethiopia invited foreign supporters to suppress them. We indicated that American experts were decisive in providing counter-insurgency trainings. Now they came in for a different mission. Patrick Gilkes has to offer this:

> Air attacks were unsuccessful and the accuracy of rebel bazookas caused some concerns. It was at this time that American experts were brought in to improve the fire power on some of the jets (Gilkes, 1975, 218).

The British army engineers were also came in to help. They built a military supply line from Nagelle Borana to Goba through the Gannale River (ibid). A Gannale River bridge was so crucial to send the U.S. donated M-41 tanks and armed cars to battle fronts. Eventually, the United States cooperation in a diplomatic front and the provision of firepower helped the emperor to quash the rebellion with the heavy-handedness. The CIA took note of the role of emperor's absolute firepower superiority in defeating them in this way: "[They] defied the Emperor and fended off a division of the Ethiopian Army for several years before yielding to military pressure" (National Intelligence Estimate 75/76-7, 1970). As Patrick Gilkes correctly put, "The activities of the army in Bale certainly played a major part in turning an essentially peasant revolt into a national revolutionary movement" (Gilkes, 1975, 226).

In general, from the Arab-Israel conflict to the election of non-hawkish Somalia Prime Minister, and from the defeat of Nasser in Yemen to the U.S. increasing military aid to Ethiopia, Hayla Sillase considerably benefited by consolidating his power and muzzling oppositions during the lull. Would his throne be tranquilized after his pyrrhic victories? Would Hayla Sillase be caving in for domestic pressure? Would a friendliness of Somalia and Ethiopia remain intact? Would Kagnew remain the overriding interest of the U.S. in the region forever? The forthcoming chapter will explore these questions?

11   The Failure of Triangular Axis and a Road to Communism

WHEREAS HAYLA SILLASE PACIFIED the rural popular uprisings, the resistance against his throne intensified and entered a new phase. The peasants had passed the torch to the students, and the center of gravity shifted from the peasants, who were neglected by his order, to students, who were created by his order, from rural to urban, and from non-ideological to ideological. As Gebru Tareke eloquently noted, the peasants' rebellions did "sap the energy of the old regime and inspire a generation of radical students who served as a catalyst in the revolution" (quoted in Tirfe, 1999, 100)

In the previous discussion, we saw the U.S. lion's share in developing the technical colleges through Point IV programs and later in establishing the Haile I Selassie University. The U.S. also fundamentally contributed for curriculum development through the Peace Corps program. These investments were designed to create the eternal triangular alliance of Hayla Sillase, Western-educated elite, and the U.S. as an iron wall against the global communism (Paulos, 2006). Why did relations of the educated class and the United States drift from cordiality to outright hostility? Why did the students elope to the orbit of communism?

One may say, and I would say that the turning point between the students and the United States was the 1960 coup. The coup, however, inept to galvanize widespread support from the mass, army, air force, and the church, it found a refuge in the hearts and minds of the intelligentsia whom the United States sponsored to shore up and secure the throne of the emperor. Since then, for the radicalized students, nothing short of revolution was palatable, even the natural death of the emperor. "I wake up screaming in the night at the thought the Emperor might die a natural death," noted an embittered student. "I want him to know a judgment is being enacted on him!" (quoted in Huntington, 2006, 189). They also rejected a tradition of bribing them by political positions. A certain student lamented, "We have been kept from acting by fear and the sweetness of office" (ibid, 187). In 1962 and 1963, to control the epidemic of anti-monarchic political fever in the student population and to deny them opportunities for political activism, the government closed dormitories.

The U.S. restoration of the Emperor changed its relations with intellectuals from coziness to acrimonious. Thus, "imperialist" America became "a friend of feudal Ethiopia" and a complicit in the perpetuation of sufferings of Ethiopian peasants (Paulos, 2006). The unconditional support the U.S. gave to the archaic absolutist state proved that America was lethargic to the genuine reform in Ethiopia, rather interested in the 'window dressing' (Marcus, 1995, 181). For the students, the university, the "gift" of the generous emperor, "with its many American personnel and its John F. Kennedy Library came to represent the sham of democratic American liberalism allied to despotic Ethiopian feudalism" (ibid, 180). A certain communist leaning newspaper wrote:

> Even if one were generously to assume that U.S. educational policy sought to produce (Jeffersonian) democrats in Ethiopia, 'the support of the West was giving to the oppressive Ethiopian regime' and ruthless dictatorship in the chain of the free world subverted and nullified it (quoted in Kebede, 2008, 173-4).

Washington's foreign policy obsession with countering communism and romanticism with dictators, to the dismay of the suffering of large-mass, failed to work in Ethiopia. The students that America funded, baptized and infused, in the Western liberal curricula, to dissuade them from embracing communism, radicalized and drifted into the cliff of socialism as an ideological opposition (alternative) to the farce of American idealism. They chanted the socialist motto of "Land to the Tiller" disregarding what they thought.

In the eyes of students, the U.S. became anything, but an enemy of progressive forces worldwide; the imperial government nicknamed an American puppet; bourgeois democracy detested as a sham. They embraced Marxism as "unchangeable," "self-evident" truth, "scientific," and the only genuine way to bring progress (see, Donham, 1986, 126-7). A term "America," which captivated and obsessed generations of Ethiopian students for its grandeur, modernity, and liberal values, and America that Hayla Sillase wished to be "the ideal cradle of instructions of the Ethiopian youth," degenerated into a pejorative term. 'You are American,' means you are selfish, materialistic, disrespectful, fake, and so on (Kebede, 2008, 174).

In 1923 letter to President Coolidge Hayla Sillase hope that Ethiopian students in the U.S. would receive "sound education" to serve their country, but contrarily, since 1965, the Ethiopian Students Union in North America (ESUNA) championed Marxist ideology and regime change. They became a catalyst of the Ethiopian students' struggles and the revolution. "Ten years, even five years ago, the emperor was a head and leading us," a young Ethiopian craving for transformation insisted in 1966, "Now, it is we, the educated elite, educated by his orders, who are leading, and the emperor who lags behind" (quoted in Huntington, 2006, 188).

Gradually, student oppositions to the Hayla Sillase regime and the U.S. presence in Eritrea sharpened. The following comment epitomized the radicalization of students and their bitterness towards the U.S:

> Tell the Americans that this is not Korea! Tell them that this is not Dominican Republic or Laos or Vietnam whom they have succeeded in dividing! Tell them that we have a long history behind us, that America is too young to outsmart us! Tell them that the President of the United States cannot determine who should rule this country in the same manner as he is determining who should rule the Dominican Republic. Tell them that ours is a land that successfully protected its independence against all intruders, that it is a proud country on a proud continent. Tell them that we are the fighting Horn of the continent whose written and unwritten histories predates the first Caucasian cave dwellers who once had the pyramids constructed, dispatched Hannibal across the Alps to vanquish Rome, gallantly combated Caesars battalions, and smashed an invading European colonial army at the battle of Adwa! (Quoted in Paulos, 2006, 142-143).

In March 1968, it was a diplomatic *faux pas* when the Addis Ababa University students forced Vice President Humphrey to cancel delivering a speech at a university campus. The students demonstrated in the campus protesting against the ongoing Vietnam War. They burned his effigy with a U.S. dollar bill. They carried a number of placards emblazoned with anti-U.S. slogans: "Yankees pull out of Vietnam;" "Yankees stop abusing our sister;" "Johnson has sent Humphrey to Prepare Africans for mass butcher, but Ethiopia has to say—down with the underhanded USA;" "withdraw from Kagnew communication base in Ethiopia;" "Down with CIA;" and "Is Harlem in the free world?" (Ebony, Vol., 23, No., 5, 1968, 53).

Humphrey saw for himself the unpopularity of the rule of the emperor and animosity of students towards the U.S., but he chose to praise him rather than appraise the policy of his government. He praised the emperor whose house was on fire as a 'revered, respected, and the great statesman of his time and our century'. "Ethiopia is eminently qualified by history, by experience and by dedication to the principle of freedom and justice to serve as the focal point in the building of the new Africa," said Humphrey (quoted in Toledo Blade, Ethiopia Chief Draws Praise by Humphrey, January 1968).

In the late 1969s and early 1970s, the students followed confrontational approaches towards the United States. Anger towards "imperialist" America was not limited to Embassy and Kagnew; it spilled over to anything that represented America including "the popular and apolitical Peace Corps." Circulations of anti-American leaflets to beating of the Peace Corps volunteers became a mundane part of students' animosity towards the U.S. Because of this, several Peace Corps volunteers abandoned their posts to save their lives (Vestal, 2011, 171). On the other hand, a U.S. director of the Peace Corps Program resigned in 1970 protesting "repressive" policy of the Ethiopian government (Skinner, 2003, 44). The Peace Corps program was closed on 20 January 1970. This radicalization of the students signaled a beginning of a new era, a failure of the United States' foreign policy on Ethiopia long before the revolution of 1974, and harbinger of what to come after the revolution.

The intellectuals identified themselves not only in opposition to the Western ideology but also in relation to the grievances of their own 'backward' countrymen (Donham, 1986, 126). They rejected the suppression of peripheral peoples, both religiously and nationally. Thus, for instance, the rebellion of Bale peasants and insurgency in Eritrea were their struggles and source of their inspirations. Walalliny Makonnin, a leader of the student movement, wrote:

> I am all for them, the ELF, the Bale movements, the Gojjam uprising, to the extent that they have challenged and weakened the existing regime, and have created areas of discontent to be harnessed later on by a genuine Socialist revolution (Wallelign, 1969).

Perhaps, nothing expresses the zeitgeist of the day like his powerful remarks in which he rejected "the fake Ethiopian Nationalism advanced by the ruling class and unwillingly accepted and even propagated by innocent fellow travelers." This is how he expounded it:

> Ask anybody what Ethiopian culture is? Ask anybody what Ethiopian language is? Ask anybody what Ethiopian music is? Ask about what Ethiopian religion is? Ask about the national dress is? It is either Amhara or Amhara–Tigre!! To be a "genuine" Ethiopian one has to speak Amharic, listen to Amharic music, accept the Amhara-Tigre religion-Orthodox Christianity, and wear the Amhara-Tigre shamma in international conferences. In short, to be an Ethiopian, you will have to wear an Amhara mask. In short to be an Ethiopian, you will have to wear an Amhara mask (to use Fanon's expression) (ibid).

When the monarchy collapsed, the Marxism ideology championed by the student was the only ready-made ideology for the military, whose only ideology was patriotism and defense of the throne. As we shall discuss in a volume two of this work, the military not only armed itself with the ideology, but it also finished proponents of the ideology once it consolidated its powers.

Why did the students reject the Emperor and the United States? Paulos Milkias, in his work, *Haile Selassie, Western Education, and Political Revolution in Ethiopia*, tries to provide causes of the radicalization of the students. He draws a conclusion similar to Professor Huntington's thesis of the dilemma of 'changing society'. Accordingly, his emphasis was on a contradictory nature of implementing liberal education in a dependent modernizing autocracy that was inherently inimical with the notion of autonomy and personal freedom. Thus, liberal education in the authoritarian system results in denunciation of the very ideology it supposed to uphold it. Thus, he concludes "that attempts to introduce Western education and all the accompanying values without changing the intrinsic character pertaining to itself carries the seed of its own destruction" [Paulos, 2006, 33]. Therefore, the following quote provides a good description of the assumption and conclusion, "The central assumption in this study is that the intrinsic contradictions between the values of metropolitan systems to which the Ethiopian intelligentsia exposed and the political realities of a modernizing autocracy triggered the Ethiopian revolution and led to the fall of Haile Selassie in December 1974" [ibid., 27-8].

He also underlined contradictions between American idealism and political realism. What the students learned in school about America, he contends, was different from American romanticism with the authoritarian and snailish government of Hayla Sillase. He explains this point in this way:

> From the outset, there was an element of contradictions in this alliance and the ideological bond that tied them. U.S. education which molded the new intellectual elite, promoted the values of metropolitan market economies which were readily accepted by the young scholars who never got tired of quoting the Magna Carta, the Bill of Rights, and particularly, Thomas Jefferson and Abraham Lincoln, the former in connection with the Declaration of Independence and the latter for his "government of the people, by the people and for the people." The intelligentsia's desire was to exercise the moral, economic, and political rights they had learned about at school--the independence, individual freedoms, and civil liberties advocated by the major liberal capitalist thinkers. For them, such bourgeois rights could be limited; they could not be restricted by any rulers whether divine or temporal. The new

elite was not prepared to accept anything else but those rights (Paulos, 2006, 23).

Unlike traditional education that manufactured legitimacy for old power institutions by promoting loyalty, sycophancy, and mediocrity, liberal education produced a host of student army that disconnected from the system they supposed to underpin. They were materialistic; individualistic (atomistic) and represented a new culture within the old culture that denied them the chance, according to their contention, to be up to their potential, a potential to be a certain bourgeois they knew in books.

Professor Messay Kebede tried to address the same question in his work *Radicalism and Cultural Dislocation in Ethiopia*. As the topic of the book suggests, radicalism and cultural dislocation are different faces of the same coin. American domination of the education system through curriculum development, supplying the manpower, provision of text books, and above all, the fact that Ethiopian education policy lacked "the goal of national development" and "lack of policy articulation" resulted in the cultural dislocation. To establish the nexus clearer, he argued that the fact that American religions (Mormonism, Catholicism, and Protestantism) dominated the university culminated in a retreat of "national culture," in the form of the Ethiopian Orthodox Christianity fleeing off campus.

> Though Orthodox Christianity was the traditional and official religion of Ethiopia, it was given a place at the university, and Ethiopian students were placed under the influence of Catholic and Protestant academic staff. The dominance of expatriate staff with alien religion affiliations indicated from the beginning that the university had forsaken the goal of defending and promoting the national culture, which was interwoven with Ethiopia's religious legacy. The main difference with traditional education occurred here (Messay, 2008, 56).

Donald Donham provided a detailed analysis of anomaly of "socialist revolution" in this typical agrarian country with a moribund mode of production. It seems like, in what he called double rejections by the Ethiopian students at the time, the students were neither necessarily socialists nor capitalist, but capitalism was a collateral damage. Firstly, there was a rejection of ancestral "backward" culture for achieving progress. Secondly, there was a rejection of domineering America who should be, at the same time, mimicked for its progress and surpassed if possible. Accordingly, he opines that Marxism not only provided a framework to reject the West that supported the monarch and "Ethiopian backwardness" but also a framework to own the West's wealth and power (Donham, 1986, 127).

12   The Culmination of Misguided Policy: The Death of the Lion

ESCALATIONS OF THE VIETNAM WAR had tormented and torn apart the White House and the Democratic Party in the late 1960s. In one of the most tumultuous conventions, the party nominated vice president Hubert Humphrey for the election of 1968 to run against the republican candidate Richard Nixon. Thanks to the public unhappiness with the war and a weak economy, the people gave their verdict. Nixon easily won the election.

Likewise, the Emperor's regime was rocked by students' activism and provincial rebellions. There was hardly peaceful means to get-rid-off from his rule as there was no election. Nor, in the first place, election was thinkable since he was the "Elect of God." His regime, now and then, proved its ineffectiveness to deal with domestic issues through peaceful means. The legitimate grievances of the Bale peasants were presented as agitation of Somalia, and their rebellion was nothing more than an offshoot of Somalia irredentism. The relentless pressure from students for radical land reform, fighting corruption, tackling the rising inflation, and improving the snail pace of development were neglected as gibberish from emotionally driven thankless youths intoxicated by luxuries provided to them by the most benevolent King. Similarly, denying the existence of the problem in Eritrea and portraying as an outgrowth of subversive activities of a few Arab sycophants was a commonplace experience.

In May 1969, a coup d'état of Gaafar Nimeiry toppled a military rule of Sudan. Sudan embarked on "socialism" inspired by Arab nationalism of Nasser variety. The new government refused to negotiate the border closure with Ethiopia and supported Eritrean rebels. At this time, the ELF established itself as robust challenger to the rule of the emperor in Eritrea through the military, financial, and propaganda supports it gained from Arab and socialist countries. Subsequently, a genie of Eritrean rebels unleashed. They controlled most of the Eritrean lowlands and displayed remarkable potency to launch an attack anywhere in Eritrea. They destroyed oil tankers, buses on the vital Asmara-Massawa highway, bombed an Ethiopian commercial jet in Frankfurt [Germany] and staged a sophisticated attack on the main electric power and water supply systems of the city of Asmara (Airgram A-30, 1969). On September 9, 1969, the members of the ELF kidnapped American Consul General Murray E. Jackson while he was riding with his driver between Aqordat and Karan. He was released unharmed after signing a statement confirming that he had listened to their complaints and that he had not been mistreated (Newton, 2002, 148). In a show of force, the Ethiopian army stormed the town where the hostage took place following his release, which made him question the timing and judgment of the military action. The ELF hostility towards the U.S. became manifest when it killed a U.S. currier on a Massawa road in 1970. Later, ELF fighters ambushed and killed General Tashoma Ergatu, a commander-in-chief of the Ethiopian army in Eritrea. A downward spiral of the security situation in Eritrea was unstoppable to the extent that the emperor had to blanket the whole province with the martial law, in the same year.

We should also indicate that while the emperor trying to control the ELF, a new player came into the playfield in 1969. The Eritrean People's Liberation Front (EPLF), which champions the formation of "revolutionary Arab" Eritrea, and which ironically claims loyalty from the Christian highlanders formed in the Palestine Liberation Organization camp in Jordan (Erlick, 2002, 147). The formation of the EPLF with leftist agenda showed the general trend of radicalization of Ethiopian students at home and in the diaspora.

Confronted with a challenge at home, the emperor had to run to his superpower patron for the military aid as always since his single solution to his "subjects" yearning for dignity was muzzling them through his modern army. We should indicate that because of the improvement of Ethiopia and Somalia relations and because of the Vietnam War, the aid the U.S. allocated to Ethiopia in 1968 declined to 9.3 million dollars from 19 million dollars in 1967. Nonetheless, Ethiopia received over 60 percent of the U.S. military aid to Africa.

Before the emperor came to White House, the President's Assistant for National Security Affairs, Henry Kissinger, wrote a memo in which he indicated the need for supporting Hayla Sillase "without being drawn into his own parochial and exaggerated view of threats to Ethiopian security." He went on to explain the psyche of the emperor: "His outlook was clearly shaped by the Italian conquest of Ethiopia," "his dramatic but futile appeal to the League of Nations," and "the traditional fear of Christian Ethiopia being overwhelmed by surrounding Moslems." This produced "a virtual siege mentality, in which Soviet arms aid to neighboring Somalia, Sudan and Yemen seems larger than life." Thus, "the Emperor brings both a passion from tragic experience and a sensitivity born of a royal self-esteem." He noted, "The Emperor will recite Soviet and Arab designs on Ethiopia and the Red Sea basin. He may exaggerate Soviet arms deliveries, and conclude Ethiopia urgently needs more U.S. military help." Enumerating his challenges at home, Kissinger advised the president to distract the emperor from drawing him into his domestic messes by inviting him to lecture on the broader state of world politics (Memorandum from Kissinger to Nixon, June 6, 1969).

On a toast to the emperor, Nixon had to scratch his head to find words of praise for the emperor whose ship of state was sinking fast. He found the notorious myth of Solomonic descent and the "wisdom," which the battered emperor inherited from his putative ancestor:

> I can think of the fact that His Majesty, of course, is a descendant of Solomon. If I can recall the Biblical phrase correctly, when King David died and the Lord asked Solomon what he wanted most, Solomon said, "Lord, give me an understanding heart." And because he asked for that, he received great wisdom, a long life and, of course, he had an understanding heart. So it is with His Majesty. He has wisdom. He has had a long life, and, I know from personal experience, an understanding heart.

Nixon narrated his recollections about his visits to Ethiopia:

> I share that with you for one moment. I had the great privilege, which some in this room have enjoyed, of visiting his country in 1957. My wife and I were received as royal guests at that time and treated royally. I returned again to his country in 1967, holding no office, having no portfolio whatever. I was received again as a royal guest and treated royally. This is a man with an understanding heart [Laughter]. ...I think there is nothing more appropriate that we can say to His Imperial Majesty tonight than that we trust he may live long for our glory (Richard Nixon Toasts, 1969).

When a real business came, Nixon got tough. Then, he posed a leading question to the emperor on what he thought a greater danger to his throne. He was all over the map, to enumerate a catalogue of his imagined foreign threats from Sudan, Somalia, Yemen, China, Egypt, and Soviet; and "their wish" to convert the Red Sea into "a Soviet-Egyptian lake" (Memorandum of Conversation, 1969). Unbeknownst to him, Kissinger had alluded to his besieged mentality syndrome.

Following the liberation of the sub-Saharan Africa, the African-Americans' passion for Ethiopia—except the Rastafarians—was a matter that history takes a little account. They abandoned identifying their interests with a political Ethiopia, but with a historic Ethiopia [the entire sub-Saharan

Africa].[1] In addition to this, new African leaders related themselves with an icon of the civil rights movement, Dr. Martin Luther King, more than the emperor did. Thus, the emperor had to play catch-up to find relevance in the civil rights movement. He wanted to lay a wreath on the MLK's grave. The White House facilitated it because it "will be appreciated by his own young elite in Ethiopia and improve the U.S. image with this important group of future Ethiopian leaders," and most of all, refusal to do so "could be misinterpreted and possibly embarrassing." This "would clearly be a plus for the U.S. image" since "King is an established hero throughout Africa, and above all, *his non-violence is particularly apt for leaders like Haile Selassie who are trying to be progressive without opening the door to left-wing radicals*" [Italics added]. (Memorandum from Palmer to Rogers, 1969; Memorandum from Roger Morris to Kissinger, 1969.)

Despite the fact that U.S. interests in Ethiopia were dwindling rapidly, the visit had a happy ending for the emperor. Thanks to his friendship with Nixon, he acquired $20 million aid from the U.S. As Kissinger noted, the U.S. wanted 'to assure the Emperor of strong continuing support in his defense needs', and "traditional relationships in security matters' (Memorandum from Kissinger to Nixon, June 6, 1969). For the time being, his absolutism secured a lifeline. The Conquering Lion pushed with his policies, so did his subjects refuse to obey his rule of the jungle. The following year, the emperor met Nixon during a White House dinner for the 25th anniversary of the United Nations and Secretary Rogers visited Ethiopia. His agenda on the table was about getting additional weapons (Skinner, 2003, 42).

In a major regional development, Somalia also began to face internal crisis. In chapter ten, we saw how Somali politicians made the notion of "Greater Somalia" a sacred agenda, and how they pursued a dangerous road of militarization to achieve it. In late 1960s, the military institution had eclipsed the nascent democratic institutions. In militarized societies, military has to win elections or claim power by force. During the 1969 elections, the ruling party and the old-guards maintained their power. As we hinted out, the advent of Igal Ibrahim rocked the balance of power between the southern and northern Somalis. This had disappointed the Hawiye clan of the southern Somalia. Moreover, his détente led to a huge dissatisfaction among the Ogaden clan.

While the U.S. heavily invested in promoting Somalia's detente with Ethiopia, it hardly foresaw the discontent it was fermenting in Somalia. In June 1969, Kissinger indicated that the détente would last since Igal was "a

---

[1] In fact, perceptions of African Americans scholars about Ethiopia had evolved a lot. This trend culminated in the work of Edmond J. Keller, *Revolutionary Ethiopia: From Empire to People's Republic*.

strong, inward-looking leader" (Memorandum from Kissinger to Nixon, June 6, 1969).

In October 1969, the rapprochement cost the life of President Sharmarke. His assassination followed by a bloodless coup that brought Siad Barre, who came from Ogaden on the maternal side, to the helm of power in the name of abolishing tribalism, wiping out widespread corruption, supporting freedom fighters, and implementing 'scientific socialism'. Whereas Lewis (1980, 14) contends that socialism was a "natural choice" for Somalia; Vestal (2011, 171) argues that Somali nationalism and socialism were "an oxymoronic combination." Whatever was the chemistry between Somalia and socialism, the military rule popularity evaporated immediately. The military dictatorship dismantled the fabric of the nation that enjoyed a legitimate claim to a democratic vibrancy. It suspended the parliament and constitution, and nationalized private companies.

The junta's anti-American stances were manifest from its actions such as allowing North Vietnam ships to trade under the Somalia flag; rendering U.S. diplomats *persona non grata*; dismissing Peace Corps volunteers, and capturing a U.S. flag carrier ship on suspicion of espionage (Lefebvre, 1991, 138). The U.S. was swiftly expressed its disappointment with the military rule since it undermined the détente with Ethiopia by "arming Arussi Galla rebels operating in Southwestern Ethiopia" (Intelligence Note No. 747, 1969).

Meanwhile, the revolutionary Arab nationalist Nasser suddenly died from the cardiac arrest in 1970. Hayla Sillase was among the dignitaries that attended his turbulent funeral ceremony. "In the last 14 years of his highly regarded leadership Nasser has probably done more for Egypt than his predecessors in 1400 years," wrote the Ethiopian Herald obituary. "While his ancestors built the pyramids for the dead, he built the Aswan dam for the living." "In him," wrote the obituary, "Ethiopia loses a great friend" (quoted in Erlick, 2002, 149).

The death of Nasser fundamentally changed the diplomatic orientation of Egypt. His brand of Arab nationalism, which amplified the significance of Hayla Sillase in the eyes of Washington bureaucrats, also died. In the dramatic volte-face, his successor (Anwar Sadat) established a secret diplomatic channel with the U.S. The secret channel culminated in the expulsion of the Soviet's 15,000 military advisors from Egypt in 1972 (Lefebvre, 1991, 136).

The beneficiary from the Egypt-Soviet diplomatic crisis was none other than Somalia thanks to its strategic location and "scientific socialism" of Siad Barre. The Soviet aids to Somalia exponentially increased reaching 100 million dollars by 1974 while Hayla Sillase secured $11.75 million and $ 10.6 million military assistances from the U.S. in 1971 and 1972 respectively (Donham, 1999, 138; Lefebvre, 1991, 141). Whereas Somalia was on the verge of signing a Treaty of Friendship and Cooperation with the Soviet,

Ethiopia's source of military aid (Kagnew) was on the verge of expiring thanks to a similar service from the Island of Diego Garcia. The status of Kagnew changed from an irreplaceable strategic asset to a burden.

In spite of the fact that Nixon campaigned on the platform of "peace with honor," he chose to escalate the war. During his administration, Washington lost its moral capital because of his political realism. The detente with the communist bloc hit a climax when the U.S. decided to formalize relations with the People's Republic of China. Vice President Sapiro Agnew sent to Addis Ababa to inform the emperor on that in advance. Thus, Washington would be no more bribing him on the Communist China question.

Because of the detente, the space for human rights shrank in the U.S. foreign policy. Numerous advocacy groups commenced protesting what they perceived impotent policy to promote human rights. Besides, the Congress challenged the established practice that leaves foreign policy to the Executive body. Article II (2) of the Constitution reads, "[The president] shall have Power, by and with the Advice and Consent of the Senate, to make Treaties ... and ... shall appoint Ambassadors..." In addition to this, the Congress has "the power of the purse" that gives it a broad influence over actions of the executive body on many foreign policy areas. The Congress was committed to "reassert its role in determining the direction of U.S. foreign policy and be more responsive to popular opinion" to heal a "breach between American values and American foreign policy" (Petro, 1983, 11).

The Fraser Subcommittee report condemned Washington for embracing "governments which practice torture and unabashedly violate almost every human right guarantee pronounced by the world committee." It underscored "the near impossibility in a democratic society of conducting, over a long period of time, a foreign policy against the opposition of a substantial segment of the people." The report found the government record "random" and "unpredictable" and suggested a list of recommendations, which were "both morally imperative and practically necessary" to improve the U.S. responsiveness to human rights considerations (ibid, 11-12).

The activism of the Congress ended the era of executive body underwriting friendly dictators with blank checks since it stepped up monitoring United States military commitment around the world. It had already placed a ceiling on the military aid to Africa because Washington should not be civilizing "primitive nations all over the world" or it would derail poor countries, like Ethiopia, from the development goals which in turn would inflame internal turmoil (Lefebvre, 1991, 144). Senate hearings revealed the extent of White House commitments, both military support and counterinsurgency trainings, to Ethiopia. Thanks to the Congress grip on the foreign aid Ethiopia received $9.3 million military assistances in 1973, the lowest aid since 1960. In addition to this, the hearings exposed the kidnapping of Consul General in Eritrea. Came at the time when America recoils from the shadow of Vietnam, also known as the "Vietnam syndrome," some believed the revelation was nothing, but a fodder for "the makings of another Vietnam" (ibid, 146). The killing of a commander-in-chief of the Ethiopian army in Eritrea at the time of the hearing augmented the threat.

When the U.S. expressed its intention to "phase out" Kagnew, the news came nothing short of panic for the emperor since he knew that an era of reaping American's weaponry goldmine would come to an end, soon. At the same time, Somalia declared that it would foil oil and gas explorations by an American company in Ogaden. Challenged by increasing insurgency at home, bothered by the Soviet turning Somalia into a regional military power, Hayla Sillase rushed to bring the matter to the attention of President Nixon. He came to the White House in May 1973.

Nixon knew the insatiable appetite of the emperor for the military hardware that brought him back-and-forth to the White House record times. On a toast for the emperor, he mentioned, "This Nation is 195 years old, this house is about 185 years old, and in the whole long history of this Nation, no chief of state, no head of government has been received more often, honored more often, than is the man we honor tonight." "Ethiopia is gratified to know that she can always count on the continuation of this assistance," said the emperor. He recommended for sustaining at increasing levels the mutual cooperation (Richard Nixon Toasts, 1973). He talked about regional peace and security, freedom of navigation and access to natural resources, and the prospect of oil and safeguarding against enemy takeover (Memorandum of Conversation, 1973). Enumerating a litany of armaments the Soviet Union donated to Somalia, the ailing emperor presented a whopping 450 million dollars military shopping lists to Nixon. He wanted sophisticated fighter jets, surface-to-air missiles, ground-to ground missiles, tanks, etc (Vestal, 2011, 180-81; Skinner, 2003, 42). Counted on his friendship with Nixon and supported by U.S. Embassy in Addis Ababa, Hayla Sillase had a strong impression that he would secure what he wanted, but to his disappointment he got too little of it. The era of extorting through Kagnew, the era of defection to the Soviet, and the era of unregulated presidential power over foreign aid were the nostalgia of yesteryears.

In August 1973, Nixon approved the Defense Department recommendation to "phase out" Kagnew. Now, the U.S. involvement in the region was keeping a regional balance of power between Ethiopia and the Soviet backed Somalia; not to mention that Ethiopia's encirclement with pro-communist Sudan to the West and South Yemen across the Red Sea. The U.S. decided to maintain grant military aid and training at previous levels under a new system based on the loan agreements for military sales, and decided to keep economic support intact (Skinner, 2003, 42).

In the meantime, in October 1973, a coalition of Arab forces led by Egypt and Syria launched a surprise attack against the State of Israel on the Yom Kippur holiday. Israel repulsed Egyptian forces and reached within a parameter of launching an attack on Cairo. The Third World countries in the show of solidarity with Egypt severed diplomatic ties with Israel. In the era of declining of U.S. commitments, Hayla Sillase was reluctant to be a left out from the wave of the Third World nations. He joined several leaders of the Sub-Saharan Africa in severing relations with Israel. He kissed strong Israel military support and counter-insurgency trainings goodbye.

On the other hand, the war led to the oil crisis that sent the world economy into the recession, which exacerbated the living conditions of the embryonic urban middle class in Ethiopia. Prices of petroleum, cooking oil, food items, and export-commodities in general skyrocketed. This was the immediate recipe for the 1974 revolution against the emperor's rule.

The Famine that Naked the Emperor

However, abject poverty and starvation are the direct consequences of government policy as Amartya Sen showed in his noble prize winning work of *Poverty and Famines*; it is "the long-established Ethiopian tradition of blaming natural calamities on the wickedness of the people," as Pankhurst (1985, 46) noted. In a traditional Ethiopian polity, a cyclical starvation plays to the advantage of the Crown since people "should be so dependent upon him" (Acemoglu & Robinson, 2012, 236), and it often used to highlight the generosity of the kings. The biblical scale starvation in Wallo and Tigray, in 1973-74, turned political because of ways the government handled it.

Firstly, the famine was clearly preventable. In the same year, the hunger claimed lives of hundreds of thousand people, eighty percent of staple grain producing provinces produced above average which led to the growth of grain export (Keller, 1989, 167). Instead of directing grain flow to the drought affected areas, Hayla Sillase's urgency was to facilitate exports to compensate for the loss of America's cash cow (ibid). The victims were selling their property and animals at extremely low prices to buy staple food items, which "first hidden by the rich and then thrown on the market at a double price, inaccessible to peasants and poor" (Kapuscinski, 1984, 140). Secondly, the famine was a failure of Hayla Sillase land policy since most of the starved were landless tenants, who lost 75 percent of their produce to landlords (Legum, 1975, 12). Thirdly, the emperor should have better prepared to address the condition since, at the time, a Wallo governor was none other than his son, Prince Asfaw Wassan. Fourthly, it was widely believed that the emperor condemned Wallo and Tigray to death because of their support to Lij Iyyasu during his struggle for the throne some sixty years ago (Lefort, 1983, 44-45).

Because of a royal prestige, the emperor refused to acknowledge the existence of the famine in his dominion. For instance, he never uttered a single word about the famine victims while he asked the U.S. for a gargantuan $450 million military aid at the same time when the starving masses were falling in thousands every passing day. Moreover, his government presented the famine as a total fabrication of the Western press and missionaries destined to tarnish the "grand" image of "three thousand years nation." They did whatever they could conceal it. As Kapuscinski (1984, 140) reported, when the beggars descended on towns, 'on the orders of local dignitaries the police finished off whole clans of still-living skeletons'.

Once the regime forced to concede the problem, the emperor convinced the U.S. Agency for International Development (USAID) "to begin shipping aid quietly so as not to cause the government undue embarrassment" (Keller, 1989, 168). The regime also downplayed the scale of the problem, and it started to use to its advantage. Whereas as the relief need stood at over 100,000 tones; the government requested 20,000 tons of grains from the international donors. To benefit the imperial treasury out of the crisis, the minister of finance imposed, high custom, fees on the aid for the famine victims (Kapuscinski, 1984 118). The regime officials were benefiting by an artificial escalation of food prices and even by selling international relief ration cards to the famine victims (Keller, 1989, 168). During the crisis, the international donors provided $25 million "for food relief while Ethiopian government spent nothing" for the relief of the famine victims (ibid, 170). Amidst an industrial scale starvation and pestilence ravaging the country, Hayla Sillase "had amassed a personal fortune of more than $1.6 billion at the expense of the Ethiopian people and stashed it away in the Swiss bank accounts" (ibid). On the other hand, he spent $35 million to celebrate his birthday in the same year (International Report, 1983, 15) and around E$200 million for military purposes (Keller, 1989, 102). At the time when the death tolls were trickling in, Hayla Sillase hosted a sumptuous wedding banquets for which a cake was flown from London. "As the 5,000 guests assembled at the Hilton Hotel for the wedding party washed down their exotic cakes with champagne, the death toll from famine in Wello was reaching the 200,000 marks" (in Gebru, 2009, 15). Whereas dead bodies and skeletons putrefied on the streets of Wallo, a Hayla Sillase's dog guaranteed statue, on which it was engraved, "To Lulu—Our Beloved dog. He has been with us to Europe, Latin America, and Asia." (Keller, 1989, 187).

"By the time of the drought of 1973, only three percent of the total populations were enrolled in school, eighty percent did not have access to medical care, ninety percent could not read or write, there were few all weather roads, Ethiopia had the lowest per capita income in Africa amidst unbelievable poverty and seventy-five percent of reported cases of disease were said to be preventable." (Robinette, 2012, 325-326). A peasant had to walk half a day to reach a motor road. There were provinces without a single hospital, and one doctor served 75,000 people.

The Gestation of the Revolution

In early 1970s, Hayla Sillase was sitting over different fault lines. Regional and tribal tensions, insurgencies, students' revolts, discontent of his army, and deteriorating economic conditions were among the notable ones. The "dying lion" was neither willing to cave in to the demands of his "subjects" nor did able to calm the growing tremors, which found epicenter in the wilderness of the Borana country, in Nagelle. Nagelle, literally means "the peaceful," is located in Liban, a ritual capital of the *Gada* system of the Borana Oromo, the last bastion of the living *gada* system. It is the Borana holy city, like Jerusalem for the Jews, Makka for the Muslims, and Aksum for the Abyssinians. The Borana people call Liban, *Lafa lafa caaltuu* [the land above all land]." Nagelle is the peripheral town, close to both Somalia and Kenya; it is a bustling town populated by Oromos and Somalis, known for its fine Borana oxen; contraband trade, and the proximity to the Adola goldmines. It is also a typical *naftanya* garrison, a home of the 4th Division that was indispensable in neutralizing endless commotions that plagued the southern Oromiya.

In January 1974, a mutiny took place in this 4th Division tormented by the Oromo and Somali peasant insurgencies. A conflict broke out between a rank and file of the army and officers over the usage of water when the former's water pump broke down, and the latter denied them access to theirs. The angry soldiers took their commanders hostage and sent a petition to the emperor for the betterment of their living conditions. He dispatched a Commander of the Land Forces, whom they detained upon arrival and forced to test their living standard. This was the first victory of the army over the monarchy. Subsequently, he dispatched an air force general who negotiated a release of the commander in return for exempting the mutineers from criminal charges and improving their living conditions.

At the time, the continuity of the throne became more uncertain as the Crown Prince Asfaw Wassan suffered a massive stroke and paralyzed. The emperor was determined, as ever, to resist designating an heir to the throne. At the eleventh hour of his rule, he chose to demand a further arms supply from the U.S. to quell the insurgencies in Eritrea and Ogaden than addressing the demands of his soldiers. Unlike the coup of 1960, the U.S. was unwilling to rescue the emperor and let the throne die a natural death. In apparent disinterest to observe the Ethiopian internal political affairs, the U.S. withdrew its ambassador from Addis Ababa. On the other hand, the Empire snubbed a lesson of the revolt as a "spontaneous outburst of disgust at living conditions in the wasteland of Sidamo Province" (Ottaway & Ottaway, 1978, 45).

Although the news of Nagelle Revolt concealed from public for a while, it was a harbinger to the danger looming larger on the throne of the emperor. The coming of the coup was foreseen in light of regime's inability to address the burning issues and the country's rapid descent into lawlessness. Of course, the mutineers primarily protested the deterioration of the living conditions, but the fact that they managed to detain their leaders revealed the regime's vulnerability in the face of military rebellion, and, hence, it had political implications (Clapham, 1990, 38). The octogenarian emperor failed to understand the situation. This could be because of his senility, or his sycophants fed him wrong information, or he was complacent with his narcissist view, "[He is] a clever, all understanding ruler who gets his ideas of how to act only from himself" (quoted in Rubinkowska, 2004, 226).

Hayla Sillase had always been too smart by half. Instead of introducing a functional parliament, he opted for single-handed style of rule. Instead of decentralizing power to regions, he built power around himself in the name of unity. Instead of introducing meaningful tax reforms, he passed the burden of nobility to peasants; instead of accommodating the Ogaden demand, he gave himself the same problem everywhere; instead of accommodating the non-violent *Macha-Tulama* association, he turned them violent; instead of killing students' demands with genuine reforms, he killed them with bullet. In his epic reign of more than half of a century, while he styled himself the father of the Ethiopian modernization, he only modernized the *naftanya* riflemen into the most mechanized and formidable military in the continent. This is a single strongest institution he built, with which he brutalized; conquered; petrified; ruled and shined. This time, he lost his iron grip over it.

In fact, with those machines he defeated them so many times, but he hardly broke their resilience and indomitable spirit. Each defeat was a victory for peasants, and each victory was a defeat for his throne. In general, unintelligently relying on heavy machines, he rode for his demise.

The Nagelle revolt was not an esoteric agenda; it was a manifestation of the zeitgeist of the day. The dismal living conditions, corruptions, and accumulated frustrations (epitomes of peasants' daily lives) had reached the emperor's army, who were well-equipped and well-fed and who rewarded with land and tenants labor. The discrimination between the foot soldiers (the sons of peasants) and the officers (the sons of the aristocrats) was a miniature copy of a ubiquitous and fundamental inequality in the distribution of power among ethnic groups of the nation. This grievance had reached a point of no return. His own army had said enough!

When the news of revolt started trickling in to the center slowly, it soon found reverberation in the army and became a lesson to be mimicked elsewhere. In a show of solidarity and to protest their own living conditions, the air force men at Bushoftu and the Second Division at Asmara replicated exactly what happened in Nagelle. A Signal Corps at Asmara broadcasted the news all over to the military (Meredith, 2011, 213). It soon spread like a wildfire; the messages of solidarity were coming in from units all over the country. Nothing drove paranoia palpable to the throne like the mutiny of the Fourth Division at Addis Ababa that detained eight ministers and sought their sacking for the corruption they committed. In the Penal Code of Hayla Sillase, the punishment for mutiny is up-to death; but owning to the weaknesses of his regime, the salaries of rebel soldiers were increased; rewards in the form of land and peasants labors were promised, and the detained ministers were sacked.[1]

The resistance was contagious, and it had infested the public. Demonstrations were mushrooming and rocking every corner of Addis Ababa: students against curriculum changes, teachers for a salary increase, taxi drivers against the increase of petroleum prices, and labor unions against the cost of living conditions. None of the demonstrations paralleled in intensity and scale the mammoth rally organized by Muslims and their supporters calling for the separation of state and church and ending discrimination based on religion. They demanded the formation of independent Islamic courts with its own budget, recognition of their holidays as national holidays, the right to establish religious organizations, to own land, to work in government, justice system, media, and military. Above all, they demanded the government to stop disfiguring Islam, to rectify that image through teaching of Islam in schools and media(Chege, 2000, 245; Levtzion, 2012, 240).

The Imperial Cabinet of Aklilu appointed Colonel Alam Zawd Tasamma, a commander of airborne brigade, as the head of the Armed Forces Coordinating Committee (AFCC) to control eruptions. He took an arduous task of defending the indefensible and safeguarding a vanishing regime. Aside from his alignment with the reviled establishment, his mission was nothing shy of witch hunting of dissenters under the pretext of returning public normalcy. He chose to pacify the emperor's style. He spearheaded the incarceration of dissidents, i.e., "foreign agents" in the military. Doing so, he

---

[1] Here are pertinent Articles of Ethiopian Penal Code of 1957 on Munity. According to article 252, mutiny is punishable with rigorous imprisonment not exceeding fifteen years. Article 260 (c), mutiny is punishable with rigorous imprisonment from three years to life, or, in cases of exceptional gravity, such as in time of war or danger of war with death. Conspiracy to raise a mutiny is punishable under Article 313, failure to report mutiny is punishable under Article 321 and 344. As per Art. 458, mutiny of prisoners is punishable by law. Mutiny was tolerated in the case of "military state of necessity," according to Article 73.

proved his unwavering support for the dying regime than finding an amicable solution. A method he followed, his intimacy to the throne put him at loggerheads with the radical officers demanding fundamental reforms. His attempt failed short of thwarting the wave of mutinies and strikes and thus, the state of anarchy was unabated.

Unappeased by his mission and direction, the low ranking military officer pulled out of the AFCC and cobbled a parallel entity called the Coordinating Committee of the Armed Forces, Police and Territorial Army on 28 January 1974. The splinter group named itself *Darg*, which means committee in Ge'ez. It comprised of 120 persons and headed by Major Mangistu Hayla Maryam and Major Atnafu Abate. It was more broad-based and representative than the AFCC as three persons represented from every army and police units. This group neither had political or administrative skills, nor tainted by the rampant corruption in the army. It was none other than this secretive, shadowy, and anonymous junior officers that took advantage of the anarchy to restore and maintain law and order due to the weakness of the civilian government. Losing the support of his battalion, Colonel Alam Zawd fled to Gondar and the AFCC demised.

The throne issued a strong warning against any attempt of overthrowing the emperor. Some loyalists suggested luring them by benefits, and others suggested bombing them during their meeting in their barrack. The splinter smartly kept a low key because they were not sure about the public support and reactions from the loyalists.

Amidst this, on 23 February 1974, the emperor announced catalogues of concessions and reforms to placate the disillusioned mass with the incompetence and hollowness of the promises of his administration. The planned unpopular curriculum change was shelved; temporary price rollbacks and inflation control was put in place; salary increase for the civil servants and army was pledged, and constitutional monarchy was promised (Meredith, 2011, 214). Pertaining to relentless pressure exerted by the low ranking officers for reform, the inefficient and ineffective Imperial Cabinet of Aklilu Habtawald collapsed.

The emperor did not get the message of the reform. He replaced a humble son of a priest (Aklilu) with a son of the prominent Shawan oligarchy, Indalkachaw Makonnin. The latter used the rhetoric of a constitutional monarchy, that is, immediate power devolution to the nobility and eventually to the level of the commoners. The new prime minister came to power at a bad time, when the rule lost the means of its rule, the army. Also, he had to fight against the byzantine games of his predecessor and convince the emperor for the need of reforms (Lefort, 1983, 56). The power transition to bourgeoisie regime was designed to soothe the enraged mass with the hope of creation of constitutional monarchy and accountable to the public indirectly. More than genuine changes, the reforms were for saving the face of the monarchy and taking the steam out of the revolutionary fervors (Chege, 2000, 245). Unresponsive to the reformists clamoring for the urgent overhauling of broken imperial systems, the aristocracy introduced a cacophony of cosmetic reforms to save themselves from the current. The emperor was playing his routine byzantine game. He was buying time for forceful come back on the aftermath of the crisis. Neither the pro-reform group accommodated in a new government nor did it change the culture of filling the ministerial portfolios with the aristocratic families. Even, in the drafting of a new constitution, representatives of the pro-reform group were missing, and the emperor proceeded with the mentality of giving a gift, but this time asked by his subjects. On March 5, he declared a new constitution that introduced prime minister's accountability to the parliament. Notwithstanding the concessions put forward, except the brief hiatus, the turmoil was not subsiding. Instead of placating the Darg, the concessions emboldened it to push the reform agenda further.

Coming into power during the climax of the weakness of government system, the Indalkachaw cabinet succumbed to inexorable pressure from the *Darg* and ceded sweeping concessions to them. Maintaining law and order, investigating the grievances of the army, unraveling the abuses of the senior army members, and dismantling the rampant corruption in the army fell within the prerogatives of *Darg* powers. Again, in July 1974, utmost concession slipped from the jaw of the absolute and supreme emperor, who tightened his control on every detail of the government operation and who controlled his ministers' activities and who stripped of the regional lords their traditional powers and eventually abolished them. The emperor and his cabinet compelled to delegate a blanket of power to the *Darg*: a power to work in tandem with government officials at all level of bureaucracies, a power to investigate and arrest senior military officers and government officials at all levels, a power to release of all political prisoners, and a power to provide assurances for a safe return of exiles. The *Darg* was pledging allegiance to the imperial bureaucracies and using them as a Trojan horse to bring the collapse of the system itself. Numerous proclamations that wrought about the demise of the monarchy were rushed through the parliament. It issued the names of prominent emperor's inner circles, official, aristocrats to either return the property they looted from the public or face confiscation and arrest. Instantaneously, the high ranking officials and armed personnel swelled prisons (Meredith, 2011, 216).

A year ago, this was unthinkable on earth. The genie was out of the bottle, and the myth of the 'Conquering Lion' was debunked. Hayla Sillase's lost control over his once-powerful propaganda machine. The Ethiopian Television broadcasted the expose about the Wallo famine by the British Journalist Jonathan Dimbleby, *the Hidden Famine*, which was tailored to fit the *Darg* narrative about him. The presentation juxtaposed horrendous images of hunger, deaths and skeletons, with previous videotapes of the emperor toasting with his loyalists, sprinkling champagne, eating caviar, and feeding his dogs on silver plates. As Kapuscinski (1984, 140-141) commented, "This situation of intense evil, of horror, of desperate absurdity, became the signal of the conspiring officers to go work. After a short period of bewilderment, shock, and hesitation, Haile Selassie began to realize that he was losing his most important instrument (the army)." The revelation of the famine, in the expression of Colin Legum of the Observer, was "stinking albatross around the neck of the emperor" (quoted in Paulos Milkias 2006, 163). This sensitized the public about the irresponsibility of emperor's regime, and his public support was on the free-fall.

The Darg pressured Indalkachaw Makonnin to relinquish power [on 22 July, 1974] and requested a left leaning Lij Mikael Immiru to form a new government. Indalkachaw and his cabinet were taken from the palace to jails. The arrests failed to quench the public yearning for justice and change. Justice would be done if the demise of the regime came from the top, deposing and arresting of Hayla Sillase. The emperor became a political piñata, and his office came under avalanches of criticisms. The Darg portrayed him as out of touch, apathetic to the plight of hunger ridden population, a corrupted leader who secretly laundered billions of dollars to foreign bank accounts and who squandered the limited resources of the country on his lavish international tours. Ensued was dismantling of the imperial edifices such as the ministry of pen, Crown Council, Imperial Courts, the Emperor's Private Exchequer, confiscation of his royal investments in the St. George Beer and the Ambassa City Buses, and nationalization of his palaces (Meredith, 2011, 215).

On 11 September 1974, his majesty forced to watch the film, *the Hidden Famine*. The next day, the proclamation of his dethronement was read to him at the national palace, and then he was driven away, not by a Rolls-Royce, but by a dilapidated Volkswagen. A man, who ordered nothing less than to be called Hayla Sillase [Power of Trinity], who referred to himself often with the imperial 'We', and who arrogantly declared, "Ethiopia without me means virtually nothing," was rubbished by his own soldiers and booed and mobbed 'thief! thief!' by very subject, who used to prostrate for him when he was passing around, who used to swear in his name (*haylasillase yimut*), and who used to considered him a moving law (*bahaylasillase adara*). A Borana dictum goes: *Qaalluu Waaqa se'ee, biraan baanan beekee*, which is freely translated, I thought that the king is God, when I approached him, he was not.

The "divine" emperor, who named himself the Conquering Lion had been conquered and placed under house arrest. The throne, which survived a myriad of regional oppositions, the Mussolini's aggression, and the palace coup of 1960, had lost the battle to the junior military officers. He was a modernizer, but he came by the coup, and went by the coup. Hayla Sillase 'chickens came home to roost'. Perhaps, learning from errors of the 1960 palace coup and uncertain about its public support, or to use monarch as legitimizing symbol, the *Darg* followed precautionary measures. Hence, it was not abolitionist initially and was insisting for a promulgation of liberal constitution that introduces a formation of figurehead monarchy. It nominated Crown Prince Asfaw Wasan as king [not emperor] who rejected the dethronement of his father and designation with less flattering title. Thanks to Hayla Sillase's totalitarian government that neither allowed the flourishing of the democratic culture nor institutions; the military became the only viable institution to fill the power vacuum he left behind. The *Darg* selected Aman Andom, a retired General, an outsider, a man with impeccable military resume to helm the Provisional Military Administration.

This picture shows Hayla Sillase being shoved off to the Volkswagen. Shemelis Image Courtesy of Shemelis Desta.

The bloodless revolution that developed a motto of "May Ethiopia progress without any bloodshed" was perceived as a downing of a new chapter in Ethiopian political process. In the face of future uncertainties, people were delighted by the smoothness of the revolution and the riddance from the totalitarian rule. As Gaitachew Bekele (1993, 172) well said, "When it was clear that the emperor could not last, the whole nation heaved a sigh of relief, not caring who replaced him, so long as he went." Unfortunately, the engineers of the coup morphed into the dictators of the nation, and, they continued with the same infamous imperial style of rule, but with the gospel of communism. They self-styled republicans, but Ethiopian changed from the Solomonic Empire to the Communist Empire.

The U.S. Response to the Coup/Revolution

Rocked by the Watergate Scandal, overwhelmed by the anti-war waves, the commander-in-chief powers curbed by the Congress, the Nixon administration was trying to scale down the military operation overseas and withdraw from the conflict with dignity. Jettisoning Washington from the notion of policing the world with the debacle of Vietnam, Henry Kissinger developed a doctrine that revolved around the orbit of self-interest. The U.S. was neither interested in salvaging the throne of the emperor from the self-inflicted wounds nor willing to defend Ethiopia from communist takeover. Unlike the 1960 coup, in which the Eisenhower administration played a crucial role to restore the emperor; the Nixon administration policy was 'Washington supplies the fire extinguisher, but not fight the fire' (Lefebvre, 1991, 142).

During his golden days, the U.S. idealized Hayla Sillase for a number of reasons. He was buttressed for Kagnew, for his statesmanship, for his significance to advance U.S. imperialist agendas in Africa. The U.S. praised him as "the chief innovator" of social change and "the towering figures of modern history" (National Intelligence Estimate 75/76-72, 1972; Memorandum from Kissinger to President Nixon, 1969). Considered, for a long time, as "the dominant force" in the Ethiopian politics," the only challenge that the national security papers had foreseen on the throne of the emperor was the challenge of nature, his death, and a subsequent succession problem.

The promptness with which he lost relevance was an unbelievable for friends and foes alike. A memorandum from Richard Kennedy, on October 16, 1974, described the Africa's elder statesman as "the symbol of sins and omissions of the old regime." He was "the cornerstone of a discredited system" based on "position, wealth, and family connections." Intelligence Note IN-47 of September 1974 explained the condition of the emperor as a man subjected "to continuing military harassment." On December 5, 1974, in his op-ed to the New York Times, the U.S. advisor of the emperor (John Spencer) condemned his government for abandoning Ethiopia.

The emperor fell out of grace, and the U.S. had several reasons to unfriend and kiss him goodbye. Firstly, defending the emperor served no strategic significance because of the obsolescence of Kagnew. As we touched earlier, the U.S. instantly overruled the emperor plea for extra arm supplies. Secondly, the diplomatic intercourse between Ethiopia and the U.S. was at a low point since the U.S. even lost the appetite to observe the incident by appointing a representative, and let alone trying to halt the tsunami of change. In fact, the decision to downgrade the diplomatic intercourse was to avoid entangling in the domestic turmoil of Ethiopia. It should be noted that Ambassador E. Ross Adair departed Addis Ababa at the time when the country was engrossed in the pandemonium; mutiny after mutiny and strikes after strikes in February 1974. Thirdly, perhaps the Washington bureaucrats did not like the fact that Hayla Sillase severed ties with Israel in solidarity with the Third World countries. Fourthly, there was no significant interest such as commerce or investment that the "Yankee traders" had to defend since the relationship with Ethiopia was purely the security diplomacy. Fifthly, there had not been any passion even from the African-American community for the regime of the emperor, which would have created a domestic pressure on the Washington. Sixthly, there was no ideological dimension to the revolution at the initial stage. Seventhly, there was a belief that the U.S. trained officers would hardly abandon their trusted patron. Eighthly, Kissinger general approach towards African affairs was keeping Africa at bay. Ninthly, because of the crisis snow balling one after another and because of the Wallo famine, supporting the government of the emperor had become "an international liability" for the U.S.

Thanks to the realpolitik of Henry Kissinger, Washington embraced the ousters of their longtime ally. A memo of Richard Kennedy on October 16, 1974 noted, "The political change set in motion by the military revolt is irreversible. The old order based on position, wealth, and family connections has been destroyed." (Memorandum from Richard Kennedy to Kissinger, 1974). This was the vindication of time honored dictum that 'nations have no permanent friends or allies; they only have permanent interests'.

A memo from the Director of Policy Planning (Winston Lord) to the Undersecretary of State for Political Affairs (Joseph John Sisco) had some fascinating take on the fall of the emperor. It began with how "the emperor tried to dissuade the U.S. from reducing the base [...] to maintain stability through him" and how he could attribute his decline to its reduction. He surmised, "If he could speak to us now, he might say, "I told you so: You phased out Kagnew; therefore I was overthrown." Lord continued, "He would be wrong. His durability was more surprising than his ouster in 1974." He cited the student of African politics who said, "It seemed unlikely that his old regime would survive himself if, indeed, it would last that long." Lord continued to find an explanation for his toppling:

> U.S. official and private aid to Ethiopia together with assistance provided by other countries created tremendous tensions between the feudal realities of the Empire and the modern expectations which western training and other exposures engendered among the thin educated elite. These tensions were not always anticipated by proponents of aid who believed in "stable development, a contradiction in terms. (Briefing Memorandum from Lord to Sisco, 1975).

While the regime came to an end mainly because of lack of human rights and its inability to realize tangible economic progress, the memo asserts that his demise was because of "development." The notion of traditional monarchies becoming the victim of their own modernization was, indeed, a page taken from Professor Samuel Huntington's book, *Political Order in Changing Societies*. He argues that correlating economic development to political stability is 'erroneous dogma' since they are "two independent goals and progress toward one has no necessary connection with progress towards the other." Contrary to bringing stability, reforms "undermine traditional sources of political authority and traditional political institutions" and "exacerbate tensions, precipitate violence, and be a catalyst of rather than a substitute for revolution" (Huntington, 2006, 5-7). One thing, nevertheless, is truer from the memorandum and Huntington's thesis, the wrong policy of the U.S. partly contributed for the sustenance and the collapse of the brutal regime.

Not only the U.S. embraced the *Darg*, but also it had positive impressions about the revolution. This can be seen from Intelligence Note IN-47 of September 25, 1974 entitled, "Ethiopia: Anatomy of a Revolution." As per this report, the domestic objectives of the *Darg* were: (a) establishing constitutional government, (b) the destruction of the feudal social order, (c) the accommodation of ethnic and regional dissidence, (d) active government encouragement of socioeconomic development, and reform of the military. On the foreign policy front, the report predicted that the *Darg* would (a) pursue rapprochement with Arabs, emphasize third-world solidarity, (b) continue to favor the U.S. as arms supplier, diversify source of arms supply, and loosen bilateral ties with the U.S. According the report, a junta's decision to loosen diplomatic ties with the U.S. was because they wanted to distance themselves from the unpopular policies of the previous regime, and not because they were communists. (Intelligence Note IN-47, 1974). Moscow, however, had foreseen a rise of their red dictator because Pravda, the official Soviet Communist party newspaper, underlined that the change was not simply "an ordinary military coup" (quoted in Donham, 1999, 138).

Summary

THE MODERN CONCEPT of human rights is a product of collective shock the world community suffered after horrendous acts of the Nazi. In other words, it was the establishment of the United Nations (UN) that heralded its birth. There was a consensus that encouraging respect of human rights will fundamentally enhance global peace and security. Accordingly, it is a duty of the states to respect, promote, prevent, and protect natural and inalienable rights of individuals.

Be that as it may, the history of human rights is as old as humankind. Hagel, Marks, and Fukuyama have noted that human beings—like animals—have natural needs and desires for food, drink, shelter, and self-preservation (see, Fukuyama, 2006). Christian Bay noted that "needs establish human rights," (quoted in Donnelly, 2013, 13) and Green equally observed that "a basic human need logically gives rise to a right" (ibid). Hagel, Marks, and Fukuyama have noted that man is intrinsically different from animals in the sense that he is not the mere slave of his needs. Man has 'a desire to be recognized as a human being' (Fukuyama, 2006, xvi). This desire empowers human being to "overcome self-preservation for the sake of higher, abstract principles and goals" (ibid). Aristocratic societies, which ruled in the form of the slave master relationship for the most part of human history, had succumbed to failure because of a human being indomitable spirit of the self-worth [prestige]. Jack Donnelly remarked, "Human rights are 'needed' for human dignity ... and violations of human rights are denials of one's humanity rather than deprivations of needs" (quoted in Buchanan, 2009, 210). Maslow has demonstrated the progression of human motivation from the lowest to the highest, from the simplest to the complex. Hence, originated from the simple concept of human needs, today we have a complex understanding of human rights and democracy.

Humanity has tried to design various mechanisms to address the issues of human needs and desires. Therefore, precepts of various religions, customary laws, moral teachings, and a plethora of legal documents attempted to address human rights issues of their time. As far back as 1500s, there were human rights agendas [individual violations of human rights] that the world community already embraced through the states usages [practices] and acquiescence to be bound [*opinion juris*] as customary international norms. A crime of piracy was such an example (Bassiouni, 515, 1919). Regrettably, it is an irony of human rights that the individual responsibility developed faster than state responsibility, which is the primary subject of international law and primary violators of human rights.

Nowhere the notion of human rights found a strong resonance like in the U.S. and the U.S. foreign policy. When the U.S. formed relations with Ethiopia, there were human rights violations [agendas] that the international community agreed on to end it. Slavery was the best case in point. However, the aspect of Minilik as a "hero" against colonialism, a modernizer, and a Christian potentate emerged on a global scale; his rule at home for the conquered peoples was unjust, exploitative, violent, and, and in brief, he was mass butcher. In dealing with him, the U.S. human rights agenda took a backseat of its diplomacy. To the embarrassment of the U.S. and an affront to humanity, its diplomat not only failed to utter a word about flourishing epidemic of the slave trade in Abyssinia, but also tried to humanize the Abyssinian enslavement of what he called the "savage" races.

The Achilles' heel of the United States foreign policy towards Africa is the absence of uniform policy. Nothing illuminates this than Peter Schraeder analogy of the pattern of the U.S. policy towards Africa than the parable of 'blind men and an elephant'. Curious to know about the elephant, the blind men touched the elephant, according to this parable. They reached at a conclusion depending where they touched. For a person who touched a large ear, an elephant was about the large ear; for a person, who touched a trunk, an elephant was all about the trunk or for a person who touched a fat leg, an elephant was all about the fat leg. Schraeder maintains that what they concluded about the various parts of the elephant could be true, but it does not provide a holistic answer as to a "nature of the beast."

As I demonstrated throughout this material, the U.S. foreign policy towards Africa is worse than that. Whereas the conclusions of the blind men about the certain part of the beast [say, ear] could be pretty much consistent, the U.S. foreign policy to a certain part of Africa [say, Ethiopia] is pretty much inconsistent. Thus, the U.S. foreign policy towards Africa is self-contradictory, lacked commitment, and contingent upon national security goals, and often thrown under the bus whenever there are overriding national security goals. It is often effective by failure because of its poor understanding [knowledge] about the continent and reactionary in nature to crisis (see, Schraeder, 1996).

Africa was the most ignored and unknown continent, designated "Dark Continent" by westerners. There is a culture that permeates scholarly works, the media, public at large, and government bureaucrats; Africa is a singular, homogenous, and holistic entity. It is far off place known for its exotic animals. "Americans fascinated with Africa," says Grubbs, "but with an artificial, culturally constructed 'Africa'" (Grubbs, 2009, 21). "This was an Africa of the mind, not the concrete, discrete, immensely large and diverse of live reality" (ibid).

Nowhere the U.S. has erroneous and shortsighted diagnoses of problems in Africa like it is a case in Ethiopia. Firstly, like elsewhere in Africa, the wrong diagnoses are so rampant because it is mainly guided by self-interest and geopolitical realities. Secondly, it is shaped by false conscience about that country than its objective reality. She was defined by the reality propagated by Abyssinian ruling class and amplified by western travellers, as well as the one imagined by the U.S. politicians, than the reality she lived it. At the beginning of the twentieth century, the U.S. politicians convinced that Abyssinia was a candidate for "Americanization" mission. She was suitable due to its Caucasian [Semitic] identity and ripe because of its victories over "barbarians." This open racism was a lighting guide of the diplomatic adventure of Robert Skinner, who established a contact with "a United States of Abyssinia" in 1903. President Roosevelt also could see Ethiopia beyond cliché of the land of big animal and "Christian" civilization.

The legacies of misguidedness and shortsightedness are innumerable. The fact that the U.S. commissioned a white man, instead of an African-American initiator, for negotiating the treaty with Minilik speaks for itself about the nature of their Abyssinia. The U.S. benign negligence of oppression of the non-Abyssinian race was a manifestation of the footprint Skinner left behind on the U.S. foreign policy towards Abyssinia: "Caucasian" vs. "savages." When Emperor Iyyasu tried to reform the totalitarian empire that stood in a stark contrast to the values of the west and human rationality, the proponents of the *status quo* and their western supporters buttressed one another to see the demise of the progressive leader. The Department of State classifying Abyssinia under the Division of Near Eastern Affairs, for a long time, shows impacts of myths of Ethiopia. A racial composition of U.S service men in Ethiopia in 1960s was another reflection of the legacy of this distortion. Out of 3,500 service men in Ethiopia, only "few U.S. Negroes hold top posts because of U.S. State Department's view that Ethiopians dislike American Negroes" (Ebony, Vol. 23, No. 5, 1968, 53). In fact, at the time when the throne of Hayla Sillase was on the fire, President Nixon used a biblical quote to express the "Solomonic" wisdom of unwise ruler.

It was this misguided policy that made the U.S. rehabilitate and reinforce an empire, which its diplomat called a semi-fascist while it was fighting Fascism and Nazism in Europe and urging its allies to abandon their imperial ambitions. When this misguided policy wed to self-interest, in the era of the Cold War, maintaining a fundamentally undemocratic empire became a concern of the U.S. as much as it was of the throne in Addis. Let alone convincing Ethiopia to embrace democratic reforms, the U.S. was unwilling/unable to pressure the regime to reform agriculture, the sector that employs 85 percent of the Ethiopian population. On the other hand, the empire entrapped the U.S. into their pernicious rifle diplomacy. By sustaining the violent throne, the U.S. sustained the traumas of the victims of the throne. With the U.S. generous hand, the "Conquering Lion" conquered his subjects.

Instead of checking his imperialistic lust, the United States eroticized Hayla Sillase to claim Eritrea disregarding the human rights of the Eritrean people. When his inhumane dictatorship became unbearable, and when the Eritreans resorted to militancy, the empire labeled them "Arab nationalists" and decided to liquidate them. Rather than advising the emperor to step back from military offensives and negotiate with them, the U.S. provided weapons and counter insurgency trainings to his commandos. The U.S. did the same thing in the case of the Bale, Borana, and Guji peasants' rebellions. U.S. armaments, counter-insurgency trainings helped the emperor to pacify them. The U.S. tangled in the conflicts to the extent of its experts improving the fire power of the jets during the Bale uprisings. These were the jests that did not discriminate between the civilian populations and the rebels. The U.S. was silent about the plights of Muslim populations, who were considered aliens by the empire. The fear that they might fall to Nasser's orbit concerned the U.S. more than their lack of human rights protections.

The U.S. unconditional military aids to Ethiopia fueled the unparalleled arm races in the Horn of Africa. The militarization drive stifled economic growth and development of other institutions in the region. During this time, no matter how the grand project of pan-Somali state faltered and no matter how Somalia locked in the incessant wars with its neighbors, a democratic vibrancy was highly visible in Somalia. Somalia was a country of blossoming free-press and a model for human rights safeguards. To facilitate the detente between Ethiopia and Somalia, the U.S. involved in the Somali political arrangement. The interference turned the equivalence of positions between different clans and regions of Somalia on its head. This led to the collapse of democratic order in Somalia, which is burning that country still today.

In Ethiopia, the imperial regime pursues military solutions for the demands of human rights from its subjects. This increased Hayla Sillase's dependency on the U.S. for heavy machinery became a life support of his regime. Whereas he was consistently dissatisfied with the amount of military aid, the students' disenchantment with the U.S. increased because of its unconditional support for 'repressive' and 'backward' regime. The students chose socialism as alternative ideology. When the U.S. withdrew its hand, his rule deflated like a balloon, and it became his turn to be conquered. The emperor, a natural fortress against the communist expansion in Africa, became a bastion of communism, and the student thought to be the iron wall against communism became a Trojan horse for communism. This is a logical end of misguided and myopic policy.

Bibliography

Abir, Mordechai (1968). *Ethiopia: The Era of the Princes: The Challenge of Islam and Re-Unification of the Christian Empire, 1769-1855*. New York: Frederick A. Praeger.

Acemoglu, Daron and Robinson, James (2012). *Why Nations Fail: The Origins of Power, Prosperity, and Poverty*. New York: Random House Inc.

Adejumobi, Saheed A. (2007). *The History of Ethiopia*. Westport: Greenwood Press.

Agyeman-Duah, Baffour (1994). *The United States and Ethiopia: Military Assistance and the Quest for Security 1953–1993*. Lanham: University Press of America.

Ahrari, Mohammed E. (1987). *Ethnic Groups and U.S. Foreign Policy*. Westport: Greenwood Publishing Group.

Alexander, Zvi (2004). *Oil: Israel's Covert Efforts to Secure Oil Supplies*. Jerusalem: Gefen Publishing House Ltd.

Alteras, Isaac (1993). *Eisenhower and Israel: U.S.-Israeli Relations, 1953-1960*. Gainesville: University Press of Florida.

Apodaca Clair (2006), *Understanding U.S. Human Rights Policy: A Paradoxical Legacy*. New York: Routledge.

Arén, Gustav (1999), *Envoys of the Gospel in Ethiopia: In the Steps of the Evangelical Pioneers 1898-1936*. Stockholm: EFS Förlaget.

Asafa Jalata (2002). *Fighting against the Injustice of the State and Globalization: Comparing the African American and Oromo Movements*. New York: Palgrave.

_____. (2005). *Oromia and Ethiopia: State Formation and Ethnonational Conflict 1868–2004*. Trenton: The Red Sea Press.

_____. (2011). "Imperfections in U.S. Foreign Policy Toward Oromia and Ethiopia: Will The Obama Administration Introduce Change?," *The Journal of Pan African Studies*, Vol., 4, No., 3.

Asante, S.K.B. (1977). *Pan-African Protest: West Africa and the Italo-Ethiopian Crisis, 1934-1941*. London: Longman Group.

Bahru Zewde (2001). *A History of Modern Ethiopia 1855-1991*, Edition 2. Oxford: James Currey.

Bairu Tafla (1994). *Ethiopia and Austria: A History of Their Relations*. Wiesbaden: Harrassowitz.

Balsvik, R.R. (1985). *Haile Selassie's Students: The Intellectual and Social Background to Revolution, 1952–1977* (East Lansing, Michigan State Univ.).

Bassiouni, M. Cherif (1999). *Crimes against Humanity in International Criminal Law*. The Hague: Martinus Nijhoff Publishers.

Beit-Hallahmi, Benjamin (1987). *The Israeli Connection: Who Israel Arms and Why*. New York: I. B. Tauris.

Berhanou Dinke, *Letters to the Editor*, The Washington Post, Feb. 24, 1964.

Bernstein, R. B. (2003). *Thomas Jefferson*. New York: Oxford Univ. Press.
Böll, Verena (2005). *Ethiopia and the Missions: Historical and Anthropological Insights*.Münster: LIT Verlag Münster.
Boyle, Peter G., ed. (2006). *Eden-Eisenhower Correspondence, 1955-1957*. Chapel Hill: University of North Carolina Press.
Brinkley, Douglas (2009). *The Wilderness Warrior: Theodore Roosevelt and the Crusade for America*. New York: HarperCollins.
Bromiley, Geoffrey (1915). *International Standard Bible Encyclopedia: E-J*. Chicago: Howard Severance Co.
Brownson, James Dunwoody, et al., (1850). *Review Agricultural, Commercial, Industrial Progress and Resources*, Vol., 9. New Orleans: J. D. B. DeBow.
Broyles, Matthew (2004). *The Six-Day War*. New York: The Rosen Publishing Group, Inc.
Brzezinski, Matthew (2008). *Red Moon Rising: Sputnik and the Hidden Rivalries that Ignited the Space Age*. New York: Holt.
Buchanan, Allen (2009). *Justice and Health Care: Selected Essays*. Oxford: Oxford University Press.
Buck, David R. (2002). *A Helping Hand?: The United States, "Questions of the Far East," & the Washington Conference, 1921—1922*. Ann Harbor: ProQuest.
Bulatovich, A.K. (2000), *Ethiopia Through Russian Eyes: Country in Transition, 1896-1898*, trans., Richard Seltzer. Trenton: Red Sea Press.
Burns, James MacGregor (1956). *Roosevelt: The Lion and the Fox: 1882–1940*. New York: Smithmark Publishing, Inc.
Carol, Steven (2012). *From Jerusalem to the Lion of Judah and Beyond: Israel's Foreign Policy in East Africa*. Bloomington: iUniverse.
Cassese, Antonio (1995). Self-Determination of Peoples: A Legal Reappraisal. Cambridge: Cambridge University Press.
Chambers, John Whiteclay, ed. (1999). *The Oxford Companion to American Military History*. New York: Oxford University Press.
Chege, Michael (2000). "The Revolution Betrayed: Ethiopia, 1974-9," in Rosemary H. T. O'Kane (ed.), *Revolution: Critical Concepts in Political Science*, Volume 3. London: Routledge.
Churchill, et al. (1899). *The Anglo-Saxon Review*, Vol., 2. London: John Lane.
Clarence-Smith, W. G. (1989). *The Economics of the Indian Ocean Slave Trade in the Nineteenth Century*. Totowa: Psychology Press.
Collins, Robert O. Burns, and James M. (2007). *A History of Sub-Saharan Africa*. Cambridge: Cambridge University Press.
Coppa, Frank J., ed. (2006). *Encyclopedia of Modern Dictators: From Napoleon to the Present*. New York: Peter Lang Publishing, Inc.
Cull, Nicholas John, et. al. (2003). *Propaganda and Mass Persuasion: A Historical Encyclopedia, 1500 to the Present*. Santa Barbara: ABC-CLIO.
Damato, Antonio (1994). *International Law Anthology*. Chicago: Anderson Publishers Co.

Daugherty, Leo J. (2009). *The Marine Corps and the State Department: Enduring Partners in United States Foreign Policy, 1798-2007*. Jefferson: McFarland.

Davison, Donald J. (2003). *The Wisdom of Theodore Roosevelt*. New York: Kensington Publishing Corp.

de Salviac, Martial (1900). *Un Peuple Antique, Ou Une Colonie Gauloise Au Pays De Ménélik: les Galla, Grande Nation Africaine*. Paris: F. Plantade.

De Waal, Alexander (1991). *Evil Days: 30 Years of War and Famine in Ethiopia*. New York: Human Rights Watch.

Donham, Donald Lewis (1999). *Marxist Modern: An Ethnographic History of the Ethiopian Revolution*. Berkeley: University of California Press.

Donham, Donald and James, Wendy (1986). *The Southern Marches of Imperial Ethiopia: Essays in History and Social Anthropology*. New York: Cambridge University Press.

Donnelly, Jack (2013). *Universal Human Rights in Theory and Practice, 3rd edition*. Ithaca: Cornell University Press.

Duignan, Peter and Gann, L. H. (1987). *The United States and Africa: A History*. Cambridge: Cambridge University Press.

Erlick, Hagai (2002). *The Cross and the River: Ethiopia, Egypt, and the Nile*. Boulder: Lynne Rienner Publishers.

_____. (2007). Saudi Arabia and Ethiopia: Islam, Christianity, and Politics Entwined. Boulder: Lynne Rienner Publishers.

Everett, Marshall (2004). *Roosevelt Thrilling Experiences in the Wildest of Africa Hunting Big Game*. London: Kessinger Publishing.

Fasil Nahum (1997) *Constitution for a Nation of Nations: The Ethiopian Prospect*. Asmara: Red Sea Press.

Feldmeth, Gregory, et. al. (2011). *AP U.S. History*: 8th Edition. Piscataway: Research & Education Assoc.

Ferris, Jesse (2003). *"Nasser's Gamble": How Intervention in Yemen Caused the Six-Day War and the Decline of Egyptian Power*. Princeton: Princeton Univ. Press.

Finaldi, Giuseppe (2009). *Italian National Identity in the Scramble for Africa: Italy's African Wars in the Era of Nation-Building, 1870-1900*. Bern: Peter Lang.

Freidle, Frank Burt (1990). *Franklin D Roosevelt: A Rendezvous with Destiny*. Boston, Toronto, London: Little, Brown and Co.

Forsythe, David P. (1989). *Human Rights and World Politics*, 2nd ed. Omaha: Univ. of Nebraska Press.

Frost, Bryan-Paul and Sikkenga, Jeffrey (2003). *History of American Political Thought*. Oxford: Lexington Books.

Fry, Michael Graham, et al. (2004). *Guide to International Relations and Diplomacy*. New York: Continuum International Publishing Group.

Fukuyama, Francis (2006). *The End of History and the Last Man*. New York: Simon and Schuster.

Gadaa Melba (1980), *Oromia: A brief Introduction*. Finfinne, Oromia.

Gaitachew Bekele (1993). *The Emperor's Clothes: A Personal viewpoint on Politics and Administration in the Imperial Ethiopian Government 1941-1974*. East Lansing: Michigan State University Press.

Gallagher, John (1982). *The Decline, Revival and Fall of the British Empire: The Ford Lectures and Other Essays, The Ford Lectures and Other Essays*. Cambridge: Cambridge University Press.

Garretson, Peter P. (2000), *A History of Addis Abäba from Its Foundation in 1886 to 1910*. Wiesbaden: Otto Harrassowitz.

Gebru Tareke (1991). *Ethiopia: Power and Protest, Peasant Revolts in the Twentieth Century*. Cambridge: Cambridge University Press.

_____. (2009). *The Ethiopian Revolution: War on the Horn of Africa*. New Haven: Yale Univ. Press.

Gellner, Ernest and Breuilly, John (2008). *Nations and Nationalism*, Second Edition. Ithaca: Cornell Univ. Press.

Getachew Metaferia (2009). *Ethiopia and the United States: History, Diplomacy, and Analysis*. New York: Algora Publishing.

Getahun Bekele, *Ethiopia: 'Judas of Wollayta' shattered as pagan TPLF warlords cancelled his bizarre Sunday mass*. 03 Feb 2013. 07 Feb. 2013 <http://indepthafrica.com/ethiopia-judas-of-wollayta-shattered-as-pagan-tplf-warlords-cancelled-his-bizarre-sunday-mass/#.USYRKKWTz2u>.

Gibbon, Edward (1841). *The Decline and Fall of the Roman Empire*, Vol., 3. New York: Harper & Brothers.

Gilkes, Patrick (1975). *The Dying Lion: Feudalism and Modernization in Ethiopia*. New York: St. Martin's Press.

Gleichen, Edward (1898). *With the Mission to Menelik*. London: E. Arnold.

Gleijeses, Piero (2004). Conflicting Missions: Havana, Washington, and Africa, 1959-1976. Chapel Hill: Univ.of North Carolina Press.

Glueck, Sheldon (2008). "The Nuernberg Trial and Aggressive War," in Guénaël Mettraux (ed.), *Perspectives on the Nuremberg Trial*. Oxford: Oxford Univ. Press.

Greenfield, Richard (1965). Ethiopia: A New Political History. London: Pall Mall Press.

Greenidge, C. W.W (1958) Slavery. London: Allen & Unwin.

Grubbs, Larry (2009). Secular Missionaries: Americans and African Development in the 1960s. Amherst: Univ. of Massachusetts Press.

Gunther, John (1954). *Inside Africa*. New York: Harper and Brothers.

Hadden, B. & Luce, H.R. (1961), *Time*, Volume 78, Part 3.

Hagedorn, Hermann (1921). *Roosevelt in the Bad Lands*, Vol., 1. Boston & New York: Houghton Mifflin Company.

Haile Selassie (1972). *Important Utterances of H. I. M. Emperor Haile Selassie I, 1963-1972*. Addis Ababa: Imperial Ethiopian Ministry of Information.

_____. (1976). *My Life and Ethiopia's Progress, 1892-1937: the Autobiography of Emperor Haile Sellassie I*, ed., Edward Ullendorff. Oxford: OUP.

_____. (1994). My *Life and Ethiopia's Progress*, trans. Ezekiel Gebissa & Tibebe Eshete, ed. H. G. Marcus. East Lansing: Michigan State Uni. Press.

Haile Selassie Gebreselassie and Volker, Edmond (2000). "Contextualizing the Establishment of the Institution of Human Rights Protection in Ethiopia," in Kamal Hossain et al. (eds.), *Human Rights Commissions and Ombudsman Offices: National Experiences*. The Hague: Kluwer.

Harlan, Louis R. ed. (1979). *Booker T. Washington: 1904-6*, Vol., 8. Chicago: University of Illinois Press.

Harland, David M. (2008). *Exploring the Moon: The Apollo Expedition*. Berlin, Heidelberg, New York: Springer-Verlag.

Harris, Jr., Brice (1964). *The United States and the Italo-Ethiopian Crisis*. Stanford: Stanford University Press.

Hart, Parker T. (2008). *Saudi Arabia and the United States: Birth of a Security Partnership*. Bloomington: Indiana University Press.

Haufler, Hervie (2006). *The Spies Who Never Were: The True Story of the Nazi Spies Who Were Actually Allied Double Agents*. New York: NAL Caliber.

Hendrickson, David C. (2009). *Union, Nation, or Empire: The American Debate over International Relations, 1789-1941*. Lawrence: Univ. Press of Kansas.

Hill, John E., (2007). *Democracy, Equality, and Justice: John Adams, Adam Smith, and Political Economy*. Lanham: Lexington Books.

Hill, Robert A. ed. (1983). *The Marcus Garvey and Universal Negro Improvement Association Papers*, Vol. VII. Berkeley: University of California Press.

Hixson, Walter L. (2008). *The Myth of American Diplomacy: National Identity and U.S. Foreign Policy*. New Haven: Yale University Press.

Holcomb, Bonnie & Sissai Ibssa (1990). *The Invention of Ethiopia*. Trenton: The Red Sea Press.

Holland, Matthew F. (1996). *America and Egypt: From Roosevelt to Eisenhower*. Westport: Greenwood Publishing Group.

Hollister, Ned (1919). *East African Mammals in the United States National Museum...: Insectivora, Chiroptera, and Carnivora*. Washington: G. P.P.

Homer (1950). *The Odyssey*, translated by E.V. Rieu. Harmondsworth, Penguin.

Hopwood, Derek (2002). *Egypt 1945-1990: Politics and Society*. London: Routledge.

Philip, Hoffman and Hough, Walter (1911). *The Hoffman Philip Abyssinian Ethnological Collection, Proceeding of U.S. National Museum*, Vol. 40, No., 1819.

Hindlip, B. C. A. (1906). *Sport and travel: Abyssinia and British East Africa*. London: T.F. Unwin.

Hubbard, James P. (2011). *The United States and the End of British Colonial Rule in Africa, 1941-1968*. Jefferson: McFarland Co.

Huntington, Samuel P. (2006). *Political Order in Changing Societies*. New Haven: Yale University Press.

Hussein Ahmed (2001), *Islam in Nineteenth-Century Wallo, Ethiopia: Revival, Reform and Reaction.* Leiden: Brill.
Hyde, Harlow A. (1988). *Scraps of Paper: The Disarmament Treaties Between the World Wars.* Lincoln: Media Publishing.
Hydén, Göran, et al. (2003). *Media and Democracy in Africa.* Piscataway: Transaction Publishers.
Ibrahim Amae Elemo (2005). *The Role of Traditional Institutions among the Borana Oromo, Southern Ethiopia: HIV/AIDS, Gender and Reproductive Health Promotion: Contemporary Issues In Boorana and the 38th Gumii Gaayoo Assembly.* Addis Ababa: Artistic Printing Enterprise.
International Report, Vol 3 (1983). Irvine: University of California,
Jensen, Derrick (2004), *The Culture of Make Believe.* New York: Chelsea Green.
Johnson, Lady Bird (2007). *A White House Diary.* Austin: Univ. of Texas Press.
Joireman, S.F. and Szayna, T.S. (2000)."The Ethiopian Prospective Case," in Thomas S. Szayna (ed.), *Identifying Potential Ethnic Conflict: Application of a Process Model.* Santa Monica, Rand Corp.
Jonas, R. Anthony (2011). *The Battle of Adwa: African Victory in the Age of Empire.* Boston: Harvard University Press.
Joseph, Frank (2010). *Mussolini's War: Fascist Italy's Military Struggles from Africa and Western Europe to the Mediterranean and Soviet Union 1935-45.* Solihull: Helion & Company.
Kapuscinski, Ryzard (1984). The Emperor: *Downfall of an Autocrat,* trans., William R. Brand and Katarzyna Mroczwska-Brand. New York: Vintage.
Keim, Curt (1999). *Mistaking Africa: Curiosities and Inventions of the American Mind.* Boulder: Westview Press.
Keller, Edmond J. (1989). *Revolutionary Ethiopia: From Empire to People's Republic.* Bloomington: Indiana University Press.
Khogali, Walied and Krajnc, Anita, *'Al-Jazeera Effect' Counters 'CNN Effect': Canadians Deserve Al Jazeera.* N.d. 05 March 2013 <http://towardfreedom.com/home/content/view/1599/1/>.
Kommers, Donald P. and Loescher, Gilbert D., (1979). Human Rights and American Foreign Policy. Notre Dame: Univ. of Notre Dame Press.
LaGumina, Salvatore John, et al., eds. (2000). *The Italian American Experience: An Encyclopedia.* New York: Garland.
Leenco Lata (1999). *The Ethiopian State at the Crossroads: Decolonization and Democratization or Disintegration?* Lawrenceville, Asmara: RSP.
Lefebvre, Jeffrey A. (1991). *Arms for the Horn: U.S. Security Policy in Ethiopia and Somalia, 1953-1991.* Pittsburgh: Univ. of Pittsburgh Press.
Lefort, René (2012). *Ethiopia: Meles rules from beyond the grave, but for how long?* 26 Nov. 2012. 21 February 2013.
http://www.opendemocracy.net/opensecurity/ren%C3%A9-lefort/ethiopia-meles-rules-from-beyond-grave-but-for-how-long.

Lefort, René (1983). *A Heretical Revolution?*, trans. A.M Berrett. London: Z-Press.
Legum, Colin (1975). *Ethiopia: The Fall of Haile Selassie's Empire*. New York : Africana Pub. Co.
Lentakis, Michael B. (2005). *Ethiopia: A View from Within*. London: Janus Publ.
Levine, Donald N. (1965). "Ethiopia: Identity, Authority, and Realism," in Lucian W. Pye and Sidney Verba, (eds.), *Political Culture and Political Development*. Princeton: University Press.
_____. (1974). *Greater Ethiopia: The Evolution of a Multiethnic Society*. Chicago: University of Chicago Press.
Levtzion, Nehemia (2012). *History of Islam in Africa*. Athens: Ohio Univ. Press.
Lewis, Neal A (1991). *U.S. Plans to Be 'Midwife' to a New Rule in Ethiopia*, the New York Times, May 26, 1991.
Lewis, I. M. (1980). A Modern History of Somaliland: Nation and State in the Horn of Africa. New York: Longmans.
Lipsky, George A. (1964). *U.S. Army Area Handbook for Ethiopia*. Washington, D.C.: U.S. Government Printing Office.
Livingston, Bernard (2000). *Zoo: Animals, People, Places*. Lincoln: iUniverse.com.
Louis, Wm. Roger (2006). *Ends of British Imperialism: The Scramble for Empire, Suez and Decolonization*. London: I. B. Tauris.
Luther, Ernest W. (1958). *Ethiopia Today*. Stanford: Stanford University Press.
Lyons, Terrence "Keeping Africa off the Agenda," in Warren I. Cohen and Nancy Bernkopf Tucker (eds.), *Lyndon Johnson Confronts the World: American Foreign Policy, 1963-1968*. New York: Cambridge Univ. Press.
Madkhli, Nawaf (2003). *"Nasser's Vietnam": The Egyptian Intervention in Yemen, 1962-1967*. Fayetteville: University of Arkansas.
Magubane, Bernard (1987).*The Ties That Bind: African-American Consciousness of Africa*. Trenton: Africa World Press.
Maier, Thomas (2009). *The Kennedys: America's Emerald Kings: A Five-Generation History of the Ultimate Irish-Catholic Family*. New York: Basic Books.
Mammo Tirfe (1999). *The Paradox of Africa's Poverty: The Role of Indigenous Knowledge, Traditional Practices and Local Institutions-The Case of Ethiopia*. Lawrenceville: The Red Sea Press.
Marcus, Harold G. (1971). "The Black Men Who Turned White: European Attitudes towards Ethiopians, 1850-1900," *Archive Orientale*, Vol., 39.
_____. (1995). *The Politics of Empire: Ethiopia, Great Britain and the United States*. Lawrenceville: Red Sea Press.
_____.(1975). *The Life and Times of Menelik II*. Oxford: Clarendon Press.
_____.(1994). *A History of Ethiopia*. Berkeley, University of California Press.
Markakis, John (2011). *Ethiopia: The Last Two Frontiers*. Oxford: James Currey.
Markakis, John and Nega Ayele (1978). *Class and Revolution in Ethiopia*. Nottingham: Spokesman Books.

Matthews, Melvin E. (2012). *Duck and Cover: Civil Defense Images in Film and Television from the Cold War to 9/11*. Jefferson: McFarland.
May, Ernest R. (1961). *Imperial Democracy: The Emergence of America as a Great Power*. New York: Harcourt, Brace & World.
McGuckin, John Anthony, ed. (2010). *The Encyclopedia of Eastern Orthodox Christianity*. Oxford: Wiley-Blackwell.
McKenna, Amy (2011). *The History of Central and Eastern Africa*. New York: Encyclopedia Britannica Inc.
McVety, Amanda (2008). "Pursuing Progress: Point Four in Ethiopia," The Journal of the Gilded Age and Progressive Era, Vol. 10, No, 2.
_____ (2012). *Enlightened Aid: U.S. Development as Foreign Policy in Ethiopia*. Oxford: Oxford University Press.
_____. (2011). "The 1903 Skinner Mission: Images of Ethiopia in the Progressive Era," *The Journal of Gilded Age and Progressive Era*, Vol., 10, No., 2.
Mekuria Bulcha (1988). *Flight and integration: causes of mass exodus from Ethiopia and problems of integration in the Sudan*. Uppsala: Scandinavian Institute of African Studies.
_____. (2002). *The Making of the Oromo Diaspora: a Historical Sociology of Forced Migration*. Minneapolis: Kirk House Publishers.
Mercury, Karen (2006). *The Four Quarters of the World*. N.P.: Medallion Press.
Mersha Alehegne (2005). The Orthodox-Protestant Relationship in Ethiopia: A Glimpse on Interaction, Attitude, Causes of Disharmony, Consequences, and Some Solutions, in Verena Boll (ed.), *Ethiopia and the Missions: Historical and Anthropological Insights*. Münster: LIT Verlag.
Messay Kebede (2008). *Radicalism and Cultural Dislocation in Ethiopia, 1960-1974*. Rochester: University Rochester Press.
Messing, Simon David (1972). *A Holistic Reader in Applied Anthropology: The Target of Health in Ethiopia*. New York: Ardent Media.
Mesthrie, Rajend (2002). *Language in South Africa*. Cambridge: Cambridge University Press.
Miscamble, Wilson D. (1992). *George F. Kennan and the Making of American Foreign Policy, 1947-1950*. Princeton, NJ: Princeton University Press.
Mockler, Anthony (1984). *Haile Selassie's War*. Oxford: Oxford Univ. Press.
Mohamed D. Abdullahi (2001). *Culture and Customs of Somalia*. Westport: Greenwood Publ. Group.
Mohammed Hassen (1999). "Ethiopia: Missed Opportunities for Peaceful Democratic Process," in Kidane Mengisteab and Cyril Daddieh (eds.), *State Building and Democratization in Africa*. Westport: Praeger Publishers.
Mojica, Monique (2009). "Stories from the Body: Blood Memory and Organic Texts," in (ed.), S.E. Wilmer, *Native American Performance and Representation*. Tucson: Arizona University Press.

Morgan, James (1919). *Theodore Roosevelt: The Boy and the Man.* New York: The Macmillan Co.
Mott, Willliam H. (2002). *United States Military Assistance: An Empirical Perspective.* Westport: Greenwood Publishing Group.
Mullan, Robert and Marvin, Garry (1999). *Zoo Culture*, Urbana Champagne: University of Illinois Press.
Murray, John (1895). *A Summary of the Scientific Results Obtained at the Sounding, Dredging and Trawling Stations of H.M.S. Challenger*, Volume 1, Part 6. London: Neill and Co.
Nathaniel, Ras (2004). *50th Anniversary of His Imperial Majesty Emperor Haile Selassie I First Visit to the United States (1954-2004).* Oxford: Trafford Publ.
Negussay Ayele (1977). "The Foreign Policy of Ethiopia," in Olajide Aluko (ed.), *The Foreign Policies of African States.* London: Hodder and Stoughton.
_____. (2003). *Ethiopia and the United States: The Season of Courtship*, Vol., 1. NJ: Ocopy.com.
Neilsen, Waldemar A. (1969). *The Great Powers and Africa. New York*: Praeger.
Newton, Michael ed. (2002). *The Encyclopedia of Kidnappings.* New York: Infobase.
Nicholl, Charles. (1999). *Somebody Else: Arthur Rimbaud in Africa 1880-91.* Chicago: University of Chicago Press, 1999.
Nichols, David A. (1956). *Eisenhower 1956: The President's Year of Crisis—Suez and the Brink of War.* New York: Simon and Schuster.
Noer, Thomas J. (2009). *Soapy: A Biography of G. Mennen Williams.* Ann Arbor: University of Michigan Press.
Naty, Alexander, (1994). "The Thief-Searching (Leba Shay) Institution in Aariland, Southwest Ethiopia, 1890s-1930s," *Ethnology*, Vol. 33, No. 3, 261-272.
Oberleitner, Gerd (2007). *Global Human Rights Institutions.* Cambridge: Polity Press.
Ofcansky, Thomas and Berry, LaVerle Bennette (2004). *Ethiopia a Country Study.* N.P.: Kessinger Publishing.
Ofcansky, Thomas P. and Berry, LaVerle B. (2004). *Ethiopia a Country Stud.* (N.P.: Kessinger Publishing.
Oguibe, Olu (2004). *The Culture Game.* Minneapolis: Univ. of Minnesota Press.
Okbazghi Yohannes (1991). *Eritrea: A Pawn in World Politics.* Gainesville: UFP.
Olusanya, Olaoluwa (2004). *Double Jeopardy without Parameters: Re-Characterisation in International Criminal Law.* Oxford: Intersentia.
Østebø, Terje (2011). *Localising Salafism: Religious Change among Oromo Muslims in Bale, Ethiopia.* Leiden: Brill.
Ottaway, Marina and Ottaway, David (1978). *Ethiopia: Empire in Revolution.* New York: Africana Pub. Co.
Pakenham, Thomas (1991). *The Scramble for Africa: White Man's of the Dark Continent from 1876 to 1912.* New York: Avon Books.

Palla, Marco (2000). *Mussolini Fascism*. New York: Interlink.
Pancoast, Jr., Omar B. (1954). "The 'Point Four Policy," in Bulletin of Atomic Scientist.
Pankhurst, Richard (1968). *Economic History of Ethiopia: 1800-1935*. Addis Ababa: Haile Sellasie I University Press.
_____. (2004). "Correspondance d'Ethiopie: The History of a Pro-Ethiopian Newspaper (1926-1933)," in Verena Boll (ed.), *Studia Aethiopica: In Honor of Siegbert Uhlig on the Occasion of His 65th*. Wiesbaden: Otto Harrassowitz Verlag.
_____. (2009). "Economic and Social Innovation during the Last Years of Emperor Menelik's Life and the Short Reign of Lij Iyasu," in Svein Ege et al. (eds.), *Proceedings of the 16th International Conference of Ethiopian Studies*. Trondheim: NUST.
Pankhurst, Richard, et. al. (2004). *Letters from Abyssinia, 1916 and 1917: With Supplemental Foreign Office Documents*. Hollywood: Tsehai Publishers.
Patman, Robert G. (1990). *The Soviet Union in the Horn of Africa: The Diplomacy of Intervention and Disengagement*. Cambridge: Cambridge Uni. Press.
Paulos Milkias (2006). *Haile Selassie, Western Education, and Political Revolution in Ethiopia*. Youngstown: Cambria Press.
Pearson, Drew, *Ethiopia May Determine Course of African Future*, June 12, 1964.
Pearson, Drew, *Ethiopian Ambassador Bolts Emperor Haile Selassie*. June 14, 1965. http://dspace.wrlc.org/doc/bitstream/2041/51271/b19f03-0614zdisplay.pdf.
Perham, Margery (1948). *The Government of Ethiopia*. London: Faber and Faber.
Perkins, Bradford (1993). *The Cambridge History of American Foreign Relations: The Creation of a Republican Empire, 1776-1865*, Vol., 1. Cambridge: Cambridge University Press.
Perkins, Dexter (1952). *The American Approach to Foreign Policy*. Cambridge: Harvard University Press.
Petro, Nicolai N. (1983). *The Predicament of Human Rights: the Carter and Reagan policies*. Washington, D.C.: University Press of America.
Philips, Matt and Carillet, Jean Bernard (2006). *Ethiopia and Eritrea*. N.P.: Lonely Planet.
Plummer, Brenda Gayle (1996). *Rising Wind: Black Americans and U.S. Foreign Affairs, 1935-1960*. Chapel Hill: University of North Carolina Press.
Prouty, Chris (1986). *Empress Taytu and Menilek II: Ethiopia, 1883-1910*. London: Ravens Educational & Development Services.
Porter, Bruce D. (1984). *The USSR in Third World Conflicts: Soviet Arms and Diplomacy in Local Wars, 1945-1980*. Cambridge: Cambridge Univ. Press.
Putnam, Aric E. (2006). *"Black Belt Millennium": Rhetorical Moments in Black Anti-colonialism during the Great Depression*. Ann Arbor: ProQuest.
Quinn, Sue and Sevareid, Eric (N.P.). *Between Wars*. New York: Taylor & Francis.
Quirk, Joel (2011). *The Anti-Slavery Project: From the Slave Trade to Human Trafficking*. Philadelphia: University of Pennsylvania Press.

Rais, Rasul Bux (1987). *The Indian Ocean and the Superpowers*. Totowa: Rowman & Littlefield.
Raustiala, Kal (2009). *Does the Constitution Follow the Flag?: The Evolution of Territoriality in American Law*. Oxford: Oxford University Press.
Redden, R. Kenneth (1968). *The Legal System of Ethiopia*. Charlottesville: The Michie Company Law Publishers.
Reid, Richard J. (2006). *Warfare in African History*. Cambridge: CUP.
Restad, Hilde Eliassen (2010). *U.S. Foreign Policy Traditions: Multilateralism vs. Unilateralism since 1776*. Oslo: Norwegian Institute for Defense Studies.
Rey, Charles Fernand (1924). *Unconquered Abyssinia as It Is Today*. London: Seeley, Service & Co.
Robinette, Glenn W. (2012). *Why Drug Wars Fail: A Study of Prohibitions*, Vol., 1. Valparaiso, Graffiti Militante Press.
Robinson, David (2004). *Muslim Societies in African History*. New York: Cambridge University Press.
Robinson, Gerald H. (2006). *Photography, History & Science*. Nevada City: Carl Mautz Publishing.
Roger, J. Augustus (1940). *Your History: From Beginning of Time to the Present*. Baltimore: Black Classic Press.
Roosevelt, Theodore (1897). *American Ideals: And Other Essays, Social and Political*. (London: Knickerbocker Press.
_____. (1897). *The Works of Theodore Roosevelt: American Ideals, with a Biographical Sketch by F. V. Greene*. New York: P.F. Collier & Son, Publishers.
Ross, Red (1998)." Black Americans and Italo-Ethiopian Relief 1935-36," in Michael L. Krenn (ed.), *Race and U.S. Foreign Policy from the Colonial Period to the Present: A Collection of Essays*. New York: Taylor & Francis.
Rossini Daniela (1999). "Isolationism and Internationalism in Perspective: Myths and Reality in American Foreign Policy," in Daniela Rossini (eds.), *From Theodore Roosevelt to FDR: Internationalism and Isolationism in American Foreign Policy*. Keele, Ryburn Publishing.
Rubinkowska, Hanna (2004). "The History That Never Was: Historiography by Hayla Sillase," in Verena Böll, (ed.), *Studia Aethiopica: In Honor of Siegbert Uhlig on the Occasion of His 65th Birthday*. Wiesbaden: Otto Harrassowitz Verlag.
Sbacchi, Alberto (1997). *Legacy of bitterness: Ethiopia and fascist Italy, 1935-1941*.Lawrenceville: Red Sea Press.
Schirmer, Daniel B. and Shalom, Stephen Rosskamm (1987). *The Philippines Reader: A History of Colonialism, Neocolonialism, Dictatorship, and Resistance*. Cambridge: South End Press.
Schivelbusch, Wolfgang (2006). *Three New Deals: Reflections on Roosevelt's America, Mussolini's Italy, and Hitler's Germany, 1933–1939*. New York: Metropolitan Books.

Schlee, Günther (1998). "Gada System on the Meta- Ethnic Level: Gabbra/Boran/Garre," in Eisei Kurimoto and Simon Simonse (eds.), *Conflict, Age, and Power in the North East Africa*. New York: James Currey.

Schlesinger, Arthur Meier (2004). *The Imperial Presidency*. New York: Houghton Mifflin Co.

Schmitt, Carl, et al., *The Leviathan in the State Theory of Thomas Hobbes: Meaning and Failure of a Political Symbol*. University of Chicago Press, 2008.

Schoultz, Lars (2009). *That Infernal Little Cuban Republic: The United States and the Cuban Revolution*. Chapel Hill: Univ. of North Carolina Press.

Schraeder, Peter J. (1996). *US Foreign Policy towards Africa: Incrementalism, Crisis and Change*. Cambridge: Cambridge University Press.

Schweizer, Bernard (2001). *Radicals on the Road: The Politics of English Travel Writing in the 1930s*. Charlottesville: University of Virginia Press.

Scott, William R. (1993). *The Sons of Sheba's Race: African-Americans and the Italo-Ethiopian War, 1935-1941*. Bloomington: Indiana University Press.

_____. 1998). "Black Nationalism and the Italo-Ethiopian Conflict, 1934-1936," in Michael L. Krenn (ed.), *Race and U.S. Foreign Policy from the Colonial Period to the Present: A Collection of Essays*. New York: Taylor & Francis.

Sen, Amartya (1981). *Poverty and Famines: An Essay on Entitlement and Deprivation*. Oxford and New York: Oxford University Press.

Shillington,Kevin (2005). *Encyclopedia of African History*, Vol., 1. New York: Taylor & Francis Group.

Shinn, David and Ofcansky, Thomas (2004). *Historical Dictionary of Ethiopia*. Oxford: Scarecrow Press, Inc.

Shuster, Richard J. (2006). "Abyssinia (Ethiopia)," in Spencer C. Tucker and Priscilla Mary Roberts, (eds.), *World War I: A Student Encyclopedia*. Santa Barbara: ABC-CLIO.

Skinner, Elliott (1979). *Blacks and U.S. Policy towards Africa*. Lafayette: Purdue Univ.

Skinner, Robert P. (1904). The National Geographic Magazine, Vol. XV.

_____. (1906). *Abyssinia of today, an Account of the First Mission sent by the American Government to the Court of the King of Kings (1903-04)*. London: Longmans, Green & Co.

_____. (2003). *The 1903 Skinner Mission to Ethiopia & A Century of American-Ethiopian Relations*, Introduction by Ambassador David H. Shinn, Preface by Ambassador Aurelia E. Brazeal. Hollywood: Tsehai Publishers.

Skinner, Robert. P. (1905). *Making a Treaty with Menelik: The Story of the American Mission to Abyssinia*. Chicago: Bible House.

Skrabec, Quentin R. (2008), William McKinley: *Apostle of Protectionism*. (New York: Algora Publishing.

Sloan, Stanley (2010). *Permanent Alliance?: NATO and the Transatlantic Bargain from Truman to Obama.* New York: The Continuum International Publishing Group Inc.
Smith, Denis Mack. 1983. *Mussolini.* New York: Vintage Books.
Somerville, Barbara (2004). *Warren G. Harding.* Minneapolis: Compass Point.
Sotiropoulos, Karen (2009). *Staging Race: Black Performers in Turn of the Century America.* Cambridge: Harvard University Press.
Spencer, John (2006). *Ethiopia at Bay: A Personal Account of the Haile Selassie Years.* Hollywood: Tsehai Publishers.
_____. (1977). *Ethiopia, The Horn of Africa, and U.S. Policy.* Washington, DC: Corporate Press, Inc.
_____. "Ethiopia: a friend of the U.S. abandoned," *The New York Times,* December 5, 1974.
Stanley, H. M. (1874). *Coomassie and Magdala: the story of two British campaigns in Africa.* London: Sampson Low, Marston, Low & Searle.
Stanton, Andrea L. (2012). *Cultural Sociology of the Middle East, Asia, and Africa: An Encyclopedia.* Los Angles, SAGE Publications.
Steffanson, Borg G., et al., *The Decline of Menelik II to the Emergence of Ras Tafari, later known as Haile Selassie 1910-1919,* Vol., 1. Salisbury: N.C. E. Wagner.
Strecker, Ivo (1994). "The Glories and Agonies of the Ethiopian Past," in *Social Anthropology,* Vol., 2, No., 3.
Taddesse Tamrat (1972). *Church and state in Ethiopia, 1270-1527.* Oxford: Clarendon Press.
Tekeste Negash (1987). *Italian colonialism in Eritrea, 1882-1941: Policies, Praxis and Impact.* Uppsala: Uppsala University.
_____. (1997). *Eritrea and Ethiopia: The Federal Experience.* Uppsala, Nordiska Afrikainstitutet.
Thesiger, Wilfred (1987). *The Life of My Choice.* New York: W. W. Norton & Co.
Thompson, Willard S. (1969). *Ghana's Foreign Policy, 1957-1966: Diplomacy, Ideology, and the New State.* Princeton: Princeton Univ. Press.
Tibebu Teshale (1995), *The Making of Modern Ethiopia, 1896–1974.* Lawrenceville, Red Sea Press.
Tvedt, Terje (2004). *The River Nile in the Age of the British: Political Ecology and the Quest for Economic Power* (London: I. B. Tauris & Co. Ltd.
Uhlig, Siegbert (ed.). (2003). *Encyclopaedia Aethiopica: A-C.* Wiesbaden: Otto Harrassowitz Verlag.
Utter, Jack (1993). *American Indians: Answers to Today's Questions.* Lake Ann: National Woodlands Publishing Co.
Van Arsdale, Peter W. (2006). *Forced to Flee: Human Rights and Human Wrongs in Refugee Homelands.* Oxford: Lexington Books.

Van Der Beken, Christophe (2012). *Unity in Diversity: Federalism as a Mechanism to Accommodate Ethnic Diversity: The Case of Ethiopia*. Zürich: LIT Verlag Münster.

Varnis, Steven (1990). *Reluctant Aid Or Aiding the Reluctant?: U.S. Food Aid Policy and Ethiopian Famine Relief.* New Brunswick, Transaction Pub.

Vaughan, Sarah (2003). *Ethnicity and Power in Ethiopia*, Ph.D. Thesis. University of Edinburgh.

Veeser, Cyrus. *H-Diplo Article Review* No. 318. July 24, 2011. <http://www.h-net.org/~diplo/reviews/PDF/AR318.pdf>.

Vestal, Theodore M. (2011). *The Lion of Judah in the New World: Emperor Haile Selassie of Ethiopia and the Shaping of Americans' Attitudes toward Africa*. Santa Barbara: Greenwood Publishing Group.

_____. (1999). *Ethiopia: A Post-Cold War African State*. Westport: Greenwood Publishing Group.

Vestal, Theodore M. *A Peace Corps History*. 28 April 2001. <http://www.fp.okstate.edu/vestal/InternationalStudy/Peace_Corps_History.htm>

Von Eschen, Penny Marie (1997). *Race against Empire: Black Americans and Anticolonialism, 1937-1957*. Ithaca: Cornell University Press.

Wallelign Mekonnen (1969). "On the Question of Nationalities in Ethiopia," *Struggle*, Vol., 17, No., 1.

Walton Jr., Hanes (2010). "African Foreign Policy before the Kissinger Years: The G. Mennen "Soapy" Williams Era 1961-1966," in Walton, Jr., Hanes, et. al. (eds.), *The African Foreign Policy of Secretary of State Henry Kissinger: A Documentary Analysis*. Lanham: Lexington Books.

Washington, George (1982). *The Writings of George Washington: 1794-1798*, Vol., xiii. New York and London: Knickerbocker Press.

Watters, Ethan. (2010), *Crazy Like Us: The Globalization of the American Psyche*. New York: Free Press.

Waugh, Evelyn (2005). *The Coronation of Haile Selassie*. London: Penguins.

_____. (2007). *Waugh in Abyssinia*. Baton Rouge: Louisiana State Univ. Press.

Weaver, Frederick S. (2011). *Economic Literacy: Basic Economics with an Attitude*, ed., 3. Lanham: Rowman & Littlefield.

Weisbord, Robert G. (1998). "Black America and the Italian-Ethiopian Crisis: An Episode in Pan-Negroism," in Michael L. Krenn (ed.), *Race and U.S. Foreign Policy from the Colonial Period to the Present: A Collection of Essays*. New York: Taylor & Francis.

Weissbrodt, David S. and de la Vega, Connie (2007). *International Human Rights Law: An Introduction*. Philadelphia: Univ. of Pennsylvania Press.

White, George (2005). Holding the Line: Race, Racism, and American Foreign Policy toward Africa, 1953-1961. Oxford: Rowman & Littlefield Publishers Inc.

Whiteman, Kaye and Yates, Douglas (2004). "France, Britain, and the United States," in Adekeye Adebajo and Ismail O. D. Rashid, *West Africa's*

Security Challenges: Building Peace in a Troubled Region. Boulder: Lynne Rienner Publishers, Inc., 2004.
Wiarda, Howard J. (1990). *On the agenda: Current Issues and Conflicts in U.S. Foreign Policy.* New York: Scott, Foresman/Little, Brown.
Williams, W. A. (1962). *The Tragedy of American Diplomacy.* New York: Dell.
Williams, J. F. (1934). *Some Aspects of the Covenant of the League of Nations.* London: Oxford University Press.
Winkler-Morey, Anne (2003). "Dollar Diplomacy," in Lee Stacy (ed.), *Mexico and the United States.* Tarrytown: Marshall Cavendish Corp.
Wittkopf, Eugene R., and Jones, Christopher M. (2008). *American Foreign Policy, Pattern and Process.* Belmont: Cengage Learning.
Woolbert, Robert Gale (1935). "The Peoples of Ethiopia," in *Council on Foreign Relations*, Vol., 14.
Worger, William H. et al. (2010). *Africa and the West: From the slave trade to conquest*, 1441-1905. Oxford: Oxford University Press.
Wrigley, C.J. and Taylor, A.J.P. (2006). *Radical Historian of Europe.* London: I. B. Tauris.
Wrong, Michela (2005). *I Didn't Do It for You.* New York: HarperCollins.
Wylde, Augustus Blandy (1901). *Modern Abyssinia.* London: Methuen & Co.
Yaqub, Salim (2004). *Containing Arab Nationalism: The Eisenhower Doctrine and the Middle East.* Chapel Hill: University of North Carolina Press.
Young, John (2006). *Peasant Revolution in Ethiopia: The Tigray People's Liberation Front, 1975-1991.* Cambridge: Cambridge University Press.
Young, William H. and Young, Nancy K. (2007). *The Great Depression in America: A Cultural Encyclopedia*, Vol., 1.Westport: Greenwood Press.

Official Publications

Congressional Serial Set 1873-74 (Washington, D.C.: United States Government Printing Office, 1873).
Foreign Relations of the United States: Diplomatic Papers, Vol., 4 (Washington, D.C.: U.S. Government Printing Office, 1964).
Monthly Consular and Trade Reports, Volume 65, Issues 244-247 (Washington, D.C.: U.S. Government Printing Office, 1901).
Monthly Consular and Trade Reports, Volume 67, Issues 252-255 (Washington, D.C.: U.S. G.P.O., 1901).
Papers Relating to the Foreign Relations of the United States, Part 1 (Washington, D.C.: United States Government Printing Office, 1873).
Papers Relating to the Foreign Relations of the United States, Volume 2 (Washington, D.C.: U.S. Government Printing Office, 1935).
Papers Relating to the Foreign Relations of the United States, Vol., 2 (Washington, D.C.:U.S. Government Printing Office, 1943).
Public Papers of the Presidents of the United States (Washington DC: G. P. O, 1999).

United States Congressional Serial Set (Washington, D.C.: G.P.O, 1902).
United States Treaties and Other International Agreements, Vol., 8, Part 2 (Washington, D.C.: Department of State, 1958).
US Department of State Dispatch, Volume 3, Issue 8 (Washington, DC: Office of Public Communication, Bureau of Public Affairs, 1992).

Online Government Documents

(All the documents were retrieved from the *Office of the Historian* website)
Airgram A-194 from the Embassy in Ethiopia to the Department of State. Addis Ababa, June 18, 1969. N.p., n.d. 19 March 2013.
<http://history.state.gov/historicaldocuments/frus1969-76ve05p1/d270>.
Airgram A-30 from the American Consulate in Asmara to the Department of State, April 10, 1969. N.p., n.d. 11 March 2013.
<http://history.state.gov/historicaldocuments/frus1969-76ve05p1/d268>.
Briefing Memorandum from the Director of Policy Planning (Lord) to the Under Secretary of State for Political Affairs (Sisco), January 24, 1975. N.p., n.d. 02 March 2013. <http://history.state.gov/historicaldocuments/frus1969-76ve06/d129>.
Circular Airgram from the Department of State to Certain African Posts, March 21, 1964. N.p., n.d. 10 February 2013.
<http://history.state.gov/historicaldocuments/frus1964-68v24/d290>.
Editorial Note of the 414th meeting of the National Security Council, July 23, 1959. N.p., n.d. 03 January 2013.
<http://history.state.gov/historicaldocuments/frus1958-60v14/d46>.
Ethiopian Prospects after the Abortive Coup, January 24, 1961. N.p., n.d. 12 December 2012.
<http://history.state.gov/historicaldocuments/frus1961-63v21/d271>.
Ethiopia: Anatomy of a Revolution: Intelligence Note IN-47 Prepared by the Bureau of Intelligence and Research, September 25, 1974. N.p., n.d. 26 March 2013.
<http://history.state.gov/historicaldocuments/frus1969-76ve06/d112>.
Intelligence Note No. 747 from the Deputy Director of the Bureau of Intelligence and Research (Denney) to Secretary of State Rogers, October 21, 1969. N.p., n.d. 19 March 2013.
http://history.state.gov/historicaldocuments/frus1969-76ve05p1/d280 .
Memorandum from Richard Kennedy of the National Security Council Staff to Secretary of State Kissinger. October 16, 1974. N.p., n.d. 27 February 2013.
<http://history.state.gov/historicaldocuments/frus1969-76ve06/d114>.
Memorandum from Robert W. Komer of the National Security Council Staff to President Kennedy, Washington. November 28, 1962. N.p., n.d. 13 April 2013.
<http://history.state.gov/historicaldocuments/frus1961-63v21/d286>.
Memorandum from Roger Morris of the National Security Council Staff to the President's Assistant for National Security Affairs (Kissinger), July 3, 1969. N.p., n.d. 19

April 2013. <http://history.state.gov/historicaldocuments/frus1969-76ve05p1/d272>.

Memorandum from the Assistant Secretary of State for African Affairs (Williams) to the President's Deputy Special Assistant for National Security Affairs (Komer), February 11, 1966." N.p., n.d. 19 April 2013. http://history.state.gov/historicaldocuments/frus1964-68v24/d310.

Memorandum from the Assistant Secretary of State for African Affairs (Williams) to the President's Deputy Special Assistant for National Security Affairs (Komer), February 11, 1966." N.p., n.d. 19 April 2013. <http://history.state.gov/historicaldocuments/frus1964-68v24/d310>.

Memorandum from the Assistant Secretary of State for African Affairs (Palmer) to Secretary of State Rogers, June 28, 1969. N.p., n.d. 19 April 2013. <http://history.state.gov/historicaldocuments/frus1969-76ve05p1/d271>.

Memorandum from the Assistant Secretary of State for African Affairs (Satterthwaite) to Secretary of State Herter, August 10, 1960. N.p., n.d. 19 April 2013. <http://history.state.gov/historicaldocuments/frus1958-60v14/d50>.

Memorandum from the President's Assistant for National Security Affairs (Kissinger) to President Nixon. July 6, 1969. N.p., n.d. 10 May 2013. <http://history.state.gov/historicaldocuments/frus1969-76ve05p1/d273>.

Memorandum from the President's Assistant for National Security Affairs (Kissinger) to President Nixon, July 6, 1969. N.p., n.d. 10 May 2013. http://history.state.gov/historicaldocuments/frus1969-76ve05p1/d273⊥ >.

Memorandum from the President's Deputy Special Assistant for National Security Affairs (Komer) to the Assistant Secretary of State for African Affairs (Williams), February 8, 1966. N.p., n.d. 15 March 2013. <http://history.state.gov/historicaldocuments/frus1964-68v24/d309>.

Memorandum from the President's Deputy Special Assistant for National Security Affairs (Komer) to the Assistant Secretary of State for African Affairs (Williams), February 18, 1966. N.p., n.d. 29 May 2013. http://history.state.gov/historicaldocuments/frus1964-68v24/d311.

Memorandum from the President's Special Assistant (Rostow) to President Johnson, October 12, 1966. N.p., n.d. 9 April 2013. <http://history.state.gov/historicaldocuments/frus1964-68v24/d318>.

Memorandum from the President's Special Assistant (Rostow) to President Johnson. Visit of Emperor Haile Selassie of Ethiopia, February 11, 1967. N.p., n.d. 07 April 2013. <http://history.state.gov/historicaldocuments/frus1964-68v24/d327>.

Memorandum from the President's Assistant for National Security Affairs (Kissinger) to President Nixon, July 6, 1969. N.p., n.d. 12 January 2013. Available at: http://history.state.gov/historicaldocuments/frus1969-76ve05p1/d273.

Memorandum from the Under Secretary of State (Katzenbach) to President Johnson, March 12, 1968. N.p., n.d. 02 May 2013. <http://history.state.gov/historicaldocuments/frus1964-68v24/d346>.

Memorandum from William H. Brubeck of the National Security Council Staff to the President's Special Assistant for National Security Affairs (Bundy), October 11, 1963. N.p., n.d. 19 March 2013.
    <http://history.state.gov/historicaldocuments/frus1961-63v21/d303>.
Memorandum of Conversation, July 8, 1969. N.p., n.d. 3 April 2013.
    http://history.state.gov/historicaldocuments/frus1969-76ve05p1/d275 >.
Memorandum of Conversation, November 27, 1962. N.p., n.d. 19 March 2013.
    <http://history.state.gov/historicaldocuments/frus1961-63v21/d285>.
Memorandum of Conversation, PSV/MC/16, October 2, 1959. N.p., n.d. 23 March 2013.
    http://history.state.gov/historicaldocuments/frus1958-60v07p2/d255 >.
Memorandum of Conversation, Somalia, October 1, 1963. N.p., n.d. 18 March 2013.<http://history.state.gov/historicaldocuments/frus1961-63v21/d302>.
Memorandum of Conversation, Tuesday, May 15, 1973. N.p., n.d. 20 March 2013.
    <http://2001-2009.state.gov/documents/organization/67407.pdf>.
National Intelligence Estimate 75/76-70, May 21, 1970. N.p., n.d. 20 March 2013.
    < http://2001-2009.state.gov/documents/organization/54651.pdf>.
National Intelligence Estimate 75/76-72, October 4, 1972. N.p., n.d. 14 March 2013. <history.state.gov/historicaldocuments/frus1969-76ve05p1/d332>.
Note by the Executive Secretary to the National Security Council on U.S. Policy toward the Horn of Africa (NSC 5903), February 4, 1959. N.p., n.d. 14 March 2013.<http://history.state.gov/historicaldocuments/frus1958-60v14/d44>.
Prospects for Ethiopia, Special Memorandum Prepared in the Central Intelligence Agency, March 31, 1966. N.p., n.d. 14 March 2013.
    <http://history.state.gov/historicaldocuments/frus1964-68v24/d312>.
Records of the Department of State Relating to Political Relations between the United States and Ethiopia (Abyssinia), 1910-29 [microfilm], 1962. N.p., n.d. 14 March 2013.
    <http://ia700504.us.archive.org/17/items/798013/798013.pdf>.
Special Memorandum Prepared in the Central Intelligence Agency, March 31, 1966. N.p., n.d. 10 March 2013.
    <http://history.state.gov/historicaldocuments/frus1964-68v24/d312>.
Telegram from the Department of State to the Embassy in Italy, April 15, 1960. N.p., n.d. 14 March 2013.
    <http://history.state.gov/historicaldocuments/frus1958-60v14/d48>.
Telegram from the Department of State to the Embassy in Somalia, February 20, 1964. N.p., n.d. 14 March 2013.
    <http://history.state.gov/historicaldocuments/frus1964-68v24/d282>.

Telegram from the Department of State to the Embassy in Somalia, January 21, 1964. N.p., n.d. 14 March 2013.
<http://history.state.gov/historicaldocuments/frus1964-68v24/d277>.

Miscellaneous Sources

JFK, "Inaugural Address," January 20, 1961. Online by Gerhard Peters and John T. Woolley, *The American Presidency Project*. N.d. 05 May 2013.
<http://www.presidency.ucsb.edu/ws/?pid=8032>.

JFK, "Special Message to the Congress on Foreign Aid," March 22, 1961. Online by Gerhard Peters and John T. Woolley, *The American Presidency Project*. N.d. 05 May 2013.
<http://www.presidency.ucsb.edu/ws/?pid=8545>.

Richard Nixon, "Toasts of the President and Emperor Haile Selassie I of Ethiopia" July 8, 1969. Online by Gerhard Peters and John T. Woolley, *The American Presidency Project*. N.d. 05 May 2013.
<http://www.presidency.ucsb.edu/ws/?pid=2118>.

Richard Nixon, "Toasts of the President and Emperor Haile Selassie of Ethiopia," May 15, 1973. Online by Gerhard Peters and John T. Woolley, *The American Presidency Project*. N.d. 05 May 2013.
<http://www.presidency.ucsb.edu/ws/?pid=3845>.

Theodore Roosevelt, "Second Annual Message," December 2, 1902. Online by Gerhard Peters and John T. Woolley, *The American Presidency Project*. N.d. 05 May 2013.
<http://www.presidency.ucsb.edu/ws/?pid=29543>.

Truman, "Inaugural Address," January 20, 1949. N.p., n.d. 15 May 2013.
<http://www.trumanlibrary.org/whistlestop/50yr_archive/inagural20jan1949.htm>.

Paul Henze Interview, Episode 17.
http://www.gwu.edu/~nsarchiv/coldwar/interviews/episode-17/henze1.html >.

Pearson, Drew, *Ethiopia May Determine Course of African Future*, Merry-go-round, June 12, 1964.

PoliticalGraveyard.com, *Robert Peet Skinner. Index to Politicians* (February 24, 2013). http://politicalgraveyard.com/bio/skinner.html

Press Release, Bay Area Author Mixes History and Romance. 8 September 2006. <http://www.prweb.com/releases/2006/09/prweb434859.htm.

Skinner's African Trip, The New York Times, October 18, 1903.

Tells of King Menelik. The New York Times, and January 1, 1904.

Glossary

Abba Gadaa—An Oromo traditional leader elected according to the Gada system. See, gada.
Abuna—bishop.
Afaan Oromoo—Oromo language.
Afarsata—Abyssinian justice system in which a collective punishment was imposed on villagers for a crime committed by an individual.
Awuchachny—a procedure of afarsata.
Balabbat—refers to a person from settlers or from the conquered peoples who worked for the Ethiopian state in return for a landholding right and other benefits.
Bariya—lit. 'slave'. It refers to people from along the Ethiopia-Sudan border (bariya hagar) or refers to all people of dark complexion. See, Shanqilla.
Blattangeta—an Abyssinian title for a feudal lord who has special literary skill.
Chisanya—lit. smoke. Refers to the ease with which the indigenous peoples were removed from their lands.
Dajjazmach—the second highest Abyssinian military /official ranking. It is one rank below ras.
Darg—lit. 'committee'. A military régime that overthrow the rule of the emperor in 1974 and ruled until 1991.
Finfinne—lit. the land of spring water. An Oromo indigenous name for the site of present day Addis Ababa before the Minilik conquest.
Gabbar—lit. a tax payer or a landless tenant. Refers to the status of the conquered peoples in relation to land
Gada—an Oromo socio-economic, political, and egalitarian administrative system before the Abyssinian conquest.
Galla—Pejorative appellation for the Oromo people.
Habasha—Abyssinian or Abyssinian land
Katama (ketema)—Lit. town. Means garrison towns established in the conquered areas.
Leba shay—lit. thief finder. A practice of intoxicating and walking a young boy, in the neighborhood, to detect a thief. In the Abyssinian sense of justice, an owner of a house (property) where the unfortunate boy collapses automatically convicted of theft
Naft—rifle, gun.

Naftanya—Lit. a gun holder, a one who enforces law and order by force. It refers to Minilik soldier who settled in the conquered areas.

Naftanya diplomacy—an Abyssinian diplomacy based upon procurement of weapons.

Naftanya system—an Abyssinia administration system introduced in the conquered areas in which the legitimacy of the rule originates from gun or use of force.

Nigus, king

Qallu—an Oromo institution. Also refers to a hereditary Oromo ritual leader.

Qur'an—Islamic Holy Book.

Quranya—An Abyssinian justice system in which a plaintiff and defendant chained together until a case resolved.

Ras—lit. head. Refers to the highest ranking in the Abyssinian military or administrative position.

Shanqilla—lit. slave. Refers to people from the Western Ethiopia, along Ethiopia-Sudan border. See, Bariya

Sharia—Islamic law.

Zamana Masafint—the era of princes(1769-1855). According to the Abyssinian historiography, it was the era in which Abyssinia engaged in endless bloodlettings.

Acronyms

EPRDF—Ethiopian Peoples' Revolutionary Democratic Front.

OLF, Oromo Liberation Front

OPDO, Oromo People's Democratic Organization.

SEPDF, South Ethiopian Peoples' Democratic Front.

SNNPR, Southern Nations, Nationalities, and People's Region

TPLF, Tigray People's Liberation Front